MW00581982

Eating on the Wild Side

Arizona Series in Human Ecology

Eating on the Wild Side

THE
PHARMACOLOGIC,
ECOLOGIC,
AND SOCIAL
IMPLICATIONS
OF USING
NONCULTIGENS

Nina L. Etkin

EDITOR

The University of Arizona Press ❋ *Tucson & London*

The University of Arizona Press
Copyright © 1994
The Arizona Board of Regents
All Rights Reserved

∞ This book is printed on acid-free, archival-quality paper.
Manufactured in the United States of America

99 98 97 96 95 94 6 5 4 3 2 1

LIBRARY OF CONGRESS CATALOGING-IN-PUBLICATION DATA

Eating on the wild side : the pharmacologic, ecologic, and social
    implications of using noncultigens / Nina L. Etkin, editor.
        p.   cm. — (Arizona studies in human ecology)
    Includes bibliographical references and index.
    ISBN 0-8165-1369-4 (acid-free paper)
        1. Ethnobotany.   2. Wild plants, Edible.   3. Materia medica,
Vegetable.   4. Man, Prehistoric—Food.   5. Food habits—History.
    1. Etkin, Nina L. (Nina Lilian), 1948–   .   II. Series.
    GN476.73.E27   1994
    581.6'1—dc20   94-12163
                                                                CIP

British Library Cataloguing-in-Publication Data
A catalogue record for this book is available from the British Library.

For my parents
Jack and Natasha Etkin

Contents

Eating on the Wild Side

1

The Cull of the Wild

✻ NINA L. ETKIN

Wild plants hold a curious position in the contemporary scholarship of human-plant relations. Located somehow liminally, the topic has been the subject of works that seemingly leap—certainly do not range—from the folksy descriptive style of an older generation of field naturalists (e.g., Ebeling 1986; Kindscher 1992) to encyclopedic compendia (e.g., Duke 1992; Iwu 1992; Kuhnlein and Turner 1991; Moerman 1986) to technical works on germplasm research and gene banks (e.g., Hoyt 1988; Workshop on Genetic Resources 1990). Despite all this attention, nothing approaching a systematic treatment of these botanicals has emerged. What does distill from these varied sources is the striking nutritional and pharmacologic potential of "wild" plants, and their cultural implications.

This introductory discussion offers a synthetic framework built on several themes addressed in the chapters of this volume. Each of us struggled with definitions of "wild," "domesticated," and in between as we reviewed the results of our research, which had been formulated with other objectives in mind and for which "wildness" was not then the key issue. The theoretical formulation advanced in these chapters links biology to culture so that researchers can comprehend the dynamics of selection and the physiologic implications of wild plant consumption. Collectively, the chapters emphasize the evolutionary process of plant selection: the approach taken by these authors spans the history of human-plant interactions, drawing on implications from nonhuman primate studies, evidence from prehistoric populations, and extensive field research among contemporary populations representing a range of subsistence strategies. Finally, this volume locates wild plants in a pivotal position in the current debate about conservation of biodiversity.

Definitions: Are "Weeds" Politically Incorrect?

Inattentive to botanical conventions, social scientists casually use terms such as *wild, supplementary,* and *semicultivated* as referents for very different types of plant foods. This lexical coupling implies a peripheral role in diet, as well as similar nutrient composition, neither of which applies. Botanists, too, find the terms difficult to standardize. This lack of consensus has been a significant obstacle for researchers striving to understand the "origins" of agriculture and the role that "wild" plants play in contemporary human diet. David Harris sheds some light on this difficulty through a continuum model of human-plant interaction, which he describes as "ecological in that the analytical target is *interaction* between people and plants, evolutionary in that the *results* of the processes involved in domestication and the emergence of agriculture . . . are assumed to be the products of selection working on both biological and cultural variation" (1989:12).

The intellectual history of these models is rather short. They gained currency during the 1960s as explanatory frameworks that emphasized the continuities between foragers' reliance on wild species for "food procurement" and agriculturists' reliance on domesticated species for "food production." Harris offered the terms *manipulation* and *transformation* to describe two aspects along a continuum of ecological change represented by increased alteration of natural habitats by human activity: chronologically the sequence ranged from hunting and gathering through domestication to agriculture. Within a decade, investigators using eco-evolutionary approaches had broadened and reconfigured the study of early agriculture to address "subsistence systems" through biological and economic paradigms, in order to explore the varieties and continuities of human interaction with "wild" and "domesticated" species.

By the early 1980s the paleoeconomic perspective of Eric Higgs (1972) and colleagues had been refined as researchers advanced more complex taxonomies for human-environment relationships, differentiating more gradations and continuing the tradition to distinguish explicitly between cultivation and domestication: for plants, casual gathering → systematic gathering → limited cultivation → developed cultivation → intensive cultivation. Later, David Rindos (1984) intellectually located domestication within a coevolutionary paradigm and offered a three-part taxonomy whose elements are distinguished both by type of human activity and by environment: incidental and specialized domestication, which eventuate in agricultural domestication. Both of these schemes accommodate blurred borders between categories and reject unidirectional and deterministic progressions. So, too, do the theoretical formulations of R. A. Hynes and A. K. Chase (1982), who introduced "domiculture," and Richard Ford (1985), who has conceived of two successive stages of procuring plant foods—"foraging" and "food production," the latter comprising "cultivation" and "domestication." Further, he has identified three successive means of food production (incipient agriculture, gardening, and field agriculture) as well as a continuum of human actions including tending, tilling, transplanting, sowing, and plant breeding.

Expanding this comprehensive scheme, Harris's model assumes that people will generally expend energy only if they consistently receive high caloric value from the foods they procure or produce using that energy. This model does not seek to explain shifting trends in plant use by factoring into the equation such sociodemographic issues as population pressure, sedentism, and social stratification. It is instead a descriptive model that focuses on a progression of increasingly intimate people-plant relations and corollary perturbations of habitat (Harris 1989:12–16). The chapters in this volume illustrate that despite a manifest logic that locates wild plant use in populations representing the "low-energy" pole of the continuum, these plants continue to be important across the full range of plant-getting technologies. Further, we expand Harris's perspective to assess foods not only for caloric value, but also for other nutrient and pharmacologic potential.

Whereas researchers generally agree that human-plant interactions are best viewed along the wild-domesticated continuum outlined above, they still dispute the number and character of the intergrading categories. Contemporary schema especially strive to address the difficulty embedded in the category "cultivated": cultivation (sowing in prepared beds) is defined by human activities, while domestication refers to the genetic response of plants to human action; thus wild plants can be cultivated, and cultivated plants may not be domesticated. Examples provided by the chapters in this volume illustrate the continuing difficulty in applying general terms to specific cases.

Weeds are difficult to position along a continuum, since they grow fully or predominantly in circumstances disturbed by human activity and so contribute significantly to our understanding of human agency and domestication. People's attention may be rather easily drawn to weeds that are adapted to a broad range of factors. This "general-purpose genotype" enables weeds to move into disturbed habitats quickly, since they do not need a period of selection to build up allelochemical defenses and competitor inhibitors. Unless they evolve more refined adaptations quickly, they may be displaced by the return of native plants, which are likely to be adapted to most local conditions (Baker 1991). But when weeds that develop from wild progenitors or from domesticates are tolerated, encouraged, or harvested they may become "weed crops" (planted for later collection) and may become genetically altered, human-dependent domesticates.

Curiously, no one appears to have systematically recorded a series comparable to a wild-domesticated continuum for a native group, even though researchers often base their distinctions (partially or entirely) on how people of the study community distinguish species (e.g., White 1989). Careful ethnography reveals that some non-Western peoples recognize a wild-domesticated continuum. For example, Hausa in Nigeria regularly consume "wild" foods but refer to them as "hunger" and "famine" foods or, especially for small fruit, "children's" foods.[1] They also regard a wild species as more potent than its cultivated counterpart (for example, as a flavoring or medicine). In the fuller ethnographic context this can be linked to Hausa knowledge of drought resistance in plants, experience with food shortage, knowledge of local ecology, children's activities, and perceptions of therapeutic merit (see also Etkin and Ross [this volume]). Similarly, indigenous peoples of Tanzania say that wild plants are not "food proper" although they regularly use these plants in their diet (Fleuret 1979). More attention to local views will advance our understanding of the potential importance of noncultigens for diet and health.

Any typology is confounded by the cultural and temporal variability that characterizes the dynamics of plant use. Differences within populations exist as well, reflecting distinct individual needs and knowledge. Species are not confined to a single category of resource management: for example, Shuar in Amazonian Ecuador plant some *Inga spectabilis* in gardens and fields, whereas other individuals of this species occur naturally in the forest; and *Bactris gasipaes* (peach-palm) and *Grias* spp. are both planted in gardens and also protected in old fallows (Bennett 1992). When other animals and microbes are factored into the equation, these definitions become more problematic still.

The authors in this volume restrict themselves largely to the wild end of the continuum, but the reader should also note departures in terminology. For example, William Vickers takes issue with the definition of "weeds" for exactly the reasons outlined here, and Nina Etkin and Paul Ross use the term *semiwild* to highlight the human-modified ecology of the Kano Close-Settled Zone in Nigeria.

Wild Plants: Why Neglected?

Diet surveys tend to ignore "wild" plants compared to dietary "staples" because of a lack of understanding regarding which plants should be included in the "wild" category and the extent to which they contribute to routine cuisine. But wherever the consumption of wild foods has been accurately assessed, they emerge as regular and important elements of diet. Even—some would say especially—agricultural populations include significant quantities of foraged plants in their diets and in fact may exploit a greater variety of plants than do some hunters and gatherers (Harlan 1992; Hayden 1981).[2] People use "greens" or "herbs" to vary cuisine, as snacks, or to flavor, stretch, garnish, or otherwise culturally mark other foods. More ambiguously, ethnographers describe the use of "wild" plants for "teas," "tonics," and "recreational drugs." None of these categories is static: plants may occupy more than one classificatory position as well as move fluidly among them depending on such factors as tastes and design of cuisine, relative availability of other types of foods (both cultivated and not), intention (satiety, promoting health, etc.), or an individual's health. Even in technologically developed societies wild plants are important for reinforcing symbolic domains and as pedagogic tools that instruct about past lifeways (Bouverot-Rothaker 1982; Kruker and Niederer 1982).

In view of the varied, often special, and subtle roles that "wild" foods play, the extent to which they contribute to diet will be elicited by only the most rigorous of methodologies applied within a specific population (Etkin and Ross 1991a; Fleuret 1986; Grossman 1991; see also Dufour and Wilson, Etkin and Ross, and Vickers [all in this volume]): diet history and recall strategies at best summon only trends and normative statements about diet; formal questionnaires, especially self-administered, lack flexibility and can be highly unreliable; in-depth inquiry using overly small samples cannot hope to plumb the range and relative importance of different dietary constituents; measures during and close to meal times may change people's cooking and eating behaviors; short-term or episodic surveys disregard seasonal and other temporal variability; failure to account for between-meal and out-of-home consumption will not capture important food events; and so on. Thus, a poor knowledge of wild foods at least partly reflects flawed research design and implementation.

Some researchers exhibit more than a methodologic deficiency in their general disinterest in "wild" plants, which might be traced to the fact that women and children typically are involved in the collection of such foods. In general, children have not figured prominently in population-based dietary research and tend to be featured only in studies that address specific issues such as infant feeding or growth and development. Nor do many researchers perceive children as important contributors to production. Granted, children are poor subjects for recall and interview methods, and they tend to get lost in food consumption surveys as some percentage of adult equivalent. But, in fact, by closely examining children's food behaviors, one gains important insight into the range and quantity of foods consumed, emphasizing that children are complex in their food behaviors, not simply the "small adults" implied by aggregated dietary surveys (Fleuret 1979; Laderman 1991). Regarding why plant collection by women has been ignored, a vast literature documents the lesser study of "women's domains" generally. The current redirection of studies to include women-centered activities (e.g., Lockwood 1993; Rubin 1992; Womack and Marti 1993) could be expanded by considering children's "work" as well.

Selection

The importance of plants in the evolution of human diets has been well established, leaving room now for us to refine our interpretations of how and why plants are selected and what different patterns of plant use signify for human health and culture. Allelochemicals have become key elements in the deconstruction of human cuisines and pharmacopoeias and are especially conspicuous in "wild" plants. Allelochemicals (produced by plant tissues, by associated microflora,[3] or by both) serve a variety of functions as attractants of pollinators or seed dispersers, as repellents of herbivores and competitors, as growth regulators, and the like. These "secondary" compounds, which human management has eliminated from some domesticates, are the nucleus of the complex coevolutionary relationships between plants and herbivores, including humans. For human societies allelochemicals have come to serve as "fingerprints" (Janzen 1978) that guide our selection of foods and medicines.

Michael Logan and Anna Dixon (Chapter 2) review generally how the distinctive attributes of plants focus human inquiry on certain species while others that lack culturally valued qualities are rejected. They compare the botanical knowledge of agricultural populations to that of hunters and gatherers and use the example of fertility-affecting plants to consider the evolution and implications of the overlapping use of such species in diet and medicine. Timothy Johns (Chapter 3) isolates the particular attribute "palatability" to consider how culturally marked foods are managed in diet and medicine and how complex biocultural interrelations shape human preferences and tolerances for particular foods. Indeed, domestication of particular plants may have been shaped more by their sensory appeal than by their potential to function as dietary staples (Farrington and Urry 1985), a premise advanced in simpler models of human cultural development. Experimentation and later incorporation into diet also may be encouraged by the attractive qualities of wild plants that enter the human domain as something very different from foods—ornamentals, for example (Laferriere 1992; North and North 1987).

Selection of plant resources appears in discussions in other chapters as well, reflecting its key role for understanding human-plant relations. Knowing what objectives people have (and presuming what needs animals have) is fundamental to that comprehension. Thus, Etkin and Ross (Chapter 5) differentiate among the selection criteria for Hausa foods and medicines. Paul Cox (Chapter 6) suggests that populations in Samoa select "wild" emergency foods based on morphological similarity with staple foods and prefer introduced flora. Darna Dufour and Warren Wilson (Chapter 7) note that their Amazonian study populations tend to select oil-rich fruit of palms or trees, while minimal overlap between wild foods and medicines suggests that different selection criteria apply to those categories. And Kenneth Glander (Chapter 12) describes the importance of smell and taste in plant selection by howler monkeys.

Emergency Foods

In commentary on selection criteria for wild foods, researchers typically make a special case for "famine foods" (or "emergency," "starvation," or "unusual" foods). Like the other categorical schemes discussed in this essay, a famine/ordinary distinction is ambiguous: although not among the preferred food-stuffs, these plants tend to be used at other times and for many reasons. Because of variability in people's physiologic capacity to taste as well as in how culture mediates the positive or negative affect of particular tastes (Johns [this volume]; Kalow 1986; Rozin 1987), studies have revealed both inter- and intra-population variability in the definition of emergency foods and the extent to which people consume them outside of critical contexts.

Ethnology, and especially ethnobotany, tend to be ahistorical, so that unless studies coincide with a period of shortage, researchers often under-record the variety of emergency foods as well as details about their preparation and use. Further, as discussed above, insufficiently rigorous dietary surveys cannot capture the full extent to which foods that are the subject of local public derision do, after all, occur in diet (Etkin 1993). Indeed, intensive longitudinal dietary studies reveal that during periods of abundance, people extensively use many, even most, of the plants recognized for emergency purposes (e.g., Etkin and Ross, Johns, and Vickers [all in this volume]). Anecdotal evidence is similarly compelling (Cox [this volume]; Laderman 1991). For herbaceous weeds especially, this regular use assures an adequate level of human protection so that species density does not diminish to nonsustainable numbers. Some wild plants are protected as well by the utilization of other, nonemergency parts of those plants or by their use in other contexts such as medicine or cosmetics (Etkin 1994).[4]

Some emergency plants, although they vanish from a locality between episodes of dire need, still appear in the intergenerational transmission of knowledge through such vehicles as myth, ritual, and oral history. Among Hausa, for example, parables, songs, and plant-specific epithets reinforce knowledge of famines, foods, and medicines (Duffill 1986; Smith 1954; Tremearne 1970). These have special significance for married Hausa women who are constrained by purdah (seclusion within the compound) and thus have less opportunity to recall the habitat and growing characteristics of plants, especially "wild" ones. Similarly, in the desert borderlands of the American Southwest, oral traditions recall the utilization of certain plants during shortage (Minnis 1991); the ritual use of some species fosters gathering foodstuffs that otherwise might disappear from local knowledge. Also, at least one community of Native Americans in California designated individual specialists as repositories for particular species, a service for which community members reimbursed them with a portion of foods collected during the day, providing them ample time to observe and experiment throughout the group's territory and to train successors (Shipek 1989).

Like other "wild" foods, emergency foods have been poorly studied to date and can only be properly understood in the context of the diet as a whole. In Chapter 4 Rebecca Huss-Ashmore and Susan Johnston review famine foods, offering a biocultural framework that links human patterns of plant use to strategies for adapting to particular ecozones. A case study of plant use in three broad ecological areas illustrates the variety of wild plants employed by indigenous North Americans and provides a foundation for future research.

Physiologic Implications of Wild Plant Consumption

The consumption of "wild" foods has been interpreted as an adaptive strategy for periods of seasonal, other irregularly periodic, and (as outlined above) long-term catastrophic shortages of cultigens. The very pursuit of wild foods generally can be construed as adaptive since, in that quest, individuals learn about new ecologies as they migrate or venture radially from a residential center (Johnson and Baksh 1987). Wild plants do not develop with the synchrony of domesticates and are thus more regularly available. Further, researchers generally concede that the use of "wild" foods adds diversity and thus improves the quality of diet by amplifying the range of nutrients consumed. Various reports catalogue measures of one or more of the standard nutrients for selected non-cultigens. Joseph Laferriere and colleagues (1991), for example, reviewed nutritional composition for "wild" foods consumed by Mountain Pima, measuring both proximate composition (for calories, protein, carbohydrate, lipid, fiber, and ash) and mineral content (iron, copper, zinc, calcium, magnesium). They noted especially high calcium concentrations for the leaf base of *Agave shrevei matapensis* (chugilla) and cladode and fruit of *Opuntia durangensis* (prickly pear); high iron content for shoots of *Hedeoma patens* and *Monarda austromontana* (oregano grande); and high protein values for *Dahlia coccinea* (kachana) tuber, *Hymenocallis pimana* (cebollin/onion) bulb, and *Jaltomata procumbens* (tulusin) fruit. A high prevalence of vitamin A and riboflavin deficiencies in India and Malaysia, respectively, provided rationales for assessments of beta-carotene and riboflavin in "wild greens" consumed in those regions (Begum and Pereira 1977; Caldwell and Enoch 1972). In addition, nutrient analyses inspired by potential dietary deficiencies of vitamins A and C, calcium, thiamine, and riboflavin document that quelites—weedy greens from cultivated fields (*Amaranthus*, *Brassica*, and *Chenopodium* spp.)—likely contain those nutrients in ample supply for Tarahumara in Mexico (Bye 1981). Similarly, in one rural district in Kenya, local "wild" and "semiwild" plants—notably *Gynandropsis gynandra* (cat whiskers), *Amaranthus* spp., and *Commelina* spp.—contain levels of vitamins A and C in excess of recommended daily intakes, as well as relatively high levels of calcium and protein (Mwajumwa et al. 1991). Still other research has sought "new" potentially nutrient-rich resources such as the high vitamin A and protein content of the fruit of a locally prized Colombian palm (*Aiphanes caryotifolia*) previously known by the researchers only for ornamental value (Balick and Gershoff 1990).

This research tacitly accepts the premise that because noncultigens contain appreciable levels of nutrients whose relationship to physiologic health has been well established, "wild" foods make important contributions to general well-being by helping to ensure that the body can muster a competent immune response when challenged by infectious diseases and to prevent vitamin or mineral deficiencies and certain chronic disorders. Although nutrient quality merits attention, researchers should explore as well the other physiologic implications of consuming these "wild" species: academic and popular literatures alike have increasingly reported preventive and therapeutic qualities of familiar foods.[5] The chapters in this volume suggest that the adaptive, disease-mitigating qualities of "wild" foods should draw attention as well.

The multipurpose use of plants provides a basis for questions of precedence and interpretations of order. Etkin and Ross (Chapter 5) suggest that Hausa acquire knowledge and use of some "wild" food plants through experience with those plants in medicine. Johns (Chapter 3) and Logan and Dixon (Chapter 2) advance the more conventional view that people learn of the medicinal value of plants during their pursuit of foods. Johns proposes that the inclusion of unpalatable foods in normative cuisines takes advantage of the health-mediating effects of pharmacologically active constituents of plants, some of which later come to be used as medicine proper. Similarly, Logan and Dixon suggest that the transition to agriculture made available for the first time an assemblage of controlled species from which people gained new medicinal knowledge. In a synthetic model of human ecology and domestication these perspectives do not, of course, dispute one other. Cuisines and pharmacopoeias are created not in toto but incrementally, so that one pattern or another may apply for a given species; moreover, the order will vary among populations depending on perceived need and environmental circumstances. Plants also function as resources other than food and medicine, including pigments, construction materials, utensils, ritual furnishings, and hunting poisons. Analogues for the Hausa "nonfood first" model illuminate this perspective: among populations ranging from the U.S. Southwest to the Andes the ritual use of red amaranth pigments was (and in some places still is) far more common than the use of these plants for grain (Fowler and Mooney 1990); soybeans (*Glycine max*) were first cultivated in China for medicinal use and only later acquired their now-prominent dietary function (Katz 1987); given the ambiguous distinction between food and medicine in Asian cultures, other Chinese and Southwest Asian plants also are likely to have been first cultivated for medicinal use (Farrington and Urry 1985; Harlan 1992); some of the plants recognized today as flavorings apparently were domesticated for therapeutic objectives—e.g., licorice (*Glycyrrhiza glabra*) in the Mediterranean and Near East (Harlan 1992). Clearly, the interconnected histories of food and medicine are reflected in contemporary overlapping contexts of use.

Chapters 5 through 9 address the physiologic implications of consuming wild plants for populations acquiring their food resources using strategies of intensive agriculture (Hausa: Etkin and Ross), horticulture (Samoans: Cox), shifting cultivation and mixed schema (Tatuyo: Dufour and Wilson; Siona and Secoya: Vickers), and hunting and gathering (North American Indians: Moerman). In Chapters 11 through 13, Ford and colleagues, Glander, and Michelle Sauther speculate as well on the health-mediating aspects of plant use among prehistoric human populations and primates. These essays provide chronological depth and help us to visualize the dynamics of the interrelated evolution of cuisines and pharmacopoeias.

Wild Plants in Prehistoric Human Environments

Plant domestication long ago captured the interest of archaeologists concerned with the origins and spread of agriculture. Frances King (Chapter 10) reviews the preservation of archaeobotanical remains, recovery techniques, and analysis; she also advances an optimal foraging model to speculate about the types of plants that may have been most desirable in particular environments. Whereas some research has challenged the argument that human societies universally rely on optimizing strategies (Winterhalder 1987), this analytic framework has proved useful for the analysis of wild plant use by some contemporary populations and in some cases shows a conflation of emic perspectives (food preferences and beliefs) with etic ecological constraints (Johnson and Baksh 1987). The model nonetheless needs to be embellished by insights such as those offered in other chapters, which speculate on the extranutritive, health-mediating potential of "wild" plants.

With important exceptions (e.g., Hillman et al. 1989; Pyramarn 1989; Reinhard et al. 1991), archaeological reconstructions tend to be compromised by the assumption that evidence of edible plants reflects use solely in diet: even when the provenience of preserved materials suggests the technology of food preparation (e.g., mortar, mealing bin), archaeologists should not discount medicinal and other uses. In cases in which archaeobotanists do consider the extranutritive uses of wild plants, they frequently extend little effort to deduce in any detail the selection, preparation, and effects of medicinal plants and the overlap between foods and medicines, cosmetics, and the like. In this context Heather Trigg, Richard Ford, John Moore, and L. D. Jessop (Chapter 11) use a unique methodology to describe not only the potential medicinal use of plants identified through coprolite analysis, but also the presence of clay, which some contemporary peoples use to reduce the toxicity of medicinal plants.

Do Other Animals Play with Their Food?

Humans most deliberately play not only with their food but with medicines as well, including their transformations of one into the other. Researchers have difficulty distinguishing pharmacologic from nutritional adaptations for animals, just as they do trying to neatly divide human dietary and medicinal uses of plants (Etkin 1986; Etkin and Ross 1982, 1991b). Johns (1990) offers insights for the apparently "medicinal" behaviors of other animals, including "pharmacophagous" insects that concentrate plant allelochemicals as protection against predators, and others (such as black swallowtail and cabbage butterflies) that depend on allelochemicals of specific plants to regulate key phases of the reproductive cycle (Nahrstedt 1989). He reviews as well the consumption of "unusual" plants by a wide array of animals as an adaptive "strategy" that takes advantage of plant allelochemicals for control of intestinal parasites and other disorders (Janzen 1978; Johns 1990). For example, wild boars, reservoirs of many intestinal parasites, are selective and avid consumers of *Boerhaavia diffusa* (pigweed), the same species used by human populations in India for anthelmintic activity. Pigs are fond of pomegranate roots (*Punica granatum*), a potent taenicide. The consumption by rhinoceros of large quantities of tannin-rich mangrove bark (*Ceriops candoleana*) may serve an antiparasitic or antimicrobial function as well. Bears seek *Ligusticum* spp. and both eat and rub onto their fur this known vermifuge and fungicide. The consumption of plants that mechanically or chemically cause purging or emesis may be a nonspecific antidote for poisoning or other excess. For example, civets, wild dogs, and jackals that feed on purgative fruits may reduce the risk of microbial infection that results from eating the intestinal contents of their prey. The list goes on, growing from what earlier was merely an entertaining catalogue of anecdotes about nonhuman animals to a serious inquiry in today's biology about "zoo-pharmacognosy," one aspect of the complex coevolutionary process involving plants, herbivores, and their respective parasites and intestinal microflora.

In addition to employing apparently defensive and antiparasitic strategies, herbivores also seem to utilize allelochemical interactions to neutralize toxins. In controlled laboratory experiments, for example, mice provided with a choice among foods containing saponins and tannins select combinations of these foods that produce none of the toxic symptoms that develop when either of these chemicals is consumed alone. (The chelation of tannins with saponins in the intestinal tract protects against both cholesterol-binding by saponin and the erosion of intestinal epithelium by tannins [Freeland et al. 1985].) This type of behavior may also be relevant for nonexperimental circumstances, although the field of choice is of course broader and the packaging or sequencing of allelochemicals more complicated.

Chapters 12 and 13 reinforce the evolutionary perspective on human-plant use to explore behaviors that researchers have until recently assumed to be nonhuman primate "feeding" behaviors. Glander's general review of primate consumption of wild plants outside of nutritive contexts highlights behaviors that we humans share with our close relations. Observing howler monkeys, he notes that individuals smell and taste plants to detect appropriate qualities, some apparently to influence birth spacing, and that primates teach these behaviors intergenerationally. Sauther offers a uniquely detailed record of wild plant consumption by lemurs, linking shifts in diet to reproductive status. These discussions suggest new interpretations of primate-plant interactions and also offer insights into our prehominid past.

Primates not only ingest but also manipulate plants, presumably to maximize their effects. The unusual nonchewing way in which chimpanzees "feed" on *Aspilia* spp. resembles the inside-cheek or under-tongue administration of drugs that is dictated by various human medical traditions, including biomedicine. Rapid absorption from the mucous membranes of the mouth into the systemic circulation results in drugs reaching target organs without passage through the stomach or liver where they may be destroyed by low pH and detoxifying microsomal enzymes (Newton 1991). Although studies have traditionally interpreted geophagy (earth eating) in animals, including humans, as a means of ensuring adequate mineral intake (Danford 1982; Reid 1992), one can entertain as well an extranutritive function in the removal of organic and potentially toxic compounds from wild plants (Johns 1990).

Control of fire marked an important transition in hominid evolution, in no small part because cooking rendered palatable and safe some plant species that otherwise contain potentially toxic allelochemicals (Stahl 1984). Perhaps humans captured the same allelochemicals for pharmacologic action by consuming them in much smaller quantities in medicinal preparations, which typically are not heated. Other animals have apparently controlled allelochemicals as well: grizzly bears unearth bulbs of yellow dogtooth violet (*Erythronium grandiflorum*) and return several days later to eat them, in much the same way that indigenous North American peoples "age" these bulbs prior to cooking, favoring the sweeter taste afforded through conversion of inulin to fructose (Kuhnlein and Turner 1991).

Physiologic variation between species also influences these behaviors. For example, animals who have forestomach fermentation (sloths, hippopotamuses, and colobine monkeys) may consume clay to buffer forestomach pH and absorb volatile fatty acids and other fermentation products. If these animals ingest plants containing antimicrobials, by contrast, they may destroy commensal bacteria, thus impairing digestion and promoting overgrowth of pathogenic bacteria. That colobine monkeys (langurs) avoid the profusely abundant dipterocarp leaves and certain ripe fruits in their forest habitats may reflect the presence in these plant organs of antibacterial oleoresins and high concentrations of organic acids, both of which may disrupt the forestomach environment. One might speculate that colobines, unlike chimpanzees, would not engage in inside-cheek "feeding" for *Aspilia* spp.; instead, swallowing the leaves would be efficient because the high (basic) pH in the colobine proximal stomach would protect the acid-sensitive antimicrobial thiarubrine. Conversely, the complex bacterial flora of the colobine forestomach may destroy other medicinal compounds, suggesting that buccal "feeding" may occur for other plants. Clearly, for all animals, the physical environment presents a chaos of nutrients, medicines, and toxins that requires some sophistication on the part of species to design feeding strategies and on the part of researchers to comprehend (Newton 1991).

As we begin to understand more about human diversity in the ability to manage xenobiotics (Kalow et al. 1986; Jackson 1991), we can apply our knowledge as well to nonhuman models of inter- and intraspecific physiologic variability, with a view toward better understanding the evolution of "feeding" strategies generally and their implications not only for health but also for geographic range, social organization, and cultural complexity. This complicates further our definitions of plants along a wild-domesticated continuum, since clearly humans are not the only animals that influence plant selection and survival.

Biodiversity

The final chapter (15) transports us back to the present by invoking the timely and increasingly politicized concern for vanishing biodiversity. Brien Meilleur offers a general review of biodiversity and further refines the issue through specific reference to each of the preceding chapters, thus linking theoretical research to global issues.

At present the rapidity and extent to which the earth's genetic resources are being depleted threatens an extinction of species of a magnitude never before experienced in human history. For example, the International Union for Conservation of Nature and Natural Resources and the World Wide Fund for Nature have estimated that

> 60,000 higher plant species could become extinct or near extinct by the middle of the next century if present trends continue. This exceeds [nearly threefold] earlier estimates . . . which were based mainly on experience in temperate countries. . . . The primary cause of this loss will be the continuing destruction of the habitats that support these species. . . . Probably the most daunting aspect of the biodiversity issue is our almost complete ignorance of both the problem itself and potential benefits that may be lost or retained. (Principe 1991:79–80)

Although species preservation is being hotly debated from a variety of Western postures, predominantly economics (Morowitz 1991), the value of those taxa has not been adequately assessed in the local contexts of their use. Instead, outsiders who are both politically and culturally detached from the threatened environments define the "interesting" or "important" species that become the subject of conservation campaigns. Conservation efforts generally lack intellectual leadership and sustained funding. Moreover, many of the conserved species exist *ex situ* in seed banks or in tissue culture or germ plasm collections (Smith et al. 1992; Soule 1991).

If *conservation of what* has reached a bewildered adolescence, *conservation for whom* is barely in its infancy. Most policy makers pay no attention to or have no interest in admonishments from social scientists to consider indigenous knowledge of biodiversity and its conservation (Moran 1992). They fail to appreciate the link between biodiversity and human activity even in putatively "natural" ecological systems (Bennett 1992). Conservation and "development" efforts to date have tended to focus on preservation of crop biodiversity, underscoring once more the importance of better establishing both the nutritive and the pharmacologic characters of "wild" plants. Those schemes typically fail to comprehend the special role that each existing and introduced species plays in a particular agro-ecological niche (or agro-pharmacological, etc.): the characteristics of any given plant will be a composite of locally defined key niche parameters—for example, balancing yield with qualities such as taste, "secondary" products such as straw, amenability to intercropping, and the like (Bergeret and Ribot 1990; Hansen 1991; Moock and Rhoades 1992; Rambo and Sajise 1986; Richards 1985).

More recent efforts to frame biodiversity efforts through a focus on medicinal plant use (e.g., Farnsworth and Soejarto 1991) still betray a Western bias that values knowledge of medicinal plants for potential development by the pharmaceutical industry, some even glibly acknowledging their own "selfish interests" (Huxtable 1992). Greater sensitivity to the medicinal, dietary, and other significance of wild plants for local cultures would better advance global efforts to sustain biodiversity and at the same time draw attention to important ethical issues such as questions regarding ownership of data, which includes protection of indigenous populations against "chemical prospecting," compensation for intellectual property, and return of data and findings to the study community.

NOTES

1. Unless otherwise indicated, statements about Hausa diet and medicine are based on unpublished field observations by Etkin, Ross, and Muazzamu.

2. This stance departs from the conventional wisdom that as people come to rely more heavily on agriculture they consume fewer types of plants and as a corollary lose knowledge of wild plant use.

3. Scientists have long known that plant-associated microbes (*Gibberella fujikuroi*) produce growth-regulating gibberellins, and recently a research team isolated a taxol-producing fungal endophyte (*Taxomyces andreanae*) from the inner bark of Pacific yew (*Taxus brevifolia*) (Stierle et al. 1993).

4. That many of these emergency foods are also medicines suggests that their increased use during stressful times may help to contain the occurrence or severity of illness.

5. These include an initiative (championed by a clinical pharmacologist-endocrinologist) to create unique federal regulations for "nutraceuticals"—constituents of common foods in U.S. cuisines for which studies have demonstrated healthful effects. For example, sulforaphane in broccoli increases enzyme levels and protects against certain cancers; folic acid diminishes the risk of cervical cancer and neural tube birth defects; the antioxidant action of vitamins E and C reduces the risk of cataracts, heart disease, and some cancers; gamma-amino butyric acid in tomatoes is hypotensive; capsaicin in chili pepper diminishes the risk of cluster headaches and stomach cancer; sulfides in garlic and onion inhibit blood clotting and promote cardiovascular integrity; vitamins B_6 and E improve immune function in the elderly; and vitamin A reduces the severity of measles (Debrovner 1992).

REFERENCES

Baker, Herbert G.
   1991   The continuing evolution of weeds. *Economic Botany* 45:445–449.

Balick, Michael J., and Stanley N. Gershoff

1990   A nutritional study of *Aiphanes caryotifolia* fruit: An exceptional source of vitamin A and high quality protein from tropical America. In *New directions in the study of plants and people*, edited by G. T. Prance and M. J. Balick, pp. 35–40. Advances in Economic Botany, Vol. 8. New York Botanical Garden, New York.

Begum, Almas, and Sheila M. Pereira

1977   The beta carotene content of Indian edible green leaves. *Tropical and Geographic Medicine* 29:47–50.

Bennett, Bradley C.

1992   Plants and people of the Amazonian rainforests: The role of ethnobotany in sustainable development. *BioScience* 42:599–607.

Bergeret, Anne, and Jesse C. Ribot

1990   *L'arbre nourricier en pays Sahelien.* Editions de la Maison des Sciences de l'Homme, Paris.

Bouverot-Rothacker, Anita

1982   Consommer l'espace sauvage. *Etudes Rurales* 87–88:131–137.

Bye, Robert A.

1981   Quelites—Ethnoecology of edible greens—Past, present, and future. *Journal of Ethnobiology* 1:109–123.

Caldwell, M. J., and T. C. Enoch

1972   Riboflavin content of Malaysian leaf vegetables. *Ecology of Food and Nutrition* 1:309–312.

Danford, Darla E.

1982   Pica and nutrition. *Annual Review of Nutrition* 2:303–322.

Debrovner, Diane

1992   Edible remedies. *American Druggist* 205:36–40.

Duffill, M. B.

1986   Hausa poems as sources for social and economic history. *History in Africa* 13:35–88.

Duke, James A.

1992   *Handbook of edible weeds.* CRC Press, Boca Raton, Florida.

Ebeling, Walter

1986   *Handbook of Indian foods and fibers of arid America.* University of California Press, Berkeley.

Etkin, Nina L.

1993   Anthropological methods in ethnopharmacology. *Journal of Ethnopharmacology* 38:93–104.

1994   Consuming a therapeutic landscape: A multicontextual framework for assessing the health significance of human-plant interactions. *Journal of Home and Consumer Horticulture* 1(2/3):61–91.

Etkin, Nina L. [Editor]

1986   *Plants in indigenous medicine and diet: Biobehavioral approaches.* Gordon and Breach Science Publishers (Redgrave), New York.

Etkin, Nina L., and Paul J. Ross

1982 Food as medicine and medicine as food: An adaptive framework for the interpretation of plant utilization among the Hausa of northern Nigeria. *Social Science and Medicine* 16:1559–1573.

1991a Recasting malaria, medicine, and meals: A perspective on disease adaptation. In *The anthropology of medicine* [second edition], edited by L. Romanucci-Ross, D. E. Moerman, and L. R. Tancredi, pp. 230–258. Bergin and Garvey, New York.

1991b Should we set a place for diet in ethnopharmacology? *Journal of Ethnopharmacology* 32:25–36.

Farnsworth, Norman R., and Djaja D. Soejarto

1991 Global importance of medicinal plants. In *Conservation of medicinal plants,* edited by O. Akerele, V. Heywood, and H. Synge, pp. 25–51. Cambridge University Press, Cambridge.

Farrington, I. S., and James Urry

1985 Food and the early history of cultivation. *Journal of Ethnobiology* 5:143–157.

Fleuret, Anne

1979 Methods for evaluation of the role of fruits and wild greens in Shambaa diet: A case study. *Medical Anthropology* 3:249–269.

1986 Dietary and therapeutic uses of fruit in three Taita communities. In *Plants in indigenous medicine and diet: Biobehavioral approaches,* edited by N. L. Etkin, pp. 151–170. Gordon and Breach Science Publishers (Redgrave), New York.

Ford, Richard I.

1985 The processes of plant food production in prehistoric North America. In *Prehistoric food production in North America,* edited by R. I. Ford, pp. 1–18. University of Michigan Museum of Anthropology, Ann Arbor.

Fowler, Cary, and Pat Mooney

1990 *Shattering: Food, politics, and the loss of genetic diversity.* University of Arizona Press, Tucson.

Freeland, W. J., P. H. Calcott, and Lisa R. Anderson

1985 Tannins and saponin: Interaction in herbivore diets. *Biochemical Systematics and Ecology* 13:189–193.

Grossman, Lawrence S.

1991 Diet, income, and subsistence in an eastern highland village in Papua New Guinea. *Ecology of Food and Nutrition* 26:235–253.

Hansen, Art

1991 Learning from experience: Implementing farming systems research and extension in the Malawi Agricultural Research Project. In *Anthropology and food policy: Human dimensions of food policy in Africa and Latin America,* edited by D. E. McMillan, pp. 40–65. University of Georgia Press, Athens.

Harlan, Jack

1992 *Crops and man* [second edition]. American Society of Agronomy and the Crop Science Society of America, Madison, Wisconsin.

Harris, David R.

1989   An evolutionary continuum of people-plant interaction. In *Foraging and farming: The evolution of plant exploitation,* edited by D. R. Harris and G. C. Hillman, pp. 11–26. Unwin Hyman, London.

Hayden, B.

1981   Subsistence and ecological adaptations of modern hunter/gatherers. In *Omnivorous primates gathering and hunting in human evolution,* edited by R.S.O. Harding and G. Teleki, pp. 344–421. Columbia University Press, New York.

Higgs, Eric S. [Editor]

1972   *Papers in economic prehistory.* Cambridge University Press, Cambridge.

Hillman, Gordon C., Susan M. Colledge, and David R. Harris

1989   Plant-food economy during the Epipalaeolithic period at Tell Abu Hureyra, Syria: Dietary diversity, seasonality, and modes of exploitation. In *Foraging and farming: The evolution of plant exploitation,* edited by D. R. Harris and G. C. Hillman, pp. 240–268. Unwin Hyman, London.

Hoyt, Erich

1988   *Conserving the wild relatives of crops.* World Wide Fund for Nature, Rome.

Huxtable, Ryan J.

1992   The pharmacology of extinction. *Journal of Ethnopharmacology* 37:1–11.

Hynes, R. A., and A. K. Chase

1982   Plants, sites and domiculture: Aboriginal influence upon plant communities in Cape York Peninsula. *Archaeology in Oceania* 17:38–50.

Iwu, Maurice M.

1992   *Handbook of African medicinal plants.* CRC Press, Boca Raton, Florida.

Jackson, Fatimah L. C.

1991   Secondary compounds in plants (allelochemicals) as promoters of human biological variability. *Annual Review of Anthropology* 20:505–546.

Janzen, D. H.

1978   Complications in interpreting the chemical defenses of trees against tropical arboreal plant-eating vertebrates. In *The ecology of arboreal folivores,* edited by G. G. Montgomery, pp. 73–84. Smithsonian Institution Press, Washington, D.C.

Johns, Timothy

1990   *With bitter herbs they shall eat it: Chemical ecology and the origins of human diet and medicine.* University of Arizona Press, Tucson.

Johnson, Allen, and Michael Baksh

1987   Ecological and structural influences on the proportions of wild foods in the diets of two Machiguenga communities. In *Food and evolution: Toward a theory of human food habits,* edited by M. Harris and E. B. Ross, pp. 387–405. Temple University Press, Philadelphia.

Kalow, Werner

1986   Caffeine and other drugs. In *Ethnic differences in reactions to drugs and xenobiotics*, edited by W. Kalow, H. W. Goedde, and D. P. Agarwal, pp. 331–341. Alan R. Liss, New York.

Kalow, Werner, H. Werner Goedde, and Dharam P. Agarwal [Editors]
1986   *Ethnic differences in reactions to drugs and xenobiotics*. Alan R. Liss, New York.

Katz, Solomon H.
1987   Food and biocultural evolution: A model for the investigation of modern nutritional problems. In *Nutritional anthropology*, edited by F. E. Johnston, pp. 41–63. Alan R. Liss, New York.

Kindscher, Kelly
1992   *Medicinal wild plants of the prairie: An ethnobotanical guide*. University Press of Kansas, Lawrence.

Kruker, Robert, and Arnold Niederer
1982   Aspects de la cueillette dans les Alpes Suisses. *Etudes Rurales* 87–88:139–152.

Kuhnlein, Harriet V., and Nancy J. Turner
1991   *Traditional plant foods of Canadian indigenous peoples: Nutrition, botany and use*. Gordon and Breach Science Publishers, Philadelphia.

Laderman, Carol
1991   Where the wild things are. In *Diet and domestic life in society*, edited by A. Sharman, J. Theophano, K. Curtis, and E. Messer, pp. 15–32. Temple University Press, Philadelphia.

Laferriere, Joseph E.
1992   Begonias as food and medicine. *Economic Botany* 46:114–116.

Laferriere, Joseph E., Charles W. Weber, and Edwin A. Kohlhepp
1991   Use and nutritional composition of some traditional Mountain Pima plant foods. *Journal of Ethnobiology* 11:93–114.

Lockwood, Victoria S.
1993   *Tahitian transformation: Gender and capitalist development in a rural society*. Lynne Rienner, Boulder, Colorado.

Minnis, Paul E.
1991   Famine foods of the northern American desert borderlands in historical context. *Journal of Ethnobiology* 11:231–256.

Moerman, Daniel E.
1986   *Medicinal plants of Native America*. University of Michigan Museum of Anthropology Technical Reports, No. 19. Ann Arbor.

Moock, Joyce Lewinger, and Robert E. Rhoades [Editors]
1992   *Diversity, farmer knowledge, and sustainability*. Cornell University Press, Ithaca, New York.

Moran, Katy
1992   Ethnobiology and U.S. policy. In *Sustainable harvest and marketing of rainforest products*, edited by M. Plotkin and L. Famolare, pp. 289–301. Island Press, Washington, D.C.

Morowitz, Harold J.
   1991   Balancing species preservation and economic considerations. *Science* 253: 752–754.

Mwajumwa, L.B.S., E. M. Kahangi, and Jasper K. Imungi
   1991   The prevalence and nutritional value of some Kenyan indigenous leafy vegetables from three locations of Machakos District. *Ecology of Food and Nutrition* 26:275–280.

Nahrstedt, Adolf
   1989   The significance of secondary metabolites for interactions between plants and insects. *Planta Medica* 55:333–338.

Newton, Paul
   1991   The use of medicinal plants by primates: A missing link? *Tree* 6:297–299.

North, J., and P. North
   1987   *Guide to cooking with edible flowers.* Paradise Farms Press, Summerland, California.

Principe, Peter P.
   1991   Valuing the biodiversity of medicinal plants. In *Conservation of medicinal plants,* edited by O. Akerele, V. H. Heywood, and H. Synge, pp. 70–124. Cambridge University Press, Cambridge.

Pyramarn, Kosum
   1989   New evidence on plant exploitation and environment during the Hoabinhian (Late Stone Age) from Ban Kao Caves, Thailand. In *Foraging and farming: The evolution of plant exploitation,* edited by D. R. Harris and G. C. Hillman, pp. 282–291. Unwin Hyman, London.

Rambo, Terry, and Percy E. Sajise
   1986   Alternative crops. *Science* 234:801–802.

Reid, Russell M.
   1992   Cultural and medical perspectives on geophagia. *Medical Anthropology* 13: 337–351.

Reinhard, Karl J., Donny L. Hamilton, and Richard H. Hevly
   1991   Use of pollen concentration in paleopharmacology: Coprolite evidence of medicinal plants. *Journal of Ethnobiology* 11:117–132.

Richards, Paul
   1985   *Indigenous agricultural revolution.* Westview, Boulder, Colorado.

Rindos, David
   1984   *The origins of agriculture: An evolutionary perspective.* Academic Press, New York.

Rozin, Paul
   1987   Psychobiological perspectives on food preferences and avoidances. In *Food and evolution: Toward a theory of human food habits,* edited by M. Harris and E. B. Ross, pp. 387–405. Temple University Press, Philadelphia.

Rubin, Deborah S.

1992   Labor patterns in agricultural households: A time-use study in southwest-
        ern Kenya. In *Diversity, farmer knowledge, and sustainability,* edited by J. L.
        Moock and R. E. Rhoades, pp. 169–188. Cornell University Press, Ithaca,
        New York.

Shipek, Florence C.

1989   An example of intensive plant husbandry: The Kumeyaay of southern Cal-
        ifornia. In *Foraging and farming: The evolution of plant exploitation,* edited
        by D. R. Harris and G. C. Hillman, pp. 282–291. Unwin Hyman, London.

Smith, Mary F.

1954   *Baba of Karo: A woman of the Muslim Hausa.* Faber and Faber, London.

Smith, Nigel J. H., J. T. Williams, Donald L. Plucknett, and Jennifer P. Talbot

1992   *Tropical forests and their crops.* Cornell University Press, Ithaca, New York.

Soule, Michael E.

1991   Conservation: Tactics for a constant crisis. *Science* 253:744–750.

Stahl, Ann B.

1984   Hominid dietary selection before fire. *Current Anthropology* 25:151–168.

Stierle, Andrea, Gary Strobel, and Donald Stierle

1993   Taxol and taxane production by *Taxomyces andreanae,* an endophytic fungus
        of Pacific yew. *Science* 260:214–219.

Tremearne, A.J.N.

1970   *Hausa superstitions and customs: An introduction to the folk-lore and the folk*
        [Second edition]. Frank Cass, London.

White, Joyce

1989   Ethnoecological observations on wild and cultivated rice and yams in north-
        eastern Thailand. In *Foraging and farming: The evolution of plant exploita-
        tion,* edited by D. R. Harris and G. C. Hillman, pp. 152–158. Unwin Hyman,
        London.

Winterhalder, Bruce

1987   The analysis of hunter-gatherer diets: Stalking an optimal foraging model.
        In *Food and evolution: Toward a theory of human food habits,* edited by M.
        Harris and E. B. Ross, pp. 311–339. Temple University Press, Philadelphia.

Womack, Mari, and Judith Marti

1993   *The other fifty percent: Multicultural perspectives on gender relations.* Waveland
        Press, Prospect Heights, Illinois.

Workshop on Genetic Resources

1990   *Report of a workshop on the genetic resources of wild Arachis species.* FAO,
        Rome.

❧ *Selection*

2

Agriculture and the Acquisition of Medicinal Plant Knowledge

ℵ MICHAEL H. LOGAN AND ANNA R. DIXON

Even a casual reading of the ethnobotanical literature reveals that peoples with simple technologies have amassed a remarkably sophisticated understanding of their ambient plant resources. Consider, for example, the Ifugao, who recognize and label more than two thousand varieties of plants (Conklin 1980); the Kuikuru of Brazil, who can accurately determine how long former garden plots have lain fallow by observing the types and relative occurrence of successional species (Carneiro 1978); or Peruvian Indians who are able to block the body's metabolism of harmine, thus potentiating the alkaloid responsible for the psychotropic effects of the beverage *ayahuasca* (Schultes and Raffauf 1992). Similar testimony to the richness of botanical knowledge clearly emerges from current research on the elaborate cultural comprehension of plants by Maya-speaking populations in Mexico (Berlin et al. 1988, 1990), investigations of indigenous resource management in Brazil where Kayapo create islands of useful vegetation within "natural" forests (Posey 1989, 1991; but see Parker 1992), and documentation of the extensive utilization of Amazon rainforest diversity (close to 100% of available species) by Ecuadoran Quechua (Bennett 1992; see also Dufour and Wilson, Etkin and Ross, and Vickers [all in this volume]).

Equally impressive is the vast number of indigenous discoveries concerning the use of plants for medicinal purposes. The Aztec, for example, treated

An earlier version of this paper was presented at the 87th Annual Meeting of the American Anthropological Association, Phoenix, 1988. The authors would like to thank Gary Crites, Nina Etkin, Richard Ford, Benita Howell, and Bernard Ortiz de Montellano for their many helpful suggestions. Any errors or ambiguities in this article are, however, solely our own.

infected wounds with the sap of the maguey or century plant (*Agave* spp.), which medical researchers now know inhibits the growth of several genera of bacteria commonly associated with infection (Davidson and Ortiz de Montellano 1983; Dimayuga and Garcia 1991). The Aztec also used the blossoms of the hand-flower tree (*Chiranthodendron pentadactylon*) as a blood or heart tonic. Researchers have shown that water-based solutions of the flowers reduce edema and serum cholesterol levels (Jiu 1966). The hand-flower tree also acts as a diuretic (due to the glycosides quercetin and luteolin) and, when ingested regularly as a decocted beverage, is most likely effective in treating cardiopulmonary insufficiency (Logan 1981).

The list of such discoveries is truly immense (e.g., Bisset 1991; Lewis and Elvin-Lewis 1977), and people in Western societies have surely benefited from the botanical knowledge of native peoples. About half of all prescriptions currently written in the United States are for medications derived from natural plant products (Farnsworth 1990). This proportion is likely to be substantially higher in Europe and elsewhere, where the licensure of phytopharmaceutical drugs has been less restrained (Artiges 1991; Keller 1991). Outside the context of biomedicine, a recent survey estimated that one in three persons in the United States used some form of "unconventional medicine" (which includes not only plant-based preparations, but also massage, chiropractic, etc.) in the preceding year (Eisenberg et al. 1993). Exemplifying the currency of this topic, the National Institutes of Health created a new agency: the Office for the Study of Alternative Medical Practices (Cassidy 1993). The plant-based knowledge of non-Western medical traditions clearly will contribute heavily to this innovative national effort.

The ethnobotanical literature leaves no doubt that traditional cultures had, and commonly still have, an impressively vast plant-based knowledge. Yet scholars have only now begun to turn their attention systematically to a question of fundamental importance: Why have so many peoples with very simple technologies been able to discover so much from the plant kingdom? Surely elements beyond chance must have been involved. Researchers can largely rule out random experimentation, where someone would ingest a little of this plant, then move on to another and another, and then wait to assess the effects. Such a scenario is only a popularized, though persistent, myth (Johns 1986:269); moreover, oral dosages in such small amounts would rarely contain enough of a plant's biologically active compounds to induce any perceptible physiologic change.

Perceptual Salience and the Acquisition of Plant-Based Knowledge

In most cases, traditional societies acquired plant-based knowledge through a nonrandom process (Johns, Moerman [both in this volume]). This process rests on a simple yet universal feature of human-plant interaction: people target only certain species for inquiry and eventual use for they, unlike countless others, are somehow distinct or unusual. Largely for this reason, as Otto Gottlieb notes, "[i]ndigenous peoples succeeded in discovering only a small proportion of all useful organisms. The number of plants containing potentially applicable compounds with biological, pharmacological or therapeutic properties they left behind is astronomical" (1982:236). Norman Farnsworth and Djaja Soejarto estimate that a mere 15% of all angiosperm species "have been examined chemically and pharmacologically, in detail or superficially, for their medical potential" (1991:38–39). By keying in on certain species (Browner 1985) and thereby largely ignoring many others, people transformed the exceedingly diverse and complex world of plants into a meaningful and manageable cultural domain. Illustrating the discriminating nature of medicinal plant selection, 25% of plants collected on the basis of ethnomedical use reveal in vitro activity against human immunodeficiency virus (HIV), whereas only 6% of plants collected randomly demonstrate such activity; similarly, in ethnomedically informed screens, researchers obtain positive responses in 29% of plants used as anthelmintics and 20% of plants used to treat cancers, whereas only 10% of randomly selected plants have anticancer activity (Farnsworth 1990; Huxtable 1992). Even non-human primates follow a similar pattern of selectivity in the species they employ to eliminate intestinal parasites and to treat other maladies (Strier 1993).

A plant's distinctiveness can arise from many factors. Ubiquity, morphology, color, aroma, and taste certainly set some plants apart from others (Alcorn 1981, 1984; Johns 1990, [this volume]; Nabhan 1985). So, too, do such attributes as the ability to produce contact dermatitis, being noticeably free of insect predation, serving as a food for some animal species, or possessing some anthropomorphic quality. These attributes all affect what Nancy Turner calls the "perceptual salience of a plant, its 'obviousness' to people within a culture." (1988:277). A recent case in point comes from Australia, where sheep breeders noticed that their ewes were failing to reproduce. Researchers also observed that the animals fed almost exclusively on a particular type of clover, a species now known to inhibit ovulation (Riddle and Estes 1992:292).

The distinctive attributes of a given plant literally become foci of inquiry, selectively narrowing and directing human attention and experimentation toward certain species and away from others (Moerman [this volume]; Schultes 1986). Once people have made the original discovery, these attributes generate additional innovations in a predictable manner. For example, the bitter taste and pungent odor of the alkaloids in one genus—*Datura* (thorn apple), for instance—were most likely used to predict the properties, and the effect of those properties on humans, in other species and genera with similar tastes and smells. Michael Brown's work with the Aguaruna Jivaro of eastern Peru provides a telling example. Each of the differing *Datura* species employed by these people to induce visions has the same bitter taste and nauseating smell (Brown 1978:124). Perhaps for this reason peoples in Mexico have given the same name, "epazote," to two morphologically distinct genera: *Chenopodium* (Chenopodiaceae) and *Lippia* (Verbenaceae) (Morton 1981:176–178, 746–747). While these plants certainly look different, both have strong, pungent odors. In this way, existing knowledge generates new knowledge, typically in a linked or linear manner. Interestingly, a recent essay by John M. Riddle and J. Worth Estes on the origins of oral contraceptives in ancient and medieval times notes, "Like Queen Anne's lace," (*Daucus carota* var. *carota*) "the *strong-smelling* woody herb 'rue' (*Ruta graveolens*) seems to turn up in many regions and, as an antifertility agent, in many times and cultures. The ancients used rue both as a contraceptive and as an abortifacient" (1992:232; emphasis added). Perhaps the shared trait of a similarly strong smell in these highly different taxa led to similar medicinal uses.

More researchers are beginning to focus on the role of taste and olfaction in indigenous patterns of plant utilization. For example, the emic concept of "irritant"—judged by the presence of a bitter taste—has structured the suite of plants used in Colombia and Mexico for regulating a woman's menstrual cycle and for inducing abortions (Browner and Ortiz de Montellano 1986). Timothy Johns (1986, 1989, [this volume]) has offered the most insightful perspective to date on the importance of taste and smell as agents of plant selection. Indeed, characteristic odors and tastes may be of particular importance in imparting perceptual salience to plants. In a survey of the scented flora of the world, Roy Genders observed that "there are 4,000 to 5,000 species of plants utilized for various purposes and of these, no more than *one-tenth* have a pleasing smell, the rest being either scentless or having an unpleasant smell" (1977:73; emphasis added). Although the perception of what makes a scent "pleasing" is subjective, Genders's observation is nonetheless significant and may in part account for the seeming bias toward particular families of plants as medicinals (Moerman [this volume]). Peoples in traditional cultures, including those in the archaeological past, certainly had long employed taste and odor to select certain species (and varieties) for medicinal use (Negbi 1992). They also used taste and smell to engineer more desirable food plants (Bye 1979; Davis and Bye 1982; Etkin and Ross 1991; Heiser 1985).

Agriculture, Disease, and the Growth of Plant-Based Knowledge

Using extensive cross-cultural data, Cecil Brown (1985) has demonstrated that agriculturists have, on average, larger plant lexicons (named vocabularies) than do hunting and gathering groups. Agricultural societies developed extensive plant lexicons, according to Brown, as fail-safe mechanisms should agriculture fall short of providing a sufficient food base (1985:49). In such cases, a society's lexicon for wild plants would allow its members to recognize and use secondary resources until local agricultural practices could once again provide sufficient food. Within the complex processes leading to agriculture lie a number of other selective agents that favored the growth of medicinal plant knowledge (Brown 1985). Brown also reports on many of these.

The first, and perhaps most obvious, aspect that advanced the growth of medicinal plant knowledge pertains to differential disease load. Sickness is much more prevalent, pervasive, and diverse among agriculturists than among hunters and gatherers (Cohen and Armelagos 1984; Logan and Hunt 1978:Section II; Stuart-Macadam and Kent 1992). Peasants in Oaxaca, for example, suffered from an average of more than five separate diagnosed diseases per patient (Rubel et al. 1984), an epidemiological picture in direct contrast to that of the nomadic Bushmen, who enjoyed excellent nutrition and health prior to forced resettlement (Howell 1979; Truswell and Hansen 1976; see also Kolata 1974; Wirsing 1985). Medicinal discoveries often arise from the need to combat newly introduced or increasingly threatening diseases, as cancer and acquired immune deficiency syndrome (AIDS) so clearly demonstrate today. Growth in botanical lexicons is clearly linked to the relative risk or prevalence of disease (Johns 1990:262–263).

Another reason pertains to human fertility and population control. Hunting and gathering groups successfully regulated their size in a number of ways: social fission, postpartum sexual taboos, delayed menarche, infanticide, prolonged breastfeeding, and later age at first marriage (Bodley 1985:145–170). Apparently they had relatively little need to manipulate reproductive behavior through botanical (or other medicinal) means. This situation changed, however, with the transition to an agricultural economy, after which populations grew rapidly (Buikstra et al. 1986). Having many children also changed from a deficit to an asset, with children making important contributions in the family work force (Thomas 1975). Yet frequent birthing and a lowering of age at menarche (Frisch and McArthur 1974; Scott and Johnston 1985) intensified maternal health problems. Warren Hern, a physician who has worked extensively with the Shipibo of eastern Peru, has observed the deleterious effects of frequent pregnancies on maternal health (1992). Shipibo women greatly desire contraceptive technology, yet Western forms are not available and the botanical resources necessary for employing traditional methods are rapidly disappearing due to acculturation and environmental change. Throughout human history, however, the concern for maternal health undoubtedly led to an increased focus on plants that could affect human reproduction: contraceptives, parturients, galactagogues, emmenagogues, and abortifacients.

Also, with an agrarian lifeway the diet changed dramatically. The number of diversified items composing the diet of hunters and gatherers (Lee 1984; Winterhalder and Smith 1981) shrank with agriculture to only two or three staple foods. In many cases, only one plant source provided the majority of all calories consumed, as with maize in Mesoamerica (Galinat 1992). With the loss of dietary breadth, many agricultural societies seem to have increasingly favored the use of spices, many of which are also used medicinally (Etkin and Ross 1982, 1991; C. Wilson 1981). The quest for spices or flavorings would surely have added to a group's botanical lexicon.

Lexical growth also resulted from the impact of agriculture on the natural environment. The clearing of forest for garden plots created a habitat ideal for "edge" species (Crites 1987; Kunstadter 1978:174). With cultivation and agriculture came weeds and, in turn, additional discoveries. Agriculturists utilized many of these herbaceous annuals as food sources (Bohrer 1991; Ford 1985; McClung de Tapia 1992). Agricultural societies even domesticated some—for example, *Iva* (Yarnell 1978), *Chenopodium* (Smith 1985; H. Wilson 1981), and *Amaranthus* (Ford 1985:356). Many also served medicinal purposes, a role owing in part to human alteration of the natural environment. That traditional cultures often use the same plants in different contexts, especially in food and medicine (Etkin and Ross 1982), provides a key for understanding the physiologic significance of those plants for human populations. Johns (1989:516) notes, "From a chemical-ecological perspective, food, condiments, medicine, stimulants, and toxins can be viewed as parts of a continuum with a chemical basis, rather than as separate entities."

As societies became increasingly dependent upon agriculture they also exhibited greater internal economic specialization (Carneiro 1967; Ford 1985; Harris 1989). Full-time healers emerged, and with them a growth in plant-based knowledge. Differences arose between laity and specialist, with the latter holding an expertise on medicinal plant use far more elaborate than what most patients commanded. Mexican folk healers and their clientele, for example, display this pattern of variation in knowledge (Finkler 1984). Similarly, Joseph Bastien observes that Bolivian herbalists "employ more than a thousand medicinal plants, 25 to 30% of which provide effective cures" (1992:47). The knowledge of medicinal plant use exhibited by patients surely cannot even remotely compare to that of their attending herbalist healers.

Agriculturists differ from hunters and gatherers in many ways, and variations in disease load, settlement pattern, fertility, diet, altered environments, and economic specialization must all have favored the acquisition of new knowledge concerning plants. This disparity in turn led to the larger botanical lexicons observed by Brown (1985).

In sum, agriculturists purposefully selected, curated, and genetically altered plants to a much greater degree than did hunters and gatherers and thereby achieved certain discoveries that remained largely unknown in nomadic groups. The terms *wild, cultivated,* and *domesticated* actually represent points on a continuum of human-plant relationships. At one end of this continuum are wild plants, defined as those "which grow outside the man-disturbed habitat, and which cannot successfully invade permanently man-disturbed habitats" (de Wet and Harlan 1975:99). Further along the continuum, the activities of hunting and gathering populations (such as repeatedly harvesting the same stand, or firing areas to encourage the growth of herbaceous taxa) can result in "incidental domestication" (Miller 1992; Rindos 1989; Shipek 1989; Yen 1989). Cultivation, where crop plants are intentionally planted, represents the next point on a continuum of increasing interference with the natural ecosystem. Finally, domestication results once a plant has "evolved into a new form under continued human manipulation so that it may have lost the ability to reproduce itself" (Miller 1992:39).

Thus, the term *wild* applies when a plant's habitat does not include secondary (disturbed) habitats such as open areas, thickets, roadsides, old fields, edges of fields, and so forth. "Controlled" plant species include not only plants regarded as disturbance indicators ("weeds"), but also cultivated and domesticated plants. However, a taxon may be "weedy" in one part of its range but wild in another, depending on factors such as temperature, moisture, edaphic conditions, and degree of competition with other plants. Further, plants may move back and forth on this continuum (cf. Harlan 1992:67), as was the case for *Iva annua* var. *macrocarpa* (large-seeded marshelder), *Chenopodium berlandieri* (lamb's quarters), *Phalaris caroliniana* (Carolina maygrass), and *Polygonum erectum* (erect knotweed) in prehistoric eastern North America (Smith 1992). Put simply, the modification of plants to meet culturally defined needs (and agriculture is really nothing more than this) favored the acquisition of new knowledge. This certainly seems to be the situation concerning one realm of medicinal plant use: gynecological aids.

Agricultural Groups and the Control of Human Fertility

Why, for example, in the suite of plants used as contraceptives, emmenagogues, galactogogues, or abortifacients by geographically and historically independent agricultural groups are many of the species either weeds, cultivars, or domesticates? American wormseed (*Chenopodium ambrosioides*), rue, and cotton (*Gossypium* spp.) are clear cases in point (Conway and Slocum 1979; Riddle and Estes 1992). Why, too, are many of these fertility agents also used as spices or condiments?

The answer to these questions lies, possibly, in the basic nature of agriculture itself. Plants are purposefully selected and manipulated because they possess culturally desired traits first identified by taste, olfaction, and frequently, of course, edibility (Farrington and Urry 1985; Johns 1990). Thus, the accumulation of plant-based knowledge follows from repeated observation of the effects certain plants have on human fertility, birthing, menstruation, and lactation. Most likely the people of Mesoamerica originally "discovered" capsicum peppers because of their taste (Eshbaugh et al. 1983) and only after continued dietary utilization and eventual domestication did they realize the oxytocic properties of these flavorings (Browner and Ortiz de Montellano 1986). Spearmint (*Mentha spicata*) would be another example (Kamboj and Dhawan 1982). Much the same can be said for many of the most commonly used gynecological aids in folk systems worldwide: onion (*Allium* spp.), garlic (*Allium sativum*), cloves (*Syzygium aromaticum*), nutmeg (*Myristica fragrans*), cumin seeds (*Cuminum cyminum*), black pepper (*Piper nigrum*), chili peppers (*Capsicum* spp.), avocado (*Persea americana*), pineapple (*Ananas comosus*), papaya (*Carica papaya*), pennyroyal (*Hedeoma pulegioides*), sesame seeds (*Sesamum indicum*), lemons and limes (*Citrus* spp.), and so forth (Farnsworth et al. 1975).[1] People most likely discovered the effects of these plants on human reproduction as a consequence of an agrarian lifeway. Moreover, they added the gynecological aids to an existing body of knowledge (and lexicon) that derived from a pre-agricultural lifestyle.

This point clearly appears in the plant knowledge that Peter Kunstadter reports for the Lua' swiddeners of Thailand. First, a majority of their economically useful plant varieties come from managed habitats (swiddens), not wild contexts. As for fertility-controlling plant agents, the greatest number are "aromatic spices or herbs, which are also used for other purposes" (Kunstadter 1978:191), notably as dietary items or flavorings.

A similar picture emerges for other cultural regions as well; many of the remedies popularly used to control reproduction involve species with similar, although distinctive, traits based on odor and taste. Many of these—for example, elderberry (*Sambucus* spp. [Moerman 1989])—have alternative, and most likely earlier, uses as spices or foods. Nina Etkin and Paul Ross report that for Hausa of Nigeria, "among the 107 Hausa plants used as medicines for gastrointestinal (GI) disorders, fully 49% are used as food as well" (1991:28).

If this hypothesis is valid—that agriculture itself led to additional discoveries of gynecological aids—then a significant proportion of the plants involved for such purposes should either be "weeds" or cultivars and domesticates. Were discovery only a chance-based phenomenon, little affected by an agrarian lifestyle, then controlled plants should not have an overriding presence in the total set of species employed by agrarian peoples for reproductive purposes. After all, in any environment, the number of wild species far overshadows the number of controlled species. Logically, then, the ratio of wild to controlled species should always favor the former, and strongly so. But do the actual patterns of plant use in traditional agrarian cultures exhibit this ratio?

Kunstadter's (1978) data from Thailand say no. So, too, do the data of Carole Browner and Bernard Ortiz de Montellano (1986) drawn from Cali, Colombia, and Oaxaca, Mexico. Sandra Orellana's (1987) data for pre-Hispanic and colonial Guatemala, Catherine Greene's (1988) for contemporary Isthmus Zapotec, and G. E. Ferro-Luzzi's for India (1980a, b) say no as well. In a randomly drawn sample from a cross-cultural list of plants reported to have uterine stimulant activity (Farnsworth et al. 1975), Anna Dixon (1989) found that all 15 plants were under some form of human management.[2]

The Control of Plants and Human Fertility in Mexico

To further test whether the pattern of domination by controlled species was simply coincidental, we consulted the volume published by the Instituto Mexicano para el Estudio de las Plantas Medicinales (IMEPLAM: Luis Diaz 1976) for information on reproductive aids. This data base provides a computerized listing of genera and species identified in major ethnobotanical works on Mexico. Each entry carries information on medicinal use, plant parts used, how the remedies are prepared and taken, and a note on efficacy. Unfortunately, only two fertility-related use categories are represented, galactogogues and emmenagogues, the latter being numerically larger and therefore the one examined here.

The IMEPLAM volume identifies 84 entries as emmenagogues. Of these, about half are native to the New World. The question explored here is how many of these indigenous species are wild and how many are controlled. To reiterate, a plant will be considered "controlled" if it is either managed, as in the case of weeds, or grown expressly for given cultural goals, whether as an ornamental plant, a spice, a food crop, or a medicinal agent. Again, if the process of discovery did not significantly involve active selection and manipulation of plants for their culturally desired traits, then the ratio of wild to controlled species should strongly favor the former, since wild species far outnumber weeds, cultivars, or domesticates on the landscape. But does such a pattern hold for the present sample?

Of the 40 entries considered here (see Table 2.1),[3] two-thirds are purposefully controlled. Some hold a prominent role in the traditional diet, notably, maize (*Zea mays*), chilies (*Capsicum annuum*), avocado (*Persea americana*), papaya (*Carica papaya*), and maguey (*Agave atrovirens*). Some also yield important flavorings, for example, vanilla (*Vanilla planifolia*) and epazote (*Chenopodium ambrosioides*). Others, such as malva (*Malvaviscus* spp.), serve as

Table 2.1 Herbal Emmenagogues Listed in the IMEPLAM Database

Genus and Species	Family	W	C	D	F
Acrostichum sorbifolium sic	Polypodiaceae	X			
Adiantum capillus-veneris L.	Polypodiaceae	X			
Adiantum tenerum Swartz	Polypodiaceae	X			
Agave atrovirens Karw.	Amaryllidaceae		X		X
Aloysia triphylla (L'Herit.) Britton	Verbenaceae		X	X	X
Ambrosia artemisiifolia L.	Asteraceae		X	X	
Aristolochia fragrantissima sic	Aristolochiaceae	X		X	
Aristolochia grandiflora Swartz	Aristolochiaceae	X		X	
Aristolochia pentandra Jacq.	Aristolochiaceae	X		X	
Bursera simaruba (L.) Sarg.	Burseraceae		X	X	
Caesalpinia pulcherrima (L.) Schwartz	Fabaceae		X	X	X
Calamintha macrostema sic	Lamiaceae		X	X	
Capparis flexuosa L.	Capparidaceae	X		X	X
Capsicum annuum L.	Solanaceae		X	X	X
Carica papaya L.	Caricaceae		X	X	X
Cassia laevigata Willd.	Fabaceae		X	X	X
Cassia occidentalis L.	Fabaceae		X	X	X
Castilla elastica Sesse	Moraceae		X		
Chenopodium ambrosioides L.	Che-nopodiaceae		X	X	X
Cosmos diversifolius Otto	Asteraceae		X		
Dorstenia contrajerva L.	Moraceae	X		X	X
Eupatorium odoratum L.	Asteraceae		X	X	
Euphorbia pulcherrima Willd. ex Klotsch	Euphorbiaceae		X	X	
Ficus petiolaris sic	Moraceae	X			
Juniperus communis L.	Cupressaceae	X		X	
Juniperus sabina L.	Cupressaceae	X		X	
Lippia scaberrima Mold.	Verbenaceae		X	X	X
Malvaviscus pentacarpus Moc. et Sesse	Malvaceae		X		X
Mikania guaco Humb. & Bonpl.	Asteraceae		X	X	
Montanoa tomentosa Cervant.	Asteraceae		X	X	

Table 2.1 Continued

Genus and Species	Family	W	C	D	F
Myroxylon balsamum L.f.	Fabaceae		X	X	X
Persea americana Mill.	Lauraceae		X		X
Piper sanctum (Miquel) Schlecht.	Piperaceae	X		X	X
Pluchea odorata (L.) Cass.	Asteraceae		X	X	
Porophyllum tagetoides sic	Asteraceae		X		
Sambucus mexicana Presl. ex A.DC.	Caprifoliaceae	X		X	X
Tagetes lucida Cav.	Asteraceae		X	X	X
Vanilla planifolia Andrews	Orchidaceae		X	X	X
Zea mays L.	Poaceae		X		X
Zephyranthes carinata (Sprengel) Herbert	Amaryllidaceae		X	X	

Source: Luis Diaz 1976
Abbreviations: W = wild; C = controlled; D = distinctive taste, odor, etc.; F = food, etc.

ornamentals. Several entries are grown almost solely for their use as medicinals: the sweet marigold or pericon (*Tagetes lucida*) and cihuapatli (*Montanoa tomentosa*) are well-known examples (Ortiz de Montellano 1990). Several plants in the IMEPLAM list are also minor dietary components, serving as flavorings for foods and beverages, smoking mixtures, and other uses. These plants include *Sambucus mexicana,* with its edible fruits (Morton 1981:296, 299); *Caesalpinia pulcherrima* (barba de barata), which has edible green seeds and seed gum (Morton 1981:284–285); *Cassia laevigata* (cafe del pais) and *C. occidentalis* (achu-poroto), the seeds of which are used as a coffee substitute (Morton 1981:335); *Aloysia triphylla,* or cedron (Morton 1981:733); and *Lippia scaberrima,* or corron-chocho (=*L. dulcis;* Morton 1981:746). In all, 19 (48%) of the plants in this sample serve as foods or flavorings.

Interestingly, 29 (73%) of the 40 plants also possess characteristic tastes, odors, or both or, less importantly, unusual appearances. These distinctive odors and tastes are probably linked with the underlying chemistry that accounts for these plants' medicinal uses. Other plants, such as ragweed (*Ambrosia artemisiifolia*), are clearly invasion species or weeds, a status no doubt enhancing their salience to agriculturists. As Darrell Posey notes for the Kayapo of Brazil, "Most of what Western agriculturalists would consider 'weeds' in a Kayapo field are, in fact, useful semi-domesticates for the Indians" (1986: 106).

The IMEPLAM data clearly illustrate that the controlled species used as emmenagogues outnumber the wild species (27 vs. 13). Given Mexico's floral diversity (Sanchez 1968; Standley 1920–1926), with several thousands of wild species from which humans could have randomly selected and assessed experimentally, one would not expect this pattern to have emerged solely by chance. The data on plants used for reproductive purposes can be better explained as a product of selection resulting from an agrarian lifeway.

Retrospect on the Origins of Plant-Based Knowledge

Agriculture obviously changed the way people perceived and interacted with plants (Ford 1985). Many species now employed in the realm of human reproduction were probably first "targeted" and used for nonmedicinal purposes, notably as foods, flavorings, and preservatives. Other species became better known because of some distinctive feature, as with the ubiquity of weeds. Only later, after a long and intimate involvement with these plants, did humans generate a new botanical environment (Crites 1987; Heiser 1985; Miller 1992; Rindos 1984; Yen 1989) from which both accumulation of medical knowledge and growth in a group's botanical lexicon occurred.

Furthermore, the economic and reproductive roles of women played center stage in determining which species became common fertility or reproductive aids. Because women typically care for children and prepare, cook, and store foods, as well as weed fields and tend house-lot gardens (Finerman 1989; Watson and Kennedy 1991), they have access to many dietary items employed medicinally as emmenagogues, abortifacients, galactagogues, and so forth. Food, in an important way, most likely gave women a degree of control over reproduction—an independence—not seen in pre-agrarian times. However, this independence may not always be fully realized in modern stratified societies, where the competing interests of husbands, health agencies, and national governments may, at times, dominate (Browner 1986).

Medicinal plant use can now be placed into a broad historical or evolutionary perspective. With the transition from hunting and gathering to agriculture, human groups entered into a novel form of botanical resource management in which the process of medicinal plant selection gained an additional dimension or focus. For the first time people derived health-related knowledge from a new pool of plants—the controlled species. Since then, agrarian peoples have exerted additional forces of selection through which they have refined the culturally valued qualities of culinary and medicinal items (Johns 1990). Random experimentation had little to do with the acquisition of plant-based knowledge in traditional cultures. Moreover, the variance between hunter-gatherers and agriculturists in the size of botanical lexicons owes as much to a changed lifestyle and women's health as to a fail-safe edge against famine and eating on "the wild side."

NOTES

1. With the apparent rise in public interest in "alternative" medicines, as well as conservative attitudes opposing abortion, the possibility exists that some women may turn to plant medicines for a solution to unwanted pregnancies (de Smet 1991).

2. The 15 taxa investigated by Dixon are *Adhatoda vasica* Nees; *Artemisia maritima* L.; *Astragalus glycyphyllos* L.; *Berberis vulgaris* L.; *Carum carvi* L.; *Citrus aurantium* L.; *Clerodendrum uncinatum* Schinz.; *Cnicus benedictus* L.; *Marrubium vulgare* L.; *Ocimum sanctum* L.; *Orthosiphon aristatus* (Bl.) Miq. (= *O. stamineus*); *Pisum sativum* var. *arvense* (L.) Poiret.; *Plumbago zeylanica* L.; *Solidago odora* Aiton; and *Withania somnifera* Dunal.

3. Several inaccuracies appear in the IMEPLAM listing of emmenagogues. Some involve the use of archaic binomials (e.g., *Persea gratissima* for *P. americana*). Others pertain to duplication due to synonymy, as in the case of *Agave atrovirens* and *A. mexicana* being listed as two separate species. Because of such problems, as well as the inability to locate sufficient reference materials on certain entries, the total size of the New World species examined here is smaller ($N=40$) than it would be if the IMEPLAM listing were taken at face value.

REFERENCES

Alcorn, Janis B.

1981   Some factors influencing botanical resource perception among the Huastec. *Journal of Ethnobiology* 1:221–230.

1984   *Huastec Mayan ethnobotany.* University of Texas Press, Austin.

Artiges, A.

1991   What are the legal requirements for the use of phytopharmaceutical drugs in France? *Journal of Ethnopharmacology* 32:231–234.

Bastien, Joseph W.

1992   *Drum and stethoscope: Integrating ethnomedicine and biomedicine in Bolivia.* University of Utah Press, Salt Lake City.

Bennett, Bradley C.

1992   Plants and people of the Amazonian rainforest: The role of ethnobotany in sustainable development. *BioScience* 42:599–607.

Berlin, Brent, Elois A. Berlin, D. E. Breedlove, T. Duncan, V. Jarra, R. Laughlin, and A. Mendez

1988   Scientific and practical contributions of traditional Mayan medicine. Paper presented at the 87th Annual Meeting of the American Anthropological Association, Phoenix, 16–20 November.

Berlin, Brent, Elois A. Berlin, D. E. Breedlove, T. Duncan, V. Jarra, R. M. Laughlin, and T. Velasco

1990   *La herbolaria medica Tzeltal-Tzotzil.* Instituto Cultura Chiapaneco, Chiapas, Mexico.

Bisset, Norman G.

1991   One man's poison, another man's medicine? *Journal of Ethnopharmacology* 32:71–81.

Bodley, John H.

1985   *Anthropology and contemporary human problems* [Second edition]. Mayfield, Palo Alto, California.

Bohrer, Vorsila

1991   Recently recognized cultivated and encouraged plants among the Hohokam. *Kiva* 56(3):227–235.

Brown, Cecil H.

1985   Mode of subsistence and folk biological taxonomy. *Current Anthropology* 26:43–64.

Brown, Michael F.

1978   From the hero's bones: Three Aguaruna hallucinogens and their uses. In *The nature and status of ethnobotany*, edited by R. I. Ford, pp. 119–136. University of Michigan Museum of Anthropology, Ann Arbor.

Browner, Carole H.

1985   Criteria for selecting herbal remedies. *Ethnology* 24:13–32.

1986   The politics of reproduction in a Mexican village. *Signs: Journal of Women in Culture and Society* 2:710–724.

Browner, Carole H., and Bernard Ortiz de Montellano

1986   Herbal emmenagogues used by women in Colombia and Mexico. In *Plants in indigenous medicine and diet*, edited by N. L. Etkin, pp. 32–47. Gordon and Breach Science Publishers (Redgrave), New York.

Buikstra, Jane E., Lyle W. Konigsberg, and Jill Billington

1986   Fertility and the development of agriculture for the prehistoric Midwest. *American Antiquity* 51:528–546.

Bye, Robert A.

1979   Incipient domestication of mustards in northwestern Mexico. *Kiva* 44:237–254.

Carneiro, Robert L.

1967   On the relationship between size of population and complexity of social organization. *Southwestern Journal of Anthropology* 23:234–243.

1978   The knowledge and use of rain forest trees by the Kuikuru Indians of central Brazil. In *The nature and status of ethnobotany*, edited by R. I. Ford, pp. 201–216. University of Michigan Museum of Anthropology, Ann Arbor.

Cassidy, Claire

1993   Unconventional thinking at NIH. *American Anthropological Association Newsletter* 34(2):25.

Cohen, Mark A., and George J. Armelagos [Editors]
  1984   *Paleopathology and the origins of agriculture.* Academic Press, Orlando, Florida.

Conklin, Harold C.
  1980   *Ethnographic atlas of the Ifugao: A study of environment, culture, and society in northern Luzon.* Yale University Press, New Haven.

Conway, George A., and John C. Slocum
  1979   Plants used as abortifacients and emmenagogues by Spanish New Mexicans. *Journal of Ethnopharmacology* 1:241–261.

Crites, Gary D.
  1987   Human-plant mutualism and niche expression in the paleoethnobotanical record: A Middle Woodland example. *American Antiquity* 52:725–740.

Davidson, J. R., and Bernard Ortiz de Montellano
  1983   The antibacterial properties of an Aztec wound remedy. *Journal of Ethnopharmacology* 8:149–161.

Davis, Tilton, and Robert A. Bye
  1982   Ethnobotany and progressive domestication of "jaltomata" (Solanaceae) in Mexico and Central America. *Economic Botany* 36:225–241.

de Smet, Peter A.G.M.
  1991   Is there any danger in using traditional remedies? *Journal of Ethnopharmacology* 32:43–50.

de Wet, J., and J. Harlan
  1975   Evolution in the man-made habitat. *Economic Botany* 29(2):99–107.

Dimayuga, Rosalba E., and Sergio K. Garcia
  1991   Antimicrobial screening of medicinal plants from Baja California Sur, Mexico. *Journal of Ethnopharmacology* 31:181–192.

Dixon, Anna R.
  1989   Acquisition of medicinal plant knowledge: A cross cultural survey. M.A. thesis, Department of Anthropology, University of Tennessee, Knoxville.

Eisenberg, David M., R. C. Kessler, C. Foster, F. Norlock, D. Calkins, and T. Delbanco
  1993   Unconventional medicine in the United States. *New England Journal of Medicine* 328(4):246–252.

Eshbaugh, W. H., S. I. Guttman, and M. J. McLeod
  1983   The origin and evolution of domesticated *Capsicum* species. *Journal of Ethnobiology* 3:49–54.

Etkin, Nina L., and Paul J. Ross
  1982   Food as medicine and medicine as food: An adaptive framework for the interpretation of plant utilization among the Hausa of northern Nigeria. *Social Science and Medicine* 16:1559–1573.
  1991   Should we set a place for diet in ethnopharmacology? *Journal of Ethnopharmacology* 32:25–36.

Farnsworth, Norman R.

1990   The role of ethnopharmacology in drug development. In *Bioactive compounds from plants*, edited by D. J. Chadwick and J. Marsh, pp. 2–21. John Wiley and Sons, Chichester.

Farnsworth, Norman R., Audrey S. Bingel, Geoffrey A. Cordell, Frank A. Crane, and Harry H. S. Fong

1975   Potential value of plants as a source of new antifertility agents. *Journal of Pharmaceutical Sciences* 64:535–589.

Farnsworth, Norman R., and Djaja D. Soejarto

1991   Global importance of medicinal plants. In *The conservation of medicinal plants*, edited by O. Akerle, V. Heywood, and H. Synge, pp. 25–51. Cambridge University Press, Cambridge.

Farrington, I. S., and James Urry

1985   Food and the early history of cultivation. *Journal of Ethnobiology* 5:143–158.

Ferro-Luzzi, G. E.

1980a   Food avoidances of pregnant women in Tamilnad. In *Food, ecology, and culture*, edited by J.R.K. Robson, pp. 101–108. Gordon and Breach Science Publishers, New York.

1980b   Food avoidances during the puerperium and lactation in Tamilnad. In *Food, ecology, and culture*, edited by J.R.K. Robson, pp. 109–118. Gordon and Breach Science Publishers, New York.

Finerman, Ruthbeth

1989   The forgotten healers: Women as family healers in an Andean Indian community. In *Women as healers: Cross-cultural perspectives*, edited by C. S. McClain, pp. 24–41. Rutgers University Press, New Brunswick, New Jersey.

Finkler, Kaja

1984   The nonsharing of medical knowledge among spiritualist healers and their patients. *Medical Anthropology* 8:195–209.

Ford, Richard I. [Editor]

1985   *Prehistoric food production in North America*. University of Michigan Museum of Anthropology, Ann Arbor.

Frisch, Rose E., and J. W. McArthur

1974   Menstrual cycles: Fatness as a determinant of minimum weight necessary for their maintenance or onset. *Science* 185:949–951.

Galinat, Walton C.

1992   Maize, gift from America's first peoples. In *Chilies to chocolate: Foods the Americas gave the world*, edited by N. Foster and L. S. Cordell, pp. 47–60. University of Arizona Press, Tucson.

Genders, Roy

1977   *Scented flora of the world*. St. Martin's, New York.

Gottlieb, Otto R.

1982   Ethnopharmacology *versus* chemosystematics in the search for biologically active principles in plants. *Journal of Ethnopharmacology* 6:227–238.

Greene, Catherine M.

   1988   Parteras, partos, y plantas: Isthmus Zapotec childbirth, ethnobotany, and perinatal traditions. M.A. thesis, Department of Anthropology, Indiana University, Bloomington.

Harlan, Jack R.

   1992   *Crops and man* [Second edition]. American Society of Agronomy and Crop Science Society of America, Madison, Wisconsin.

Harris, David R.

   1989   An evolutionary continuum of people-plant interaction. In *Foraging and farming,* edited by D. R. Harris and G. C. Hillman, pp. 11–26. Unwin Hyman, London.

Heiser, Charles B.

   1985   *Of plants and people.* University of Oklahoma Press, Norman.

Hern, Warren M.

   1992   Family planning, Amazon style. *Natural History* 101(12):30–38.

Howell, Nancy

   1979   *Demography of the Dobe Kung.* Academic Press, New York.

Huxtable, Ryan J.

   1992   The pharmacology of extinction. *Journal of Ethnopharmacology* 37:1–11.

Jiu, James

   1966   A survey of some medicinal plants of Mexico for selected biological activities. *Lloydia* 29:250–259.

Johns, Timothy

   1986   Chemical selection in Andean domesticated tubers as a model for the acquisition of empirical plant knowledge. In *Plants in indigenous medicine and diet,* edited by N. L. Etkin, pp. 266–288. Gordon and Breach Science Publishers (Redgrave), New York.

   1989   A chemical-ecological model of root and tuber domestication in the Andes. In *Foraging and farming,* edited by D. R. Harris and G. C. Hillman, pp. 504–519. Unwin Hyman, London.

   1990   *With bitter herbs they shall eat it: Chemical ecology and the origins of human diet and medicine.* University of Arizona Press, Tucson.

Kamboj, V. P. and B. N. Dhawan

   1982   Research on plants for fertility regulation in India. *Journal of Ethnopharmacology* 6:191–226.

Keller, K.

   1991   Legal requirements for the use of phytopharmaceutical drugs in the Federal Republic of Germany. *Journal of Ethnopharmacology* 32:225–229.

Kolata, Gina B.

   1974   Kung hunter-gatherers: Feminism, diet, and birth control. *Science* 185:932–934.

Kunstadter, Peter

    1978   Ecological modification and adaptation: An ethnobotanical view of Lua' swiddeners in northwestern Thailand. In *The nature and status of ethnobotany*, edited by R. I. Ford, pp. 168–200. University of Michigan Museum of Anthropology, Ann Arbor.

Lee, Richard B.

    1984   The hunters: Scarce resources in the Kalahari. In *Conformity and Conflict* [Fifth edition], edited by J. P. Spradley and D. W. McCurdy, pp. 183–199. Little, Brown and Company, Boston.

Lewis, Walter H., and Memory P. F. Elvin-Lewis

    1977   *Medical botany: Plants affecting man's health.* John Wiley and Sons, New York.

Logan, Michael H.

    1981   Ethnography and the empirical validity of Mesoamerican folk medicine: Some methodological and research considerations. In *Aspects of American Hispanic and Indian involvement in biomedical research,* edited by J. V. Martinez and D. I. Martinez, pp. 89–103. SACNAS Publications, Bethesda, Maryland.

Logan, Michael H., and Edward E. Hunt [Editors]

    1978   *Health and the human condition: Perspectives on medical anthropology.* Duxbury Press, Scituate, Massachusetts.

Luis Diaz, Jose [Editor]

    1976   *Usas de las plantas medicinales de Mexico.* Instituto Mexicano para el Estudio de las Plantas Medicinales, Mexico City.

McClung de Tapia, Emily

    1992   The origins of agriculture in Mesoamerica and Central America. In *The origins of agriculture: An international perspective,* edited by C. W. Cowan and P. J. Watson, pp. 143–172. Smithsonian Institution Press, Washington, D.C.

Miller, Naomi

    1992   The origins of plant cultivation in the Near East. In *The origins of agriculture: An international perspective,* edited by C. W. Cowan and P. J. Watson, pp. 39–58. Smithsonian Institution Press, Washington, D.C.

Moerman, Daniel E.

    1989   Poisoned apples and honeysuckles: The medicinal plants of native America. *Medical Anthropology Quarterly* 3:52–61.

Morton, Julia F.

    1981   *Atlas of medicinal plants of Middle America: Bahamas to Yucatan.* Charles C. Thomas, Springfield, Illinois.

Nabhan, Gary P.

    1985   *Gathering the desert.* University of Arizona Press, Tucson.

Negbi, Moshe

    1992   A sweetmeat plant, a perfume plant and their weedy relatives: A chapter in the history of *Cyperus esculentus* L. and *C. rotundus* L. *Economic Botany* 46(1):64–71.

Orellana, Sandra L.

1987   *Indian medicine in highland Guatemala: The Pre-Hispanic and Colonial Peri-
       ods.* University of New Mexico Press, Albuquerque.

Ortiz de Montellano, Bernard R.

1990   *Aztec medicine, health, and nutrition.* Rutgers University Press, New Bruns-
       wick, New Jersey.

Parker, Eugene

1992   Forest islands and Kayapo resource management in Amazonia: A reap-
       praisal of the *Apete. American Anthropologist* 94:406–428.

Posey, Darrell A.

1986   Topics and issues in ethnoentomology with some suggestions for the de-
       velopment of hypothesis-generation and testing in ethnobiology. *Journal of
       Ethnobiology* 6:99–120.

1989   Brazil's Kayapo Indians and the conservation of Amazonia's tropical forests.
       Lecture presented at the University of Tennessee, Knoxville, 28 March.

1991   Importance of semi-domesticated species in post-contact Amazonia: Ef-
       fects of the Kayapo Indians on dispersal of flora and fauna of the region.
       Paper presented at the Annual Meeting of the American Anthropological
       Association, Chicago, 20–24 November.

Riddle, John M., and J. Worth Estes

1992   Oral contraceptives in ancient and medieval times. *American Scientist* 80:
       226–233.

Rindos, David

1984   *The origins of agriculture: An evolutionary perspective.* Academic Press, New
       York.

1989   Darwinism and its role in the explanation of domestication. In *Foraging and
       farming,* edited by D. R. Harris and G. C. Hillman, pp. 27–41. Unwin
       Hyman, London.

Rubel, A. J., C. W. O'Nell, and R. Collado-Ardon

1984   *Susto: A folk illness.* University of California Press, Berkeley.

Sanchez, Oscar S.

1968   *La flora del Valle de Mexico.* Editorial Herrero, Mexico City.

Schultes, Richard E.

1986   Recognition of variability in wild plants by Indians of the Northwestern
       Amazon: An enigma. *Journal of Ethnobiology* 6:229–255.

Schultes, Richard E., and Robert F. Raffauf

1992   *Vine of the soul: Medicine men, their plants and rituals in the Colombian
       Amazon.* Synergetic Press, Oracle, Arizona.

Scott, Eugenie C., and Frances E. Johnston

1985   Science, nutrition, fat, and policy: Tests of the critical-fat hypothesis. *Cur-
       rent Anthropology* 26:463–473.

Shipek, Florence C.

1989   An example of intensive plant husbandry: The Kumeyaay of southern California. In *Foraging and farming*, edited by D. R. Harris and G. C. Hillman, pp. 159–170. Unwin Hyman, London.

Smith, Bruce D.

1985   The role of *Chenopodium* as a domesticate in pre-maize garden systems in the Eastern United States. *Southeastern Archaeology* 4:51–72.

1992   Prehistoric plant husbandry in Eastern North America. In *The origins of agriculture: An international perspective*, edited by C. W. Cowan and P. J. Watson, pp. 101–120. Smithsonian Institution Press, Washington, D.C.

Standley, Paul C.

1920–   *Trees and shrubs of Mexico*. United National Herbarium, Smithsonian In-
1926   stitution, Washington, D.C.

Strier, Karen B.

1993   Menu for a monkey. *Natural History* 102(3):34–42.

Stuart-Macadam, Patricia, and Susan Kent [Editors]

1992   *Diet, demography, and disease: Changing perspectives on anemia*. Aldine de Gruyter, New York.

Thomas, R. Brook

1975   The ecology of work. In *Physiological anthropology*, edited by A. Damon, pp. 59–79. Oxford University Press, New York.

Truswell, A. S., and J.D.L. Hansen

1976   Medical research among the Kung. In *Kalahari hunter-gatherers*, edited by R. B. Lee and S. Washburn, pp. 166–194. Harvard University Press, Cambridge.

Turner, Nancy J.

1988   The importance of a rose: Evaluating the cultural significance of plants. *American Anthropologist* 90:272–290.

Watson, Patty Jo, and M. Kennedy

1991   The development of horticulture in the Eastern Woodlands of North America: Women's role. In *Engendering archaeology*, edited by J. Gero and M. Conkey, pp. 255–275. Basil Blackwell, Oxford.

Wilson, Christine S.

1981   Food in a medical system: Prescriptions and proscriptions in health and illness among Malays. In *Food in perspective*, edited by A. Fenton and T. M. Owen, pp. 391–400. John Donald, Edinburgh.

Wilson, Hugh

1981   Domesticated *Chenopodium* of the Ozark Bluff Dwellers. *Economic Botany* 35:233–239.

Winterhalder, Bruce, and Eric A. Smith

1981   *Hunter-gatherer foraging strategies*. University of Chicago Press, Chicago.

Wirsing, Rolf L.

1985   The health of traditional societies and the effects of acculturation. *Current Anthropology* 26:303–322.

Yarnell, Richard A.

    1978   Domestication of sunflower and sumpweed in eastern North America. In *The nature and status of ethnobotany,* edited by R. I. Ford, pp. 289–300. University of Michigan Museum of Anthropology, Ann Arbor.

Yen, Douglas E.

    1989   The domestication of environment. In *Foraging and farming,* edited by D. R. Harris and G. C. Hillman, pp. 55–75. Unwin Hyman, London.

3

Ambivalence to the Palatability Factors in Wild Food Plants

❧ TIMOTHY JOHNS

Wild food plants often contain chemical constituents that make them pungent, astringent, sour, or bitter; for someone unaccustomed to a particular plant food its ingestion can be a unpleasant experience. Persons who routinely use a plant may not share the subjective judgment of unpalatability, but many wild food plants do contain appreciable amounts of alkaloids, terpenes, phenolics, and other organic compounds that can provide a strong, sometimes disagreeable taste. Where human groups have limited food options, an important part of their diet includes resources that might seem to others to be only marginally edible. Nonetheless, many human populations consume by choice foods that are by most accounts distasteful.

From a cultural ecological perspective, the ambivalence of humans to the allelochemicals that occur in wild plant foods calls for a brief examination of the types of chemical factors involved, the extent of their consumption by humans (including efforts to avoid or retain them), and the sensory aspects of human responses to bitter, astringent, and pungent principles. People have logical reasons, understandable from an ecological and evolutionary perspective, for consuming intrinsically unpalatable substances even when other options are available. Moreover, the possible adaptive value of allelochemicals has important implications for indigenous populations experiencing dietary, economic, and social change.

Unpalatability Factors in Indigenous Wild Foods

Various classes of allelochemicals produce a bitter taste in plants. Best known are the alkaloids, which are diverse in structure and characterize many plant families (Robinson 1981). Among the alkaloids are several well-known bitter compounds such as quinine and caffeine, and although plant chemicals of this class generally taste bitter, individual compounds differ widely in their chemical properties and the way they are perceived. Flavonoids, an example of phenolics, are ubiquitous in higher plants (Swain 1986). A number of these, such as naringin found in grapefruit peel, taste intensely bitter, although many have no taste (Horowitz 1986). Other examples of bitter principles include the cyanogenic glycosides (another widespread group of compounds) and cucurbitacins, terpenoid compounds restricted to the family Cucurbitaceae, including wild relatives of pumpkin and squash (Johns 1990).

Bitter compounds produce a "taste" by interacting with receptors located in the taste buds on the tongue and other areas of the oral cavity (Plattig 1988). Other common types of plant allelochemicals such as tannins and saponins, although often called bitter, in reality generate a bitter taste through their astringent effects on oral membranes and by their stimulation of the trigeminal nerve (Johns 1990). Tannins are common plant phenolics, and saponins are a complex and also widely distributed group of triterpenoid glycosides. Glycoalkaloids (steroidal alkaloids), common in plants of the Solanaceae (nightshade) family, are nitrogen-containing analogues of the saponins (Johns 1990). They also are astringent (Maga 1980). The perception of alkaloids such as capsaicin and piperine involves irritation of the trigeminal nerve. This nerve has receptors in the oral and nasal cavities, which are sensitive to chemical stimuli, and is responsible also for pain, touch, and temperature perception (Silver 1987). Capsaicin is the source of the "hot" taste of chili peppers, and piperine confers the pungency of black pepper.

Unpalatable constituents of foods may exercise their effects in the nasal cavity, either on the trigeminal nerve or on olfactory receptors. Glucosinolates, the mustard oil glycosides, impart pungency to a number of foods from the Cruciferae family such as radish, mustard, and horseradish when they break down to release the highly volatile isothiocyanates. Other volatile plant constituents such as the sulfurous compounds of onions and garlic are also perceived through the olfactory system (Tyler 1987).

Sourness, particularly if it is much above the threshold level of detection, can contribute to the unpalatability of foods. Organic acids, such as tartaric acid in tamarind, occur in high concentrations in some plants and produce sourness (Windholz 1983).

Unpalatability can reflect a lack of positive stimuli as well as the presence of irritating and unpleasant principles. Local anesthetics can reduce sensory responses, and several triterpenoidal saponins depress sweetness perception in humans (Kennedy and Halpern 1980). Because sweetness is a preferred taste, reduced ability to taste sweet substances would make the foods that contain them less acceptable.

One should not be surprised that humans and other animals react to the compounds described above as unpleasant. Plants apparently produce allelochemicals to deter herbivores from feeding on them (Harborne 1988). In many cases these compounds are toxic, and any animal that ingests them receives through its chemical sensors a crucial message of unpalatability. Indeed, researchers generally accept that perceptions of bitter and its associated senses have evolved as a means of avoiding potentially toxic constituents contained in plants (Garcia and Hankins 1974).

Strategies to Reduce Exposure to Unpalatable Substances

Humans are highly selective in the plants and plant parts that they choose as food; most plants are very successful, through chemical and other defenses, in deterring humans from eating them in any quantity. Discrimination of the most desirable foods from those that are unpleasant is one way to reduce the amounts of toxins encountered. Humans, like other intelligent animals such as chimpanzees and other nonhuman primates, seem particularly adept at selecting desirable foods (Johns 1990). The folk knowledge of most cultures transmits extensive information about the properties of plants on which individuals base the decision of whether to avoid them or not.

Most people process plant foods with the explicit purpose of detoxifying foods or making them more palatable (Johns and Kubo 1988). Various processing methods for wild and cultivated plant parts, including cooking, leaching, and adding various physical adsorbents such as clay, neutralize plant constituents. In general the people who go to the effort to employ these methods obtain potential concentrated sources of carbohydrate and protein.

Domestication is another important means by which agriculturists have reduced the unpalatable constituents present in the plant components of their diets (Johns 1990). Agrarian societies have improved the palatability of many major crop plants (Johns and Galindo Alonso 1990), yet people having access to domesticated crops often continue to use wild plants in their diet as well.

Most humans should be able to formulate their diets in such a way that they consume minimal amounts of plant allelochemicals. However, despite having the means to avoid allelochemicals, most traditional peoples consume diets that contain some and often many components that taste bitter, pungent, astringent, or sour. Rather than avoiding unpleasant flavors humans seem often to seek them out.

Sensory Physiology and Preference

In experiments using pure chemical compounds in aqueous solution or as part of foods, humans show a preference for sweet substances that increases as the concentrations rise above the threshold detection level (Johns 1990). By contrast, they are ambivalent toward salt and dislike increasing concentrations of sour and bitter substances. The distaste for bitter substances is an innate human characteristic demonstrated even by newborn babies (Desor et al. 1975).

Nonetheless, the actual levels at which an individual perceives a particular bitter stimulus vary. A well-known dimorphism appears in human populations for sensitivity to phenylthiocarbamate (PTC), the related compound phenylthiourea, and 6-n-propylthiouracil (PROP): individuals are tasters or nontasters, and the proportion of nontasters varies among races and ethnic groups (Molnar 1992). Several other compounds are perceived in a similar fashion, including isohumulones, naturally occurring compounds that give a bitter taste to beer (Mela 1990). The differences between individuals in their ability to detect quinine at threshold levels appears to have a genetic basis (Smith and Davies 1973). Bitterness is the only one of the four basic tastes for which researchers have found genetic components that could explain individual and cross-cultural differences in hedonic response or preference (Johns 1994). On a population level these genetic differences could account for an apparent ambivalence among individuals for the foods that contain certain potentially bitter stimuli.

However, studies of human populations have demonstrated few genetically based differences in food preferences related to PTC/PROP or other stimuli (Johns 1994). Indeed, researchers have had difficulty in verifying direct links to taste perception and preference of single compounds in complex food items. Although in certain circumstances genetically based responses determine the preferences of humans for foods that contain bitter and otherwise unpalatable substances, learning also plays a significant role in determining hedonic responses for bitter and other stimuli. Clearly humans can and do acquire tastes for unpalatable substances such as caffeine, isohumulones, and capsaicin. Mere exposure and familiarity, social learning, and associative conditioning may all play roles in the development and modification of food preferences (Sullivan and Birch 1990). Why are these preferences maintained at a population level, distinguishing one cultural group from another?

Consumption of Allelochemicals

Most humans consume allelochemicals with some noticeable flavor as part of their regular food intake, including such well-known items as horseradish, mustard, chili pepper, and black pepper. People generally consume these pungent foods in only small amounts, strictly as condiments. However, eating larger quantities produces the sensation that one would experience from ingesting such chemicals in the levels in which they occur in unprocessed food. Certain groups of people eat chili peppers, for example, as part of their normal cuisine in excess of the levels that cause other peoples obvious pain. Still other cultural groups go further, consuming as staple parts of the diet those plants that most of us would reject out of hand.

For example, the Aymara and Quechua Amerindians of Bolivia and Peru rely on indigenous tuber crops (e.g., *Oxalis tuberosa,* oca; *Solanum* spp., potatoes; *Tropaeolum tuberosum*; and *Ullucus tuberosus,* ollucos) for subsistence at altitudes exceeding 3,000 meters above sea level. Although the Aymara and Quechua have detoxified many of these tubers through domestication or undertake elaborate processing methods that remove palatability-reducing factors, they still eat many tubers in a form that outsiders find unpleasant. The potato (*Solanum* spp.) is the most important of these crops, and these Amerindians consume many varieties that contain significant levels of glycoalkaloids on a routine basis without processing (Johns 1990). The tubers of *Tropaeolum tuberosum* (añu, mashua, isaño), the roots of *Lepidium meyenii* (maca), and bitter forms of the seed grains *Chenopodium quinoa* (quinoa) and *C. canihua* (cañihua) are also rather unpalatable for outsiders.

Similarly, Indians in North America and peoples across Europe and Asia relied historically on acorns, nuts of the genus *Quercus,* as staple foods (Johns and Duquette 1991a). Again, the traditional cultures made some efforts to reduce the astringency of many of these nuts, but the acorn dishes with which I am familiar from California and Sardinia are by no means free of the characteristic tannic acid or its astringent properties.

In East Africa indigenous wild and cultivated leafy greens form a large part of the diet of many tribes of subsistence agriculturists. A number of these (Table 3.1) contain allelochemicals at levels sufficient to make them unpalatable. Agrarian peoples appear to have selected certain genotypes exhibiting chemical differences and do perform some processing. Nevertheless, people continue to consume the most bitter vegetables, often explicitly preferring them. In a survey we conducted among the Luo of Tarime District, Tanzania (Uiso 1991), the most preferred vegetable—*Gynandropsis gynandra* (akeyo)—tastes quite strong and contains glucosinolates; an encouraged weed, *G. gynandra* is also cultivated. Similarly, *Crotalaria brevidens* (mitoo) is considered bitter, but more people reported liking it than disliking it. *C. brevidens* is widely cultivated in western Kenya, although in Tarime District we primarily recorded the use of wild forms. Among the Luo in Kenya (Johns and Kokwaro 1991) and Tanzania (Uiso 1991) we have documented 33 species of wild leafy vegetables, most of which ethnobotanists have not evaluated for bitterness or secondary chemistry.

The Maasai, Batemi (Sonjo; see Johns, Mhoro et al. 1994), and other tribes in East Africa routinely add roots, root bark, stem bark, and other plant parts to meat-based soups. In a recent survey in Ngorongoro District, Tanzania, we

Table 3.1 Some Bitter Leafy Vegetables from East Africa

Genus and Species	Major Bitter Constituent	Citation
Cassia occidentalis L.	anthraquinones	Rai & Shok 1983
Crotalaria brevidens Benth.	pyrrolizidine alkaloids	Uiso 1991
Gynandropsis gynandra (L.) Briq.	glucosinolates	Hasapis et al. 1981
Solanum nigrum L.	glycoalkaloids	Oliver-Bever 1986
Sonchus schweinfurthii Oliv. & Hiern	sesquiterpene lactones	Tomb 1977

identified 33 plants that are added to food. Generally speaking these people consider these additives to be medicine, but the Maasai, at least, generally make no soup without them. The East African tribes consume these additives on a routine basis and in situations of both health and illness. (Besides food additives we have also identified to date 19 wild fruits, 9 wild roots, 10 wild vegetables, and 10 barks and gums that are eaten in addition to the more than 25 food plants cultivated in the area.)

Reasons for Maintenance of Unpalatable Constituents in the Diet

Necessity certainly provides the simplest explanation for why some people eat wild and cultivated plants that others find unpalatable. In the absence of alternative resources, wisdom dictates meeting one's basic needs from what is available. In times of shortage, human populations eat edibles that they avoid under less stressful circumstances. Famine foods, often bitter and potentially toxic, can be considered only marginally edible.

Nonetheless, necessity does not explain many of the circumstances under which humans ingest significant amounts of plant allelochemicals. Many of these plants serve as important dietary components of particular ethnic groups. As ingredients of a shared cuisine to which one becomes accustomed as a child, they are part of the experience of members of the group, and their consumption proceeds more or less as a matter of course. These dietary patterns may have adaptive significance, since the patterns of consumption of unpalatable plants may have arisen over time to meet the needs of the population.

Nutrient Sources

Unpalatable plants can provide carbohydrate, fat, vitamins, and minerals. Leafy vegetables—whether cultivated varieties, garden weeds, or wild plants—are important sources of vitamins and minerals (FAO 1988). We recently examined a number of indigenous leafy vegetables, many that have both wild and cultivated forms, used by the K'ekchi in Guatemala (Booth et al. 1992). Among East African leafy vegetables, *Crotalaria brevidens* stands out as a food that, although containing pyrrolizidine alkaloids, is a very rich source of beta-carotene (Uiso 1991). *Gynandropsis gynandra*, the vegetable most preferred by the Luo, is a good dietary source of beta-carotene (Gomez 1981), protein (Imbamaba 1973), and vitamin C (Sreeramula et al. 1983).

The plants that the Maasai and Batemi add to their foods may make a nutrient contribution as well. The Maasai staple diet of animal-derived products and maize (Nestel 1989) provides little vitamin C (Gatenby Davies and Newson 1974), and additive products may contribute this nutrient. However, most of these additives are roots or bark that are not as likely to be sources of vitamin C as are leaves and fruit. The Maasai probably eat much more fruit outside of meals than ethnobotanists and nutritionists generally recognize, although children seem to make the most use of the wild fruits in Ngorongoro District.

Even if unpalatable plants are good sources of nutrients, most people are unlikely to consciously consume them for this reason. People eat food, not nutrients. At the same time, individuals must have a diet containing all essential nutrients, and consumption of these foods can be considered adaptive.

Pharmacological Sources

Pharmacologic explanations seem most appropriate in the case of the Maasai and Batemi addition of barks and roots to food. Most of these plants are explicitly referred to as medicine. Particularly during the ritual training associated with Maasai warriorhood (Rigby 1985), members of the *moran* age group preferentially consume the additive foods. These plants, although cathartics, also induce a frenzied state considered important for battle readiness. The most renowned of these food additives, ol kiloriti (*Acacia nilotica*), has these properties but is considered to be a digestive aid as well. The *moran* engage in bouts of slaughtering animals and consuming meat in large quantity, purportedly as a strengthening exercise traditionally undertaken prior to battle. They say that ol kiloriti, either eaten in soup or drunk in water, facilitates digestion so that they can consume more meat.

The Luo and other tribes in the Lake Victoria area attribute medicinal properties to bitter species of leafy vegetables, although the actual medicinal value of the plant may not be clear. Some of them, such as *Cassia occidentalis* (nyayado), have laxative value, and a large number are felt to aid the gastrointestinal tract in some way. Some people attribute to them protective effects against malaria and other diseases. We have examined five of these leafy species in bioassays against *Giardia lamblia,* an important human gastrointestinal parasite, and also with brine shrimp, an organism that provides a convenient test of biological activity in the field. Only *Sonchus schweinfurthii* (achak) and *Solanum nigrum* (osuga) show activity against *Giardia,* although leaves of *C. occidentalis* and *G. gynandra* kill brine shrimp.

Plants consumed as food or as additives are just as likely to exhibit medicinal properties as if they were taken explicitly as plant remedies (Etkin and Ross 1991). Culture groups could theoretically treat any number of conditions through diet, although researchers would need to examine and test each case individually to verify efficacy.

Sensory Variety

Variety plays an important role in determining the food intake of humans and animals. Humans develop selective satiety to specific foods (Rolls 1986) and prefer variety in their diet. In a foraging situation this behavior ensures the consumption of a range of essential nutrients and may minimize the ingestion of any one particular dietary toxin as well. Subsistence diets of agriculturists, dominated by a few carbohydrate staples, often seem bland and monotonous. While simply changing the sensory characteristics of food does not change its fundamental quality, by providing sensory variety wild plants can make the diets of agriculturists more palatable.

Pest Resistance

A bitter plant chosen for consumption over another less bitter genotype could be more resistant to insects, fungi, and other plant parasites, thus bearing a higher yield. Plants from which allelochemicals have been selected against in the domestication process are more susceptible to disease (Johns 1990); chemical pesticides added to crops compensate for this deficit in natural defenses. Wild plants have sufficient chemical defenses to survive, and to exploit them people learn to accept the associated bitterness.

Traditional agriculturists may exploit more wild plants in times of famine, whether caused by climatic or biological factors. After crops have succumbed to the ravages of insects or disease, wild plants may survive.

Maintenance of Indigenous Knowledge

Wild plants are not necessarily easy to distinguish as either famine or non-famine foods. Reliance on wild plants in times of shortage may be a matter of degree rather than a total behavioral change. Many of the marginally edible wild plants consumed by a population may in less stressful times be eaten in small amounts, either on an infrequent basis or as minor components in complex dishes. This behavior maintains the knowledge of the usefulness of the plants. When the preferred foods become scarce, people simply adjust their diet by increasing the proportion of available food resources.

The consumption of leafy vegetables in East Africa illustrates this point. People like to mix leafy vegetables, sometimes several species at a time. They mix bitter and nonbitter vegetables for sensory reasons, sometimes mixing cultivated with wild species to produce the right amount of bitterness. When they collect leafy vegetables from the wild they do not focus on one species unless it is predominant; instead, they gather a variety of edibles as they encounter suitable species. If the relative abundance of plants changes for climatic reasons, so does the portion of each species in the mix.

Taste and smell are also important in the recognition of medicinal properties of plants. The inclusion of medicinal plants in food may facilitate their recognition and acceptance when they are needed.

Culture and Identity

While outsiders may label a group of people by their dietary habits (e.g., anthropologists [Gray 1963] and neighbors of the Batemi call them Sonjo after their own name for *Lablab purpureus*, the hyacinth bean), for the people themselves the consumption of foods that other people consider unpalatable can become a point of identity, even of pride. Cultural and social factors are powerful forces in establishing the learned preferences that people have for food; they can easily overcome the innate ways in which humans react to bitter and otherwise unpalatable substances.

Evolutionary Considerations

Humans may have little explicit understanding of their own behaviors, whether these are biologically or culturally defined. Regardless of the underlying cause, behaviors that involve the consumption of plants containing allelochemicals may be beneficial. They may have developed over time and may be adaptive either in general or in response to specific environmental conditions.

Where foods that contribute in an essential way to satisfying nutritional needs are unpalatable, a cultural group may consume them because they provide an otherwise unavailable nutrient. The associated flavors then become characteristic of the cuisine. The responsible principles may even become associative signals by which the population identifies valuable foods. By eating the cuisine to which they are introduced as children, people may consume their defined resources in a manner proven by time to ensure survival through cycles of both abundance and shortage.

Similarly, pharmacologically active substances may contribute to the overall health of people in the circumstances in which they find themselves. Thus, although the Maasai and Batemi have culturally defined the list of plants accepted as food additives, the plants (and thus pharmacologically active non-nutrient chemicals) remain part of collective knowledge because their consumption has had positive biological effects for generations of the community.

Many other animals exhibit pharmacophagous behaviors that have adaptive significance. Researchers have observed "self-medication" in chimpanzees and other primates (Glander [this volume]). Herbivorous animals consume active chemicals as an inevitable part of their diet, and when the properties of these chemicals are positive their consumption could offer a selective advantage. Indeed, I based my conceptual model of the evolution of human medicine (Johns 1990) on the presumed importance of similar phenomena to the survival of our plant-eating ancestors prior to the development of detoxification techniques and the origin of agriculture.

Primates and humans also widely practice the consumption of clay, which has an important role in modulating gastrointestinal function, primarily through adsorbance of toxic and irritating chemicals. Many of these chemicals are the toxins found in diet, and geophagy may be the earliest form of medicine (Johns 1990; Johns and Duquette 1991b).

The effects of plant compounds on the gastrointestinal tract, particularly on gastrointestinal parasites and infections, probably had a primary influence on the evolution of medicine. The same properties that protect plants against attack from microorganisms, nematodes, and insects may make these chemicals efficacious in controlling diseases and parasites of humans. Humans and animals may also select plants for their effects, direct or indirect, on the nervous system, although perhaps more through associative learning than through genetically defined medicinal behavior. Other compounds may have become parts of dietary physiology in ways that make their ingestion normal and even preferred. Antioxidative compounds, for example, may protect against cancer and other diseases (Diplock 1991). Tannins seem to affect digestive processes in positive ways (Mole and Waterman 1985) and appear to control dental caries (Kakiuchi et al. 1986). Salivary factors that bind with tannins suggest that the ingestion of these compounds is a normal part of our dietary ecology (Butler et al. 1986).

Although food processing technology and domestication may have given humans the capacity to reduce the amount of allelochemicals in their diet, the positive benefits afforded by these compounds may have ensured that people continue to consume them. The deliberate use of plants as medicines and the consumption of pure drugs in modern medicine thus simply elaborates on a more fundamental behavior.

Certainly allelochemicals can be toxic, as can modern pharmaceuticals. In selecting substances to ingest, therefore, people must ensure that they achieve a balance between nutritional or health status and toxicity. Toxic chemicals are generally unpalatable. However, unpalatability is the messenger, not the message itself. Humans interpret the message in the context of many ecological factors and in so doing define palatability in relative rather than absolute terms. Not surprisingly, what is unpalatable for one group is desirable for another.

Attitudes Toward Indigenous Foods in a Rapidly Changing World

In the modern world, subsistence and food procurement patterns of indigenous populations can be altered profoundly, but at the same time they can buffer change. My subjective experience is that as humans have access to new foods and—as they move to urban areas—less access to traditional resources, they modify not only their diet but also their food preferences. Nonetheless, people continue to consume traditional "unpalatable" foods in many urban centers. For example, some markets of Nairobi display leafy vegetables such as *C. brevidens, G. gynandra,* and *S. nigrum.* These perishable commodities must be brought from a distance, but as a result they become items of increased economic and cultural value because of the difficulty in procuring them.

The desire for these bitter plants may decrease incrementally from one generation to another (Johns and Kuhnlein 1990), reflecting the axiom that the generation is the fundamental unit of change in culturally defined behavior. I have heard people complain in Peru that members of the younger generation do not want to eat tubers such as *T. tuberosum* or *O. tuberosa* but instead prefer pasta, rice, and fried potatoes. These changes are inevitable in most cities of the south (Latin America, Africa, and Asia) for economic reasons and perhaps also because of the influence of contact with dominant industrial cultures.

In a dietary situation of rapid flux people face the danger of consuming nutritionally deficient foods. In the traditional situation, sensory cues (whether for sweet or bitter substances) are likely to be relevant in the process of selecting a nutritionally adequate diet. In a new context, by contrast, sensory cues may be irrelevant to the nutrient content of a food and inappropriate for guiding people in their eating behavior. When culturally mediated cues fall aside, what remains are biologically defined cues: preferences for sweet, fat, bland, and salty foods. People generally avoid foods containing bitter, astringent, and sour substances, particularly unfamiliar tastes. Modern diets in industrialized or urban settings are typically high in sugar, carbohydrate, fat, and salt; and even when good sources of other nutrients are available, our innate preferences for foods high in energy can supersede balanced consumptive behavior. With the availability of enough total food, people have little difficulty in meeting their needs for calories, protein, or essential fatty acids. However, few cues guide an individual to sources of essential vitamins, minerals, and amino acids. In a highly processed diet the situation leads even more directly to states of deficiency of nutrients such as iron, zinc, vitamins A and C, and folic acid. These problems are likely to beset populations moving from subsistence to market systems and from rural to urban settings.

The conservative side of culture offers some hope for countering the destructive dietary trends associated with modernization. People do like the familiar, and learned preferences can be as strong as innate ones. That populations continue to consume indigenous plant foods in many rapidly changing situations supports this notion. These resources of the past, both cultivated and wild, can contribute to human well-being in the present and the future. From a dietary basis these plants can be sensory beacons to good health and nutrition in a sea of multiple confusing forces.

The factors that will determine the survival of these adaptive reference points are economic and social. People cannot eat what they cannot afford. In situations that place urban poor and middle classes under increased economic stress, cultural groups have more and more difficulty in consuming a balanced diet. As well, the social value attached to traditional plant foods has a profound influence on peoples' consumption of these foods. Traditional foods often become stigmatized, particularly if associated with poverty (Johns et al. 1992).

In this context numerous issues need to be addressed. Researchers should assess the biological properties (nutrient content, toxicity, palatability, pharmacologic value) of most wild and indigenous cultivated plants, along with issues of production, distribution, storage, social attitudes, and consumption. Increasing attention has been directed to the place of wild edible and medicinal plants in relation to the economics of forest conservation (Vasquez and Gentry 1989). Both from the environmental perspective and for the benefit of human populations, humanity has good reason to encourage the continued use of these plants in changing circumstances (Johns, Chan et al. 1994). The apparent opposition between environmental preservation and human needs is a factor in an equation that is coming to characterize the human situation in local settings as well as on a global scale. One step toward solving this equation to the benefit of humans in the future is a holistic approach that understands wild food plants in relation to their place in traditional human ecology in the past and the forces that determine their use in the present.

REFERENCES

Booth, S., R. Bressani, and T. Johns
    1992   Nutrient content of selected indigenous leafy vegetables consumed by the

Kekchi people of Alta Verapaz, Guatemala. *Journal of Food Composition and Analysis* 5:25–34.

Butler, L. G., J. C. Rogler, H. Mehansho, and D. M. Carlson

1986 Dietary effects of tannins. In *Plant flavonoids in biology and medicine: Biochemical, pharmacological, and structure-activity relationships,* edited by V. Cody, E. Middleton, and J. B. Harborne, pp. 141–158. Alan R. Liss, New York.

Desor, J. A., O. Maller, and K. Andrews

1975 Ingestive responses of human newborns to salty, sour and bitter stimuli. *Journal of Comparative Physiology and Psychology* 89:966–970.

Diplock, A. T.

1991 Antioxidant nutrients and disease prevention—an overview. *American Journal of Clinical Nutrition* 53:S189–193.

Etkin, N. L., and P. J. Ross

1991 Should we set a place for diet in ethnopharmacology? *Journal of Ethnopharmacology* 32:25–36.

FAO

1988 *Traditional food plants.* Food and Nutrition Paper 42. Food and Agricultural Organization of the United Nations, Rome.

Garcia, J., and W. G. Hankins

1974 The evolution of bitter and the acquisition of toxiphobia. In *Fifth international symposium on olfaction and taste,* edited by D. A. Denton and J. P. Coghlan, pp. 39–45. Academic Press, New York.

Gatenby Davies, J. D., and J. Newson

1974 Low ascorbate status in the Masai of Kenya. *American Journal of Clinical Nutrition* 27:310–314.

Gomez, M. I.

1981 Carotene content of some green leafy vegetables of Kenya and effects of dehydration and storage on carotene retention. *Journal of Plant Foods* 3:231–244.

Gray, R. F.

1963 *The Sonjo of Tanganyika.* Oxford University Press, London.

Harborne, J. B.

1988 *Introduction to ecological biochemistry* [Third edition]. Academic Press, London.

Hasapis, X., A. J. Maclead, and M. Moreau

1981 Glucosinolates of nine Cruciferae and two Capparaceae species. *Phytochemistry* 20:2355–2358.

Horowitz, R. M.

1986 Taste effects of flavonoids. In *Plant flavonoids in biology and medicine,* edited by V. Cody, E. Middleton, and J. B. Harborne, pp. 163–176. Alan R. Liss, New York.

Imbamaba, S. K.

1973   Leaf protein content of some Kenya vegetables. *East Africa Agricultural and Forestry Journal* 38:246–251.

Johns, T.

1994   Sensory perception, preference and classification in relation to cross-cultural differences in food consumption patterns. In *International perspectives on sensory analysis: Theory and applications,* edited by A. Goldman and B. Watts. Elsevier Applied Science Publishers, London (in press).

1990   *With bitter herbs they shall eat it: Chemical ecology and the origins of human diet and medicine.* University of Arizona Press, Tucson.

Johns, T., S. L. Booth, and H. V. Kuhnlein

1992   Factors of influence and programmes for improvement of vitamin A status. *Food and Nutrition Bulletin* 14:20–33.

Johns, T., H. M. Chan, O. Receveur, and H. V. Kuhnlein

1994   Commentary on the ICN World Declaration on Nutrition: Nutrition and the environment of indigneous peoples. *Ecology of Food and Nutrition* (in press).

Johns, T., and M. Duquette

1991a   Traditional detoxification of acorn bread with clay. *Ecology of Food and Nutrition* 25:221–228.

1991b   Detoxification and mineral supplementation as functions of geophagy. *American Journal of Clinical Nutrition* 53:448–456.

Johns, T., and J. Galindo Alonso

1990   Glycoalkaloid change during the domestication of the potato, *Solanum* section *Petota. Euphytica* 50:203–210.

Johns, T., and J. O. Kokwaro

1991   Food plants of the Luo of Siaya District, Kenya. *Economic Botany* 45:103–113.

Johns, T., and I. Kubo

1988   A survey of traditional methods employed for the detoxification of plant foods. *Journal of Ethnobiology* 8:81–129.

Johns, T., and H. V. Kuhnlein

1990   Cultural determinants of food selection and behavior. In *Diet and behavior: Multidisciplinary approaches,* edited by G. H. Anderson, pp. 17–31. Springer-Verlag, London.

Johns, T., E. B. Mhoro, P. Sanaya, and E. K. Kimanani

1994   Herbal remedies of the Batemi of Ngorongoro District, Tanzania: A quantitative appraisal. *Economic Botany* 48:90–95.

Kakiuchi, N., M. Hattori, M. Nishizawa, T. Yamagishi, and T. Okuda

1986   Studies on dental caries prevention by traditional medicines. VII: Inhibitory effects of various tannins on glucan synthesis by glucosyltransferase from *Streptococcus mutans. Chemical and Pharmaceutical Bulletin* 34:720–725.

Kennedy, L. M., and B. P. Halpern

1980   A biphasic model for action of the gymnemic acids and ziziphins on taste receptor cell membranes. *Chemical Senses* 5:149–158.

Maga, J. A.

    1980   Potato glycoalkaloids. *CRC Critical Reviews in Food Science and Nutrition.* 12:371–405.

Mela, D. J.

    1990   Gustatory perception of isohumulones: Influence of sex and thiourea taster status. *Chemical Senses* 15:485–490.

Mole, S., and P. G. Waterman

    1985   Stimulatory effects of tannins and cholic acid on tryptic hydrolysis of proteins. *Journal of Chemical Ecology* 11:1323–1332.

Molnar, S.

    1992   *Human variation: Races, types and ethnic groups* [Third edition]. Prentice Hall, Englewood Cliffs, New Jersey.

Nestel, P. S.

    1989   Food intake and growth in the Maasai. *Ecology of Food and Nutrition* 23:17–30.

Oliver-Bever, B.

    1986   *Medicinal plants in tropical West Africa.* Cambridge University Press, Cambridge.

Plattig, K.-H.

    1988   The sense of taste. In *Sensory analysis of foods* [Second edition], edited by J. R. Piggott, pp. 1–24. Elsevier Applied Science, London.

Rai, P. P., and M. Shok

    1983   Anthraquinone glycosides from plant parts of *Cassia occidentalis. Indian Journal of Pharmaceutical Science* 45:87–88.

Rigby, P.

    1985   *Persistent pastoralists: Nomadic societies in transition.* Zed Books, London.

Robinson, T.

    1981   *The biochemistry of alkaloids.* Springer-Verlag, New York.

Rolls, B. J.

    1986   Sensory-specific satiety. *Nutrition Reviews* 44:93–101.

Silver, W. L.

    1987   The common chemical sense. In *Neurobiology of taste and smell,* edited by D. Walcher and N. Kretchmer, pp. 65–87. John Wiley and Sons, New York.

Smith, S. E., and P.D.O. Davies

    1973   Quinine taste thresholds: Family study and twin study. *Annals of Human Genetics* 37:227.

Sreeramula, N., G. D. Ndossi, and K. Mtotomwema

    1983   Effect of cooking on the nutritive value of common food plants of Tanzania. Part 1: Vitamin C in some of the wild green leafy vegetables. *Food Chemistry* 10:205–210.

Sullivan, S. A., and L. L. Birch

    1990   Pass the sugar, pass the salt: Experience dictates preference. *Developmental Psychology* 26:546–551.

Swain, T.

    1986   The evolution of flavonoids. In *Plant flavonoids in biology and medicine*, edited by V. Cody, E. Middleton, and J. B. Harborne, pp. 1–14. Alan R. Liss, New York.

Tomb, A. S.

    1977   Lactuceae—systematic review. In *The biology and chemistry of the Compositae*, edited by V. H. Heywood, J. B. Harborne, and B. L. Turner, pp. 1067–1079. Academic Press, London.

Tyler, V. E.

    1987   *The new honest herbal.* George F. Stickley Company, Philadelphia.

Uiso, F. C.

    1991   Determination of toxicological and nutritional factors of Crotalaria species used as indigenous vegetables. M.Sc. thesis, McGill University.

Vasquez, R., and A. H. Gentry

    1989   Use and misuse of forest-harvested fruits in the Iquitos area. *Conservation Biology* 3:350–361.

Windholz, M. [Editor]

    1983   *The Merck index.* Merck, Rahway, New Jersey.

4

Wild Plants as Cultural Adaptations to Food Stress

❅ REBECCA HUSS-ASHMORE AND SUSAN L. JOHNSTON

Food shortage, occasionally amounting to famine, is a widely re-ported characteristic of preindustrial and subsistence-oriented economies. While the past 25 years have seen famine restricted to Africa and parts of Asia, ample historical evidence indicates that severe food shortages once affected almost all regions inhabited by humans (Robson 1981). In addition, mild to moderate food shortage has probably occurred in every human society at some time in its past, whether regularly or on rare occasions, triggered by social and natural upheaval (Gaulin and Konner 1977; Whiting 1958). Because food shortage has been so pervasive, subsistence societies often have an array of strategies for combatting hunger (Messer 1989). These strat-egies range from short-term, low-cost options such as a shift to less preferred foods, to long-term and more drastic solutions such as permanent migration. Presumably, the regularity and severity of food shortages influence the strat-egies used.

One of the most common strategies for coping with both short- and long-term shortage is the consumption of wild plants. Even in foraging societies, where wild plants often make up a high proportion of the normal diet, inten-sified gathering of a wider range of species accompanies increasing food scar-city. Cultivators may exploit wild plants seasonally to protect staple food sup-plies and may intensify their use in times of poor agricultural yield (Watts 1983). While the type of plants used varies by ecological zone, subsistence type,

Susan L. Johnston is supported by a National Science Foundation Graduate Research Fellowship.

and length of food shortage, a broad array of roots, leaves, fruits, bark, and seeds has been recorded as famine foods.

This chapter presents a conceptual framework for the study of famine foods in which human strategies for plant use are linked to plant strategies for environmental adaptation. Case studies can provide comparative information on the use of wild plants as famine foods for cultivators and foragers, such as in the three broad ecological zones of aboriginal North America discussed later in this chapter. These regions have a documented history of food shortage and considerable historical and ethnographic information on wild plant use. In the discussion we suggest potential biological impacts of plant use in these regions. Because little information is currently available on which to judge biological effects, understanding the adaptive value of famine foods will require targeted studies of actual plant use and biochemistry.

Wild Plants as Famine Adaptations

A number of authors have outlined the strategies by which nonindustrial societies cope with the threat of food shortage (e.g., Colson 1979; DeGarine and Harrison 1988; Messer 1989; Watts 1983). Because shortage occurs frequently in subsistence societies, such groups anticipate and plan for scarcity, employing mechanisms such as food storage and foraging, crop diversity, wage labor, and broad social networks to ward off hunger. They often employ strategies hierarchically, from easily reversible, low-cost options to those involving irrevocable loss of household productive capacity (Watts 1983, 1988).

Households exposed to the threat of food shortage may adopt strategies that protect both current food supply and future productive assets (Corbett 1988). One of the first responses households invoke is the collection of wild foods, a low-cost strategy involving only minimal commitment of household resources. Among groups for whom food shortage is regular and frequent, wild foods often become a standard component of the diet, even during times of "normal" food supply. While wild foods include foods of animal origin, such as mammals, fish, and insects (Cowen 1992; Dufour 1987, 1992), people place the greatest reliance on wild plants. F. R. Irvine (1952) has shown the variety of plant organs and products used as emergency foods for West Africa, and researchers have documented a similar variety for other parts of the world.

Unlike the abundant research on medicinal plants, studies have produced little systematic information on the use of wild plants as famine food. Few researchers have investigated either the cultural rules for their selection or the biological consequences of their ingestion. Although some researchers (Etkin 1986; Etkin and Ross [this volume]; Jackson 1991) have advocated an integrated biocultural approach to the study of wild plant use, famine foods have not yet been included in this framework. Nevertheless, the widespread use of wild plants as emergency foods gives them the potential to influence human evolution.

An evolutionary approach to famine foods would include the plants used and the cognitive categories by which populations encode their use, as well as methods of preparation, amount and frequency of ingestion, and the biological impacts of ingestion. This last factor should depend on both the nutritive and the pharmacologic or toxic qualities of the plant, and on the biology and health of the human population. The nutritive value of plant foods is obviously critical, but other aspects of plant biochemistry may also be important for human adaptation. Wild plants appear to have had a significant evolutionary impact on the human species through the ingestion of secondary plant compounds, or allelochemicals (Jackson 1991; Johns [this volume]). These secondary compounds include alkaloids, glycosides, and phenolics, among others, and are part of the plants' own defenses against predators. While many of these compounds are both bitter and toxic, some may also be toxic to human pathogens and thus have medicinal value. Hence, the ingestion of wild plant foods carries the potential for a variety of positive and negative biological effects.

Although the selection of specific plants as emergency foods may have wide-ranging biological impact, investigators have conducted almost no research on the criteria by which people choose emergency foods. Taste may be paramount generally in determining which plants will be included in the human diet but may be less important when food is scarce (Jackson 1991; Johns [this volume]). People generally dislike bitter foods, for example, and often use bitterness to gauge toxicity. However, the inclusion of bitter foods in famine diets, often after extensive processing, indicates that other considerations may take precedence over taste under these circumstances. Ritual, tradition, and perceived social costs may influence the choice of famine foods, as do other criteria such as availability, facility of collection, ease of preparation, taste, texture, toxicity, and sustaining power or perceived efficacy (Fox and Norwood Young 1982; Minnis 1991; Riley and Brokensha 1988a, b).

Availability of a plant, an obvious criterion for use, hardly seems to need further comment. However, the availability of famine foods during times of shortage varies. To some degree this variation hinges on the cause of food shortage, whether social disruption such as warfare or climatic factors that might affect wild as well as cultivated vegetation. Probably the majority of food shortages, especially short-term shortages, involve climatic or environmental factors, although the role of political disruption and resource control in famine etiology should not be ignored (Downs et al. 1992; Steegman 1983).

The availability of specific wild plants during periods of climatic or environmental stress reveals how well those plants are adapted to their environment, including their ability to withstand heat, cold, drought, flooding, wind, and a variety of pests and predators. Indigenous plants should logically be better adapted to environmental conditions than are introduced cultigens. Human populations reliant on wild plants during periods of environmental perturbation are merely taking advantage of the superior adaptation of indigenous plant species.

Plants have evolved a variety of strategies for dealing with environmental hazards. These strategies include structural features, biochemical composition, and life-history tactics. For example, various studies (Nabhan 1989; Solbrig and Orians 1977) describe adaptations to drought and seasonal desiccation that include dormancy, rapid energy cycling, broad root networks, resistance to dehydration, and a variety of organs for storage of water and nutrients (roots and tubers, woody trunks, fleshy stems, fruits, and seeds). Plants subjected to seasonal cold use many of these same strategies, including prolonged dormancy, rapid germination, and rapid energy capture and storage (Billings 1978; Moran 1979). The ability to withstand freezing and desiccation is an important adaptation, although in extreme cold much of the plant biomass lies below the ground, as protection from cold, snow abrasion, and herbivores (Savile 1972). Plants may further discourage predators by tough, fibrous texture and by bitter tastes and toxins.

Emergency plant foods are therefore the products of well-defended plants and those whose storage strategies allow them to survive where more fragile plants cannot. Although these plants provide humans with needed nutrients or water, they may be costly to use: processing costs are often high, due to toxins or cellulose; and collection costs may be high, due to plant scarcity or low nutrient density of available plant organs. Palatability of emergency foods is often rated as low, and some are so toxic as to cause illness or even death in human consumers.

We suggest that although availability is a critical factor, famine foods may be chosen according to a calculus that weighs desirability (perceived nutritional value, taste) against negative features (time and energy to collect and process, potential toxicity). If food shortage persists, a population should increasingly use less palatable foods with higher processing costs and greater health risk. The calculus involved in the selection of famine foods has not been explored previously but constitutes a research priority if the adaptive and evolutionary significance of famine foods is to be understood.

Data from aboriginal North America afford the opportunity to explore wild plant use during food shortage in a variety of ecological contexts. The cases presented here, using data drawn from ethnobotanical and historical accounts, represent a broad spectrum of environmental conditions and subsistence types.

North American peoples experienced hunger in climates and biotypes ranging from the Subarctic to the southwestern desert, including ecosystems limited by both rainfall and temperature. Many of the people discussed were foragers or practiced limited and shifting cultivation, although some, such as the mobile Plains Indians, could be considered as pastoralists. These contrasting cases thus show the variety of plant types used under widely differing cultural and ecological circumstances.

Famine Foods in North America

No published work to date has focused on the biological consequences of famine food use in North America, past or present. Although many Native North Americans continue to gather and use wild plants for a variety of purposes, the availability of store-bought foods has limited the practice of gathering wild plants as a strategy for coping with food scarcity. Native Americans and people of other ethnic backgrounds in North America may still deal with hunger or food shortage by using wild plants to supplement diet, but researchers have not documented present-day, shortage-induced use on this continent.

Investigators have shown increasing interest in the nutritional and healthful properties of traditional foods, as well as their continued importance within the various indigenous cultures of North America (e.g., Kuhnlein and Turner 1991; Nabhan 1985, 1989; Stoffle et al. 1990). However, unlike the development literature on Africa, South America, and Asia, studies on North America have placed little emphasis on resurrecting and documenting the potential uses of wild plants and traditional cultigens to prevent or obviate food shortage. Exceptions have presented information on the survival value of plants to the traveler, outdoors enthusiast, or military personnel in potentially extreme environments or emergency situations (e.g., Porsild 1937; Szczawinski and Hardy 1962; Weiner 1972). Some researchers have recorded nutrient analyses for traditional foods among specific indigenous groups, including foods used in scarcity situations (Crites and Terry 1984; Kaye and Moodie 1978; Keely 1980; Kuhnlein and Turner 1991; Scrimsher 1967). However, the plants or plant parts used as famine foods are under-represented in nutritional analyses, perhaps because many of them were not regular dietary items and are no longer in use.

Population-level food shortage in indigenous North America occurred in several contexts: as a consequence of the disruption of the annual seasonal cycle of temperature or moisture changes; as a result of more major, periodic disruptions, such as multiple-year drought cycles; and as a result of environmentally or culturally induced disasters, such as floods, depletion of game resources by the fur trade, and the disruption of traditional subsistence with forced settlement on reservations (Steegman 1983; Steward 1938). The marginality of a particular indigenous ecological adaptation determined to some extent the susceptibility of that group to food scarcity on a cyclical basis. Among the Kumeyaay of southern California during the 1700s, for example, drought was an expected event for which elaborate plant knowledge and management existed; foreign contact disrupted these adaptations and increased starvation rates (Shipek 1981).

The diversity of plant foods used apparently varied among regions due to geographical, ecological, and cultural factors. For example, Canadian indigenous peoples consumed fewer plant foods, in terms of both species and quantity, in northern latitudes; the greatest use occurred in the montane and plateau areas, as well as in eastern Canada (Kuhnlein and Turner 1991). Other authors have noted similar variations in the extent of wild plant food use, and types of plants used, by latitude (e.g., Yarnell 1964, for the Great Lakes region); in the Great Basin, the proportion of roots, tubers, and berries used as foods was greater among more northerly indigenous groups (Steward 1938). Knowledge of plants that could be used in times of crop or foraging failure apparently existed among most Native North American groups for their particular ecological zones. Considering the continent as a whole, famine and emergency foods represented most of the major taxonomic categories, including algae, lichens, pteridophytes (ferns and related plants), gymnosperms, and angiosperms (monocotyledons and dicotyledons). Plant parts used in times of scarcity included, most prominently, perennial greens (stems, leaves, and shoots), bark/cambium, fruits, subterranean organs (roots, rhizomes, tubers, and bulbs), and seeds, including nuts and grains (Castetter 1935; Ebeling 1986; Kindscher 1987).

The following sections adopt a regional approach to the discussion of strategies for the employment of wild plants as famine foods in order to reflect a range of climatic conditions and subsistence adaptations in North America. The Subarctic or boreal forest; arid areas of the United States Southwest and Great Basin; and the more temperate zones of the East, midcontinent, and Pacific Northwest provide the framework for a discussion of the kinds of wild plant resources used in situations of famine or food scarcity, possible reasons for plant choices, and the biological implications of such choices.

Subarctic/Boreal Forest

This region is characterized by extreme seasonality, with a brief fall and spring, abrupt season changes, and pronounced temperature differences between winter and summer (Nelson 1982; Winterhalder 1983). The potential exists for extremes of, for example, 34° C in July and −47° C in January in northern Ontario (Winterhalder 1983:18). Annual precipitation is low to moderate (35–60 cm), falling as summer rain and winter snow (Nelson 1982:16; Winterhalder 1983:19). Native peoples of these areas traditionally relied largely on hunting and secondarily on gathering for subsistence. The Woods Cree of Saskatche-wan, for example, used a wide variety of plant foods, but these foods made only a small contribution to their overall diet (Leighton 1985).

Late winter was the time of potential food scarcity, depending on the length of winter, the amount of snow, and the adequacy of preserved and stored food quantities (Hurlich 1983; Mautner 1982). Hunger and starvation reported among the Forest Algonkian peoples in the ethnohistoric record for the seven-teenth to nineteenth centuries may be attributable to disruptions in population locations, disease epidemics, and depletion of animals resulting from the fur trade (Steegman 1983; see also Young 1988). Algonkian last-resort foods in-cluded (in descending order of frequency of mention in historical reports) lichen, hide (clothing, skins, snowshoe webbing), entrails and carrion, and dogs. In addition, they ate acorns and tree bark during hungry times (Steegman 1983). The plant foods used in famine situations by northern Algonkians were apparently not ordinary dietary staples.

Among northern indigenous peoples, several Eskimo and coastal Indian groups consumed marine algae (seaweeds) in their diets; for the Eskimo sea-weed was primarily a famine food, although available in both summer and winter (Kuhnlein and Turner 1991). Algae can be difficult to digest due to complex carbohydrates, but regular consumption reportedly conditions the digestive tract (Kuhnlein and Turner 1991:27). Some algae were processed by decomposition and cooking. These plants provide several vitamins and min-erals, notably iodine.

Lichens have been an important famine food in northern North America (Arctic, Subarctic, northern Plains, Plateau, Pacific Northwest, Great Lakes) and other parts of the world (Airaksinen et al. 1986; Kuhnlein and Turner 1991). Lichens are composite organisms, consisting of algae symbiotically associated with a fungus, making them among the most durable and adaptable of plants. They can withstand extreme desiccation and cold without damage and resume metabolic functioning within minutes when conditions improve (Savile 1972). Several edible lichens occur in "great abundance" in northern Canada, utilizing a range of microhabitats, including rocks, sandy soils, and slopes with consis-tent snow cover (Porsild 1937:16). In North America, black tree lichen (*Bryoria fremontii*), reindeer moss (*Cladina* spp.), and rock tripe (*Actinogyra* and *Um-bilicaria* spp.) served as emergency or famine foods (Kuhnlein and Turner 1991). Lichens contain complex polysaccharides and generally taste bitter; some are toxic due to vulpinic and usnic acids. Indigenous northern peoples usually processed fresh lichens by soaking them in water or an alkaline solution (ash and water) and boiling them to minimize the bitter taste and improve di-gestibility; reindeer moss was sometimes collected in a partially digested state from caribou rumens (Kuhnlein and Turner 1991).

Although researchers have not reported specific nutrient data on lichen for North America, they may have the greatest food value of edible plants growing in the north (Porsild 1937). Iceland lichen (*Cetraria islandica*) contains 80% carbohydrate, and reindeer lichen (moss) contains something less than that; both are used as famine foods in Finland (Airaksinen et al. 1986). Lipid and protein levels are low in both species, and iron is relatively high, especially in reindeer moss. Reindeer moss contains greater levels of lichen toxins than Iceland moss. Lichens collect heavy metals from air and water, which probably presents more of a health threat in modern times than in the past. Ash-soaking appeared to diminish the lichen acid toxicity of Iceland lichen fed to rats (Airaksinen et al. 1986).

Bark and root foods were also important in the Subarctic, where people apparently consumed them raw. In starvation situations Woods Cree and northern Chipewyan peoples used the fresh inner bark (cambium) of paper birch (*Betula papyrifera*), and Slave Indians that of cottonwood (*Populus balsamifera*); these were also regular springtime foods. Little information is available about the nutritional value of inner bark tissues of trees, but these tissues should be high in sap, and therefore carbohydrate energy value, in the spring (Kuhnlein and Turner 1991). Other foods eaten raw to forestall starvation included the roots of lousewort (*Pedicularis langsdorfii*), eaten by the Slave, and roots of American milkvetch (*Astragalus americanus*) and sweet vetch (*Hedysarum alpinum*), eaten by other peoples in the Subarctic. American milkvetch, poisonous due to alkaloids and other toxins, was apparently consumed only when necessary and in small quantities; innocuous sweet vetch was a regular dietary item but is similar in appearance to a poisonous relative.

Southwest and Great Basin

In the Southwest (New Mexico, Arizona, southern Colorado, and southern Utah) and the Great Basin, the primary ecological limiting factor is moisture, including the amount and seasonal timing of precipitation. Most of this region receives less than 50 cm of precipitation per year. Temperature and altitude as reflected in the length of the frost-free season are additional factors of importance. The area agriculturally useful to Native Americans was limited by these factors and by their ability to irrigate it. A variety of plant zones exist within these regions (Carter 1945; Steward 1938). Aridity does not necessarily imply paucity of plant life; plants of the dry subtropics display diverse architectural strategies for dealing with infrequent and unpredictable moisture, including dwarfism, short lives, and tough outer layers, among others (Nabhan 1989).

Indigenous peoples of the Southwest and Great Basin varied in their relative reliance on cultivation, gathering and hunting, and pastoral subsistence strategies. Even the primarily agricultural peoples utilized wild plants for food needs, particularly in times of crop failure (Castetter 1935). Both agriculturists and hunter-gatherers in the Southwest utilized "cool-season" grasses, such as Indian ricegrass (*Oryzopsis hymenoides*), in early summer when their stored food supplies were at the lowest level (Ebeling 1986). Great Basin groups depended largely on gathering and hunting for their regular subsistence needs, although the Owens Valley Paiute practiced some irrigated cultivation (Steward 1938). The potential existed for food scarcity on an annual basis. For example, the Nevada Shoshoni depended on pinyon nuts, a crop that varied greatly in annual yield, as a stored staple and scarcity preventive; they commonly endured starvation in early spring.

Periodic drought and disasters were also a problem in the Southwest. For the New Mexico Pueblos from 1540 to 1896, for example, a number of extreme winters, floods, crop failures, and droughts resulted in starvation (Zubrow 1974). The Pima experienced failure of the water supply from the Gila River in midwinter about every fifth year and resorted to wild animal and plant foods (Castetter 1935).

For the Southwest and Great Basin, recorded famine foods show a dominance of greens, including stems, crowns, leaves, and shoots (Castetter 1935; Ebeling 1986). Greenstripe (*Acanthochiton wrightii*) plants were a famine preventive for the Hopi because they became available before maize ears ripened. The Navajo used guaco, the Rocky Mountain bee plant (*Cleome serrulata*), as a famine preventive; this plant was also a dietary staple for several Southwest groups. Many Southwest culture groups ate leaves, stems, and seeds of *Chenopodium* (e.g., goosefoot) and *Amaranthus* (e.g., pigweed) species, both ceremonially and to offset food shortage (Minnis 1991). The Pima roasted crowns of mescal (*Agave parriyi*) in times of shortage. Similarly, Pueblo peoples used the crowns and young leaves of yucca or soapweed (*Yucca bacchata* and *Y. glauca*). The bog orchid (*Habenaria sparsiflora*) was used in times of scarcity by the San Felipe, who also mixed cattail (*Typha latifolia*) shoots with maize to deal with shortage. The flowers, fruits, and stems of several cacti (*Opuntia* spp.) were dietary staples in the Southwest; cholla cactus buds provided the only vegetable food available in early spring. In times of scarcity, cactus fruits, stems, and the less desirable but readily available joints were important resources for Puebloan groups such as the Acoma and Laguna (Castetter 1935; Ebeling 1986). The saguaro cactus (*Carnegiea gigantea*) fruit probably was a "life-saver in ancient times" for the Papago (Tohono O'odham) when other food sources failed and was also an important regular dietary item (Castetter and Bell 1937:13).

Several barks and berries provided food or water (Castetter 1935; Ebeling 1986). The barrel cactus (*Echinocactus* or *Ferocactus* spp.), for example, served as an emergency water source for the Pima. The Navajo chewed the inner bark of the one-seeded juniper (*Juniperus monosperma*) and the aspen (*Populus trem-uloides*) to obtain the juice (Minnis 1991). Other Arizona and New Mexico groups used western yellow pine (*Pinus ponderosa,* var. *scopulorum*) bark as famine food. Juniper berries were regular as well as famine foods for Pueblo peoples. Juniper mistletoe (*Phoradendron juniperinum*) berries, largely a famine food, were generally considered by some groups to be unpalatable. The Acoma and Laguna also used cutleaf nightshade (*Solanum triflorum*) berries as a fam-ine food.

Roots and tubers used as famine foods by Puebloan peoples included *Di-chelostemma* (bluedick), *Habenaria* (bog orchid) and *Solanum* species (e.g., nightshade, wild potato). *Solanum* roots were often boiled with clay by New Mexico Puebloan groups, presumably to reduce bitterness or toxicity (Johns and Kubo 1988; Minnis 1991).

Several seeds provided a dependable food resource in times of scarcity, in-cluding sand bunchgrass or Indian millet (*Oryzopsis hymenoides*) for the Zuni, mesquite and screwbean (*Prosopis* spp.) in the Sonoran Zone of the Great Basin, and paloverde (*Cercidium microphyllum*) for the Mojave and Yuma in the lower Colorado River Basin. This last was not a usual dietary item (Castetter 1935; Ebeling 1986). Ramah Navajo used roasted groundsel (*Senecio multi-capitatus*) seeds mixed with ground maize and goat's milk in famine times (Vestal 1952). The Apache ate seeds of yellow pine ground but raw (Castetter and Opler 1936). Seeds of sagebrush (*Artemisia* spp.), consumed by most groups in the Great Basin as a famine food, were considered bitter (Steward 1938). Mesquite and screwbeans have abundant carbohydrate and protein (Ebeling 1986:125).

The kinds of scarcity foods used by peoples of the Southwest and Great Ba-sin, such as cactus, agave, juniper berries, and sagebrush, represent the human ability to take advantage of plant strategies of drought resistance. In some cases, these famine foods are plants that indigenous people generally do not consider desirable (e.g., sagebrush); in others, they are the less desirable parts of plants that provide other, more valued parts used in better times (e.g., cactus joints as opposed to flowers or fruits). A third pattern is more intensive use of plant parts that are habitually used (e.g., crowns of the agave, a plant that endures drought conditions). Wild plants seem to be better adapted and less affected by adverse weather than are introduced, domesticated plants in any region; they also mature and can be gathered over much of the year (Ebeling 1986).

Temperate Areas

Although the more temperate areas of North America, including the Prairie/ Plains, Great Lakes/East, and Pacific Northwest, differ in climatic features, they all have moderate seasonality and more than marginal annual precipitation. Subsistence strategies in these areas varied from gathering and hunting (e.g., many Plains and Northwest peoples) to a predominantly agricultural adaptation (e.g., Hidatsa, Iroquois). Indigenous peoples in all these areas have had to deal with food shortage.

On the Prairies and Plains, spring was the time when game, stored foods, and crops were most scarce and when wild plant foods provided respite (Kindscher 1987). The Omaha used Jerusalem artichoke tubers (*Helianthus tuberosus*) as spring emergency foods, presumably because of their consistent availability; they also constituted part of the normal diet of a number of Plains groups. The tuber is more desirable in the spring when the usually indigestible carbohydrate inulin has been changed to fructose to enhance plant growth. The raw tuber is also high in iron and low in fat.

Episodic shortage also affected peoples in the Prairie bioregion. Hunting failure affected groups that relied on game, and both foragers and horticulturists endured periodic drought (Kindscher 1987). Drought-resistant plants such as prostrate pigweed (*Amaranthus graecizans*), which were staples in drier regions like the Southwest, became important to Prairie peoples at those times (greens and seeds). Amaranth greens contain significant protein, calcium, phosphorus, iron, potassium, and vitamins A and C. Drought-resistant cactus species (*Coryphantha vivipara, Opuntia macrorhiza*) likewise were emergency food sources for some groups, such as the Hidatsa and Dakota, presumably because of the constant availability of cacti regardless of season. A number of Prairie and Plains groups also consumed them in good times. The Kiowa recognized gayfeather (*Liatris punctata*) for its resistance to drought and used it for emergency food into the 1930s. This plant's strategy involves a very long taproot (up to three feet) with lateral water-seeking roots at various levels; indigenous peoples do not appear to have used it as a regular food source. Another plant with a large root used during famine by several Plains groups is the bush morning glory (*Ipomoea leptophylla*), but it was difficult to extract due to its size. Rose hips served as a scarcity food for many Plains groups; the wild rose has very deep roots, and the hips, which may still adhere to the bushes in winter, are an excellent source of vitamin C. Kelly Kindscher (1987:201), citing E. T. Denig, a fur trader of the upper Missouri during the early nineteenth century, presents a sequence of food resorted to by the Assiniboin when no preferred meat was available: dried berries and roots, rawhide scrapings boiled with rose hips, grease extracted from pounded old bones, then dogs and horses.

Various other wild plants also provided emergency food to Plains peoples. Montana Indians made use of the inner cambium of lodgepole pine (*Pinus contorta*) when necessary (Blankinship 1905). Plains peoples who ordinarily prized *Psoralea esculenta*, the prairie turnip, as a dietary staple, resorted to its less desirable but more prolific relative, *P. argophylla*, in times of scarcity. This tuber was smaller, more difficult to harvest, more fibrous, and less suitable for making flour, and also caused intestinal upset; lower in carbohydrate, it is not as good a source of energy as *P. esculenta* (Kaye and Moodie 1978). This affords an example of famine food choice based on availability. Other Plains famine foods included soapberries (*Shepherdia canadensis*), which are a favored food of some indigenous peoples, and silverberries (*Elaeagnus commutata*), which are dry and mealy and were not highly regarded (Kuhnlein and Turner 1991). Besides soap-berries, the Blackfoot ate the berry of Oregon creeping grape (*Berberis repens*) when nothing else was available (Hellson and Gadd 1974). The new leaves of the willow (*Salix glauca*), eaten raw by the Stoney, provide another example of a survival food (Kuhnlein and Turner 1991). The Kiowa chewed sunflower (*Helianthus annuus*) stems to diminish thirst (Vestal and Schultes 1939).

As on the Prairies and Plains, food scarcity in the Great Lakes and East occurred seasonally, episodically, or in the course of travel or other activities. The Iroquois, whose primary subsistence strategy involved cultivation of maize and other crops, had several strategies employing wild plant foods for coping with scarcity (Parker 1968). They stored a variety of nuts, including hickory and chestnuts, against the event that sown crops (e.g., maize, beans) should fail. The Iroquois primarily utilized root foods in times of scarcity, although they consumed a few as regular dietary items. Lichens and bark, such as that of the elm (*Ulmus americanus*) and basswood (*Tilia americana*), were only consumed in emergencies. Annual food shortage in the upper Great Lakes region usually occurred in late winter and early spring (Yarnell 1964); during this time, indige-nous people made use of two cambiums (woodbine, *Parthenocissus quinquefolia*, and climbing bittersweet, *Celastrus scandens*), four lichens (rock tripe, *Um-bilicaria* spp.; reindeer moss, *Cladonia rangiferina;* spreading leather lichen, *Sticta amplissima;* and puffed shield lichen, *Parmelia physodes*), and one berry that overwintered well. The bittersweet vine, used by several groups in the western Great Lakes region, may be unique among cambium foods in that it provides as much carbohydrate during the winter as in spring, thus serving as a valuable famine resource (Jones 1965). Researchers hold differing opinions re-garding the possible toxicity of this plant (Jones 1965; Kuhnlein and Turner 1991).

Northwest Coast peoples, who subsisted largely on fishing, gathering, and hunting, used food preservation and storage as a major strategy for coping with seasonal resource variation. The Coast Salish gathered foods year-round, but unusual weather conditions, such as repeated storms with heavy seas or deep snows, could result in both a shortage of fresh foods and depletion of stored resources (Rivera 1969). The Gitksan of northwestern British Columbia state that starvation was always a threat and adequate storage a necessity that in-volved all members of the community (People of 'Ksan 1980).

Peoples of the Pacific Northwest made use of a wide variety of plants under scarcity circumstances, including, most prominently, greens and roots; these represented both increased or different use of "usual" plants and plants consumed only in scarcity (Gunther 1973; Kuhnlein and Turner 1991). Several of the greens, when chewed, functioned as hunger suppressants: deer fern (*Blechnum spicant*) and hemlock (*Tsuga heterophylla*) shoots as well as salal (*Gaultheria shallon*) leaves (Kuhnlein and Turner 1991). Crowberries (*Empetrum nigrum*), which remain on the plant throughout winter, and red twinberries (*Lonicera utahensis*) served as emergency water sources, as did horsetail (*Equisetum telmateia*) stems. A number of the famine foods in this region, both greens and roots, contain toxic substances requiring specific processing (e.g., calcium oxalate crystals in skunk cabbage, *Lysichitum americanum*, are dispelled by cooking) or use of immature forms only (Kuhnlein and Turner 1991). Some also have extremely poisonous close relatives (e.g., members of the bean family such as locoweed, *Oxytropis* spp.).

Among the Thompson (Nlaka'pamux) people of British Columbia in the nineteenth century, famine occurred occasionally, usually in spring if the salmon run failed, game was scarce, and stored food became depleted (Turner et al. 1990). People then resorted to seeking plant foods (probably roots, bulbs, or young shoots) such as cow parsnip (*Heracleum lanatum*), spring beauty (*Claytonia lanceolata*), avalanche lily (*Erythronium grandiflorum*), tiger lily (*Lilium columbianum*), and thistle (*Cirsium* spp.). People who did not eat these wild plants reportedly died. Bracken fern (*Pteridium aquilinum*) rhizomes were available during winter scarcity, and cactus stems, available all year, were also used.

Famine Food Use in Biocultural Perspective

This case material illustrates the variety of plant organs and products used as famine foods across a range of ecological zones and subsistence types. For aboriginal North America, ecozone seems to have been the most important factor determining the pattern of famine food use, with lichens, barks, and roots prominent in the colder regions and greens and cactus salient in the Southwest and Great Basin. The greater reliance on barks and cambiums in more northerly areas may reflect the greater nutrient availability for these structures in trees adapted to seasonally cold climates. Similarly, the reliance on greens and cactus in arid areas relates to the ability of succulents and deep-rooted perennials to resist desiccation and thus to maintain their productive capacity even during drought. In all cases, indigenous peoples seem to have been primarily concerned with sources of food energy, with taste, toxicity, and time to collect and process as secondary considerations.

Biological Consequences

Broadly speaking, we can view the biological consequences of famine food consumption from two perspectives: altered nutrient balance from eating a diet limited in quantity or variety, and the effects of consuming foods that may, due to their own strategies for dealing with climate and predators, contain toxic compounds. However, generalizing about nutrient deficiencies from famine food use in indigenous North America poses difficulties because of the largely historical nature of the problem and because of the variety of foods used by different groups. Biological and evolutionary consequences of wild plant use are therefore speculative.

Harriet V. Kuhnlein and Nancy J. Turner (1991) summarize generally the nutrient value of traditional plant foods; from this one can derive some idea of the nutritional impact of using a predominance of one or two food types. They state that root vegetables, as plant storage organs, are generally high in carbohydrates, some of which humans cannot readily digest. Cooking converts one of these carbohydrates, inulin, to fructose, making it digestible. Root foods are generally low in vitamins, but the skins provide some minerals. Greens (stems, leaves, shoots, and buds) are usually only palatable and digestible in their young stages; they are generally high in moisture, some vitamins (e.g., carotene, vitamin C, and folic acid), and minerals such as calcium, iron, and magnesium. Wild fruits may contain large amounts of vitamins A and C, calcium, and folic acid. Flowers are high in moisture but usually low in protein and fat; some contain carotene or ascorbic acid. Seeds, nuts, and grains are generally good sources of protein, carbohydrates, fat, minerals, and vitamins. The inner bark tissues of trees may be high in sap and therefore carbohydrates and energy, especially in the spring or early in the growing season. Algae provide several vitamins and minerals, notably iodine. Lichens contain complex polysaccharides and proteins.

A number of famine and emergency foods contain toxic substances. Toxins appear to be especially common in algae, lichens, and storage organs, such as roots and seeds, of flowering plants. Processing decreases the toxic effect in some instances but does not always eliminate it (Corkill 1948; Irvine 1952); nor can foods always be fully processed under emergency conditions. Poor selection or pretreatment of emergency foods such as lichen and water plants may have contributed to the deaths of famine victims in the past (Airaksinen et al. 1986). Children seem especially likely victims of incompletely detoxified famine foods (Sukkary-Stolba 1989). The ability to detoxify plant foods metabolically undoubtedly varies among human populations, perhaps as a result of repeated exposure (Jackson 1991). The selective impact of toxins in famine foods is obviously unknown, but survival during famine should be enhanced for those groups with both superior biological resistance to plant toxicity and effective cultural encoding of rules for plant selection and processing.

Future Research Directions

At present, understanding the importance of famine foods is hampered by a lack of data on almost all aspects of the process of their selection, ingestion, and biological utilization. Research to remedy this situation should concentrate on the following issues.

Foods Ingested During Seasonal Shortages and Severe or Long-term Famine Conditions. The nutritional and biological impact of wild foods depends on the amount and composition not only of the plants themselves, but also of the diet as a whole. Nutritional studies should therefore document amounts and types of foods actually consumed during "normal" times and during periods of scarcity. Research also should document the distribution of these foods among and within households. Observing food intake under conditions of scarcity and famine undeniably poses logistical and ethical difficulties. However, researchers involved in famine monitoring may be able to improve knowledge in this area by combined observation and respondent recall of food consumption.

Selection of Famine Foods. Research in this area should document the choices made by individuals collecting wild foods and the hierarchy of resort as conditions worsen. In addition, indigenous concepts of what constitutes a famine food and the qualities used in its selection need to be understood. Ethnobotanical understanding of plant traits and habits (e.g., drought resistance) may influence which species are protected, cultivated, and stored against times of shortage. Multiple uses of emergency plants, for example, as medicines or as animal fodder, may also influence plant availability and selection.

Processing Techniques. Food processing is crucial for human adaptation to nutritional resources (Johns and Kubo 1988; Katz 1987). Processing (peeling, cooking, leaching, fermenting, etc.) changes both the chemical content and the palatability and digestibility of foods. Since people may observe preparation and processing guidelines less strictly under famine conditions, researchers must investigate the contents of both completely and incompletely processed foods.

Biochemical Composition of Famine Foods. This category subsumes both nutrient content and the nature of secondary compounds. Although researchers have yet to analyze the chemical composition of many famine plants, existing information should be compiled on the proximate composition of known emergency foods.

Biological Variability in Response to Wild Plant Foods. Almost nothing is known about the variability among populations in nutrient needs, nutrient utilization, or tolerance of plant toxins. Some researchers have investigated differences in energy and protein needs according to body size, climate, and health status (e.g., Leslie et al. 1984; National Research Council 1980, 1986), but little is known about population variation in metabolism of other nutrients or plant secondary compounds. This constitutes a major area for potential cooperation between physiologists and human biologists.

Applications. Integrated biocultural studies of famine food use can provide information on human adaptability under conditions of nutritional stress. In addition, such studies should prove useful for predicting the biological impact of drought and hunger on populations exposed to regular or periodic food shortage. Because responses to shortage are hierarchical, the use of famine foods may also indicate the stage of deterioration of the food supply. Providing relief before emergency foods and household assets are exhausted should improve the ability of shortage-prone populations to recover from drought and other interruptions of expected food supply.

REFERENCES

Airaksinen, M. M., P. L. Peura, Liisa Ala-Fossi-Salokangas, Seija Antere, J. Lukkarinen, M. Saikkonen, and F. Stenback

    1986   Toxicity of plant material used as emergency food during famines in Finland. *Journal of Ethnopharmacology* 18:273–296.

Billings, W. D.

    1978   *Plants and the ecosystem.* Wadsworth, Belmont, California.

Blankinship, J. W.

    1905   *Native economic plants of Montana.* Montana Agricultural College Experiment Station, Bulletin No. 56. Bozeman, Montana.

Carter, George F.

    1945   *Plant geography and culture history in the American Southwest.* Viking Fund, New York.

Castetter, Edward F.

    1935   *Ethnobiological studies in the American Southwest: I. Uncultivated native plants used as sources of food.* University of New Mexico Bulletin, No. 266, Biological Series 4(1). University of New Mexico Press, Albuquerque.

Castetter, Edward F., and Willis H. Bell

    1937   *Ethnobiological studies in the American Southwest: IV. The aboriginal utilization of the tall cacti in the American Southwest.* University of New Mexico Bulletin, No. 307, Biological Series 5(1). University of New Mexico Press, Albuquerque.

Castetter, Edward F., and M. E. Opler

    1936   *Ethnobiological studies in the American Southwest: III. The ethnobiology of the Chiricahua and Mescalero Apache: A. The use of plants for foods, beverages and narcotics.* University of New Mexico Bulletin, No. 297, Biological Series 4(5). University of New Mexico Press, Albuquerque.

Colson, E.

1979   In good years and bad: Food strategies of self-reliant societies. *Journal of Anthropological Research* 35:18–29.

Corbett, J.

1988   Famine and household coping strategies. *World Development* 16(9):1099–1112.

Corkill, N. L.

1948   The poisonous wild cluster yam, *Dioscorea dumetorum* pax, as a famine food in the Anglo-Egyptian Sudan. *Annals of Tropical Medicine and Parasitology* 42:278–287.

Cowen, R.

1992   Butterflies in their stomachs. *Science News* 141(15):236.

Crites, Gary D., and R. Dale Terry

1984   Nutritive value of maygrass, *Phalaris caroliniana. Economic Botany* 38:114–120.

DeGarine, I., and G. A. Harrison [Editors]

1988   *Coping with uncertainty in food supply.* Clarendon Press, Oxford.

Downs, R. E., D. O. Kerner, and S. P. Reyna [Editors]

1992   *The political economy of famine.* Gordon and Breach Science Publishers, New York.

Dufour, Darna

1987   Insects as food: A case study from the Northwest Amazon. *American Anthropologist* 89:383–397.

1992   Nutritional ecology in the tropical rain forests of Amazonia. *American Journal of Human Biology* 4:197–207.

Ebeling, Walter

1986   *Handbook of Indian foods and fibers of arid America.* University of California Press, Berkeley.

Etkin, Nina L.

1986   Multidisciplinary perspectives in the interpretation of plants used in indigenous medicine and diet. In *Plants in indigenous medicine and diet: Biobehavioral approaches,* edited by N. L. Etkin, pp. 2–30. Gordon and Breach Science Publishers (Redgrave), New York.

Fox, F. W., and M. E. Norwood Young

1982   *Food from the Veld.* Delta Books, Johannesburg.

Gaulin, S. J., and M. Konner

1977   On the natural diet of primates, including humans. In *Nutrition and the brain,* Vol. 1, edited by R. J. Wurtman and J. J. Wurtman, pp. 1–86. Raven Press, New York.

Gunther, Erna

    1973   *Ethnobotany of western Washington: The knowledge and use of indigenous plants by Native Americans.* University of Washington Press, Seattle.

Hellson, John C., and Morgan Gadd

    1974   *Ethnobotany of the Blackfoot Indians.* Canadian Ethnology Service, Paper No. 19. National Museums of Canada, Ottawa.

Hurlich, Marshall G.

    1983   Historical and recent demography of the Algonkians of northern Ontario. In *Boreal forest adaptations: The northern Algonkians,* edited by A. T. Steegman, pp. 143–199. Plenum Press, New York.

Irvine, F. R.

    1952   Supplementary and emergency food plants of West Africa. *Economic Botany* 6:23–40.

Jackson, F.L.C.

    1991   Secondary compounds in plants (allelochemicals) as promoters of human biological diversity. *Annual Review of Anthropology* 20:505–546.

Johns, Timothy, and Isao Kubo

    1988   A survey of traditional methods employed for the detoxification of plant foods. *Journal of Ethnobiology* 8:81–129.

Jones, Volney H.

    1965   The bark of the bittersweet vine as an emergency food among the Indians of the western Great Lakes Region. *Michigan Archaeologist* 11:170–180.

Katz, S. H.

    1987   Food and biocultural evolution: A model for the investigation of modern nutritional problems. In *Nutritional anthropology,* edited by F. E. Johnston, pp. 41–63. Alan R. Liss, New York.

Kaye, Barry, and D. W. Moodie

    1978   The *Psoralea* food resource of the northern Plains. *Plains Anthropologist* 23:329–336.

Keely, Patrick B.

    1980   Nutrient composition of selected important plant foods of the pre-contact diet of the northwest Native American peoples. M.S. thesis, University of Washington.

Kindscher, Kelly

    1987   *Edible wild plants of the prairie: An ethnobotanical guide.* University Press of Kansas, Lawrence.

Kuhnlein, Harriet V., and Nancy J. Turner

    1991   *Traditional plant foods of Canadian indigenous peoples: Nutrition, botany and use.* Gordon and Breach Science Publishers, Philadelphia.

Leighton, Anna L.

    1985   *Wild plant use by the Woods Cree (Nihithawak) of east-central Saskatchewan.* National Museums of Canada, Ottawa.

Leslie, P., J. Bindon, and P. Baker
    1984   Calorie requirements of human populations: A model. *Human Ecology* 12:137–162.

Mautner, Kathleen H.
    1982   Part III. The role of Koyukon Athabaskan women in subsistence. In *Tracks in the wildland: A portrayal of Koyukon and Nunamiut subsistence,* edited by R. K. Nelson, K. H. Mautner, and G. R. Bane, pp. 132–151. Anthropology and Historic Preservation Cooperative Parks Studies Unit, University of Alaska, Fairbanks.

Messer, E.
    1989   Seasonal hunger and coping strategies: An anthropological discussion. In *Coping with seasonal constraints,* edited by R. Huss-Ashmore with J. Curry and R. Hitchcock, pp. 29–44. MASCA, University of Pennsylvania, Philadelphia.

Minnis, Paul E.
    1991   Famine foods of the northern American desert borderlands in historical context. *Journal of Ethnobiology* 11:231–257.

Moran, Emilio F.
    1979   *Human adaptability: An introduction to ecological anthropology.* Duxbury Press, North Scituate, Massachusetts.

Nabhan, Gary P.
    1985   *Gathering the desert.* University of Arizona Press, Tucson.
    1989   *Enduring seeds: Native American agriculture and wild plant conservation.* North Point Press, San Francisco.

National Research Council
    1980   *Recommended dietary allowances.* Food and Nutrition Board, National Academy of Sciences, Washington, D.C.
    1986   *Nutrient adequacy: Assessment using food consumption surveys.* Food and Nutrition Board, National Academy Press, Washington, D.C.

Nelson, Richard K.
    1982   Part I. The setting. In *Tracks in the wildland: A portrayal of Koyukon and Nunamiut subsistence,* edited by R. K. Nelson, K. H. Mautner, and G. R. Bane, pp. 13–21. Anthropology and Historic Preservation Cooperative Parks Studies Unit, University of Alaska, Fairbanks.

Parker, Arthur C.
    1968   Iroquois uses of maize and other food plants. In *Parker on the Iroquois,* edited by W. N. Fenton, pp. 5–119. Syracuse University Press, Syracuse, New York.

People of 'Ksan
    1980   *Gathering what the Great Nature provided: Food traditions of the Gitksan.* Douglas and McIntyre, Vancouver; University of Washington Press, Seattle.

Porsild, A. E.

1937   *Edible roots and berries of northern Canada.* Canada Department of Mines and Resources, National Museum of Canada, Ottawa.

Riley, B. W., and D. Brokensha

1988a   *The Mbeere of Kenya.* Volume 1, *Changing rural ecology.* Institute for Development Anthropology, University Press of America, Lanham, Maryland.

1988b   *The Mbeere of Kenya.* Volume 2, *Botanical identities and uses.* Institute for Development Anthropology, University Press of America, Lanham, Maryland.

Rivera, Trinita

1969   Diet of a food-gathering people, with chemical analysis of salmon and saskatoons. In *Indians of the urban Northwest,* edited by M. W. Smith, pp. 19–36. AMS Press, New York.

Robson, J.R.K. [Editor]

1981   *Famine: Its causes, effects and management.* Gordon and Breach Science Publishers, New York.

Savile, D.B.O.

1972   *Arctic adaptations in plants.* Canada Department of Agriculture, Monograph No. 6. Ottawa.

Scrimsher, Leda S.

1967   Native foods used by the Nez Perce Indians of Idaho. M.S. thesis, University of Idaho.

Shipek, Florence C.

1981   A Native American adaptation to drought: The Kumeyaay as seen in the San Diego Mission records 1770–1798. *Ethnohistory* 28:295–312.

Solbrig, O. T., and G. H. Orians

1977   The adaptive characteristics of desert plants. *American Scientist* 65:412–421.

Steegman, A. T.

1983   Boreal forest hazards and adaptations: The past. In *Boreal forest adaptations: The northern Algonkians,* edited by A. T. Steegman, pp. 243–267. Plenum Press, New York.

Steward, Julian H.

1938   *Basin-Plateau aboriginal sociopolitical groups.* Bureau of American Ethnology Bulletin 120. United States Government Printing Office, Washington, D.C.

Stoffle, Richard W., David B. Halmo, Michael J. Evans, and John E. Olmsted

1990   Calculating the cultural significance of American Indian plants: Paiute and Shoshone ethnobotany at Yucca Mountain, Nevada. *American Anthropologist* 92:416–432.

Sukkary-Stolba, S.

1989   Indigenous institutions and adaptation to famine: The case of the Western Sudan. In *African food systems in crisis. Part One: Microperspectives,* edited by R. Huss-Ashmore and S. H. Katz, pp. 281–294. Gordon and Breach Science Publishers, New York.

Szczawinski, Adam F., and George A. Hardy

    1962   *Guide to common edible plants of British Columbia.* British Columbia Provincial Museum, Handbook No. 20. Victoria.

Turner, Nancy J., Laurence C. Thompson, M. Terry Thompson, and Annie Z. York

    1990   *Thompson ethnobotany: Knowledge and use of plants by the Thompson Indians of British Columbia.* Royal British Columbia Museum, Memoir No. 3. Victoria.

Vestal, Paul A.

    1952   *Ethnobotany of the Ramah Navaho.* Papers of the Peabody Museum of American Archaeology and Ethnology, Harvard University, Vol. 40(4). Cambridge, Massachusetts.

Vestal, Paul A., and Richard E. Schultes

    1939   *The economic botany of the Kiowa Indians as it relates to the history of the tribe.* Botanical Museum, Cambridge, Massachusetts.

Watts, M.

    1983   *Silent violence.* University of California Press, Berkeley.

    1988   Coping with the market: Uncertainty and food security among Hausa peasants. In *Coping with uncertainty in food supply,* edited by I. DeGarine and G. A. Harrison, pp. 260–289. Clarendon Press, Oxford.

Weiner, Michael A.

    1972   *Earth medicine—earth foods: Plant remedies, drugs, and natural foods of the North American Indians.* Macmillan Company, New York.

Whiting, M. G.

    1958   A cross-cultural nutrition survey. Ph.D. dissertation, Harvard School of Public Health, Cambridge, Massachusetts.

Winterhalder, Bruce

    1983   History and ecology of the boreal zone in Ontario. In *Boreal forest adaptations: The northern Algonkians,* edited by A. T. Steegman, pp. 9–54. Plenum Press, New York.

Yarnell, Richard A.

    1964   *Aboriginal relationships between culture and plant life in the upper Great Lakes region.* Anthropological Papers, Museum of Anthropology, University of Michigan, No. 23. Ann Arbor.

Young, T. Kue

    1988   *Health care and cultural change: The Indian experience in the Central Subarctic.* University of Toronto Press, Toronto.

Zubrow, Ezra B. W.

    1974   *Population, contact, and climate in the New Mexican Pueblos.* Anthropological Papers of the University of Arizona, No. 24. University of Arizona Press, Tucson.

*❧ Physiologic Implications
of Wild Plant Consumption*

5

Pharmacologic Implications of "Wild" Plants in Hausa Diet

❊ NINA L. ETKIN AND PAUL J. ROSS

Our study of the use of "wild" plant foods by a Hausa population in northern Nigeria exhibits two salient features. The first is the unlikely setting for a discussion of "wild" foods—a relatively remote but heavily populated and intensively farmed area within one hour's drive from the ancient metropolis of Kano. Yet within this area that has long been characterized by intensive cultivation and land scarcity we have documented a surprisingly large number of noncultivated plants that find their way into the local resource base. Second, almost all the "wild" plants we discuss as foods appear on our master sample of plants used for medicinal purposes. While the design of this data base reflects our longstanding interest in the overlapping uses of plants, it gives shape in turn to a perspective that suggests not only how we can better consider the pharmacologic and nutritional implications of the dietary inclusion of wild plants, but also how the local pharmacopoeia informs food selection. Within a broader context, this design is a useful point of departure for our examination of the dynamics of "wild" food use, local views of biodiversity, and the health implications of changes imposed in the name of agricultural "development."

Our research was supported in part by grants from the National Science Foundation (BNS-8703734), the Committee on African Studies of the American Council of Learned Societies and the Social Science Research Council, the Fulbright Senior Research Scholars Program, the Bush Foundation, and the University of Minnesota. Additional support was provided by the Social Science Research Institute of the University of Hawaii; the Department of Pharmacognosy and Drug Development, Ahmadu Bello University, Zaria; Wudil Local Government; and the Kano State Department of Health.

The Setting

Since 1975 we have conducted a comprehensive investigation of diet, health, and medicine among a Hausa community in northern Nigeria, returning most recently to Hurumi, the study village, during 1987–88 (Etkin and Ross 1991a; Etkin et al. 1990; Ross 1987; Ross et al. 1991). The economic base of Hurumi is intensive, nonmechanized agriculture supplemented by livestock raising and trade in locally manufactured and other commodities. Situated 50 km southeast of urban Kano, Hurumi falls within the Kano Close-Settled Zone (Mortimore 1967)—a concentration of rural population in an area having a radius of 48–56 km that has experienced dense settlement for hundreds of years (Hill 1982). The village core features a nucleated settlement of 400 residents; dispersed compounds in the outlying hamlets bring the population total to approximately 4,000.[1] Compound size in this rural settlement ranges from 2 to nearly 40 occupants. These living units typically include a compound head, his wife (or wives), his sons and their wives, and children; frequently these compounds comprise more than one "household" (people who "eat from the same pot"), adding the potential for intracompound variability in access to resources, including knowledge of plants and composition of diet.

The general ecology of our research site is a topographically uniform landscape of Sudanian mixed Combretaceous woodland with savanna-type vegetation of scattered shrubs and small trees, once interspersed by grass cover (Barbour et al. 1982). Generations of intensive small-plot cultivation and livestock browsing, and a host of recent changes attendant on the incorporation of this region into the wider economy,[2] have disturbed the natural vegetation. Despite pressures toward biotic simplification, Hausa still have the opportunity to select from among a large number of local species as well as plants collected or purchased from more distant locales.

In broad outline, the vegetation of West Africa is relatively simple, defined by generally low-lying terrain with vegetation falling into natural latitudinal zones determined by climate. At 12° N and in the interior of Nigeria, Kano is hot and dry for most of the year; rainfall is highly variable and averages less than 75 cm annually (Barbour et al. 1982) but is sufficient to support a regime of rain-fed cultivation. The major food crops so produced are bulrush millets (*Pennisetum americanum:* gero and the late-maturing maiwa), guinea corn (*Sorghum bicolor:* dawa), groundnut (*Arachis hypogaea:* gyada), cowpea (*Vigna unguiculata:* wake), and although dramatically reduced in recent years, cassava (*Manihot esculenta:* rogo or doya). Cultivation, weeding, and harvest are labor-intensive, nonmechanized human activities assisted only, and unevenly, by hired draft oxen.[3]

Crop planting follows closely the onset of rains in late May or early June.

This time is especially critical because unless rain falls again within 7–10 days, seed is wasted and its replacement entails financial investment. This period also poses the substantial risk of mistiming, which may result in plants not achieving sufficient growth to survive a rainy season that is foreshortened by the vagaries of this local ecology. Noncultivated plants, many of which are less sensitive to desiccation than are domesticates, remain relatively unaffected by the (mis)timing of human decisions. Further, wild plants are more regularly available than domesticated species, which tend to reproduce synchronously so that individual plants are all available "at once." Rains continue through August or early September. Hausa reap most of the millet in September; harvest of sorghum, the late-maturing variety of millet, and legumes follows over the next one to two months. The dry season sets in in earnest by late October. In its advance, forbs and grasses wither, and all but one of the acacias (*A. albida*) lose leaves. Hausa store their harvests in granaries within compounds; depending on resources and perceived need, they may preserve quantities of dried nondomesticates in the same way.

Seasonally flooded riverbank gardens (*kwari*) 3 km from the village center are managed year-round by human-powered (and more recently generator-assisted) irrigation. (Individual ownership of land produces uneven access to these and other preferred farm plots.) Other areas that retain ground cover through the dry season are close to water courses that dry out completely only late in the dry season. Cattle paths—once the domain of nomadic Fulani herders—are never cultivated, providing public access where foliage remains throughout the dry season. These paths spill intermittently into small open areas, neglected because of their dry sandy habitat but nonetheless sustaining sufficient vegetation to attract grazing cattle (as well as encroaching farmers whose lands adjoin these areas). The borders of some of the larger paths that link human activities (e.g., between hamlets) share these features of year-round vegetative cover and botanical diversity. This description of population and land use in the Kano Close-Settled Zone makes it clear that undisturbed "bush" no longer exists, although the term is still in use (see below).

Population density and intense demand for land dictate that virtually no cultivable land lies fallow in a given year. This need for land is reinforced by a fluid and flexible system of land tenure in which ownership is not rigidly bound to land use, so that unexpected circumstances that might otherwise eventuate in fallowing (e.g., death, temporary migration) do not preclude a variety of arrangements by which one can cultivate land that one does not own: for example, *riko*, land rights held "in trust"; *kyauta*, simple "free" seasonal loan; *jingina*, transfer of usufruct as collateral for a cash loan, with usufruct restored after the land owner repays the loan to the land user. These arrangements for land use also involve women in farming concerns. In this Moslem population women are substantial landowners but are constrained from actually cultivating by the dictum of purdah ("seclusion" within the compound).[4] Nonetheless, the options for land use ensure that women can actively participate in shaping farming strategies. Indeed, women constitute about half of the donors (an increase from one-third a decade earlier) and allocate more than half of the land area originating from Hurumi owners—patterns not significantly different from those of household heads, the "traditional" decision makers and conventional subjects of land-use surveys (Ross 1987). As a result, Hausa women have more knowledge of crops, border plants, and other resources than researchers of Hausaland typically portray (e.g., Callaway 1987). This fluidity of land use as well as a variety of farm and off-farm activities (e.g., the manufacture of crafts, cosmetics, etc.) ensure a continued discourse in, and use of, a wide variety of plants. Participation in an ever-widening market economy affords the means by which new botanicals enter the village while some local species are transported out, thus compounding the long-standing botanical diversity.

Hausa Understandings of "Wild" and "Domesticated"

As set out in the introduction to this volume and illustrated by other chapters, the assignment of plants to one or another locus along the wild-domesticated continuum exhibits considerable disarray. Although perhaps less complicated than in tropical rainforest habitats, the issue demands clarification in Hausaland as well. Whereas the major crop domesticates resolve easily, and we have established in the foregoing discussion that truly "wild" species no longer exist in Hausaland, the intermediate categories remain problematic. For example, do plants that Hausa deliberately introduce into farm borders not qualify as "cultivated" simply because they do not grow in prepared seedbeds? Do the human actions that protect a "managed" plant result in no genetic changes that signify "semidomesticates"? Clearly, the existing schema are unsatisfactory and vary both regionally and among plants within northern Nigeria. To fine-tune this definition for Hausaland, we (re)introduce the term *semiwild*—that is, plants neither explicitly cultivated nor actively tended but nevertheless affected by human activities—without making assumptions regarding whether, or to what extent, genetic changes may have occurred. This term further conflates the connotations of "semidomesticated" and "wild." ("Semi-" is about as wild as plants can be in this densely populated, intensively farmed part of Hausaland.)

From a Hausa perspective, however, definitions are not engaged at this level of detail. They distinguish among plants found in the "bush," along cattle paths, on farms, and in gardens, terms that reflect the axes of distance and wildness and are specified by their particular context. For example, although *bakin daji,* the true ("dark," foreboding) bush that traditionally was home to wild animals, spirits, and the like, no longer exists, it continues to be a powerful metaphor in Hausa ideology—a liminal area representing death, risk, and the unknown at the same time that, paradoxically, it is potentially a vast and best resource of foods and medicines. Today Hausa widely apply the term *daji* to uncultivated (nonfarm) land and to sparsely wooded tracts within the vicinity of the village, including the areas that serve both cattle grazing and the collection of "wild" plants. Hausa distinguish as well whether a plant on a farm has been deliberately planted or will be subject to weeding, or something in between—i.e., useful plants that are deliberately missed during weeding. Discrete lexical categories refer to adventitious plants—plants that one wants sometimes but not necessarily just here or now. This concept extends to both opportunistic "weeds" or "wild" plants and to cultivated plants whose stray seeds find their way onto a farm designated for other purposes or sprout only the year following their planting. Those plants take on special cultural salience for use in food and medicine.

We were initially drawn to Hausa "wild" food plants through our study of indigenous medicines. Later we formalized that concern as part of detailed, year-long dietary surveys conducted simultaneously with investigations of local therapeutics during the 1975–76 and 1987–88 field sessions.

Medicinal Plants

Villagewide interviews yielded nearly 5,000 medicinal preparations (Etkin and Ross 1991a). Excluding replications, Hausa produce 3,165 distinct remedies, defined by a unique combination of constituents or each time a specific combination is used for another illness category. Table 5.1 lists the most common categories of illness for which Hausa administer these preparations. The majority of distinct remedies involve a total of 374 plants defined here as medicinal plants (Table 5.2). Excluding those plants identified through markets only or otherwise incompletely assessed, almost three-quarters of the medicinal plants are semiwild. These semiwild plants can be distinguished into two types: those that treat illnesses with physiologic manifestations—localized pain, discharge, fever, and so on; and those used for less tangible concerns including (largely preventive) sorcery and the mediation of spirits and witches. (Some plants appear in both categories.)

Locally Available Medicinal Plants. Of the medicinal plants, nearly three-fourths are available locally (Table 5.3). Most are found within the village proper, while a few grow in the area devoted to irrigated gardening. Nonlocal sources include regional "bushland" within a day's journey and various market venues. Consideration of only locally secured plants underscores the impor-

Table 5.1 Most Common Categories for Medicinal Preparations

Hausa Nosology	General Analogue	Medicinal Preparations (N)
Iska	spirit-caused illness	104
Sammu	sorcery	103
Ciwon ciki	general GI disorders	94
Ciwon ciki kaba	acute GI disorders	90
Shawara	hepatitis, malaria	72
Kyanda	measles	70
Maye	witch-caused illness	66
Zazzabi	febrile disorders	64
Danshi	pediatric malaria	59
Mayankwaniya	"wasting," anemia	59

tance of "wild" species, even in this area of intensive cultivation: of the locally growing medicinal plants, only one-tenth are cultivated; the other nine-tenths are semiwild.

Farms. Nearly half the medicinal plants that are protected but not planted originate from farms (Table 5.4). Some are sufficiently scarce or important to be retained under all circumstances; Hausa safeguard others for dietary motives or because of anticipated use for an ongoing illness, for illnesses whose seasonal occurrence portends need, and for other anticipated conditions such as pregnancy. These include 65 small and 13 large annuals, plants typically removed during cultivation as "weeds." Also found on farms are 38 large and 5 small perennials—trees and shrubs.

Farm Borders. Farm borders are strips 1–2 m wide that demarcate the myriad small plots and provide one-sixth of the semiwild plants (Table 5.4). These consist of 25 small and 4 large annuals, including the Guinea grasses, and are represented as well by 1 large and 12 small perennials.

Uncultivated Land. The remaining semiwild plants are found primarily on the nearly 10% of village land designated for cattle paths, (a very few) abandoned home and farm sites, and areas of sufficiently poor soil quality to preclude cultivation (Table 5.4). These plants include 39 small and 7 large annuals as well as 18 small and 8 large perennials.

Medicinal Foods

The inventory of medicinal plants accounts for nearly all botanicals that appear in diet: all but 5 of the 119 plants identified as foods appear in the master sample of 374 medicinals. Moreover, of the 235 local semiwild plants in the pharmacopoeia, one-fourth also serve dietary needs. About half of all food plants consumed by this community are noncultigens collected from the local environment. We turn now to these "medicinal foods."

Designating these medicinal foods is not to suggest that for Hausa the therapeutic properties of plants account for their role in diet. In fact, foods and medicines are conceptually quite discrete; Hausa understand them at different levels of detail regarding how they affect health. With few exceptions, local assessments of the health implications of foodstuffs are rather vague: a food may be "good for you," or "keep the body strong," or "fortify the blood"—but Hausa elaborate little beyond this. Even many of these interpretations are recent introductions through exposure to health campaigns issued from the district hospital, which seek to instruct, for example, about the merits of particular vitamin- and protein-rich foods. This perspective on foods stands in marked contrast to the elaborate explications of the same plants as medicines: these promote disease egress through the skin or mouth, neutralize stomach cold, reduce swelling, dislodge phlegm, and so on. As foods, plants are assessed with regard to palatability and satiety relative to the effort necessary to procure them; as potential contributors to meal appearance, taste, smell, and texture; and as fuel for increased work effort—criteria that are not integral to the selection of plants as medicine (although those qualities may be later used to mark the efficacy of a plant medicine).[5]

Table 5.2 Plant Medicines

Intended Use	Semiwild Plants		All Plants	
	Plants	Remedies	Plants	Remedies
Overtly Physiologic	254	1,854	345	2,275
Other	215	452	266	526
Total	272[a]	2,306	374[a]	2,801[b]

Source: Data from 1987–88 season.
[a]Totals are less than the sums due to multiple plant uses.
[b]Excluded are 5 remedies that specify plant location or situation rather than species.

Table 5.3 Primary Source Areas of Medicinal Plants

	Plants	
Location	N	%
Local	264	70.6
Central hamlet	(215)	(57.5)
Kwari	(49)	(13.1)
Regional	32	8.6
Market	78	20.9
Total (N)	374	

As we have described elsewhere (Etkin and Ross 1982, 1991a), the local grains sorghum and millet and to a much lesser extent the legumes cowpea and groundnut most prominently shape the diet: in 1988 grains provided 72% of the population's calories, and legumes 10%. At least once a day, meals feature grain-based, dense porridges and a companion soup containing diverse ingredients that impart flavor and variety. Legumes, by contrast, function in the diet as occasional meals and snacks by themselves, as soup constituents, and as supplementary and very highly valued additions for dishes that center on various other foodstuffs (both cultivated and not).

Against this backdrop we can appreciate the dietary roles of the 61 local semiwild medicinal foods (listed in Appendix 5.1).[6] As elements of diet, these plants tend to contribute only nominally to calorie and protein intake (although some do contain high concentrations of protein, minerals, and vitamins [Humphry et al. 1993]). During 1988, for example, these semiwild plants accounted for only 3% of total calorie consumption. In that respect they are clearly overshadowed by the more ubiquitous cultigens. Despite their often limited availability, pressure on resources increasingly fosters the inclusion of many of these plants into diet as substitutes not only for grains and legumes, but also for each other, particularly for plants used to mediate flavor.[7] Thus, through diet this Hausa population is exposed to a multitude of plant substances—and in significant frequency, if not quantity. This is an important issue, given the potentially pharmacologically loaded sample from which these botanicals are drawn: our research on the Hausa pharmacopoeia continues to uncover the rich potential of these plants. We have already reported the pharmacologic profile of plants used in the treatment of malaria, disorders of the gastrointestinal tract, and oral pathology (Etkin 1980, 1981; Etkin and Ross 1982, 1991a); those findings are further reinforced by the (not yet published) results of our inquiries into Hausa treatment of ocular disorders, wounds and skin disease, and fractures and dislocations.

The diversity of medicinal foods is illustrated in Table 5.5. One-third of the medicinal foods appear in soups that accompany the primary grain-based dishes for the main evening meal. Of these, many substitute for one another and for other, more preferred cultigens that serve similar roles. Some act as thickeners or confer glutinous texture; and as flavorings they may mediate the odor and taste of other ingredients, especially fish and meats that have "gone off." In several of the grain-based gruels that are popular for morning and midday meals, 2 of the plants provide the chief flavor, and 5 others appear as substitutes if those 2 are not available. For other, primarily midday, meals that feature combinations of legumes or uncooked but processed grains, 10 plants serve as primary flavorings: 2 are used regularly, 4 as substitutes, and 4 others as supplementary seasonings. Two others alter the meal's texture—one tenderizes, the other makes the food glutinous. One of the primary flavorings also stretches grain supplies by adding bulk to a dish. Other meals feature 10 semiwild plants as primary ingredients; used interchangeably and rarely in combination, these add variety as well as conserve the more valued grains and legumes.

In our sample, one-fourth of the plants also appear as snacks. Cow milk, appearing variably with and within meals and snacks, involves 4 of the plants in our sample: 1 to brighten, 1 to increase volume, and 2 used interchangeably to promote curdling and souring, forms in which milk is most popularly consumed.

Table 5.4 Primary Source Areas for Local Medicinal Plants

Plant Type and Location	Plants	
	N	%
Noncultigens	235	89.0
Farm	(121)	(45.8)
Farm border	(42)	(15.9)
Public lands	(72)	(27.3)
Cultigens	29	11.0
Total	264	

Table 5.5 Food Uses of Local Semiwild Medicinal Plants

	Plants	
Food Type	N	%
Meals	46	75.4
Soups	(20)	(32.8)
Gruels	(7)	(11.5)
Midday meals, primary	(10)	(16.4)
Midday meals, secondary	(12)	(19.7)
Snacks	15	24.6
Prepared mixture	(12)	(19.7)
Raw	(5)	(8.2)
Sweet beverages	(2)	(3.3)
Milk	(4)	(6.6)
Emergency	7	11.5

In a special category, a small portion of our sample includes "emergency" foods used during famine or other shortage, although only one plant is used exclusively so (*Eragrostis ciliaris:* komarya).[8] This category is more salient for the more distant history of this region (Mortimore 1989).

The relative importance of source areas from which these medicinal foods are drawn approximates that of the larger sample of medicinal plants: two-thirds originate on farms, one-tenth on borders, and one-fourth from the remaining uncultivated areas (Table 5.6). (Comparable figures for the larger sample are 51%, 18%, and 31% respectively.) However, medicinal food plants differ significantly from their nonfood counterparts in one respect: more than half of the medicinal foods are perennials, compared to less than one-third of the semiwild nonfood medicinals. This preponderance of perennials among medicinal foods should not be surprising, perhaps, in view of the seasonal pressures imposed by a short, four- to five-month growing season juxtaposed with the year-round need for dietary input.

As one other significant difference between the semiwild medicinal foods and their nonfood counterparts, plants used as both food and medicine appeared in $1^1/_2$ times as many remedies as those used only medicinally (Table 5.6). This ratio suggests that at least for the population studied, awareness of semiwild plants as medicinals informs their selection as dietary constituents.

Awareness of the Biotic Environment

We have documented the extensive use of semiwild food plants and suggest that the paradigm through which members of this Hausa population comprehend their biotic environment has been partly configured by their concern with plants as medicines. Certainly, other needs also influence the interpretation of plants (diet, construction, etc.), but the specific case we present here suggests that Hausa first "discovered" many of their "wild" plant foods as medicines. We do not contend that this perspective can be transposed wholesale to other societies, where the cultural and environmental circumstances under which cuisines and pharmacopoeias develop may shape different patterns of need and knowledge about particular plants. Instead, we challenge the conventional unilineal view—that people learn about medicines only secondarily to their search for food. A more synthetic perspective better characterizes the interconnected histories of human food and medicine and accommodates both "nonfood first" and "food first" models to explain the acquisition and transformation of botanical knowledge.

Our position finds general support in our medicinal plant inventory, which

Table 5.6 Source Areas and Plant Types of Medicinal Foods and Nonfoods

Plant Type and Location	Medicinal Nonfoods		Medicinal Foods		Total Medicinals	
	N	%	N	%	N	%
Source Areas						
Farm	82	47.1	39	63.9	121	51.5
Farm border	36	20.7	6	9.8	42	17.9
Public land	56	32.2	16	26.2	72	30.6
Total	174		61		235	
Plant Type[a]						
Annual	124	71.3	29	47.5	153	65.1
Perennial	50	28.7	32	52.5	82	34.9
Total	174		61		235	
Remedies[b] per Plant		14.0		21.6		16.0

[a]$x^2 = 11.16$, p<.01
[b]t = 2.34, p<.01

is substantially more comprehensive of local flora than our corollary catalogues for foods and economic plants and also subsumes plants from those other categories—whereas the reverse is not the case. A second point, mentioned earlier, is that all the criteria that Hausa use to evaluate the appropriateness of plants for food are influenced by long-term experience with botanicals used in medicinal preparations. By contrast, Hausa consider food plants—even those drawn from the pool of medicinals—for qualities of taste and satiety and only superficially with regard to health value. While knowledge of medicinal plants guides the selection of foods (hence the impressive proportion of medicinal plants that also appear in diet), the converse is less true: intimate knowledge of a food will not inform its medicinal use, because whereas taste, texture, suspending qualities, and even toxicity are all primary to food selection, they are only secondary to medicinal properties. An argument that suggests that medicinals have a primary function in guiding the selection of "wild" food plants not only adds to our understanding of how populations select dietary elements, but also draws attention to the health implications of dietary change.

We and others have remarked that very little is known about the pharmacology of food plants and have argued that, given the overlap of medicines and foods, investigation of the pharmacologic qualities of medicines remains incomplete until researchers pay attention to all contexts of exposure to those plants (Etkin and Ross 1991b; Johns 1990). Here we contend further that, given the dietary elaboration inspired by plants that first serve medicinal concerns, their pharmacologic cum nutritive implications become more explicit and the need for phytochemical investigation more compelling.

Recognizing the importance of medicinal needs in shaping local awareness of the biotic environment also provides us with a better understanding of human impact on biodiversity. Sustained interest in particular plants may either inhibit or encourage simplification; we must identify what those interests are and whether and how they are sustained. A predominant concern with medicinals may help to contain pressures that promote simplification, particularly those imposed by a dietary regimen dependent upon intensive land use. In the Kano Close-Settled Zone, for example, diet has been overwhelmingly dominated by a few plants for many generations, predating even colonial incursions (Hill 1982). While some supplemental gathering of foodstuffs has always occurred, the circumstances surrounding cultivation and diet did not foster an appreciation for biodiversity—rather, they worked in the opposite direction, focusing attention on a small number of food plants.

Nonetheless, categories of plant use are neither exclusive nor static, and as specific interests in plants shift over time, so do behaviors that affect species diversity. Given this tendency, we can appreciate why plant species introduced years ago to satisfy a specific need can be sustained for a substantial time after that need has dissipated. Thus, Hausa still maintain indigo (*Indigofera arrecta: baba*) as an important medicinal although it has long outlived its value as a dye source. In the same way, pressures to diversify the diet focus interest on local medicinal plants and, consequently, further encourage their conservation.

To date, local resistance to certain agricultural developments also has sustained species diversity. The most imposing threat comes from "development" strategies that promote the mechanized and chemical-supported cultivation of a small number of plants and thus encourage the elimination of "nonstaple" and "noncrop" species (e.g., Olasantan 1992). In the name of efficiency those same schema encourage the consolidation of land holdings, with a corollary elimination of the farm borders that serve as habitat to so many semiwild plants. Similarly, as the incursion of pharmaceuticals drives a growing disaffection for some indigenous therapies (Etkin et al. 1990), one might expect that such a trend would contribute to diminished interest in certain species of "wild" plants. If regard for those plants has already been transposed to their dietary attributes, however, their availability continues to be a priority for the local population. It remains to be seen how tenuous is this implicitly environmentally protective relationship between Hausa and their "wild" plants.

NOTES

1. The population is scattered over 18 km^2, with an average population density of 222 per km^2.

2. Especially marked are infrastructure adjustments defined by transportation, communication, and primary health care that have contributed to changes related to increased availability and diversity and more facile circulation of goods and information. Those changes have profoundly affected diet (Ross and Etkin 1991).

3. Recently, a few of the more progressive farmers have started to employ tractor service for the initial plowing of fields for groundnuts.

4. During the years intervening between our two studies, this trend became even more explicit: fewer farmers were women in 1988 (4.5% compared to 9.4% in 1976), yet more farm owners were women (24% compared to 21%).

5. The Hausa dictum that bitter taste (*daci*) signals good medicine for gastrointestinal (GI) disorders illustrates how these qualities become emblematized as markers of effective plant medicines. In fact, careful appraisal of the plants selected for GI treatments from among a larger pool of bitter-tasting plants (which vary in the quality and intensity of that taste) demonstrates that other considerations also mediate the selection of effective treatments. Some plants promote the vomiting that signals disease egress, while others are antimicrobial and can diminish symptoms of bacillary or amoebic dysenteries (Etkin and Ross 1982).

6. Humphry and coresearchers (1993) also record the common dietary uses of many of these species among Hausa in Niger, although they have apparently not distin-

guished those beyond edible/not edible and have not examined overlapping contexts of use.

7. One could argue, and Hausa would concur, that the very nature of Hausa staples— their seasonal shortages, lack of variety, and unrelenting blandness (*gahoho*)—further promotes diversification of diet and reliance on a variety of semiwild plants distinguished by taste, texture, and related properties. Those same qualities identify an overlapping subset of those plants as medicines; that is, astringent, bitter, and pungent tastes flavor foods and identify medicines for gastrointestinal disorders, and mucilaginous substances mark medicines for childbirth and for catarrh.

8. Second only to cultigens, this category has been paid the most attention by other researchers of food or plant availability in Hausaland.

REFERENCES

Barbour, K. Michael, Julius S. Oguntoyinbo, J.O.C. Onyemelukwe, and James C. Nwafor
  1982   *Nigeria in maps.* Africana Publishing Company, New York.
Callaway, Barbara J.
  1987   *Muslim Hausa women in Nigeria: Tradition and change.* Syracuse University Press, Syracuse.
Etkin, Nina L.
  1980   Indigenous medicine in northern Nigeria. Oral hygiene and medical treatment. *Journal of Preventive Dentistry* 6:143–149.
  1981   A Hausa herbal pharmacopoeia: Biomedical evaluation of commonly used plant medicines. *Journal of Ethnopharmacology* 4:75–98.
Etkin, Nina L., and Paul J. Ross
  1982   Food as medicine and medicine as food: An adaptive framework for the interpretation of plant utilization among the Hausa of northern Nigeria. *Social Science and Medicine* 16:1559–1573.
  1991a   Recasting malaria, medicine, and meals: A perspective on disease adaptation. In *The anthropology of medicine* [Second edition], edited by L. Romanucci-Ross, D. E. Moerman, and L. R. Tancredi, pp. 230–258. Bergin and Garvey, New York.
  1991b   Should we set a place for diet in ethnopharmacology? *Journal of Ethnopharmacology* 32:25–36.
Etkin, Nina L., Paul J. Ross, and Ibrahim Muazzamu
  1990   The indigenization of pharmaceuticals: Therapeutic transitions in rural Hausaland. *Social Science and Medicine* 30(8):919–928.
Hill, Polly
  1982   *Dry grain farming families.* Cambridge University Press, Cambridge.
Humphry, Carol M., Michael S. Clegg, Carl L. Keen, and Louis E. Grivetti
  1993   Food diversity and drought survival: The Hausa example. *International Journal of Food Sciences and Nutrition* 44:1–16.

Johns, Timothy

    1990   *With bitter herbs they shall eat it: Chemical ecology and the origins of human diet and medicine.* University of Arizona Press, Tucson.

Mortimore, Michael J.

    1967   Land and population pressure in the Kano Close-Settled Zone, northern Nigeria. *Advancement of Science* 23:677–688.

    1989   *Adapting to drought: Farmers, famines and desertification in West Africa.* Cambridge University Press, Cambridge.

Olasantan, F. O.

    1992   Vegetable production in traditional farming systems in Nigeria. *Outlook on Agriculture* 21:117–127.

Ross, Paul J.

    1987   Land as a right to membership: Land tenure dynamics in a peripheral area of the Kano Close-Settled Zone. In *State, oil, and agriculture in Nigeria,* edited by M. Watts, pp. 223–247. Institute of International Studies, University of California, Berkeley.

Ross, Paul J., and Nina L. Etkin

    1991   A changing Hausa dietary: Digesting a perspective on disease adaptation. Paper presented at the 90th Annual Meeting of the American Anthropological Association, as part of the Invited Session "Thinking About Eating," Chicago, 20–24 November.

Ross, Paul J., Nina L. Etkin, and Ibrahim Muazzamu

    1991   The greater risk of fewer deaths: An ethnodemographic approach to child mortality in Hausaland. *Africa* 61(4):501–512.

Appendix 5.1. Semiwild Medicinal Food Plants in Hausa Diet

Hausa Name	Genus and Species	Family
Aduwa	*Balanites aegyptiaca* (L) Del	Zygophyllaceae
Alilliba	*Cordia africana* Lam.	Boraginaceae
Baba	*Indigofera arrecta* Hochst	Fabaceae
Baba rodo	*Rogeria adenophylla* J. Gay	Pedaliaceae
Bado	*Nymphaea lotus* L.	Nymphaeaceae
Bagayi	*Cadaba farinosa* Forssk.	Capparaceae
Baure	*Ficus gnaphalocarpa* Steud ex Miq	Moraceae
Cediya	*Ficus ovata* Vahl.	Moraceae
Dabino	*Phoenix dactylifera* L.	Palmae
Daddoya	*Hyptis suaveolens* (L.) Poir.	Lamiaceae

Hausa Name	Genus and Species	Family
Dakwara	*Acacia senegal* Willd.	Mimosaceae
Danya	*Sclerocarya birrea* (A. Rich) Hochst	Anacardiaceae
Dashi	*Commiphora africana* (A. Rich) Engl.	Burseraceae
Dinya	*Vitex doniana* Sweet	Verbenaceae
Dorawa	*Parkia filicoidea* Welw ex Oliv	Fabaceae
Durumi	*Ficus polita* Vahl.	Moraceae
Ganji	*Ficus platyphylla* Delile	Moraceae
Garahunu	*Momordica balsamina* L.	Cucurbitaceae
Gasaya	*Gynandropsis gynandra* (L.) Briq	Capparaceae
Gauta	*Solanum incanum* L.	Solanaceae
Giginya	*Borassus aethiopum* Mart.	Palmae
Gurjiya	*Bombax buonopozense* P. Beauv.	Bombacaceae
Gwanda	*Carica papaya* L.	Caricaceae
Gwandai	*Stylochiton warneckei* Engl.	Araceae
Gwandar jeji	*Annona senegalensis* Pers.	Annonaceae
Haṇtsar giwa	*Amorphophallus abyssinicus* (A. Rich) N.E. Br.	Araceae
Ingidido	*Clerodendrum capitatum* (Willd) Schum. & Thonn.	Verbenaceae
Kaba	*Hyphaene thebaica* Martius	Arecaceae
Kadanya	*Vitellaria paradoxa* (Gertn. f) Hepper	Sapotaceae
Ka fi rama	*Urena lobata* L. cf. *Malvastrum coromandelianum* (L.) Garcke	Malvaceae Malvaceae
Kaikaikuwa	*Hibiscus asper* Hook f.	Malvaceae
Kanya	*Diospyros mespiliformis* Hochst. ex A DC.	Ebenaceae
Kargo	*Bauhinia reticulata* DC. *Bauhinia thonningii* Schum.	Fabaceae Fabaceae
Karkashi	*Sesamum radiatum* Schum. & Thonn.	Pedaliaceae
Kawari	*Ficus ingens* (Miq) Miq	Moraceae
Kokiya	*Strychnos spinosa* Lam.	Loganiaceae
Komarya	*Eragrostis ciliaris* R.Br.	Poaceae
Kuka	*Adansonia digitata* L.	Bombacaceae

Hausa Name	Genus and Species	Family
Kurna	*Zizyphus spina-christi* (L.) Desf	Rhamnaceae
Ludiya	—	—
Magarya	*Zizyphus spina-christi* L.(Desf)	Rhamnaceae
Malaiduwa	*Cissus populnea* Guill & Perr	Vitaceae
Mandewa	*Maerua angolensis* DC.	Capparaceae
Mangwaro	*Mangifera indica* L.	Anacardiaceae
Masarar yan kiko	*Amorphophallus* sp.	Araceae
Nannaho	*Celosia trigyna* L.	Amaranthaceae
Rimi	*Ceiba pentandra* (L.) Gaertn.	Bombacaceae
Sansan	*Ludwigia erecta* (L.) Hara	Onagraceae
Shirinya	*Ficus thonningii* Blume	Moraceae
Soso	*Luffa aegyptica* Miller	Cucurbitaceae
Tafasa	*Cassia tora* L.	Fabaceae
Tamba	*Eleusine corocana* (L.) Gaertn.	Poaceae
Tarfai	—	—
Tsamiya	*Tamarindus indica* L.	Fabaceae
Tsidau	*Tribulus terrestris* L.	Zygophyllaceae
Turgunnuwa	*Corchorus tridens* L.	Tiliaceae
Yadiya	*Leptadenia hastata* (Pers) Decne	Asclepiadaceae
Yandi	*Ficus abutifolia* (Miq) Miq	Moraceae
Yumbururu	*Ipomoea aquatica* Forssk.	Convolvulaceae
	Aniseia martinicensis (Jacq) Choisy	Convolvulaceae
Zaki banza	*Amaranthus spinosus* L.	Amaranthaceae
	Amaranthus viridis L.	Amaranthaceae
Zogale	*Moringa oleifera* Lam.	Moringaceae

Note: Vouchers were identified at the Missouri Botanical Garden Herbarium and are deposited there as part of the permanent Africa collection.

6

Wild Plants as Food and Medicine in Polynesia

❧ PAUL ALAN COX

The importance of the interaction between plants and people cannot be overstated in the case of Polynesia, where plants play a disproportionately large role in the cultural landscape, compared, for example, to pastoral peoples of continental areas. Lacking all domestic animals save pigs, chickens, and dogs, Polynesians depended on plants for their food, shelter, religious rituals, and healing practices. From the construction of the large oceangoing rafts that carried them, to the crops and agricultural strategies they introduced to the islands they colonized, Polynesians celebrated plants in practice and legend, intertwining the origin of plants with the genesis of cultural heroes. To understand the development, expansion, and intensification of Polynesian cultures, an appreciation of Polynesian plants is not only desirable but necessary (Cox and Banack 1991).

Polynesian Prehistory and Plant Environments

In Polynesian legends, cultivated and wild plants are not of equal salience, with Polynesian mythology focusing on the origin of cultivated plants. Clearly the cultigen "kit" developed and carried by the Lapita ancestors of the Polynesians was the technological innovation that allowed the colonization of perhaps the largest, most ecologically diverse, and environmentally unpredictable area on the surface of the earth: the islands of the South Pacific. The major Polynesian cultivars—particularly yams, taro, and breadfruit—exerted a strong influence on the nature of Polynesian human and material culture. This influence was potent in the intensification phase of the Polynesian cultures, where the agricultural surpluses generated from Polynesian crops were governed by chiefly classes (Kirch 1984). In the hierarchical cultures of pre–European contact Hawaii, Tahiti, and Tonga, carefully designed plantings of cultigens determined the trajectory of society, with wild plants playing only a peripheral role. Yet earlier in the colonization and establishment phases of Polynesian cultures, wild plants played a much more important role, providing not only food and shelter, but also the complete material basis of the large oceangoing rafts (Banack 1991; Banack and Cox 1987). Although the material artifacts associated with cultivated plants—such as the massive breadfruit fermentation pits of the Marquesas or the taro pounders of Hawaii—have long played a prominent role in Polynesian archaeology (Davidson 1979; Kirch 1984; Kirch and Yen 1982), the importance of wild plants has only recently garnered attention.

The wild plants (meaning here all noncultivated plants) utilized by Polynesians prior to European contact have three different possible origins, listed in reverse chronological order: (1) some were introduced subsequent to human colonization as a product of voyaging and trade; (2) others were introduced, deliberately or inadvertently, during the colonization process, and (3) many species predated human presence on the islands. Trying to distinguish between aboriginal plant introductions and truly indigenous plants is occasionally a difficult process, but recently Art Whistler (1991) made a contribution to this inquiry.

The first category, wild plants used as items of exchange during Polynesian trade, has received little consideration. The biological consequences of such plants remain poorly understood. For example, extensive commerce in Lauan oceangoing canoes by Fijians and Tongans depended upon the existence of wild stands of large *Intsia bijuga* (Leguminosae) trees on Kabara island, Lau, Fiji (Banack and Cox 1987), which were used to create large single-piece canoe hulls renowned for their remarkable strength and durability. Yet there is no evidence that this trade resulted in the introduction of *Intsia bijuga* to other islands. Similarly, ethnohistorical accounts from Samoa suggest trade within and between archipelagos in *ie toga* (gloss: "fine mats," lit.: "Tongan mats") woven from wild *Freycinetia* (Pandanaceae) leaves, but again there is no evidence that this trade furthered the spread of *Freycinetia* throughout the islands. Commerce in *kato halu*, ceremonial baskets woven from the aerial roots of *Rhapidophora* (Araceae), was also important throughout Tonga, but again transplantation of plants from one point to another as a result of this trade seems unlikely.

The reason that the products of wild plants, but not the plants themselves, were disseminated during trade is likely morphological: leaves and shoots but not fruits and seeds were the usual items of exchange. Thus, there was little possibility that a reproductive propagule would be transported and possibly inadvertently released into the natural environment. But there were perhaps a few exceptions to this general pattern. The sweet, colorful syncarps of certain wild *Pandanus tectorius* (Pandanaceae) may have been carried from island to island as confections or decorative necklaces. Certain varieties of *Aleurites moluccana* (Euphorbiaceae), the oily seeds of which were ignited to provide light, may also have been disseminated in this manner.

The second category, wild plants introduced during the colonization process, has also received little comment. Certainly the origin, modification, and intensification of agricultural materials introduced by the Polynesians has been the focus of much distinguished research (Kirch 1991; Yen 1991). Yet to my knowledge, only Whistler (1991) has attempted a broad botanical analysis of the introduction of wild plants, including weeds, during Polynesian colonization episodes. Many of us researchers hope that he and others will continue to search for the story contained within the weeds, which, unlike cultivars, were not subject to intentional genetic manipulation by the Polynesians. Analysis with new genetic techniques may therefore shed new light on the pattern and timing of early Polynesian migrations by allowing biogeographic analysis of cultivar origins and distributions (Yen 1991).

In this chapter I focus on the third class of wild Polynesian plants, those that occurred on the islands prior to human advent. This topic is of particular interest since, unlike continental areas, Polynesia was subject to human intervention only within the last two to three thousand years (Jennings 1979). Also, unlike many cultures that developed in continental areas, Polynesian subsistence sprang from an already sophisticated agricultural system. With the exception of subsistence reef foraging and fishing (which continues to this day), there was never a hunter-gatherer phase in Polynesian prehistory (Jennings 1979). Instead the islands, with their wild plant communities, were colonized by people carrying exotic cultivars and well-developed agricultural systems, particularly arboriculture and cultivation of rhizomatous aroids (Yen 1991). In some ways the Polynesian settlement of Oceania resembles the rapid European colonization of America more than the slow Amerindian development of the same continent.

The early Polynesian colonists were faced with wild plant environments that were largely superfluous to their attempts to establish dependable plantings of the crops they brought with them. On any given island, the first colonists were likely already familiar with some of the wild plants they encountered, particularly pan-Pacific and pantropical species in the strand and littoral communities. But plant species of the interior forests, many of which are endemic, were likely unfamiliar to the new settlers, requiring careful investigation to discover possible utility. Uses for new species of an already familiar genus might have presented themselves, but possible uses of species of endemic genera or endemic families likely took some time to determine.

Polynesian Wild Plants: Endemic, Indigenous, or Introduced?

We can divide Polynesian plants into two groups based on the probable familiarity of colonists with them: (1) indigenous plant materials with which the Polynesians were familiar on arrival, and in fact may have had a reasonable expectation of finding in the new locality, and (2) endemic plants that were not known to Polynesians prior to colonization. These two groups can be distinguished ecologically as well as ethnobotanically: the first category is characterized largely by strand and littoral species that form a more or less continuous flora throughout island Polynesia, while the second category is largely composed of inland rainforest and cloud species where rates of endemism are the highest.

Upon this template of two differing wild plant types can be superimposed Polynesian plant uses. For convenience I divide these uses into three types: (1) wild plants used to make durable goods, (2) wild plants used as food, and (3) wild plants used as medicine. To facilitate discussion, I concentrate on Samoa, although many of these examples are applicable to other island groups as well.

Wild Plants as Durable Goods

The use of wild plants to produce durable goods ranging from kava bowls to canoes has been well documented in Polynesia. For example, Sandra Banack and I (1987) detailed the use of many species of wild plants in the construction of large oceangoing canoes in Lau, Fiji. Each of these species was carefully selected for texture, tensile strength, buoyancy, and other structural qualities in much the same manner as contemporary engineers select materials for aircraft manufacture. But specialized uses of wild plants are of limited saliency within the general population: in the case of Lauan canoes, only a few hereditary clans of Polynesian shipwrights had the knowledge necessary to identify, select, and use the plants necessary for ship construction.

The types of Samoan durable goods constructed from wild plants include canoes and kava bowls from *Intsia bijuga* wood; fine mats made anciently from wild *Freycinetia* leaves; ceremonial skirts from *Sterculia fananiho* (Sterculiaceae) leaves; digging and fruit harvesting implements from various timbers; salt water–resistant fish traps from *Freycinetia* roots; fish nets, drills, and various toys such as darts formed from *Miscanthus floridulus* (Gramineae); and, of course, house timbers from *Intsia bijuga* and *Securinega flexuosa* (Euphorbiaceae) (Hiroa 1930). Although the production of these goods from wild plants was important, it may not have been deterministic in a cultural sense except in a few cases. For example, Samoans claim that *ifi lele* (*Intsia bijuga*) is essential for material culture, since it is the preferred wood for kava bowls; and the production of *'enu*, specialized fish traps, has recently waned in Ofu island, due to the lack of the necessary *Freycinetia reineckei* roots.

Wild Plants as Famine Foods

The use of wild plants as food in Samoa is rare. They are resorted to only in times of famine, with the exception of *Cordyline terminalis* (Agavaceae), which is infrequently used as a confection (Cox 1982). Wild plants used as famine foods include species shunned by all except children in times of plenty (such as *Aleurites moluccana* [Setchell 1924]), as well as plants reported to have been used in ancient times as either staple foods such as *Tacca leontopetaloides* (Taccaceae) or as confections such as *Cordyline terminalis*.

Although the list of wild plants used as famine foods presented in Table 6.1 is not exhaustive, it illustrates several principles that characterize how Samoans select wild famine foods. First, and somewhat surprisingly, indigenous wild plants are not used as famine foods in Samoa. All but two of the species listed in Table 6.1 are clearly aboriginal introductions that now persist in a semiferal state (Whistler 1991). And of these two, the diploid seeded banana—*Musa acuminata* ssp. *banksii* (Musaceae), called in Samoan *tae manu* (lit.: "animal excrement")—may have also been transported to Samoa through human agency in prehistoric times (Purseglove 1972; Simmonds 1962). Only *Terminalia catappa* (Combretaceae), a strand tree that is pantropical in its distribution, likely occurred in Samoa prior to Polynesian colonization.

Although this pattern of reliance for famine foods on an introduced flora rather than an indigenous one contrasts greatly with the situation of continental peoples, it is consistent with the belief that agriculture did not independently evolve in situ within Samoa. Instead, probably Samoa was first colonized by Lapita potters traveling from the west who carried with them a highly developed cultivar kit based on extensive development of starchy aroid cultivation and arboriculture prior to their arrival in Samoa (Davidson 1979; Yen 1991). Given the obvious superiority of the crops they carried with them, these colonists saw little need to explore for new cultivars from the indigenous flora of Polynesia.

The second selective principle is that the use of wild plants as famine foods in Samoa demonstrates the preference for plant taxa that collectively form a culinary analogue to the plants used as staples in the regular Samoan diet. Under this view, the rhizomes of *Cyrtosperma chamissonis* (Araceae) are analogous to the *Colocasia* (Araceae) and *Alocasia* (Araceae) rhizomes that are staples in times of plenty, and would be cooked and prepared the same way. In fact,

Table 6.1 Wild Plants as Samoan Famine Foods

Taxonomic Reference	Family	Samoan Name	Edible Part	Preparation
Monocotyledons				
Cordyline terminalis (L.) Kunth	Agavaceae	ti vao	rhizomes	cooked
Cyrtosperma chamissonis (Schott) Merrill	Araceae	pula'a	rhizomes	cooked
Dioscorea alata L.	Dioscoreaceae	ufi vao	roots	cooked
Dioscorea esculenta (Lour.) Burkill	Dioscoraceae	ufi lei	roots	cooked
Musa acuminata Simmonds	Musaceae	tae manu	fruits	cooked
Metroxylon upoluense ? Beccari	Palmae	niu lotuma	stem	starch extraction?
Cocos nucifera L.	Palmae	niu/toala	meristem	cooked/raw
Tacca leontopetaloides (L.) Kuntze	Taccaceae	masoa	roots	starch extraction
Dicotyledons				
Terminalia catappa L.	Combretaceae	talie	seeds	cooked
Inocarpus fagifer (Park.) Fosberg	Leguminosae	ifi	seeds	cooked
Adenanthera pavonina L.	Leguminosae	lopa	seeds*	raw
Syzygium samarangense (Bl.) Merr. & Perry	Myrtaceae	nonu fi'afi'a	fruits	raw

*Early European introduction

their required inclusion in the very large ovens used to cook *Cordyline terminalis* rhizomes may trace to an early time when both species were used more extensively as food (Cox 1982; Kramer 1903). Similarly, tubers of *Dioscorea alata* and *D. esculenta* (Dioscoreaceae) are analogous to the yam cultivars of the same genus that are prestige foods in traditional Samoan culture and that require little, if any, alteration in processing and preparation techniques. Thus, ordinary culinary practices as well as preparation techniques require only minimal adjustment during the shift to such famine foods. The relative lack of use of the feral sago palm *Metroxylon upoluense* (Palmae) as a starch source in Samoa, even during times of famine, strengthens the hypothesis that the famine foods, in some sense, are a mirror image of the regular Samoan diet during times of plenty. The only cultural analogue for *Metroxylon* starch is *Tacca lentopetaloides*, also a famine food.

The third selective principle for wild famine foods in Samoa is that the wild plants used in the famine diets of Polynesia may consist largely of previous prototype cultivars that may have been discarded in favor of the new improved models. The inclusion of a few nut crops such as *Inocarpus fagifer* (Leguminosae) and *Terminalia catappa* may, for example, harken back to the long-forgotten days of *Canarium* (Burseraceae) cultivation by the Lapita ancestors of the Polynesians, while the denigration of the seeded banana by the appellation *tae manu* may perhaps disguise its former importance in the evolution of more recent seedless banana cultivars. Certainly the trend toward seedlessness in Polynesian crops such as bananas and breadfruit would result in a greater likelihood of the earlier, seeded varieties persisting in a feral state; the more "advanced" seedless cultivars would obviously require active human intervention for their perpetuation.

Of course the use of wild plants in obtaining food is not limited to food plants themselves. Wild ichthyotoxic plants such as *Barringtonia asiatica* (Barringtoniaceae) and *Tephrosia piscatoria* (Leguminosae) were used to poison reef fish (Cox 1979). Fish nets woven from wild *Hibiscus tiliaceus* (Malvaceae) were able to withstand the ravages of seawater. Wild plants were even used to preserve harvests of cultivated plants: the leaves of *Heliconia paka* (Heliconiaceae) were used to provide airtight linings for breadfruit fermentation pits (Cox 1980a), while the leaves of *Barringtonia asiatica* were used to form durable baskets in which the fermented product *masi* could be stored underground (Cox 1980b).

Wild Plants in Polynesian Ethnomedicine

Perhaps the most complex and sophisticated use of wild plants in Samoa can be found in traditional herbal medicine. Most Samoan medicinal plants are gathered from the wild, although some cultivated plants such as breadfruit and certain banana and *Hibiscus* (Malvaceae) cultivars play a role as well. This pattern extends throughout Polynesia; Bernhard Zepernick (1972) found that 427 plant species from more than 300 genera had been reported to be used in Polynesian medicine. Of these 427 species, 55 are officinal in Western medicine, 1 was used in European folk medicine, 16 were used in Chinese and Tibetan folk medicine, and 72 were used in Melanesian folk medicine (excluding Fiji). Thus, in Polynesia 67% of the Polynesian ethnopharmacopoeia is used for medicine only. (Such data argue against the view that Polynesian traditional medicine in general and Samoan ethnopharmacology in particular were derived from the early European missionaries and explorers [Cox 1991].) But even more convincing is an analysis of the status of the plant species used in Samoan ethnopharmacology, which reveals that a majority of Samoan medicinal plants are indigenous. Over the last several years, my interviews with Samoan traditional healers about medicinal plants have revealed that 81 ethnotaxa comprising 75 different species are used in traditional therapies. Of these 75 species, 41 (55%) are plants indigenous to Samoa, and 4 (5%) are endemic. Of interest in the context of this essay is the number of wild species within the Samoan ethnopharmacopoeia; 50 (67%) are wild or feral species. These high percentages of wild and indigenous species are indicative of a healing tradition that continued to grow after initial colonization but remained somewhat diffuse and unformalized. Otherwise wild medicinal species might have been brought into cultivation in a manner similar to that of the physic gardens of Europe during the early Renaissance.

Unlike some Oriental traditions, Samoan ethnopharmacology relies almost exclusively on fresh plant material in the formulation of plant remedies. This, in turn, requires that a healer be able to locate, identify, and gather pharmacologically active plants as needed. Such expertise requires, as in the case of Lauan shipwrights (Banack and Cox 1987), maintenance of a specialist tradition of wild plant use. In Samoa, this guild is composed largely of *taulasea*, women herbalists who pass on their knowledge matrilineally.

I use the term *guild* in a rather loose sense since there is no economic advantage in becoming a *taulasea*. Samoan *taulasea* do not accept payment for their healing services, contending that the plants they use are gifts from God and that their skill in using them is a calling from God (Cox 1990a). Using a precise botanical lexicon in discussion of their work, the *taulasea* are far more knowledgeable about plants than other members of Samoan society. Having served informal but lengthy apprenticeships with their mothers or other female mentors, they command numerous details of disease diagnosis and etiology, plant taxonomy, and formulation.

During these apprenticeships, they learn how and where to collect wild medicinal plants. Preparation of Samoan medicines usually involves macerating the plants and infusing them in either water or, less frequently, coconut oil. Multispecies formulations are the rule. Most infusions are then rubbed directly on the forehead, back, and chest; and some are drunk. Treatments continue daily, sometimes with exhortations to observe certain types of dietary prohibitions called *sa*. Typical *sa* include avoidance of sweet or fatty foods.

The knowledge and skill of a healer increases with her age and experience. Unfortunately, the infirmities of age also reduce a healer's ability to journey into the forests for wild plants. Older healers must rely either on trained assistants who retrieve plants from the forest or upon small gardens of wild medicinal plants that they transplant to areas near their residences.

Although space precludes a detailed analysis, it is perhaps useful to analyze the Samoan ethnopharmacopoeia using the principles presented at the beginning of this chapter. Thus we can illustrate the Samoan ethnopharmacopoeia by presenting examples of medicinal plants that the ancestors of the Samoans may have brought with them to the islands, medicinal plants that they might reasonably have expected to find growing on the island when they arrived, and medicinal plants that they may have discovered only after arrival on the island.

An example of a medicinal plant deliberately introduced to Samoa during early aboriginal migrations is *Aleurites moluccana*. Known in Samoa as *lama,* the leaves are used to treat thrush, an infection of the oral cavity caused by the fungus *Candida albicans*. The seeds of *lama* or candlenut tree were used in ancient times to provide illumination for homes and night fishing; to this day, nighttime fishing in Samoa is still called *lama*. Although the large trees were perhaps at one time cultivated, today in Samoa they are feral, found on the outskirts of villages and along roadsides.

The beach morning glory, *Ipomoea pes-caprae* (Convolvulaceae), is an example of the second type of medicinal plant—i.e., one that was not carried by the Polynesians on voyaging but could be reasonably expected to occur wherever they journeyed throughout island Polynesia. Famed for its anti-inflammatory properties throughout the Pacific and Southeast Asia, this plant is used topically in Samoa to treat rashes, swellings, and various inflammatory processes. In Samoa it is called *fue moa* (lit.: "chicken vine"), and children use the immature floral buds as toplike toys.

Homalanthus nutans (Euphorbiaceae), an example of the third type of medicinal plant, was probably not exploited by the ancestors of the Samoans prior to colonization. A small tree that grows along the edge of the interior forests, *Homalanthus* is used by healers to treat *fiva samasama,* which may be translated as either "yellow fever" or "jaundice with fever"—hence, hepatitis. In either case, the stem wood is said to be useful against diseases whose counterparts in Western medicine are known to be of viral origin. My collaborators and I at the Natural Products Branch of the National Cancer Institute have found that extracts of *H. nutans* are active against the human immunovirus HIV-I in human cell culture. Fractionation yielded the phorbol prostratin (12-deoxyphorbol 13-acetate), which is currently being investigated by the National Cancer Institute as a drug candidate for acquired immune deficiency syndrome (AIDS) therapies (Gustafson et al. 1992)

Regardless of the eventual success or failure of prostratin as a clinical antiviral therapy in Western medicine, its discovery vindicates the ethnopharmacological approach to drug discovery (Cox 1990b). The study of indigenous uses of wild plants is now transcending purely ethnographic or ethnobotanical value and is taking a place in Western biomedical research. For example, more than 86% of the medicinal plants used by Samoan healers show some type of pharmacologic activity in broad-based screens (Cox et al. 1989). Indeed, even earlier studies indicated the possible antibiotic activity of the Samoan ethnopharmacopoeia (Norton et al. 1973). And yet it is puzzling that ethnopharmacology, a topic of such antiquity, would have been paid so little attention by the academic community.

It is important, now that possible commercial utility has been discovered in the Samoan ethnopharmacopoeia, that ethnobotanists not repeat the previous depredations of European sandalwood traders upon Polynesians. Specifically, it is crucial that the intellectual property rights of indigenous Polynesian peoples be explicitly recognized in light of potential Western development of Polynesian pharmaceuticals. In the case of prostratin, strenuous efforts have been made to ensure that the Samoan people are treated fairly. First, prior to the discovery of prostratin, written agreements concerning the disposition of any possible royalty income from Samoan medicinal plants were negotiated and signed with village chiefs. Second, prior to obtaining a use patent for prostratin, both the National Cancer Institute and Brigham Young University guaranteed that a significant portion of any royalties would be returned to the people of Samoa. Of course, at this early stage of research on prostratin, it would be just as cruel to prematurely raise villagers' expectations of financial return as it would be to raise AIDS patients' hopes of a cure. But even in the early stages of ethnobotanical research, it is important that the rights of indigenous people always be explicitly considered and protected.

Throughout Polynesia, as in the rest of the world, knowledge of wild plant uses is vanishing at a rapid rate. Perhaps this book will encourage others to join in studying the uses of wild plants before all opportunities to do so have vanished.

REFERENCES

Banack, S. A.
1991   Plants and Polynesian voyaging. In *Islands, Plants, and Polynesians*, edited by P. A. Cox and S. A. Banack, pp. 25–39. Dioscorides Press, Portland, Oregon.

Banack, S. A., and P. A. Cox
1987   Ethnobotany of oceangoing canoes in Lau, Fiji. *Economic Botany* 41:148–162.

Cox, P. A.
1979   Use of indigenous plants as fish poisons in Samoa. *Economic Botany* 33:397–399.

1980a   Two Samoan technologies for breadfruit and banana preservation. *Economic Botany* 34:181–185.

1980b   Masi and tanu 'eli: Two Polynesian technologies for breadfruit and banana preservation. *Pacific Tropical Botanical Garden Bulletin* 4:81–93.

1982   Cordyline ovens (umu ti) in Samoa. *Economic Botany* 36:389–396.

1990a   Samoan ethnopharmacology. In *Economic and medicinal plant research* Volume 4, *Plants and traditional medicine,* edited by H. Wagner and N. R. Farnsworth, pp. 123–139. Academic Press, London.

1990b   Ethnopharmacology and the search for new drugs. In *Bioactive molecules from plants,* edited by A. Battersby and J. Marsh, pp. 40–47. Wiley, Chichester, England.

1991   Polynesian herbal medicine. In *Islands, plants, and Polynesians,* edited by P. A. Cox and S. A. Banack, pp. 147–169. Dioscorides Press, Portland, Oregon.

Cox, P. A., and S. A. Banack [Editors]

1991   *Islands, plants, and Polynesians.* Dioscorides Press, Portland, Oregon.

Cox, P. A., L. R. Sperry, M. Tuominen, and L. Bohlin

1989   Pharmacological activity of the Samoan ethnopharmacopoeia. *Economic Botany* 43:487–497.

Davidson, J. M.

1979   Samoa and Tonga. In *The prehistory of Polynesia,* edited by J. D. Jennings, pp 82–109. Harvard University Press, Cambridge, Massachusetts.

Gustafson, K. R., J. H. Cardellina, J. B. McMahon, R. J. Gulakowski, J. Ishitoya, Z. Szallsi, N. E. Lewin, P. M. Blumberg, O. S. Weislow, J. A. Beutler, R. W. Buckheit, G. M. Cragg, P. A. Cox, J. P. Bader, and M. R. Boyd

1992   A non-promoting phorbol from the Samoan medicinal plant *Homalanthus nutans* inhibits cell killing by HIV-1. *Journal of Medicinal Chemistry* 35:1978–1986.

Hiroa, T. R. [P. H. Buck]

1930   Samoan material culture. *Bernice P. Bishop Museum Bulletin* 75:1–724.

Jennings, J. D. [Editor]

1979   *The prehistory of Polynesia.* Harvard University Press, Cambridge, Massachusetts.

Kirch, P. V.

1984   *The evolution of the Polynesian chiefdoms.* Cambridge University Press, Cambridge.

1991   Polynesian agricultural systems. In *Islands, plants, and Polynesians,* edited by P. A. Cox and S. A. Banack, pp. 113–133. Dioscorides Press, Portland, Oregon.

Kirch, P. V., and D. E. Yen

1982   Tikopia: The prehistory and ecology of a Polynesian outlier. *Bernice P. Bishop Museum Bulletin* 238:1–416.

Kramer, A.

1903   *Die Samoa-Inseln. II Band. Ethnographie.* E. Nagele, Stuttgart.

Norton, T. R., M. L. Bristol, G. W. Read, O. A. Bushnell, M. Kashiwagi, C. M. Okinaga, and C. S. Oda

1973   Pharmacological evaluation of medicinal plants from Western Samoa. *Journal of Pharmaceutical Sciences* 62:1077–1082.

Purseglove, J. W.

1972   *Tropical crops: Monocotyledons.* Longman, London.

Setchell, W. A.

1924   American Samoa. Part 1, Vegetation of Tutuila Island; Part 2, Ethnobotany of the Samoans. *Proceedings of the Carnegie Institute of Washington* 20:1–224.

Simmonds, N. W.

1962   *The evolution of the bananas.* Longman, London.

Whistler, W. A.

1991   Polynesian plant introductions. In *Islands, plants, and Polynesians,* edited by P. A. Cox and S. A. Banack, pp. 41–66. Dioscorides Press, Portland, Oregon.

Yen, D. E.

1991   Polynesian cultigens and cultivars: The questions of origin. In *Islands, plants, and Polynesians,* edited by P. A. Cox and S. A. Banack, pp. 67–95. Dioscorides Press, Portland, Oregon.

Zepernick, B.

1972   *Arzneipflanzen der Polynesier.* Verlag von Deitrich Reimer, Berlin.

7

Characteristics of "Wild" Plant Foods Used by Indigenous Populations in Amazonia

⚕ DARNA L. DUFOUR AND WARREN M. WILSON

The collection of "wild" plant foods constitutes an integral part of the subsistence strategies of indigenous peoples throughout the tropical rainforests of Amazonia (Balée 1988; Beckerman 1977; Dufour and Zarucchi 1979; Metraux 1948a, b; Stearman 1989; Wilbert 1972). These foods appear to play a varied role in traditional Amerindian diets ranging from trail snacks to major meal elements. Although researchers have not determined the nutritional value of "wild" plant foods for most Amerindian diets, these foods appear to be important sources of vitamins, minerals, protein, and fats (Beckerman 1977; Dufour and Zarucchi 1979; Vickers 1983). Another generally overlooked role of "wild" plants may be therapeutic; that is, some of the "wild" plants consumed as foods may have beneficial medicinal properties (Etkin and Ross 1991a).

Despite the apparent importance of "wild" plant foods in indigenous diets, researchers have only an incomplete understanding of these resources. Much of the literature identifies plants only by family, and investigators often do not clearly know the degree of management to which indigenous peoples subjected these "wild" plant foods. Of those studies that do describe the use of "wild" plant foods, few have examined their nutritional composition or significance in the diet. The lack of data on "wild" plant foods may be due to a number of factors, but perhaps the primary reason is that few researchers have studied the resource-gathering habits of the hundreds of groups that live in Latin American tropical rainforests (Clay 1988).

Whatever causes may have contributed to the current situation, an improved understanding of Amerindian use of "wild" plants has at least two important applications. First, it has the potential to enhance our understanding of how the original, as well as the extant, inhabitants of Amazonia adapted (and still adapt) to the environment. Second, these "wild" plant foods "are at most risk of depletion through reduced species diversity and other biotic simplifications that have become the signature of agricultural 'development' programs" (Etkin and Ross 1991a:27–28), lending a sense of urgency to the examination of this issue.

What Is a "Wild" Plant?

The distinction between "wild" and domesticated plants is problematical in Amazonia because, as Claude Lévi-Strauss noted in 1950, many intermediate stages lie between the utilization of plants in their wild state and true domestication. Domestication is an evolutionary process exhibiting all degrees of plant-human association; in the plants themselves, we see a range of morphological differentiation from "forms identical to wild races to fully domesticated races" (Harlan 1975).

Researchers have used a variety of terms to describe these points along the continuum. For Amazonia, Charles R. Clement (1990; following Harlan 1975), has proposed using the terms *domesticated, semidomesticated, cultivated, managed,* and *wild.* He has defined them as follows:

A domesticated plant is a genetically modified species completely dependent on humans for survival

A semidomesticated plant has been significantly modified but is still not completely dependent on humans for survival

A cultivated plant has been introduced into human agro-ecosystems and is nurtured in a prepared seed bed

A managed plant is protected from human actions that might harm it, is liberated from competition with other species, or is planted in areas other than prepared seedbeds

A wild plant may be used but is neither managed nor cultivated.

The Clement-Harlan definition of domestication is strict but would apply to a crop such as manioc (*Manihot esculenta*), the traditional staple of many Amerindians. Semidomesticates would include a species such as *Psidium guajava* (guava) that has been modified by human selection and is widely cultivated but also grows spontaneously—that is, in a feral state (Cavalcante 1974). Cultivated plants would include those purposefully planted into prepared beds, as well as those planted by the Runa at a carefully chosen site (Irvine 1989), and also those that the Kayapo transplant from primary forest and encourage to grow in successional forest stands (Posey 1984). Managed plants would include those referred to as "protected" or "tolerated" by some authors. For example, a number of trees with edible fruits are protected from harm during the weeding of gardens (Irvine 1989). Managed plants would also include plants that grow in cultivated areas or around living sites from seeds discarded after a snack.

A further difficulty in understanding the use of "wild" plants is that the interaction between a given plant species and humans might vary considerably among different Amerindian groups. For example, *Theobroma cacao* (chocolate) is a semidomesticate cultivated by the Kayapo (Posey 1984) but a wild plant used for fruit collection by the Runa (Irvine 1989) and can be found both cultivated and wild in the northwest Amazon (Dufour, unpublished observations). A second example is "wild" bananas collected by the Yora in Peru (Hill and Kaplan 1989). These are actually feral bananas, the fruits of vegetative seeds that had washed downriver from an area of cultivation and become established on riverbanks. Ethnobotanists generally consider the banana (*Musa* spp.) a domesticate, but in this case it would be best classified as a semidomesticate because of its ability to propagate itself; also, from the point of view of the Yora it is a wild plant.

In addition to identifying differences between Amerindian groups in the quality of plant-human interactions, investigators have reported plants in what appears to be a wild state although they have actually been cultivated or managed at some point. This might be the case, for example, of managed trees growing in a forest that is in fact an old garden fallow. Given these problems in categorizing plants, we refer to all nondomesticated plants simply as non-domesticates, or "wild" plants, and indicate (where possible) which of those seem to be actually wild.

Defining "Wild" Food Plants in Amazonia

We use the term *Amazonia* in the broad sense to refer to the tropical lowlands and plateaus of South America east of the Andes and north of the Tropic of Capricorn, except for the Gran Chaco area. (This area is equivalent to "greater Amazonia" as defined in Denevan 1976.) Amazonia, although often thought of as a broad expanse of homogeneous forest, is not uniform geologically, topographically, or climatologically. Rather, it contains a wide range of forest and other vegetation types, the phytogeographic patterns of which have yet to be fully described (Daly and Prance 1989). Thus, the generalizations we can make from this review of the literature are only as accurate as the regions we review are representative of Amazonia.

We based our overview of nondomesticated food plants on the published literature for Amazonia (primarily the anthropological literature), the unpublished literature of which we are aware, and some personal communications. We used four criteria to assemble a list of "wild" food plants. First, the plants had to be identified to at least the genus level; second, they had to be used by a named Amerindian group. Third, the plants had to be considered "wild" by the researchers. An exception to this was the case of the Yora in which the plant in question, the banana (*Musa* spp.), was described as wild but is generally considered a domesticate. In cases where the researcher did not specifically distinguish between wild and domesticated plants we have assumed that plants other than well-known domesticates are not domesticates and have included them. We refer to most plants simply as nondomesticates. Fourth, the part of the plant used as food had to be specified. This information is essential for understanding the role of the plant in the diet, but researchers do not always report it. For example, although both the heart (immature apical shoots) and fruits of palms such as *Jessenia* species are consumed, they are quite different foods nutritionally: palm hearts are a low-energy, low-nutrient-density vegetable, while palm fruits are an oil-rich, high-energy food. Distinctions as to part consumed are also important with regard to medicinal uses because secondary compounds (allelochemicals) of pharmacologic value are not usually evenly dispersed throughout the plant, and one part of a plant may be used medicinally while a different part is used for food.

Types of "Wild" Plants Used as Food by Amerindians

Our review of the available literature generated a preliminary list of 414 species. Of these, less than one third—131 species in 83 genera and 41 families—satisfied the four criteria outlined above. A list of these plants is provided in Appendix 7.1.

The 17 Amerindian groups associated with the use of these "wild" food plants live on the periphery of the Amazon basin in seven different ecological regions (Table 7.1). Most of the research on plant use by these groups was completed within the past 20 years. Approximately half of the groups inhabited or still inhabit very moist to extremely moist evergreen forest, and the other half evergreen seasonal forest. Territories of a limited number of groups included scrub savanna, grassland, or swamp forest.

Of the 130 food plants, 41% are trees and 28% are palms. The remaining plants include shrubs (2%), herbs (7%), and vines (2%); we were unable to classify the remaining 20%. Although the number of species of trees and palms is similar, trees show much greater diversity at the genus level. The predominance of trees and palms in the inventory of Amerindian food plants is not surprising, given that these vegetative types dominate the plant communities in moist tropical environments. Over half (56%) of the trees for which we were able to obtain size data were small to medium in size, and many of them were reported from garden fallows. This suggests that successional vegetation is an

Table 7.1 Habitats of Amerindian Groups

Amerindian Group[a]	Habitat[b]	Dates of Data Collection	Reference
Achuar	very moist tropical evergreen lowland forest	–	Lewis et al. 1991
Amahuaca	tropical evergreen seasonal lowland forest	–	Carniero 1988
Apinajé	tropical evergreen seasonal lowland forest; degraded formations and cultivated land mosaic; medium tall grassland with woody broad-leaved evergreen synusia	–	Anderson et al. 1991
Bari	tropical evergreen seasonal lowland forest	1970–72	Beckerman 1977
Bora	very moist tropical evergreen lowland forest	1981	Denevan et al. 1984
Ka'apor	tropical evergreen seasonal lowland forest	1985	Balée 1988 Balée pers. comm. Balée and Gely 1989
Kayapo	tropical evergreen seasonal lowland forest and scrub savanna	1972–	Posey 1984 Anderson & Posey 1989
Parakana	tropical evergreen seasonal lowland forest	1986	Milton 1991
Piaroa	very moist tropical evergreen lowland forest	1952	Boza and Baumgartner 1962
Runa	very moist tropical evergreen lowland forest	1982–84	Irvine 1989
Siona-Secoya	very moist tropical evergreen lowland forest	1973–75	Vickers 1983, 1989
Surui	very moist tropical evergreen lowland forest	1979–83	Coimbra 1985
Tukanoan	extremely moist tropical evergreen lowland forest	1976–78	Dufour & Zarucchi 1979 Dufour 1981, 1989 Zarucchi 1980

Table 7.1 Continued

Amerindian Group[a]	Habitat[b]	Dates of Data Collection	Reference
Tukuna	extremely moist tropical evergreen lowland forest	1941–42 1972–73	Nimuendaju 1952 Glenboski 1975
Tupinamba	tropical evergreen seasonal lowland forest	—	Lévi-Strauss 1950
Warao	tropical evergreen swamp forest	early 1700s	Gumilla 1791 cited in Lévi-Strauss 1950
Yanomamo	very moist tropical evergreen lowland forest; tropical submontane evergreen forest; tall grassland with woody broad-leaved evergreen synusia	— 1970 —	Wilbert 1972 Smole 1976 Lizot 1977

[a] Amerindian names are as given by researcher cited. Tukanoans are Tatuyo-Tukanoans and Kubeo-Tukanoans. The name Piaroa as used here includes Piaroas as well as neighboring groups such as the Guahibas, Piapocus, Cuibas and Macos. Warao is also spelled Warrau.
[b] Habitat types are based on UNESCO 1990 and the researchers' descriptions.

important source of food. However, these results may be biased since some of the recent research has focused specifically on garden fallows.

Amazonia is very rich in palms (Balick et al. 1982), and the ethnographic literature on Amerindian subsistence patterns contains innumerable references to the use of palms, especially *Bactris gasipaes,* or pejibaye (Anderson 1978; Beckerman 1977), which we have assumed is a domesticate. Locally important palms have often been called "the tree of life" in Amazonia (Anderson and Anderson 1985; Carniero 1988) as well as in other parts of the world. The tendency of some palms—such as *Mauritia* spp., *Euterpe* spp., and *Orbignya phalerata*—to form large dense stands makes them a concentrated, easily exploited resource. This characteristic of palms contrasts with trees, which are typically more widely dispersed. Stands of *Mauritia* and *Euterpe* species usually grow in inundated areas or along river margins (Cavalcante 1974), and they appear to have been intensively exploited by Amerindians (Anderson 1978; Wilbert 1980). *Orbignya phalerata,* or babassu, also grows in large stands. This palm does very well in disturbed areas, and its occurrence in large stands probably dates to after the arrival of Europeans (Anderson and Anderson 1985).

The small number of nondomesticated herbaceous plants used as food is not surprising given the relative rarity of these plants in tropical rainforest communities. Some of the herbaceous plants used are clearly associated with human disturbance. *Phytolacca* spp., for example, are early successional plants, among the first to sprout in newly burned gardens. *Clidemia* spp. and *Sabicea* spp. are small bushy plants that typically grow along footpaths in the northwest Amazon.

Many species of vines thrive in tropical rainforest communities, but these appear to have been exploited by Amerindians more for their structural than their nutritive characteristics (Paz y Miño et al. 1991).

Parts of Plants Consumed

Amerindians consumed various plant parts (Table 7.2). Fruit (including seed aril) accounts for 73% of all nondomesticated plant foods identified. Tree fruits represent about 38% of all fruits consumed, and palm fruits 31%. Many of the tree fruits appear to be oil-rich as opposed to succulent fruits. Palm fruits are also typically high in oils. Seeds (including nuts) are the next most common but account for only 8% of all "wild" plant foods consumed. Most of the plants used for their edible seeds are trees (Table 7.3). Researchers have reported only a few instances of Amerindians consuming the seeds (nuts) of palms; however, the Siona-Secoya eat palm seeds (nuts) after germination (Vickers 1989). The Apinajé in the Brazilian state of Maranhã use the mesocarp of the palm fruit to make a flour (Anderson et al. 1991). Hearts and shoots are the next most common after seeds, representing 7% of all "wild" plant foods consumed.

Edible plant parts other than fruits, seeds, and palm starch and hearts include leaves, roots, bark, and sap. Researchers have reported the use of leaves for only six plants. One is a tree found in garden fallows, *Ilex guayusa*, the leaves of which are used to make an infusion or "tea" (Irvine 1989). Two others are herbaceous plants with spinachlike leaves in the genus *Phytolacca*, found in newly burned gardens. Tukanoans in the northwest Amazon cook the immature leaves and stems as a vegetable (Dufour 1981). Amerindians have consumed the leaves of at least two other plants in the form of ash: Tukanoans mix the leaf ash of *Cecropia* sp. with coca leaves (Dufour 1981); the Kayapo used leaf ash of *Maximiliana maripa* (inajá) as salt (Anderson, unpublished field notes). The relative rarity of leaves in the diets of Amerindians stands in sharp contrast to the wide variety of uncultivated edible greens, or "wild greens," in the diets of many subsistence horticulturalists outside of the rainforest. The "wild" greens reported are typically plants of the early successional stages of local plant communities, and continual human disturbance maintains their presence (Bye 1981). In parts of Africa their use appears to be associated with heavily modified

Table 7.2 "Wild" Plants Used as Food, by Type and Part Consumed

Plant Part Consumed	Growth Habit						Total	
	Trees	Palms	Shrubs	Vines	Herbs	Unknown	N	%
Bark	0	0	0	0	0	1	1	1
Fruit	41	33	3	1	7	22	107	73
Heart/Shoot	0	10	0	0	0	0	10	7
Leaf	2	1	0	0	2	1	6	4
Starch (Pith)	0	2	0	0	0	0	2	1
Root	0	0	0	0	0	1	1	1
Sap	0	0	0	1	0	0	1	1
Seed*	7	5	0	0	1	0	13	9
Seed aril	6	0	0	0	0	0	6	4
Total							147	

Note: Numbers refer to number of species counted.
*The kernels and germinated palm seeds referred to in Appendix 7.1 are included with seeds.

environments (Etkin and Ross 1991b, [this volume]; Fleuret 1979). Most of the Amerindian groups reviewed here were or are occupying forested, less heavily modified environments.

We found a minimal use of palm starch, although palms such as *Mauritia flexuosa* (buriti) and *Euterpe* spp. appear to be good sources of starch. Recent ethnographic reports of the use of palm starch are associated with peoples practicing minimal horticulture, such as the Ache of Paraguay (Hurtado et al. 1985). The ethnographic literature provides innumerable references to the use of palm hearts as food, but the species used are rarely identified. Various Amerindians used the hearts of six palm species as food—*Astrocaryum muru- muru*, *A. tucuma* (star nut palm), *Euterpe oleracea* (açai), *Bactris gasipaes*, *Max- imiliana maripa*, and *Orbignya phalerata* (babassu). The Surui, a group that was being heavily impacted by colonists, used all but *E. oleracea*. A number of authors (e.g., Beckerman 1977; Carniero 1988; Chagnon 1968; Lévi-Strauss 1950; Stearman 1989; Wilbert 1972) have suggested that palms may have been more important in the past for both fruit and starch, especially in the floodplain where they grow in large stands. For the Warao, who lived in the mangrove swamps of the Orinoco delta, palm starch appears to have been the staple food before they were introduced to rootcrop horticulture (Wilbert 1980).

Table 7.3 Plants Used for Their Edible Seeds

Species	Edible Portion
Trees	
Bertholletia excelsa	large nut
Caryocar amydaliferum	large nut
Caryodendron orinocense	3 large seeds per fruit
Erisma japura	nut, toxic
Hevea spp.	3 large seeds per fruit
Micrandra spruceana	seed, toxic??
Monopteryx angustifolia	large pulse, bitter tasting
Herbs	
Phenakospermum guyanense	many small seeds per fruit
Palms	
Astrocaryum munbaca	seed
Astrocaryum tucuma	nut
Astrocaryum sp.	germinated seed
Orbignya aff. *polystricha*	seed kernel

We identified only two edible roots. One, of the genus *Monotagma*, was used by the Kayapo (Parker et al. 1983; Posey 1984), whose territory includes scrub savanna vegetation. The general absence of nondomesticated roots is notable because roots are a good source of carbohydrate and roots of domesticated plants such as cassava, or manioc (*Manihot esculenta*), are major food crops in many rainforest areas. Researchers have more frequently reported the use of nondomesticated roots for groups living in the savanna regions to the north and south of the rainforest, such as the Yaruro in the *llanos* of Venezuela and the Xavante in the scrub savanna vegetation of the Brazilian *cerrado* (Maybury-Lewis 1967).

Nutritional Characteristics of Nondomesticated Plant Foods

Researchers have determined the nutritional characteristics of the fruits of nondomesticated Amazonian trees for a limited number of species: *Couma macrocarpa* (sorva grande), *Poraqueiba sericea* (umari), *Pouteria ucuqui* (ucuqui), *Spondias mombin* (taperebá), *Psidium guajava* (guava), and *Inga* species (ingá). The first three produce large fruits with relatively small edible mesocarps (Dufour, unpublished data) that are all very high in fats (Figure 7.1a). One of the fruits, *Poraqueiba sericea*, is rich in texture and taste and has a fat content similar to that of palm fruits. *Spondias mombin*, or yellow mombin, produces a cherrylike fruit, moderately high in fat. In contrast, the nutritional composition of fruits of *Psidium guajava* and *Inga* spp. resembles that of succulent fruits—that is, they are high in moisture (around 90%) and carbohydrate. *Psidium guajava* has one of the highest levels of vitamin C of any fruit: 200 mg/100 g of edible portion (ICBF 1967). The fruits of the genus *Inga* are long pods whose edible portion is the sweet, watery pulp surrounding the seeds.

The composition of the fruits of herbaceous plants, such as *Clidemia* species, is not known; but they are described as "berries" and are probably similar in composition to cultivated berries such as *Solanum quitoensis* (lulo), a succulent fruit. Some of the other tree fruits consumed by Amerindians appear to be quite distinctive, and it is difficult to make any assumptions regarding their nutritional composition. For example, the fruits of *Dacryodes belemensis* are described as having a resinous quality and a green color (Zarucchi 1980). The fruits of *Parkia* species are pods, the edible portion of which is a thin resinous seed aril reminiscent of tamarind (*Tamarindus indica*) in texture (Dufour, unpublished observations).

The edible portion of palm fruits such as *Jessenia* sp. and *Euterpe* spp. is the thin, oil-rich mesocarp surrounding the palm nut. Fat provides more than half of the energy in palm fruits, while protein provides less than one-twelfth; nevertheless, at least in the case of *Jessenia bataua* (patauá), the quality of the protein is high (Balick and Gershoff 1981). The fruits of *Mauritia flexuosa* and *Astrocaryum vulgare* (tucumá) are high in beta-carotene (Anderson 1978 citing Pechnik at al. 1947; Dufour 1981).

Researchers have also defined the nutritional composition of some edible seeds (Figure 7.1b). Four of the trees—*Bertholletia excelsa* (Brazil nut tree), *Caryocar amydaliferum* (butternut tree), *Caryodendron orinocense* (orinoconut), and *Erisma japura* (japura)—produce either edible nuts or large seeds that are very high in fat (providing 76–88% of the food energy). *Hevea* spp. (rubber), *Micrandra spruceana* (wapuh) and *Monopteryx angustifolia* (jimio) have seeds that are moderately high in fats (36–45% of food energy) and provide more than 10% of the food energy as protein. In *Hevea* spp., protein quality resembles that of the peanut, *Arachis hypogaea* (Giok et al. 1967). The seeds of *Phenakospermum guyanense* (yebao), a large herb, are similar in composition to cultivated legumes such as chickpeas (*Cicer arietinum*), which are low in fat (less than 15% of energy) and high in protein (more than 25% of energy).

Researchers have reported toxicity for some of the seeds. For example, *Hevea brasiliensis* (rubber) seeds contain cyanide (Giok et al. 1967; Schultes 1956) and require processing before they are consumed (Siebert 1948 citing Bentham 1854). Tukanoan Indians recognize the seeds as toxic and process them by

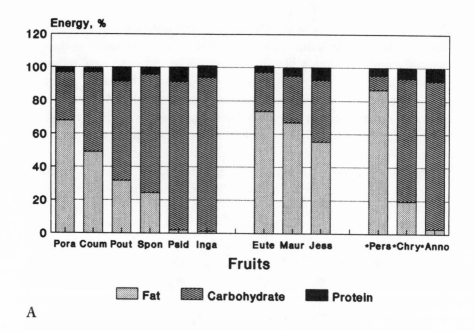

Fruits

Fat · Carbohydrate · Protein

A

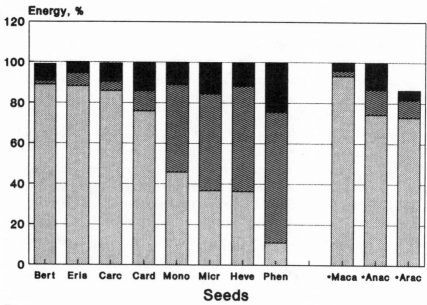

Seeds

B

grating and cooking (Dufour 1989). Tukanoans also consider the seeds of *Micrandra spruceana* and *Erisma japura* (bati, or japura) toxic and process them before eating (Dufour and Zarucchi 1979).

Leaves of *Phytolacca* spp. are similar in composition to dark green leafy vegetables such as spinach (*Spinacia oleracea*). They are good sources of vegetable protein, iron, and beta-carotene (Dufour 1981). Palm hearts are a low-nutrient-density vegetable similar in composition to cabbage (*Brassica oleracea*) (Wu-Leung and Flores 1961).

Role of "Wild" Plant Foods in Amerindian Diets

Researchers have not fully delineated the role of "wild" plant foods in Amerindian diets. Only in the case of Warao utilization of palm starch and Apinajé use of palm fruits do nondomesticated plants serve as the dietary staple. In all other cases they appear to function as supplementary foods, that is, foods added to a diet based on horticultural staples. However, to refer to nondomesticated plant foods as supplementary is not to deprecate their cultural significance or to deny their nutritional importance. Culturally, particular nondomesticated foods can be highly valued for their taste (Dufour and Zarucchi 1979), can form an integral part of a traditional ritual cycle (Hugh-Jones 1979), or can mark a group's cultural identity (Milton 1991). Many of the fruits are rich in oils and could function as an important source of fat in Amerindian diets, which typically provide very little fat (Dufour 1992). Protein content of most of the "wild"

Figure 7.1. Composition of some nondomesticated fruits and seeds used by Amerindians compared with common domesticates. Composition is in terms of the percentage of total food energy derived from fats, carbohydrate, and protein. Abbreviations are the first four letters of the genus for the species listed below. Domesticates are starred. Composition data were taken from ICBF 1967 for *Persea, Chrysophyllum, Psidium,* and *Annona;* Holland et al. 1991 for *Bertholletia, Macadamia, Anacardium,* and *Arachis;* Balick and Gershoff 1981 for *Jessenia;* Wu Leung and Flores 1961 for *Spondias mombin;* and Dufour 1988 for the remainder.
Figure 7.1a. Tree fruits are *Poraqueiba sericea, Couma macrocarpa, Pouteria ucuqui, Psidium guajava, Spondias mombin,* and *Inga* sp.; palm fruits are *Euterpe derasia, Mauritia flexuosa,* and *Jessenia bataua;* common domesticates are *Persea americana* (avocado), *Chrysophyllum cainito* (caimo), and *Annona muricata* (guanabana).
Figure 7.1b. Seeds are from five trees, *Bertholletia excelsa* (Brazil nut), *Erisma japura, Caryocar amydaliferum, Caryodendron orinocense, Monopteryx angustifolia, Micrandra spruceana, Hevea* aff. *nitida* (rubber tree); one large herb is included, *Phenakospermum guyanense;* common nuts are *Macadamia integrifolia* (macadamia), *Anacardium occidentale* (cashew), and *Arachis hypogaea* (peanut).

plant foods is not very high, but some of it is of quite good quality. The vitamin and mineral content of some foods is noteworthy, such as from the genera *Mauritia* and *Phytolacca*.

Although nondomesticated plant foods clearly have the potential to make important contributions to the diet, researchers have been unable to determine their actual contribution, given the limited data available on either the amounts consumed or the frequency of their use. Anthropologists have compiled information on dietary intake of "wild" plant foods for only a few groups of Amerindians. For these groups (Siona-Secoya, Tukanoans, and Yanomamo) "wild" plant foods provide approximately 1%, 4%, and 7% respectively of all dietary energy (Dufour 1992).

For Tukanoans, the relatively low energy contribution on an annual basis of "wild" plant foods belies their importance on a day-to-day basis. A number of these foods were not simply "snack" foods but components of regular meals on more than one-third of all days surveyed (Dufour 1989). Extracts of palm fruits, for example, were frequently added to the traditional starch-water drink or mixed with cassava meal. Tukanoans also stored large nuts such as those of the genus *Caryocar* for long periods and served the nuts at meals when fish or meat was not available. This added diversity to cassava-based meals, as well as concentrated energy in the form of fats. Although many nondomesticated foods were highly valued for their taste, a few, such as *Phenakospermum guyanense*, were not highly regarded and were only used to supplement meals when little else was available. Tukanoans used other "wild" plant foods, particularly berries and tree fruits collected in small quantities, primarily as snacks for children.

Experience with Tukanoan Indians suggests that a number of factors limit the gathering of "wild" plant foods, and hence their role in the diet. One is the high heterogeneity of the forests, which makes the collection of any given plant food time-consuming. A second factor is the seasonality of rainforest fruits. Although trees tend to fruit in the early to middle rainy season, not all individuals of a species fruit simultaneously and not all species fruit every year. A third factor is the sharply delimited time during which ripe fruits, nuts, and seeds are available to human foragers before they either sprout or are eaten by other animals. These factors combine to make nondomesticated foods less predictable resources, spatially and temporally, than they are in many other environments. Probably as a result, Tukanoan women did not devote a lot of time to foraging and tended to forage only when they could reasonably expect to find particular nondomesticated foods near the village.

For some groups an additional determinant of wild food use may be the stage of the settlement cycle of the group. The Siona and Secoya, for example, consumed more "wild" foods when the group had relocated and had not yet established gardens (Vickers, personal communication). This pattern appears to be true of the Yora as well (Hill and Kaplan 1989).

Pharmacologic Properties of Nondomesticated Plant Foods

"Wild" plant foods included in the diet may also serve a therapeutic role (Etkin and Ross 1991, [this volume]); that is, some plants consumed as foods simultaneously exhibit pharmacologic properties that reduce morbidity. We found reports of a large number of plants with medicinal uses but identified only a small overlap between the species of plants used for food and those explicitly used as medicinals. This lack of overlap may be due to the fact that investigators have only recently begun to look at food plants as potential sources of medicine.

Of all the "wild" plant foods listed in Appendix 7.1, we found relatively few used for both food and medicine (Table 7.4) and only four plants for which the same part provides both food and medicine (albeit not always for a single culture group): leaves of *Phytolacca rivinoides* and fruits of *Carica cauliflora, Psidium guyanense,* and *Spondias mombin.* With three plants the part used for medicine differed from those parts used for food: *Anacardium occidentale, Psidium guajava,* and *Spondias mombin.* In the case of *A. occidentale,* the "wild" cashew, for example, Amerindians consume the fruits as food, use the flower stem to treat influenza, and exploit the bark both as a cure for diarrhea and as a contraceptive (Glenboski 1975). For many of the plants reported to have both food and medicinal uses we were unable to determine which parts were utilized and thus did not include them in Appendix 7.1.

Some "wild" plants used as food by Amerindians serve as medicinals in other places. For example, the Igbo of Nigeria use the seed aril of *Dialium guianense* as an antispasmodic, oral antiseptic, and analgesic; the fruit of *Spondias mombin* as both a laxative and an external application for swelling; and the fruit pod of *Theobroma cacao* as both a stimulant and a galactagogue (Iwu 1986).

The difference between plant parts used for food and those used medicinally is, in part, a function of which are believed to contain secondary compounds, or allelochemicals. Secondary compounds constitute chemical defense mechanisms for plants. Amerindians utilize some of these allelochemicals as psychotropic drugs and others as poisons (Holmstedt et al. 1980). The bark of trees or vines generally contains the highest concentrations of these defense chemicals. The importance of bark as a chemical storehouse is reflected in the pharmacopoeia of rainforest peoples such as the Baka pygmies of West Africa (Lewington 1990), who prepare more than three-quarters of their remedies from trees or lianas using the bark or sap. Leaves and seeds also often contain high concentrations of secondary compounds, since plants can ill afford to lose

Table 7.4 Plants Used as Both Food and Medicine

		Uses		Medicinal	Indigenous
Genus and Species	Part	Food	Medicine	Application	Group
Anacardium occidentale	fruit	X	X	?	Yanomamo
	peduncle		X	diarrhea	Tukuna
	bark & leaves		X	diarrhea	Tukuna
	bark		X	contraceptive	Tukuna
	flower stem		X	influenza	Tukuna
Carica cauliflora	fruit with seeds	X	X	purgative	Piaroa
Phytolacca rivinoides	leaf	X		—	Ka'apor, Tatuyo
	leaf		X	fever, anti-emetic	Ka'apor
Psidium guajava	fruit	X		—	Ka'apor
	bark		X	diarrhea	Tukuna
	leaf		X	diarrhea	Tukuna
Psidium guyanense	fruit	X		—	Parakana
	fruit		X	?	Tukuna
	seed	X		—	Tatuyo
Spondias mombin	fruit	X		—	Ka'apor
	fruit	X		—	Siona-Secoya
	fruit		X	antiscorbutic	Tukuna
	bark		X	menstrual bleeding	Tukuna
	bark		X	diarrhea	Tukuna
	bark		X	wounds	Tukuna
	bark		X	contraceptive	Tukuna

Note: References for indigenous groups are Ka'apor (Balée, pers. comm.; Balée and Gely 1989); Piaroa (Boza and Baumgartner 1962); Parakana (Milton 1991); Siona-Secoya (Vickers 1989); Tatuyo (Dufour 1981); Tukuna (Glenboski 1975).

these to predation. Most fruits, by contrast, have evolved to facilitate seed dispersal by animals and thus contain generally low levels of secondary compounds. This characteristic may partly explain the predominant use of fruits as foods.

Researchers also have not thoroughly studied the ability of native Amazonians to recognize and deal with toxic secondary compounds in the "wild" plant food component of their diet. Tukanoan Indians in the northwest Amazon, however, provide an interesting example of how one group deals with toxic secondary compounds in nondomesticated plant foods. Tukanoans use 33 "wild" plants in their diet, 25 of which have been identified by researchers (Appendix 7.1). Of these 25, about half are trees, and Tukanoans harvest the nuts and seeds from 6. Tukanoans value all of these for their taste and routinely incorporate them into the diet, sometimes in relatively large amounts. However, 4 of the 6 species of seeds the Tukanoans considered toxic, and treated them to mitigate those effects prior to consumption: *Hevea* sp., *Micrandra spruceana, Monopteryx angustifolia,* and *Erisma japura. Hevea* sp. and *M. spruceana* are of the family Euphorbiaceae, which contains toxic cyanogens (Schultes 1956); botanical investigators have not reported toxicity for the other two plants. Tukanoans process these seeds using traditional techniques that involve some combination of grating, cooking, leaching, or fermentation. These techniques should eliminate secondary compounds or significantly reduce their concentration. However, researchers have not determined whether the treated seeds retain compounds with pharmacologic properties.

Why the Lack of Data on Nondomesticated Plant Foods?

Given the abundance and diversity of flora in Amazonia we were surprised to identify only 130 species of "wild" food plants. Even taking into consideration the restrictions imposed by the criteria we used, we found fewer data than we had anticipated.

This lack of information may be largely due to the fact that few studies have focused on the use of plants by Amerindians (Clay 1988). Those studies that have looked carefully at the use of nondomesticated plants have identified impressive numbers of economically useful plants (Anderson and Posey 1989; Balée and Gely 1989; Beckerman 1977). However, in these studies the nonfood uses of plants typically exceeds the food uses. Further, of all the plant foods identified, those judged "important" in the diet are few: 7 of 133 for Ka'apor (Balée and Gely 1989), and 7 of 33 for Tukanoans (Dufour 1989). Appendix 7.1 may reflect this relatively small number of "important" nondomesticated food plants. Probably many more foods are or were collected opportunistically and consumed as snacks in the forest, while others come from plants that fruit on other than yearly cycles, that have escaped notice during short periods of fieldwork, or that have not been considered important enough to warrant attention. Ethnographic accounts typically name only a limited number of "wild" plant foods and often do not include adequate identification.

Another factor contributing to the relatively small number of food plants reported is that all of the Amerindian groups had been heavily impacted by nonindigenous peoples prior to the collection of the data reviewed here. The Warao had probably the least contact of any of the groups referred to in this paper but had still been in contact with missionaries for 15 years prior to Johannes Wilbert's arrival in 1954 (Wilbert 1980). During that time they had moved from a hunter-gatherer subsistence pattern based on palm starch and other "wild" plants to subsistence agriculture. Even the Tupinamba, for whom we have Joseph Gumilla's ethnography from the 1700s, had been hard hit by European disease following the arrival of the Portuguese on Brazil's shores in 1540, and it is difficult to estimate the impact of contact on plant food gathering.

A third factor that may also contribute to our lack of understanding of "wild" plant foods in Amazonia is gender. The collection of some nondomesticated foods is the work of women and children, whose daily activities have not received the same amount of scrutiny as those of men (Etkin and Ross 1991a). For Tukanoans the division of labor by sex depends on the particular food: men collect the majority of palm fruits and other fruits that require climbing or felling trees, while women pick fruits from small trees, bushes, and shrubs and collect nuts and seeds from the litter on the forest floor. Of those items collected by women, the foods that can be eaten without preparation and those collected in small amounts are most likely to escape the notice of investigators.

A fourth factor may be termed the "temperate bias." As Charles Clement (1990) has pointed out, many researchers working in Amazonia come from temperate climates and may as a result believe that annual crops are the most important foods and that plant foods should be incorporated into an ordered garden of some sort and not scattered individually on "noncultivated" land, as many are in Amazonia. A fifth factor may simply be the tremendous floral diversity of Amazonia, coupled with a lack of training in field botany on the part of many investigators. The high diversity (high species richness and equitability) has probably contributed directly to the difficulty of documenting all nondomesticated plant foods. Operating hand in hand with these factors has been the difficulty of determining what is "wild." As a consequence, much of the literature on plant food use in Amazonia is vague on this point.

The complex and sophisticated subsistence systems of Amerindians incorporate a wide variety of plant resources. Nondomesticated plants, part of this diversity, have the potential to enhance our knowledge of human adaptation to Amazonia and sustainable agro-ecosystems in the wet tropics. To understand the saliency of nondomesticated plants, however, anthropologists and ethnobotanists must design further research into nondomesticated food plant use by Amerindians.

REFERENCES

Anderson, A. B.
  1978   The names and uses of palms among a tribe of Yanomama Indians. *Principes* 22:30–41.
Anderson, A. B., and S. Anderson
  1985   A "tree of life" grows in Brazil. *Natural History* 94(12):40–47.
Anderson, A. B., and D. A. Posey
  1989   Management of tropical scrub savanna by the Gorotire Kayapo of Brazil. In *Resource management in Amazonia: Indigenous and folk strategies,* edited by D. A. Posey and W. Balée, pp. 159–173. Advances in Economic Botany, Vol. 7. New York Botanical Garden, New York.
Anderson, A. B., P. H. May, and M. J. Balick
  1991   *Subsidy from nature: Palm forests, peasantry and development on an Amazon frontier.* Columbia University Press, New York.
Balée, William
  1988   Researcher calls for immediate step up in new crop studies. *Garden* November/December:25–26.
Balée, William, and Anne Gely
  1989   Managed forest succession in Amazonia: The Ka'apor case. In *Resource management in Amazonia: Indigenous and folk strategies,* edited by D. A. Posey and W. Balée, pp. 129–158. Advances in Economic Botany, Vol. 7. New York Botanical Garden, New York.
Balick, M. J., and S. N. Gershoff
  1981   Nutritional evaluation of *Jessenia batau* palm: Source of high quality protein and oil from tropical America. *Economic Botany* 35(3):261–271.
Balick, M. J., A. B. Anderson, and M. Freitas da Silva
  1982   Palm taxonomy in Brazilian Amazonia: The state of systematic collections in regional herbaria. *Brittonia* 34:463–477.
Beckerman, Stephen
  1977   Use of palms by the Bari Indians of the Maracaibo Basin. *Principes* 21(4): 143–154.
Boza, F. V., and J. Baumgartner
  1962   Estudio general, clinco y nutricional en tribus indígenas del territorio Federal Amazonas de Venezuela. *Archivos Venezulanos* 2:144–225.
Bye, Robert A.
  1981   Quelites—Ethnoecology of edible greens—Past, present and future. *Journal of Ethnobiology* 1(1):109–123.

Carniero, Robert L.

1988   Indians of the Amazonian forest. In *People of the tropical rainforest*, edited by J. S. Denslow and C. Padoch, 73–86. University of California Press, Berkeley.

Cavalcante, Paulo B.

1972   *Frutas comestivas da Amazonia 1*. Museu Paraense Emilio Goeldi, Belém.

1974   *Frutas comestivas da Amazonia 2*. Museu Paraense Emilio Goeldi, Belém.

Chagnon, N. A.

1968   *Yanomamo: The fierce people*. Holt, Rinehart and Winston, New York.

Clay, Jason

1988   *Indigenous peoples and tropical forests*. Cultural Survival, Cambridge, Massachusetts.

Clement, Charles R.

1990   Fruit trees and the origin of agriculture in the neotropics. Paper presented at the Second International Congress of Ethnobiology, Yunnan, People's Republic of China.

Coimbra, Carlos E. A.

1985   Estudos de ecologia humana entre os suruí do Parque Indígena Aripuanã Rondonia. Aspectos alimentares. *Bolletim Do Museu Paraense Emilio Goeldi Antropologia* 2(1):57–87.

Daly, Douglas C., and Ghillian T. Prance

1989   Brazilian Amazon. In *Floristic inventory of tropical countries*, edited by D. G. Campbell and H. D. Hammond, pp. 401–426. New York Botanical Garden, New York.

Denevan, William M.

1976   The aboriginal population of Amazonia. In *The Native population of the Americas*, edited by W. M. Denevan, pp. 205–234. University of Wisconsin Press, Madison.

Denevan, William M., John M. Treacy, Janis B. Alcorn, Christine Padoch, Julie Denslow, and Salvador Flores Paitan

1984   Indigenous agroforestry in the Peruvian Amazon: Bora Indian management of swidden fallows. *Interciencia* 9(6):346–357.

Dufour, Darna L.

1981   Household variation in energy flow in a population of tropical rainforest horticulturalists. Ph.D. dissertation, State University of New York at Binghamton. University Microfilms, Ann Arbor.

1988   The composition of some foods used in northwest Amazonia. *Interciencia* 13(2):83–86.

1989   Factors determining wild plant use in Amazonia. Paper presented at 88th Annual Meeting of the American Anthropological Association, Washington, D.C., 15–19 November 1989.

1992   Nutritional ecology in the rainforests of Amazonia. *American Journal of Human Biology* 4(2):197–208.

Dufour, Darna L., and James Zarucchi

1979   *Monopteryx angustifolia* and *Erisma japura*: Their use by indigenous peoples in the northwestern Amazon. *Botanical Museum Leaflets, Harvard University* 27(3–4):69–91.

Etkin, Nina L., and Paul J. Ross

1991a   Should we set a place for diet in ethnopharmacology? *Journal of Ethnopharmacology* 32:25–36.

1991b   Recasting malaria, medicine and meals: A perspective on disease adaptation. In *The anthropology of medicine: From culture to method* [Second edition], edited by L. Romanucci-Ross, D. E. Moerman, and L. R. Trancredi, pp. 230–258. Bergin and Garvey, New York.

Fleuret, A.

1979   The role of wild foliage plants in the diet: A case study from Lushoto, Tanzania. *Ecology of Food and Nutrition* 8:87–93.

Giok, T. L., Husaini Samsudin, and I. Tarwotjo

1967   Nutritional value of rubber-seed protein. *American Journal of Clinical Nutrition* 20(12):1300–1303.

Glenboski, Linda L.

1975   Ethnobotany of the Tukuna Indians, Amazonas, Colombia. Ph.D. dissertation, University of Alabama.

Harlan, Jack R.

1975   *Crops and man.* American Society of Agronomy, Madison, Wisconsin.

Hill, Kim, and Hillard Kaplan

1989   Population and dry-season subsistence strategies of the recently contacted Yora of Peru. *National Geographic Research* 5(3):317–334.

Holland, B., A. A. Welch, I. D. Unwin, D. H. Buss, A. A. Paul, and D.A.T. Southgate

1991   *The composition of foods* [Fifth edition]. HMSO, London.

Holmstedt, B., J. E. Lindgren, T. Plowman, L. Rivier, R. E. Schultes, and O. Tovar

1980   Indole alkaloids in Amazonian Myristicaceae: Field and laboratory research. *Botanical Museum Leaflets, Harvard University* 28(3):215–234.

Hugh-Jones, Stephen

1979   *The palm and the Pleiades.* Cambridge University Press, Cambridge.

Hurtado, Ana M., Kristen Hawkes, Kim Hill, and Hillard Kaplan

1985   Female subsistence strategies among Ache hunter-gatherers of eastern Paraguay. *Human Ecology* 13:1–28.

ICBF (Instituto Nacional de Nutrición)

1967   *Tabla de composición de alimentos Colombianos* [Third edition]. Instituto Nacional de Nutrición, Bogotá, Colombia.

Irvine, Dominique

1989   Succession management and resource distribution in an Amazonian rain forest. In *Resource management in Amazonia: Indigenous and folk strategies,* edited by D. A. Posey and W. Balée, pp. 223–227. Advances in Economic Botany, Vol. 7. New York Botanical Garden, New York.

Iwu, Maurice M.

1986   Empirical investigations of dietary plants used in Igbo ethnomedicine. In *Plants in indigenous medicine and diet: Biobehavioral approaches*, edited by N. L. Etkin, pp. 131–150. Gordon and Breach Science Publishers (Redgrave), New York.

Lévi-Strauss, Claude

1950   The use of wild plants in tropical South America. In *Handbook of South American Indians*, Vol. 6, edited by J. H. Steward, pp. 465–486. Smithsonian Institution Press, Washington, D.C.

Lewington, Anna

1990   *Plants for people*. Oxford University Press, New York.

Lewis, W. H., E. J. Kennelly, G. N. Bass, H. J. Wedner, M. P. Elvin-Lewis, and D. Fast W.

1991   Ritualistic use of the holly *Ilex guayusa* by Amazonian Jivaro Indians. *Journal of Ethnopharmacology* 33:25–30.

Lizot, J.

1977   Population, resources and warfare among the Yanomami. *Man* (n.s.) 12:497–517.

Maybury-Lewis, David

1967   *Akwe-Shavant society*. Clarendon Press, Oxford.

Metraux, Alfred

1948a   The Tupinamba. In *Handbook of South American Indians*, Vol. 3, edited by J. H. Steward, pp. 95–136. U.S. Government Printing Office, Washington, D.C.

1948b   Tribes of the western Amazon Basin. In *Handbook of South American Indians*, Vol. 3, edited by J. H. Steward, pp. 657–713. U.S. Government Printing Office, Washington, D.C.

Milton, Katharine

1991   Comparative aspects of diet in Amazonian forest dwellers. *Philosophical Transactions of the Royal Society of London* 334:253–263.

Nimuendaju, Curt

1952   *The Tukuna*. University of California Press, Berkeley.

Parker, Eugene, Darrell Posey, John Frechione, and Luiz Francelino Da Silva

1983   Resource exploitation in Amazonia: Ethnoecological examples from four populations. *Annals of the Carnegie Museum* 52:163–203.

Paz y Miño C., G., H. Balslev, R. Valencia R., and P. Mena V.

1991   *Lianas utilizadas por los indigenas Siona-Secoya de la Amazona del Ecuador*. EcoCiencia, Quito, Ecuador.

Posey, D. A.

1984   A preliminary report on diversified management of tropical forest by the Kayapo Indians of the Brazilian Amazon. In *Ethnobotany in the Neotropics*, edited by G. T. Prance and J. A. Kallunki, pp. 112–126. Advances in Economic Botany, Vol. 1. New York Botanical Garden, New York.

Schultes, R. E.

    1956   The Amazon Indian and the evolution in *Hevea* and related genera. *Journal of the Arnold Arboretum* 37:123–152.

Siebert, R.

    1948   The uses of *Hevea* for food in relation to its domestication. *Annals of the Missouri Botanical Garden* 35:117–121.

Smole, W.

    1976   *The Yanomama Indians: A cultural geography.* University of Texas Press, Austin.

Stearman, Allyn M.

    1989   *Yuqui: Forest nomads in a changing world.* Holt, Rinehart and Winston, New York.

UNESCO (United Nations Educational, Scientific, and Cultural Organization)

    1980   *Vegetation map of South America.* UNESCO, Toulouse, France.

Vickers, William T.

    1983   The territorial dimensions of Siona-Secoya and Encabellado adaptation. In *Adaptive responses of Native Amazonians,* edited by R. B. Hames and W. T. Vickers, pp. 451–478. Academic Press, New York.

    1989   *Los Sionas y Secoyas: Su adaptación al ambiente Amazonico.* Ediciones Abya-Yala, Quito, Ecuador.

Wilbert, J.

    1972   *Survivors of Eldorado: Four Indian cultures of South America.* Praeger Publishers, New York.

    1980   The Warao Indians of the Orinoco Delta. In *Demographic and biological studies of the Warao Indians,* edited by J. Wilbert and M. Layrisse, pp. 3–12. UCLA Latin American Center Publications, Los Angeles.

Wu Leung, W. T., and M. Flores

    1961   *Food composition table for use in Latin America.* Interdepartmental Committee on Nutrition for National Defense, NIH, Bethesda, Maryland.

Zarucchi, James

    1980   Ibapichuna: An edible *Dacryodes* (Burseraceae) from the northwest Amazon. *Botanical Museum Leaflets, Harvard University* 28(1):81–85.

Appendix 7.1. "Wild" Plant Foods Used by Indigenous Peoples in Amazonia

Genus and Species	Family	Growth Habit[a]	Part Used[b]	Indigenous Group[c]
Acrocomia sclerocarpa	Palmae (Arecaceae)	palm	fruit	Yanomamo
Aiphanes caryotifolia	Palmae (Arecaceae)	palm	fruit	Yanomamo
Albertia edulis	Rubiáceae	sm. tree	fruit	Piaroa

Genus and Species	Family	Growth Habit[a]	Part Used[b]	Indigenous Group[c]
Ambelania acida	Apocynaceae	?	fruit	Ka'apor
Anacardium occidentale	Anacardiaceae	?	fruit	Yanomamo
Ananas ananassoides	Bromeliaceae	?	fruit	Yanomamo
Aniba canelilla	Lauraceae	?	bark	Piaroa
Annona montana	Annonaceae	?	fruit	Ka'apor
Annona purpurea	Annonaceae	tree	fruit	Siona-Secoya
Arrabidaea inaqualis	Bignoniaceae	vine	sap	Kayapo
Astrocaryum chambria	Palmae (Arecaceae)	palm	fruit	Tukuna
Astrocaryum mumbaca	Palmae (Arecaceae)	palm	fruit seed	Surui Ka'apor
Astrocaryum murumuru	Palmae (Arecaceae)	palm	fruit shoot	Surui Surui
Astrocaryum tucuma	Palmae (Arecaceae)	palm	fruit shoot seed	Surui Surui Siona-Secoya
Astrocaryum vulgare	Palmae (Arecaceae)	palm	fruit	Ka'apor, Yano-mamo
Astrocaryum sp.	Palmae (Arecaceae)	palm	starch germ. seed	Bari Siona-Secoya
Attalea humboldtiana	Palmae (Arecaceae)	palm	fruit	Piaroa
Bactris cubaro	Palmae (Arecaceae)	palm	seed	Piaroa
Bactris maraja	Palmae (Arecaceae)	palm	fruit	Ka'apor, Piaroa
Bactris setulosa	Palmae (Arecaceae)	palm	fruit	Yanomamo
Bactris spp.	Palmae (Arecaceae)	palm	fruit	Bari, Ka'apor, Surui
Banafousia sananho	Apocynaceae	tree	fruit	Siona-Secoya
Bertholletia excelsa	Lecythidaceae	lg. tree	fruit seed	Yanomamo Tukuna, Yanomamo
Brosimum aubletti	Moraceae	?	fruit	Tukuna
Byrsonima amazonica	Malphighiaceae	?	fruit	Ka'apor
Byrsonima cf. *nitida*	Malphighiaceae	?	fruit	Ka'apor

Genus and Species	Family	Growth Habit[a]	Part Used[b]	Indigenous Group[c]
Calyptranthes spp.	Myrtaceae	tree	fruit	Runa
Carica cauliflora	Caricaceae	tree	fruit	Piaroa
Carica microcarpa	Caricaceae	tree	fruit	Siona-Secoya
Carpotroche linguifolia	Flacourtiaceae	sm. tree	fruit	Tukuna
Caryocar amydaliferum	Caryocaraceae	lg. tree	seed	Tukanoans
Caryocar villosum	Caryocaraceae	lg. tree	fruit	Yanomamo
Caryodendron orino-cense	Euphorbiaceae	lg. tree	seed	Siona-Secoya, Tukanoans
Cecropia sp.	Urticaceae	tree	leaf	Runa, Tuka-noans
Chrysophyllum sparsi-florum	Sapotaceae	?	fruit	Ka'apor
Clathrotropis villosum	Leguminosae	?	fruit	Yanomamo
Clavija lancifolia	Theophrastaceae	?	fruit	Ka'apor
Clidemia octava	Melastomataceae	herb	fruit	Tukanoans
Clidemia rubra	Melastomataceae	herb	fruit	Tukanoans
Cordia spp.	Boraginaceae	sm. tree	fruit	Ka'apor
Couma macrocarpa	Apocynaceae	tree	fruit	Tukanoans
Coumarouna odorata	Leguminosae/ Papilionoideae	?	fruit	Piaroa
Dacryodes belemensis	Burseraceae	sm. tree	fruit	Tukanoans
Dialium guianense	Leguminosae/ Caesalpinoideae	lg. tree	aril	Ka'apor
Dicranopygium bolivarense	Cyclanthaceae	?	leaf	Piaroa
Dioscorea sp.	Dioscoreaceae	?	fruit	Yanomamo
Erisma japura	Vochysiaceae	lg. tree	seed	Tukanoans
Euterpe edulis	Palmae (Arecaceae)	palm	fruit heart	Piaroa Piaroa
Euterpe oleracea	Palmae (Arecaceae)	palm	fruit shoot	Ka'apor Piaroa, Yano-mamo

Genus and Species	Family	Growth Habit[a]	Part Used[b]	Indigenous Group[c]
Euterpe precatoria	Palmae (Arecaceae)	palm	heart	Yanomamo
Euterpe spp.	Palmae (Arecaceae)	palm	fruit	Bari, Bora, Tukanoans, Tukuna
			heart	Siona-Secoya
Genipa americana	Rubiaceae	sm. tree	fruit	Piaroa
Genipa caruto	Rubiaceae	sm. tree	fruit	Piaroa
Grias neuberthii	Lecythidaceae	tree	fruit	Runa, Siona-Secoya
Herrania aff. *nitida*	Sterculiaceae	tree	fruit	Tukuna
Herrania sp.	Sterculiaceae	tree	fruit	Runa, Siona-Secoya
Hevea spp.	Euphorbiaceae	lg. tree	fruit seed	Piaroa Tukanoans
Humiria balsamifera	Humiriaceae	?	fruit	Kayapo
Hymenaea courbaril	Leguminosae/ Caesalpinoideae	tree	aril	Ka'apor
Hymenaea cf. *intermedia*	Leguminosae/ Caesalpinoideae	tree	aril	Ka'apor
Ilex guayusa	Aquifoliaceae	tree	leaf	Runa
Inga alba	Leguminosae/ Mimosoideae	tree	aril	Ka'apor
Inga spp.	Leguminosae/ Mimosoideae	tree	aril	Siona-Secoya, Tukanoans, Yanomamo, Tukuna
Iryanthera ulei	Myristicaceae	lg. tree	fruit	Siona-Secoya
Iryanthera sp.	Myristicaceae	lg. tree	fruit	Siona-Secoya
Jacaratia spinosa	Caricaceae	?	fruit	Ka'apor
Jessenia bataua	Palmae (Arecaceae)	palm	fruit	Siona-Secoya, Surui, Tukanoans, Tukuna, Yanomamo
			heart	Yanomamo

Genus and Species	Family	Growth Habit[a]	Part Used[b]	Indigenous Group[c]
Jessenia polycarpa	Palmae (Arecaceae)	palm	fruit	Yanomamo
Jessenia sp.	Palmae (Arecaceae)	palm	fruit	Bari, Tukanoans
Lacmellea lactescens	Apocynaceae	tree	fruit	Runa
Lacmellea oblongata	Apocynaceae	tree	fruit	Runa
Leopoldinia piassaba	Palmae (Arecaceae)	palm	fruit	Piaroa, Yanomamo
Macoubea pancifolia	Apocynaceae	tree	fruit	Siona-Secoya
Malpighia sp.	Malpighiaceae	?	fruit	Piaroa
Mauritia aculeata	Palmae (Arecaceae)	palm	fruit	Yanomamo
Mauritia flexuosa	Palmae (Arecaceae)	palm	fruit	Piaroa, Siona-Secoya, Surui, Tukanoans, Tukuna, Yanomamo
			starch	Tupinamba, Warao
Mauritia spp.	Palmae (Arecaceae)	palm	fruit	Yanomamo
Maximiliana maripa	Palmae (Arecaceae)	palm	fruit	Ka'apor, Piaroa, Surui
			shoot	Piaroa, Surui
			leaf	Kayapo
Micrandra spruceana	Euphorbiaceae	tree	seed	Tukanoans
Minusops elata	Sapotaceae	?	fruit	Piaroa
Minusops sp.	Sapotaceae	?	fruit	Piaroa
Monopteryx angusti-folia	Leguminosae	lg. tree	seed	Tukanoans
Monotagma sp.	Maranthaceae	?	root	Kayapo
Myrcia sp.	Myrtaceae	tree	fruit	Kayapo
Myrciaria tenella	Myrtaceae	?	fruit	Ka'apor
Oenocarpus bacaba	Palmae (Arecaceae)	palm	fruit	Piaroa, Tukuna, Yanomamo
			heart	Piaroa, Tukuna, Yanomamo

Appendix 7.1. Continued

Genus and Species	Family	Growth Habit[a]	Part Used[b]	Indigenous Group[c]
Oenocarpus distichus	Palmae (Arecaceae)	palm	fruit	Ka'apor, Kayapo
Oenocarpus sp.	Palmae (Arecaceae)	palm	fruit	Bari, Piaroa
Ogcodeia ulei	Moraceae	?	fruit	Tukuna
Orbignya phalerata	Palmae (Arecaceae)	palm	fruit	Apinajé, Ka'apor, Surui
			shoot	Ka'apor, Surui
Orbignya aff. polysticha	Palmae (Arecaceae)	palm	kernel	Tukuna
Orbignya spectabilis	Palmae (Arecaceae)	palm	fruit	Yanomamo
Orbignya sp.	Palmae (Arecaceae)	palm	fruit	Parakana
Parkia sp.	Leguminosae/ Mimosoideae	lg. tree	aril	Tukanoans
Passiflora cf. nitifa	Passifloraceae	?	fruit	Ka'apor
Paullinia bracteosa	Sapindaceae	herb	fruit	Siona-Secoya
Phenakospermum guyanense	Strelitziaceae	lg. herb	fruit seed	Parakana Tukanoans
Physalis angulata	Solanaceae	herb	fruit	Siona-Secoya, Tukanoans
Phytelephas microcarpa	Palmae (Arecaceae)	palm	fruit	Tukuna
Phytelephas sp.	Palmae (Arecaceae)	palm	fruit	Siona-Secoya
Phytolacca isconsandra	Phytolaccaceae	herb	leaf	Tukanoans
Phytolacca rivinoides	Phytolaccaceae	herb	leaf	Siona-Secoya, Tukanoans
Poraqueiba sericea	Icacinaceae	sm. tree	fruit	Tukanoans, Tukuna
Pourouma mollis	Moraceae	tree	fruit	Ka'apor
Pourouma sp.	Moraceae	tree	fruit	Siona-Secoya
Pouteria macrophylla	Sapotaceae	tree	fruit	Ka'apor
Pouteria spp.	Sapotaceae	tree	fruit	Tukanoans
Prestoea spp.	Palmae (Arecaceae)	palm	fruit	Tukanoans
Pseudolmedia laevis	Moraceae	tree	fruit	Siona-Secoya
Psidium guajava	Myrtaceae	sm. tree	fruit	Ka'apor

Genus and Species	Family	Growth Habit[a]	Part Used[b]	Indigenous Group[c]
Psidium guyanense	Myrtaceae	sm. tree	fruit	Kayapo
Psidium sp.	Myrtaceae	sm. tree	fruit	Ka'apor, Pia-roa, Yano-mamo
Pyrenoglypis sp.	Palmae (Arecaceae)	palm	fruit	Siona-Secoya
Quararibea cordata	Bombacaceae	?	fruit	Siona-Secoya
Quararibea obliquifolia	Bombacaceae	?	fruit	Siona-Secoya
Quararibea sp.	Bombacaceae	?	fruit	Siona-Secoya
Renealmia nicolaioides	Zingiberaceae	herb	fruit	Siona-Secoya
Rheedia brasiliensis	Clusiaceae	tree	fruit	Ka'apor
Sabicea amazonensis	Rubiaceae	herb	fruit	Tukanoans
Sabicea villosa	Rubiaceae	vine	fruit	Tukuna
Scheelea sp.	Palmae (Arecaceae)	palm	fruit	Bari
Solanum liximitante	Solanaceae	shrub	fruit	Tukuna
Solanum sessiliflorum	Solanaceae	shrub	fruit	Amahuaca
Solanum stramoni-folium	Solanaceae	shrub	fruit	Ka'apor
Spondias mombin	Anacardiaceae	tree	fruit	Ka'apor, Siona-Secoya
Spondias tuberosa	Anacardiaceae	tree	root	Tupinamba
Theobroma cacao	Sterculiaceae	tree	fruit	Runa, Tukuna
Theobroma grandi-florum	Sterculiaceae	sm. tree	fruit	Ka'apor
Theobroma speciosum	Sterculiaceae	sm. tree	fruit	Ka'apor, Runa
Theobroma subincanum	Sterculiaceae	sm. tree	fruit	Runa
Theobroma spp.	Sterculiaceae	sm. tree	fruit	Piaroa, Tuku-na, Yanomamo

Note: In counting the number of different plants, named species were counted individually, while plants in any given genus not identified to the species level were combined and counted as one species. For example, our initial list included the following: *Euterpe oleracea, Euterpe preca-toria, Euterpe* sp., and *Euterpe* spp. Thus, *Euterpe* sp. and *Euterpe* spp. were combined and counted as one species.

ᵃGrowth habits are based on the author's description, and when that was not available sources such as Cavalcante (1972, 1974) were particularly useful. The relative sizes of trees and herbs are listed when available.

ᵇBark, fruits (including berries), germinated seeds, heart of palm, leaf, starch (i.e., starch extracted from pith), root, sap, seeds (including nuts), aril (i.e., pulp surrounding seeds), kernel (used with references to palms and is probably the same as seed), shoots, vine.

ᶜReferences for indigenous culture groups are Amahuaca (Carniero 1988), Apinajé (Anderson et al. 1991), Bari (Beckerman 1977), Bora (Denevan et al. 1984), Ka'apor (Balée 1988; Balée and Gely 1989; Balée personal communication 1991), Kayapo (Anderson unpublished field notes; Anderson and Posey 1989; Parker et al. 1983; Posey 1984), Parakana (Milton 1991), Piaroa (Boza and Baumgartner 1962); Runa (Irvine 1989), Siona-Secoya (Vickers 1983, 1989), Surui (Coimbra 1985), Tukanoans (Dufour 1981, 1989; Dufour and Zarucchi 1979; Zarucchi 1980), Tukuna (Nimuendaju 1952; Glenboski 1975), Tupinamba (Gumilla 1791 cited in Lévi-Strauss 1950; Lévi-Strauss 1950; Metraux 1984a), Warao (Lévi-Strauss 1950); Yanomamo (Anderson 1978; Lizot 1977; Smole 1976; Wilbert 1972).

8

The Health Significance of Wild Plants for the Siona and Secoya

❦ WILLIAM T. VICKERS

The Siona and Secoya of the northwest Amazon basin base their traditional subsistence on slash-and-burn cultivation and foraging.

Although they derive most of their diet from garden plants, hunting, and fishing, they also frequently consume wild plant foods that add variety and important nutrients to the diet. During migrations and other periods of scarcity, wild plant foods become critically important. Siona and Secoya medicine requires many wild plants for various purposes, including use as therapeutic agents, hallucinogens, and materials for ritual paraphernalia. The Siona and Secoya also use a large number of feral plants as materials for tools, crafts, furnishings, construction, and cosmetic and toilet articles (Vickers and Plowman 1984; Vickers 1989).[1]

Today, the Siona and Secoya have growing contacts with Ecuador's economy due to frontier expansion. Some households are experimenting with cash cropping and livestock raising to supplement their incomes (Vickers 1993). Such "modernization" of the native lifestyle may well lower the health status of these people. Recent research indicates that colonists farming in the same region as the Siona-Secoya have poorer diets, slower rates of child development, and greater parasite infestation than do native people (Bénéfice and Barral 1991; Bénéfice et al. 1989a, 1989b). In part, these health differences between the two

This research has been supported by the Henry L. and Grace Doherty Charitable Foundation, the National Institute of Mental Health (Research Fellowship No. 1F01 MH 58552-01), the Florida International University Foundation, Cultural Survival, the Center for Latin American Studies of the University of Florida, and the Latin American and Caribbean Center and College of Arts and Sciences of Florida International University.

populations reflect their differential knowledge and use of tropical forest resources, including wild plants.

One purpose of this chapter is to document traditional wild plant use in the hope that increased awareness of these resources will promote conservation of the rainforest and native expertise. Tropical plants already are important economic and medical resources for people around the world, and more will contribute to human welfare once researchers have described them and identified their properties.

The Cultural and Ecological Setting

The Siona and Secoya speak closely related dialects belonging to the western branch of the Tukanoan language family. The two groups are culturally similar, and in the Aguarico River basin of northeastern Ecuador they now share a common territory and intermarry frequently (Figure 8.1). Related Siona and Secoya communities exist in adjacent areas of Colombia and Peru. At the time of European contact approximately 16,000 speakers of western Tukanoan languages inhabited an area of 82,000 km² (31,652 mi²) between 1°N–4°S latitude and 73°–77°W longitude (Steward 1949:663). The present Siona and Secoya population in all three countries probably does not exceed 1,500.

The Siona and Secoya live in scattered households or small villages along rivers and streams. They clear gardens nearby or at more distant locations that can be reached by canoe. People forage for wild resources over an extensive territory of approximately 1,150 km² (444 mi²). Most settlement sites are moved after periods of habitation ranging from 5 to 20 years, but people usually relocate within their established territory.

The main rivers of this region are the Napo and the Putumayo, and both are tributaries of the Amazon. The Aguarico is an important tributary of the Napo. The elevation of the study area is 250 m (823 ft). The climate corresponds to Köppen's Af or tropical wet. The mean annual rainfall is 3,375 mm (132 inches). The "dry season" spans December through February, and the "wet season" from March through July.

According to the Holdridge life zone system, the vegetation of the study area is tropical wet forest, characterized by trees with heights ranging from 24 to 45 m (89–150 ft), large woody climbers, and frequent occurrence of epiphytes and buttressed trees. In addition to this primary growth, other plant communities develop under specific conditions. These include the secondary growth developing from abandoned gardens and house sites, associations of perennially flooded soils, and liana associations (*bejucales*), among others.

Researchers often divide plants into the categories of "wild" and "domesticated" (i.e., plants that occur "naturally" versus those that are propagated by

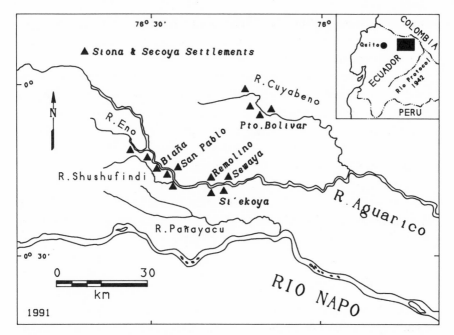

Figure 8.1. Siona and Secoya settlements in northeastern Ecuador, 1991. Additional Siona communities are located in adjacent areas of Colombia, and additional Secoya communities are in Peru.

humans). The term *semidomesticated* sometimes applies to an intermediate class of plants that occur "naturally" but are also propagated by humans (e.g., transplanted from forest to garden, or benefiting from human actions such as making clearings and dispersing seeds). The botanist Homer Pinkley suggests another terminology for characterizing these plant and human interactions:

> Since the word "weed" is relative . . . I would like to abandon its use. . . .
> [P]lants which grow around human occupations and to which no conscious
> attention is given for their growth I shall call "anthropophytes." . . . [I]t is
> plausible that for some anthropophytes the original ancestral forms no
> longer exist . . . [that] these plants have undergone domestication through
> no conscious efforts of man. These plants may or may not be used by man.
> . . . [W]henever [the Kofán] . . . move a plant from the primary forest to
> their village, this plant . . . must be referred to as a "cultivated" plant. I dif-
> ferentiate a cultivated species from a domesticated species. A domesticated
> species is one which has changed genetically, through either natural or ar-
> tificial selection, from its original native population. Hence, all domesti-
> cated plants are cultivated plants, but not all cultivated plants are
> domesticated plants. (1973:30–32)

Indeed, nearly one-eighth of the Amazon forest may be anthropogenic, including certain plant communities of palms, bamboo, Brazil nut, and liana forests (Balée 1989).

The Siona and Secoya distinguish between plants that come from *'aíro* (forest) and *siō* (garden). They also delineate many other microhabitats and plant communities, including *sitara* (swamp, permanently flooded), *dayawɨ* (swamp, seasonally flooded), *siáya* (river), *hai'ra* (lake, oxbow type), *mehawɨ* (beach), *aikūnti* (hills), *tutupɨ yihá* (lit.: vine-land; gloss.: plant communities dominated by vines), and *sɨtowa* (secondary growth).

In this chapter I use the term *wild* as shorthand to refer to plants that the Siona-Secoya collect in the forest or microhabitats other than gardens. Some of these plants may be what Pinkley refers to as "anthropophytes" or "anthropogenic," and I discuss these possibilities in certain cases.

Wild Plant Foods

Foraging for plant foods, an essential component of the Siona-Secoya's adaptation to their rainforest environment, provides many of their fruits, nuts, condiments, and stimulants. Some forest plants make important contributions to the diet on a seasonal basis, and others offer the advantage of being available during hunting trips or migrations. The Siona-Secoya use a large number of "wild" plant foods (see Appendix 8.1 for a partial listing).

The most frequently collected food during my 1973–75 fieldwork was from the dwarf banana or watí noka (lit.: demon banana). This is not a true feral species but rather a type of banana (*Musa* x *paradisiaca*, Musaceae) able to propagate itself. The watí noka grows along the banks of rivers where, according to respondents, the clones are deposited by floods. No other variety of plantain or banana known to the Siona-Secoya survives under the marginal conditions in which the watí noka thrives. The Siona-Secoya gave it the name "demon banana" because they believe that the stands of watí noka on deserted beaches and riverbanks are planted by spirits. Watí noka is not a preferred food, but during migrations it becomes an important substitute for cultivated plantains. In 1973, when the main Siona-Secoya village in Ecuador was moved from the Cuyabeno River to the Aguarico River, the people depended on watí noka for the 14–18 months that the plantains in their gardens required before beginning to produce.

Among the most important "wild" food plants are seasonal producers such as the ne'e palm (*Mauritia flexuosa*), the ñūkwa palm (*Astrocaryum tucuma*) that produces small petó (coconuts), and súni nuts (from *Caryodendron orinocense*, Euphorbiaceae). In January and February the *Mauritia* palm produces fruit that are the size of hen's eggs and very hard when green. These palms grow in areas of wet forest known as *ne'e dayawɨ* (*Mauritia* palm swamp). The people fell the palms and bury the fruit clusters in the ground for four days. Then the fruits are dug up, steamed in pots, peeled and eaten, or made into a beverage called *ne'e kõnõ̃*. The *Astrocaryum tucuma* palm provides its golf-ball-sized petó nuts in November and December. The Siona-Secoya cut off the tops of the nuts with a machete, drink the liquid, and remove and eat the white meat. These "coconuts" serve as a snack food. Súni, or *maní del monte* (lit.: peanuts of the forest), are nuts produced by large, buttressed trees (*Caryodendron orinocense*) during the dry season (December–February). The roundish, brittle súni pods contain three kidney-shaped seeds, which the people extract and roast in the fire before eating.

The Siona-Secoya cultivate many varieties of *Inga* (Leguminosae) but also collect several "wild" varieties such as goɨ bẽnẽ́ (*I. macrophylla*) and noka bẽnẽ́ (*I. thibaudiana*). These trees produce long fruit pods whose seeds are covered by a moist, white pulp. This pulp has a delicate texture and sweet taste. At least two varieties of apasí or *zapote* (*Quararibea* spp., Bombacaceae) are collected. These primary forest trees produce a brown, leathery-skinned fruit that has a delicious yellow meat inside. Another large forest tree that produces an important fruit is *Pseudolmedia laevis* (Moraceae). The Siona-Secoya call these small, red, berrylike fruits yahi and collect them in December. Additional wild fruits commonly eaten are 'aíro kwi ya'i (*Pourouma* sp., Moraceae) and sunori (*Herrania balaensis*, Sterculiaceae). The fruit of kãsɨ (*Grias neuberthii*, Lecythidaceae), when baked in coals, has a texture and taste similar to domesticated breadfruit (*Artocarpus altilis*, Moraceae).

The Siona-Secoya also eat plant parts other than nuts and fruits from trees. Two weedy herbs ("anthropophytes") occur in secondary growth: siri bia (*Physalis angulata*, Solanaceae), which has edible fruits; and bohó (*Phytolacca rivinoides*, Phytolaccaceae), which provides edible leaves and is one of the few "greens" consumed by the Siona-Secoya. The people derive heart of palm, or wiña tɨkubɨ (lit.: young shoot), from orá (*Iriartea* sp.), gõsa (*Jessenia bataua*), si'ra (*Astrocaryum huicungo*), and imi pu'e (*Euterpe edulis*).

The use of yoko (*Paullinia yoco*, Sapindaceae) is one of the diagnostic traits of western Tukanoan culture. Yoko is a woody vine with a high caffeine content (Schultes 1942) used primarily as an early morning stimulant, although Tukanoans sometimes also utilize it in curing rituals. Upon rising Siona-Secoya men scrape the bark of the vine into a gourd containing a little water and then squeeze the scrapings until the water turns brown. Then they remove the bark and drink the bitter infusion. People refer to yoko as "our coffee."

Based on observations made during 1973–75, I estimate that foods from collected plants provide approximately 5% of the calories in the Siona-Secoya diet, while cultivated plants provide 72%, hunting and fishing 20.5%, and purchased foods (e.g., rice and sugar) 2.5%. Wild plant foods contribute an average of about 110 kcal to each individual's daily diet.

One Siona household of four that I followed closely collected an estimated 592.4 kg of "wild" plant foods (with an edible portion of 422 kg) per year, but 500.8 kg consisted of the dwarf banana watí noka. As discussed earlier, this banana self-propagates in the floodplain of the Aguarico River, and the Siona-Secoya view it as a feral variety. The remaining 91.6 kg of collected plant foods (32.4 kg edible portion) consisted primarily of the aforementioned *Mauritia flexuosa, Astrocaryum* spp., *Caryodendron orinocense, Quararibea* spp., *Pseudolmedia laevis,* and *Pourouma* sp.

Although this level of consumption of collected plant foods may seem low, it is nevertheless important. The Siona-Secoya get most of their calories from their gardens, and especially from their starchy staples, which are manioc (*Manihot esculenta,* Euphorbiaceae), plantains (*Musa x paradisiaca,* Musaceae), and maize (*Zea mays,* Gramineae). Although the people have many domesticated (or semidomesticated) fruit trees and palms, "wild" plant foods make the diet more varied and interesting. Many wild fruits are excellent sources of vitamins and minerals. Palm fruits and nuts, highly esteemed for their taste, are also good sources of oils and proteins.

For example, the gõsa palm (*Jessenia bataua*) produces fruit from July to September and is one of the Siona-Secoya's most valued forest resources. The people use the fruits to make an extremely delicious and rich beverage or process them for their oil. Indeed, *Jessenia bataua* oil contains a significant amount of oleic acid and is very similar in chemical composition to olive oil (Balick 1986:33). Amino acid analysis of the protein from the fruit mesocarp and epicarp suggests that it "is comparable in quality to that of good animal protein and considerably better than most grain and legume proteins" (Balick 1986:35). The fruits of the *Astrocaryum* palm also have significant nutritional value. Analysis of *Astrocaryum* palm kernel press cakes indicates that they are 58.31% digestible carbohydrates, 8.27% protein, and 7.5% oil by weight (Pesce 1985:37). The people also collect various palm hearts, including *Euterpe edulis, Astrocaryum tucuma, Jessenia bataua,* and *Iriartea* sp. Fresh *Euterpe* hearts contain 4.1% protein (49.4% dry weight) (Instituto Nacional de Nutrición 1965:12). The most important palm, *Bactris gasipaes* (peach palm), is properly considered a domesticate because its ability to self-propagate in the wild is greatly diminished or lost. Regardless, this key resource originated in the neotropical forest. Analyses of fresh *Bactris* fruit show average protein contents ranging from 1.37 to 6.30% (3.10 to 12.8% dry weight), with seven of the eight essential amino acids present (Beckerman 1979:549–551). The fruit is also a good source of oil (4.4%), vitamin A value (670 mcg per 100 g edible portion), and vitamin C (35 mg ascorbic acid per 100 g edible portion) (Wu Leung and Flores 1961:60).

The Siona-Secoya eat the berrylike fruit of *Physalis angulata* as a snack. It is likely to be a good source of phosphorus and vitamins A and C, since analysis of the related species *P. peruviana* noted 55 mg of phosphorus, 730 mcg vitamin A value, and 43 mg ascorbic acid per 100 g edible portion. The apasí tree (*Quararibea cordata*) fruits from February to April and is another source of vitamin A value (Instituto Nacional de Nutrición 1965:16).

A recent medical study of the Siona-Secoya in Ecuador concludes that their multifaceted subsistence activities give them an excellent and well-rounded diet (Bénéfice and Barral 1991). The garden crops are reliable producers of carbohydrates, while hunting and fishing provide "extra protein, iron, thiamin, niacin and retinol" (Bénéfice and Barral 1991:320). Fat consumption is low (11% of total energy intake) but sufficient. The people also obtain substantial amounts of vitamins A and C from garden and forest fruits that are rich in carotenoids (Bénéfice and Barral 1991).

"Wild" plant foods usually serve as snacks or enhancements to meals based on starchy staples; however, they serve a key role when people are hunting or traveling since other foods are often unavailable. During migrations or flight from enemies, wild foods are the difference between survival and starvation.

Wild Plants as Medicines

The Siona-Secoya term that comprehends "disease" is *dawu*. It contrasts with *wahi*, which implies life and well-being. Local shamans diagnose illnesses and usually blame them on distant shamans who are seen as sorcerers. Diagnosis and treatment occur within the setting of communal *yahé* ceremonies, which are conducted in special ceremonial houses located away from villages. The hallucinogenic medium of yahé (*Banisteriopsis caapi*, Malpighiaceae) enables the shaman to visualize the source of the illness and to contravene the harmful activities of the sorcerer and his spirit helpers.

To become a shaman a person must undergo an apprenticeship and then develop his abilities over a period of years. He must also demonstrate the correct attitudes of asceticism, generosity, concern for others, and dignified bearing. Most of all, he must demonstrate proficiency in conducting the yahé ceremony, in experiencing visions, and in establishing contact with super-natural beings. The use of yahé and the other hallucinogenic plants is very important and highly ritualized. The Siona-Secoya believe that vision-producing substances provide the media through which a shaman contacts spirits, and the shaman is said to undergo physical transformation and soul flight when using them (e.g., becoming a jaguar or flying off to visit the spirits who reside in the various heavenly and underworld realms).

Many apprentices fail to become respected shamans because they do not experience visions of sufficient intensity or lack the discipline to continue the strict regimen of fasting, sexual abstinence, and physical isolation required in their training. The apprenticeship is also a period of active study of plants and their properties. Not only must apprentices prepare and consume potions of the more familiar medicinal and psychotropic plants, they also are expected to venture into the forest to seek unknown plants and make experimental potions from them. When asked about his apprenticeship, an established shaman once replied, "I drank all the leaves" (i.e., "I tried all of the plants in the forest"). This claim, although probably exaggerated, was nevertheless a statement of the cultural ideal that, having experienced the effects of all of the plants, the apprentice will gain an understanding of their properties and thus be able to prescribe the proper remedies for people who are ill.

The Siona-Secoya use many plants in their medicine, and a large number are domesticated or semidomesticated species (Vickers and Plowman 1984). (Appendix 8.2 provides a partial listing of Siona-Secoya wild plant medicines. The list is certainly incomplete because each field trip reveals the existence of additional plants known to the people.) Siona-Secoya medical and religious practices are intertwined, so plants that have ritual uses can be considered as part of their medical system. (Appendix 8.3 includes feral varieties of hallucinogens as well as plants used to make shamanic and ritual paraphernalia and those employed for personal adornment [a necessary preparation for rituals].) Undoubtedly, some Siona-Secoya medicines derived from "wild" plants are efficacious because of their chemical and physical properties. Others contribute to the patient's well-being through a placebo effect.

The biochemical analysis of native Amazonian medicines is still in a preliminary stage. Researchers have done some work on the hallucinogenic plants. For example, the principal active component of yahé is the alkaloid harmine; additional minor components include harmaline, tetrahydroharmine, harmol, harmic acid methylester, harmic amide, acetyl norharmine, harmine N-oxide, harmalinic acid, and ketotetrahydronorharmine (Schultes and Hofmann 1980: 171–174). The *Banisteriopsis* drink produces a range of visual, auditory, and tactile hallucinations. Among the Siona-Secoya such effects are interpreted and given cultural meaning in the context of a communal religious and curing ceremony presided over by the learned shaman, who is referred to as *yahé unkuki* (lit.: drinker of yahé).

The leaves of *Diplopterys cabrerana* (Malpighiaceae), or yahé 'okó (lit.: yahē water), serve as an admixture to the hallucinogenic yahé potion and contribute Betacarboline alkaloids and N,N-dimethyltryptamine. Additional minor components include N-methyltryptamine, 5-methoxy-N,N-dimethyltryptamine, bufotenin, and N-methyltetrahydrobetacarboline (Schultes and Hofmann 1980:175). According to native respondents, this admixture heightens and lengthens the visual hallucinations of the potion. (Another plant with powerful hallucinogenic properties, pehí [*Brugmansia* x *insignis*], is not discussed here because it is a cultivar.)

Brunfelsia grandiflora subsp. *schultesii* (Solanaceae), or uhahai, is a narcotic or hallucinogen that the Siona-Secoya use to treat fevers and is said to induce cold and tingling sensations in the extremities. Researchers have made only preliminary chemical analyses of *Brunfelsia,* and the plant's pharmacologic effects remain poorly understood (Schultes and Hofmann 1980:279–282). However, the Alpha Helix Amazon Expedition, Phase VI, conducted analyses that showed the presence of scopoletine, quinic acid, tartaric acid, lactic acid, salicylic acid, and various sugars (Schultes and Hofmann 1980:281–282). Salicylic acid is a crystalline phenolic acid commonly used as an analgesic and antipyretic (e.g., in aspirin).

The many purgatives, remedies for diarrhea, and treatments for intestinal parasites (see Appendix 8.2) likely contain various items that are efficacious. One example, the cultivated plant wasi ɨkó, or "worm remedy" (*Chenopodium ambrosioides,* Chenopodiaceae), contains the compound ascaridol that is effective against roundworms (Ayala Flores 1984:7). The Siona-Secoya ingest the latex of the tree *Ficus yoponensis* (Moraceae), kã'ko to treat intestinal parasites and diarrhea. Its congeneric *F. insipida* contains phylloxanthine, Beta-amyrine or lupeol, lavandulol, phyllanthol, and eloxanthine, the last of which is probably the toxic agent for parasites (Ayala Flores 1984:7, citing López and Kiyán de Cornelio 1974).

Eric Bénéfice and Henri Barral's comparative medical study of the Siona-Secoya and nearby colonists in Ecuador revealed that while both populations have indications of parasites, the Indians have lower rates of infestation than do the settlers:

> Nine types of helminths and protozoa were identified. . . . The settlers suffer most from ascaris and the Sionas-Secoyas from hookworm (probably *Necator americanus*). *Bilantidium coli* trophozoa and *Strongyloides stercoralis* larva were found only in the child settlers. The prevalence rate of infestation is significantly higher for the settlers than for the Indians (82% against 50%; Chi^2=27.2 for 1 df), as is their likelihood of harboring more than one parasite (64% against 26%; Chi^2=28.8 for 1 df). (1991:313–314)

Bénéfice and Barral interpret these results primarily in terms of factors such as differences in lifestyle, domestic water supply, sanitation, and housing. However, Bénéfice (personal communication 1991) has also suggested that the Siona-Secoya use of plant remedies may be a factor contributing to their lower rate of parasite infections.

Ethan B. Russo (1992) suggests that Amazonian Ecuador may be a fertile hunting ground for headache remedies because of its biodiversity and varied native pharmacopoeias that include many agents taken internally for headache treatment. The Siona and Secoya are notable in this regard because they use at least five forest species to prepare headache medicines: *Fittonia albivenis* (Acanthaceae), *Anthurium* cf. *uleanum* (Araceae), *Anthurium* sp. Sect. *Pachyneurium* (Araceae), *Erythroxylum ulei* (Erythroxylaceae), and *Codonanthopsis dissimulata* (Gesneriaceae). Russo proposes that these and other native headache remedies should be biochemically screened for serotonin receptor activity, which is a key factor in the treatment of headache, including migraine. Such research may lead to "the discovery of more effective, less toxic headache drugs . . . [and] the development of a new industry for the local economy that could promote conservation of an endangered ecosystem" (Russo 1992:193).

Conclusion

As mentioned earlier, many other forest plants provide materials for Siona-Secoya crafts, construction, furnishings, tools, weapons, fish baits, and so forth. Future studies should collect, describe, and identify additional plants used by the Siona and Secoya. A vast amount of work remains to be done on the nutritional and pharmacologic properties of plants throughout Amazonia, and this chapter reflects the sketchiness of our knowledge in these areas. Although this analysis is suggestive rather than definitive, it can leave no doubt that tropical forest plants are vitally important to native peoples. Many tropical forest species also contribute to the well-being of people living in nontropical regions of the world, and many more applications await discovery and development. However, at the current rate of clearing, all of the world's tropical forests will disappear within 100 years, thus destroying our greatest source of biological diversity. Our challenge is to prevent this tragedy.

NOTES

1. Most of the plants discussed in this chapter were collected during research on the human ecology of the Siona and Secoya of northeastern Ecuador in 1973–75. Additional observations on this community's plant use were made in 1979, 1980, and 1990–91. In

1984 I collected plants among the Secoya of the Santa María River in Peru, who are relatives of the Secoya in Ecuador.

I owe a great debt of gratitude to my friend and colleague Timothy Plowman (deceased) of the Department of Botany of the Field Museum of Natural History for organizing the effort to identify the plants collected in the field. The many botanists who assisted in this task are listed in Vickers and Plowman 1984. A nearly complete set of voucher specimens for this study is deposited at the Field Museum of Natural History, Chicago. Eight single specimens, as well as selected duplicates, are preserved at the Department of Botany, University of Florida. Some duplicate specimens have been deposited at the Instituto de Ciencias, Pontificia Universidad Católica del Ecuador, Quito.

Most importantly, I thank my many Siona and Secoya friends who have been my teachers. Their generosity and enthusiasm in sharing their botanical knowledge is remarkable.

REFERENCES

Ayala Flores, F.
    1984   Notes on some medicinal and poisonous plants of Amazonian Peru. In *Ethnobotany in the neotropics,* edited by G. T. Prance and J. A. Kallunki, pp. 1–8. Advances in Economic Botany, Vol. 1. New York Botanical Garden, New York.

Balick, Michael J.
    1986   *Systematics and economic botany of the Oenocarpus-Jessenia (Palmae) complex.* Advances in Economic Botany, Vol. 3. New York Botanical Garden, New York.

Balée, William
    1989   The culture of Amazonian forests. In *Resource management in Amazonia: Indigenous and folk strategies,* edited by D. A. Posey and W. Balée, pp. 1–21. Advances in Economic Botany, Vol. 7. New York Botanical Garden, New York.

Beckerman, Stephen
    1979   The abundance of protein in Amazonia: A reply to Gross. *American Anthropologist* 81(3):533–560.

Bénéfice, Eric, and Henri Barral
    1991   Differences in life style and nutritional status between settlers and Siona-Secoya Indians living in the same Amazonian milieu. *Ecology of Food and Nutrition* 25:307–322.

Bénéfice, E., H. Barral, and Z. Romo-Nuñez
    1989a   Écologie de la santé et de la nutrition en Amazonie Équatorienne (Province du Napo): I. Les Indiens Sionas-Sécoyas du Rio Aguarico. *Bulletin de la Société de Pathologie Exotique* 82:531–543.
    1989b   Écologie de la santé et de la nutrition en Amazonie Équatorienne (Province du Napo): II. Les colons de la zone pétrolière. *Bulletin de la Société de Pathologie Exotique* 82:544–557.

Instituto Nacional de Nutrición

1965   *Tabla de composición de los alimentos Ecuatorianos.* Ministerio de Prevision
        Social y Sanidad, Quito, Ecuador.

King, Steven R.

1991   Among the Secoyas. *Nature Conservancy* 41(1):6–15.

López G., J. E., and I. Kiyán de Cornelio

1974   Plantas medicinales del Peru. *Biota* 10:28–41, 76–84.

Paz y Miño C., G., H. Balslev, R. Valencia R., and P. Mena V.

1991   *Lianas utilizados por los indígenas Siona-Secoya de la Amazonía del Ecuador.*
        Ecociencia Reporte Técnico 1. Fundación Ecuatoriana de Estudios Ecoló-
        gicos, Quito, Ecuador.

Pesce, Celestino

1985   *Oil palms and other oilseeds of the Amazon,* translated and edited by D. V.
        Johnson. Reference Publications, Algonac, Michigan. (Originally pub-
        lished in 1941.)

Pinkley, Homer Virgil

1973   The ethno-ecology of the Kofán Indians. Ph.D. dissertation, Biology De-
        partment, Harvard University.

Russo, Ethan B.

1992   Headache treatments by native peoples of the Ecuadorian Amazon: A pre-
        liminary cross-disciplinary assessment. *Journal of Ethnopharmacology* 36:
        193–206.

Schultes, Richard Evans

1942   Plantae Colombiane II. Yoco: A stimulant of southern Colombia. *Botanical
        Museum Leaflets, Harvard University* 10(10):301–324.

Schultes, Richard Evans, and Albert Hofmann

1980   *The botany and chemistry of hallucinogens* [Second edition]. Charles C.
        Thomas, Springfield, Illinois.

Steward, Julian H.

1949   The native population of South America. In *The comparative ethnology
        of South American Indians,* in the *Handbook of South American Indians,*
        Vol. 5, edited by J. H. Steward, pp. 655–668. Bureau of American Eth-
        nology, Bulletin 143. U.S. Government Printing Office, Washington, D.C.

Vickers, William T.

1989   *Los Sionas y Secoyas: Su adaptación al ambiente Amazónico.* Ediciones Abya-
        Yala, Quito, Ecuador.

1993   Changing tropical forest resource management strategies among the Siona-
        Secoya Indians. In *Tropical forests, people, and food: Biocultural interac-
        tions and applications to development,* edited by C. M. Hladik, A. Hladik,
        O. F. Linares, H. Pagezy, A. Semple, and M. Hadley. Man in the Bio-
        sphere, Vol. 15. UNESCO/Parthenon Publishing Group, Paris and Lon-
        don.

Vickers, William T., and Timothy Plowman
    1984   *Useful plants of the Siona and Secoya Indians of eastern Ecuador.* Fieldiana
            Botany, n.s. 15. Field Museum of Natural History, Chicago.
Wu Leung, Woot-Tsuen, with Marina Flores
    1961   *Food composition table for use in Latin America.* Interdepartmental Commit-
            tee on Nutrition for National Defense, National Institutes of Health, Beth-
            esda, Maryland.

Appendix 8.1. Wild Plant Foods Utilized by the Siona and Secoya

Scientific Name	No.[a]	Native Name[b]	Growth Habit	Edible Part
Anacardiaceae				
Spondias mombin L.	V111	rohí	tree	fruit
Apocynaceae				
Bonafousia sananho (Ruiz & Pavon) Mark-graf	V46, V299	baĩ su'u	tree	fruit
Couma macrocarpa Barb.		wãnsoka	tree	fruit
Macoubea pancifolia Spreng.?		mĩũ wito	tree	fruit
Bignoniaceae				
Jacaranda copaia (Aubl.) D. Don?		wẽkineo	tree	wood (chewed for sweet taste)
Bombacaceae				
Quararibea cordata (H. & B.) Vischer	V50 V68	apasí tãnke apasí	tree	fruit
Quararibea obliquifolia (Standl.) Standl.	V85	tãnke apasí	tree	fruit
Quararibea sp.	V163	naso apasí	tree	fruit
Caricaceae				
Carica microcarpa Jacq. subsp. *heterophylla* (Poepp. & Endl.) Badillo	V126	'aíro watihĩko	treelet	fruit
Euphorbiaceae				
Caryodendron orinocense Karsten	V57	súni	tree	seed

Scientific Name	No.[a]	Native Name[b]	Growth Habit	Edible Part
Guttiferae				
Rheedia acuminata (R. & P.) Planch. & Triana	V203, V303	pɨrɨ maharo	small tree	fruit
Lecythidaceae				
Grias neuberthii Macbride	V84	kāsɨ	tree	fruit (edible when roasted)
Leguminosae				
Inga chartacea P. & E.	K527A	"nea bēnế"	tree	white seed coats eaten
Inga macrophylla H. & B. ex Willd.	V142	goɨ bēnē	tree	fruit
Inga marginata Willd.	V59 V80 V121	bēnē siri bēnế kwiṁa bēnế, sisi bēnế	tree	fruit
	V224	'airo yoko pēnế		
Inga thibaudiana DC.	V140	noka bēnế	tree	fruit
Inga sp.	V206	do'kɨ bēnế	tree	fruit
Inga sp.		'emu bēnế	tree	fruit
Inga sp.		pa'pa bēnế	tree	fruit
Inga sp.		sēse bēnế	tree	fruit
Inga sp.		tɨrɨ bēnế	tree	fruit
Inga sp.	V134	wāso bēnế	tree	fruit
Menispermaceae				
Orthomene schomburgkii (Miers) Barneby & Krukoff	K419	"anka weight su" (ākawesɨ?)	vine	fruit
Moraceae				
Pourouma sp.	V86 V123	'aíro kwi ya'i kwi ya'i	tree	fruit (several other varieties are domesticates or semi-domesticates)
Pourouma sp.?		hū'hū sɨka	tree	fruit

Appendix 8.1. Continued

Scientific Name	No.[a]	Native Name[b]	Growth Habit	Edible Part
Pseudolmedia laevis (R. & P.) Macbride	V56	yahi	large tree	fruit
	V185, V231	tõto yahi		
Myristicaceae				
Iryanthera ulei Warburg	V71, V230	wirisaká	tree	fruit
Iryanthera sp.	V235	sisiri	tree	fruit
Myrtaceae				
Psidium acutangulum D.C.	V156	arari	tree	fruit
Palmae				
Astrocaryum huicungo Damm. ex Burret	V61	si'ra	palm	seed, heart
Astrocaryum tucuma Mart. Vel. aff.	V141	ñũkwa	palm	seed
Euterpe edulis Mart.		imi pu'e	palm	heart
Iriartea sp.		orá	palm	heart
Jessenia bataua (Mart.) Burret		gõsa	palm	fruit, heart
Jessenia sp.?		bo gõsa	palm	fruit
Jessenia sp.?		ñaho gõsa	palm	fruit
Mauritia flexuosa L.f.	V43	ne'e	palm	fruit
Mauritia sp.		kãti ne'e	palm	fruit
Mauritia sp.		ma ne'e	palm	fruit
Mauritia sp.		soto ne'e	palm	fruit
Oenocarpus mapora Karsten		wi gõsa	palm	fruit
Phytelephas sp.	V79	sewa	palm	seed
Pyrenoglypis sp.?		ñũkwe	palm	fruit
Passifloraceae				
Passiflora quadrangularis L.	V102	tasiri	vine	fruit
Passiflora quadriglandulosa Rodschied	K383B	"anto wa yu"	vine	fruit

Scientific Name	No.[a]	Native Name[b]	Growth Habit	Edible Part
Phytolaccaceae				
Phytolacca rivinoides Kunth & Bouche	V39	bohó	herb	leaves
Rubiaceae				
Genipa americana L.	V223	'aíro toa	tree	fruit
Sapindaceae				
Paullinia bracteosa Radlk.	V67 V119	'oko yoko ōkwe yoko	woody liana	fruit
Paullinia yoco R.E. Schult. & Killip	V109	yoko	woody liana	caffeine-rich beverage made from bark
Solanaceae				
Physalis angulata L.	V101	siri bia	herb	fruit
Sterculiaceae				
Herrania balaensis Preuss	V94	sunori	tree	fruit
Zingiberaceae				
Renealmia nicolaioides Loesener	V209	wēkɨho	herb	fruit
Family Unknown				
Indeterminate		dei	tree	seed
Indeterminate		du'i	tree	fruit
Indeterminate		gāhe	tree	fruit
Indeterminate		sayaro	?	fruit
Indeterminate		tīto repa	tree	fruit

[a]"V" indicates plant collected by W. Vickers; "K" indicates plant collected by S. King. Unidentified plants from Vickers' research.

[b]Transcriptions of native names by W. Vickers appear without quotation marks. Those by S. King appear with quotation marks.

Appendix 8.2. Wild Plant Medicines Utilized by the Siona and Secoya

Scientific Name	No.[a]	Native Name[b]	Growth Habit	Medical Use
Acanthaceae				
Fittonia albivenis (Lindley ex Veitch) Brummitt	V213	minakoro[c]	herb	remedy for headache
Araceae				
Anthurium cf. *uleanum* Engl.	V220	karɨcho[c]	epiphytic herb	remedy for headache
Anthurium sp. Sect. *Pachyneurium*	V254	kaho; Shushufindi karɨ[c]	epiphytic herb	remedy for headache
Monstera cf. *adansonii* Schott	V251	sōso ɨkó	climbing epiphyte	remedy for headache
Syngonium podophyllum Schott	V96 V112	ñãta hu'hu ñãta kaho	vine	treatment for bite of *Paraponera* ant
Boraginaceae				
Tournefortia angustifolia R. & P.	V107	hetu bīsi	vine	purgative
Commelinaceae				
Geogenanthus ciliatus Bruckn.	V253	turu; paparohe khaki[c]	herb	liniment for joints, remedy for intestinal parasites (ingested)
Compositae				
Adenostemma platyphyllum Cass.	V179	tuwi yasi[c]	herb	remedy for pimples (leaf ashes rubbed on pimple)
Neurolaena lobata (L.) R. Br.	V180	de'a ɨkó; o'si si sehepa[c]	shrub	treatment for leshmaniasis
Spilanthes alba L'Her.	V183	gūhī sɨrɨ	herb	remedy for toothache
Erythroxylaceae				
Erythroxylum ulei O.E. Schultz	V144 V238	suara ɨkó; awɨ itɨ fasi[c] na'nyame ɨkó; itɨ fasi[c]	shrub	remedy for diarrhea, body pain, head, stomach- and toothaches, sore throat

Scientific Name	No.[a]	Native Name[b]	Growth Habit	Medical Use
Euphorbiaceae				
Chamaesyce hirta (L.) Millspaugh	V33	wito sa'wi taya	weedy herb	milky sap treats toe fungus
Gesneriaceae				
Codonanthopsis dissimulata (H.E. Moore) Wiehler	V161, V256	hūku ɨkó kūgi kɨsi[c]	herb	remedy for toothaches and headaches
Dalbergaria picta (Karsten) Wiehler	V72	soma mūto	herb	a tobacco substitute for smoking and curing rituals
Drymonia coriacea (Oerst. ex Hanst.) Wiehler	V120	mačeiõsi[c]	woody vine	remedy for mouth ulcers, toothache
Labiatae				
Hyptis capitata Jacq.	V182	nohabianyono[c]	weedy herb	remedy for diarrhea
Lecythidaceae				
Grias neuberthii Macbride	V84	kāsɨ	tree	purgative prepared from raw fruit
Leguminosae				
Brownea loretensis Standl.?	K494	"anya puki mwa"	tree	red inner bark scraped and masticated, liquid of quid squeezed on cuts
Brownea sp.?	V218	aña pɨkɨ mao	tree	medicine for cuts made from bark
Brownea sp.	K9	"anya pu ki ma"		
Inga sp.		kosi bēné	tree	treatment for earache (heated leaf applied to ear)
Marantaceae				
Calathea sp. (*C. ornata* [Linden] Koern. group)	V202	kosiri ha'o	herb	remedy for sore throat

Scientific Name	No.[a]	Native Name[b]	Growth Habit	Medical Use
Melastomataceae				
Blakea sp. aff. *B. ciliata* Mgf. or *B. rosa* (R. & P.) Don	V255	yayurua; hɨrɨ khaki[c]	shrub	treatment for burns (bathed with infusion made from leaves)
Triolena pluvialis (Wurdack) Wurdack	V219	kóshasi[c]	herb	remedy for toothache
Monimiaceae				
Mollinedia sp.	V81	hu'hu	shrub	remedy for stom-achache
Moraceae				
Ficus yoponensis Desv.	V90	kã'ko	tree	latex is remedy for diarrhea and intestinal para-sites
Myrtaceae				
Myrtaceae cf. *Plinia duplipilosa* McVaugh	K495 K6	"ai ki hen yo" "aykiuhenyo"	shrub	remedy for stom-achache and diar-rhea
Orchidaceae				
Encyclia fragrans (SW.) Lemee	K417		epiphyte	remedy for skin disorders
Piperaceae				
Piper amazonicum (Miq.) C. DC.	V257	gou pipi; čarapa sikihečuᶜ	shrub	remedy for fever; also a purgative
Piper augustum Rudge	K431	"kwepe weoko"	shrub	purgative
Rubiaceae				
Hamela axillaris Swartz	V137	sa'i bia	shrub	remedy for diar-rhea and stom-achache
Rutaceae				
Zanthoxylum cf. *tachu-elo* Little	V118	minakoro[c]	shrub	liniment made from bark

Appendix 8.2. Continued

Scientific Name	No.[a]	Native Name[b]	Growth Habit	Medical Use
Solanaceae				
Brunfelsia grandiflora D. Don subsp. *schultesii* Plowman	V138, V190	uhahai	shrub	narcotic or hallucinogen
Solanum diffusum R. & P.	V273, V143	āhi ɨta ɨkó ofa kɨhī[c]	vine	remedy for diarrhea
Solanum kioniotrichum Bitter	V110	betá	tree	purgative made from bark
Solanum leptopodum Van Heurck & Muell. Arg.	V232	oyo ha'o	shrub	treatment for "crybabies" (bathed in infusion made from leaves)
Solanum sp. aff. *nemorense*	V118	minakoro[c]	shrub	liniment for muscles
Urticaceae				
Pilea sp. aff. *hydrocotyliflora* Killip	V87, V169	ka'mi ɨkó; sisi pakɨpi[c]	herb	remedy for mouth ulcers
Urera baccifera (L.) Gaudichaud	V164	nyanami susi	herb	treatment for muscular pain (nettles rubbed on afflicted part)
Urera caracasana (Jacq.) Griseb.	V162, V204	be'su susi paɨ susi	herb	treatment for muscular pain (inflorescense rubbed on afflicted part)
Verbenaceae				
Petrea peruviana var. *acuminata* Mold.	K3, K493	"ana yo ki"; (aña ɨkó?)	vine	remedy for snakebite, used with "ana ka ho"
Family Unknown				
Indeterminate		pakūhi[c]	?	diarrhea remedy
Indeterminate		pi'hesai	aquatic plant	toothache remedy

Appendix 8.2. Continued

Scientific Name	No.ᵃ	Native Nameᵇ	Growth Habit	Medical Use
Indeterminate		sẽse bɨkɨmoa	woody vine	remedy for common cold

ᵃ"V" indicates plant collected by W. Vickers; "K" indicates plant collected by S. King.
ᵇTranscriptions of native names by W. Vickers appear without quotation marks. Those by S. King appear with quotation marks.
ᶜPlant name in Kofán, the language of a neighboring Indian group.

Appendix 8.3. Wild Plants with Ritual Uses among the Siona and Secoya

Scientific Name	No.ᵃ	Native Nameᵇ	Growth Habit	Ritual Use
Acanthaceae				
Justicia sp.	V69	weoko	herb	leaf chewed to color mouth purple for rituals
Caryocaraceae				
Caryocar glabrum (Aubl.) Persoon	V114	tuã uo	tree	bark used in scarification ritual to improve luck in hunting and fishing
Cucurbitaceae				
Fevillea cordifolia L.	V116	hukú	herbaceous vine	seed oil used as base for face painting; seeds also used as candles
Gramineae				
Bambusa subgen. *Guadua* sp.	V264 K526	mame "mame"	giant grass	used to make ceremonial flutes
Gynerium sagittatum (Aubl.) Beauv.	V16	wigãtɨ	giant grass	stem sections used to make earplugs and bases of feather "flower" necklace ornaments

Appendix 8.3. Continued

Scientific Name	No.[a]	Native Name[b]	Growth Habit	Ritual Use
Pariana aurita Swallen	V64	mamekoko	grass	plants bound to
Pariana sp.	V262	mamekoko		make shaman's rattle
Leguminosae				
Ormosia cf. *amazonica* Ducke	V270	tuku	tree	red seeds used as necklace beads
Malpighiaceae				
Banisteriopsis caapi (Spruce ex Griseb.) Morton	V250	'aíro yahé	woody vine	most important hallucinogen (many varieties are semidomesticates or domesticates)
Diplopterys cabrerana (Cuatr.) Gates	V212	yahé 'okó	woody vine	hallucinogen and admixture to basic yahé potion
Myristicaceae				
Iryanthera ulei Warburg	V71, V230	wirisaká	tree	aromatic bark used for armbands, flowers and leaves used as perfume and ornamentation
Myrtaceae				
Campomanesia lineatifolia R. & P.	V234	masíka ma'nya, arari ma'nya	aromatic shrub	perfume
Palmae				
Chamaedorea sp. aff. *integrifolia* (Traill) Dammer	V97	wakó	small palm	fruits used as perfume, placed in armbands
Palmae gen. indet. cf. *Attalea* or *Orbignya*	V267	ya'pɨ	palm	seeds used as necklace beads
Piperaceae				
Piper nudilimbum C. DC.	V252	karɨwačo[c]	shrub	foliage placed under armbands as ornament

Appendix 8.3. Continued

Scientific Name	No.[a]	Native Name[b]	Growth Habit	Ritual Use
Piper sp.	V37	bupɨ weo ha'o	shrub	leaves chewed to tint mouth purple
Polypodiaceae				
Thelypteris sp. aff. *T. berroi* (C. Chr.) Reed	V181	ka'wi	fern	leaves woven into headbands
Rubiaceae				
Genipa americana L.	V223	we'e	tree	fruit juice used as body paint (*we'e* refers to body paint, *'airo toa* to edible fruit)
Pentagonia williamsii Standley	V95	muhõ	treelet	admixture to *Genipa* body paint (see above)
Sapotaceae				
Pouteria sp. aff. *caimito* (R. & P.) Radlk.	V269	sõkɨ sewe	tree	seeds used as beads
Selaginellaceae				
Selaginella exaltata (Kze.) Spring	V75	ka'wi	herbaceous vine	wiry stems used for headbands
Violaceae				
Rinorea viridiflora Rusby	V217	pɨheri	small tree	leaves bound to make shaman's rattle
Unknown				
Indeterminate		yakuri	?	plant used in curing rituals

[a]"V" indicates plant collected by W. Vickers; "K" indicates plant collected by S. King.
[b]Transcriptions of native names by W. Vickers appear without quotation marks. Those by S. King appear with quotation marks.
[c]Plant name in Kofán, the language of a neighboring Indian group.

9

North American Food and Drug Plants

❦ DANIEL E. MOERMAN

Flambeau Ojibwa declare that [Aster macrophyllus] . . . *leaves are fine flavored and good to eat because they act as medicine at the same time they are food.*
(Huron H. Smith 1932:398)

In several papers I have argued that there was a clear difference between the botanical sources of food plants and of drug plants. In 1979, while noting that a few families with many medicinal species produced a few foods (I mentioned sunflower seeds and pine nuts), I nonetheless concluded that "most do not. Food and medicine appear . . . to be substantially discontinuous categories" (Moerman 1979:118). At that time, I had no particular explanation for why this might have been the case.

Ten years later, I elaborated on this proposition by noting that although the grass family (Poaceae) includes a few medicinal species (notably sweetgrass, *Hierochloe odorata*, often used as a pleasant or cleansing incense), generally speaking this very large family contributes far fewer than its share. I explained this characteristic by noting that, unlike families that contain a disproportionate share of medicinal species, the grass family generally produces very few biologically active substances (or allelochemicals) to inhibit browsing or to enhance seed dispersal or pollination. Indeed, "the reaction of many grasses to being browsed (or mowed) is simply to grow back. . . . Some species . . . [are] so

The data base MPNA was produced with the support of the National Endowment for the Humanities, grant number RT-20408-04. The analysis of the medicinal plant data was supported by the National Science Foundation, grant number BNS-8704103. Current work on food plants is being supported by the National Science Foundation, grant number BNS-9200674. Stanwyn Shetler of the Missouri Botanical Garden provided the computer tape for the indispensable Flora North America data, for which I am deeply grateful. Nina Etkin commissioned this chapter; her comments materially improved it.

nontoxic and nutritious that . . . they have become the dominant plant species over vast regions of the temperate zones" (Moerman 1989:57).

At that point I compromised and noted that the Rosaceae family—which includes apples (*Pyrus*), pears, peaches, cherries, and almonds (all *Prunus*)—displays a sort of poisoned-apple syndrome: "Many members of the rose family produce nutritious and attractive fruits, as do the grasses; many species also produce quite toxic substances in the leaves, bark and pits" (Moerman 1989:57). But the general point I was making was that this family was an exception. I did not back away from the more general notion that foods and drugs were discontinuous categories, even though I had ample reason by then for doing so. Nina Etkin and Paul Ross, in a pioneering paper published in a book I coedited, had by 1983 described the medicinal value of wild foods collected by the Hausa of Nigeria. The demonstration was so ingenious and so unlikely, associating a reduced consumption of grains (high in vitamin E) and an increased consumption of leafy herbs, which apparently minimized plasmodial infections (all occurring just as the malaria season developed [Etkin and Ross 1983]), that it seemed it just could not be a general case. The same book contained a paper on dietary antibiotics (Keith and Armelagos 1983), and I was well aware of the antimalarial effects of fava beans.

It is clear enough that some foods have medicinal value; that is, like vitamins, they provide us with health-enhancing substances other than the calories and protein that we usually think of as nutritional. Nevertheless, some medicines are *not* foods: the example of chimpanzee ingestion of leaves from *Aspilia* is interesting precisely because it illustrates ingestion of a nonfood plant. Chimpanzees occasionally seek out the leaves of this otherwise neglected species, which they "eat" curiously, without chewing; the chimpanzees clearly eat them not for their "nutritional" value, since they are excreted largely whole (Glander [this volume]). *Aspilia* apparently contains active anthelmintics (Wrangham and Goodall 1987). Similarly, some foods are distinctly *not* medicines. While a few people are "allergic" to wheat or other grains (that is, the grains are biologically active for these people), their primary value as dietary staples derives precisely from their pharmacological neutrality for the great preponderance of people.

No wonder this is an ambiguous situation. I will try to provide an approach to the problem that will clarify these issues and give us a better grip on them.

In this chapter, I present a preliminary analysis of the food flora of North America as constructed by Native Americans and compare it to the medicinal flora of the same region. The medicinal flora described is, generally speaking, a census of the medicinal plants of native North America; it is for all intents a complete list of the plants used medicinally by Native Americans (Moerman

1991). The food plants described are a more tentative listing based on Harriet Kuhnlein and Nancy Turner's *Traditional Plant Foods of Canadian Indigenous Peoples* (1991) and on Elias Yanovsky's classic *Food Plants of the North American Indians* (1936). I have restricted these lists to those taxa that can be cross-referenced with the preliminary checklist of the Flora North America (FNA), which includes essential information about plant distribution and character (Shetler and Skog 1978). Of the 2,095 medicinal species listed in my catalog (Moerman 1986; published as *Medicinal Plants of Native America* [MPNA]), 1,901 occur in the FNA listing. Of approximately 1,117 food species considered by Kuhnlein and Turner, 946 appear in FNA; and of 1,112 species listed by Yanovsky, 854 appear in FNA. Combining Kuhnlein and Turner's list with Yanovsky's we find 1,424 different species of food plants used by Native Americans.

The entire North American flora as listed in the preliminary FNA catalog comprises 16,270 species that are, in this context, of four sorts. The largest portion by far (13,624; 84%) provided neither food nor medicine (whatever else we may say about the manner in which Native Americans traditionally used plants, we must always remember that as far as we know they were very selective in their use of the flora; most species were not used). Of the remainder, 1,222 (7.5%) were used only as medicines, 745 (5%) only as foods, and 679 (4%) as both foods and medicines. Of the 2,646 utilized flora, then, nearly half were used exclusively as medicines, while the remainder is split between those used exclusively as foods and those used for both purposes.

Note that these are very large numbers. Native Americans used many plant species for food. Most of these plants were not produced in gardens in the strict sense but were instead gathered from the "wild." What does this mean? There is ample evidence to allow one to suggest that foraging peoples manage the territories in which they gather food. They replant bits of gathered roots so the plant will regenerate. They regularly burn substantial areas in prairies to encourage the growth of desirable plants and animals and to prevent the accumulation of fuel that leads to destructive irregular hot fires (Lewis 1989). They manage extremely complex environments that to the untutored eye may seem to be "climax forest." "Few indigenous Amazonians are resource foragers. They are resource managers" (Balée 1989). The distinction between "wild" and "domesticated" plants is not clear, admitting instead a complex continuum. Most of the plants considered here probably lie somewhere in the middle of that continuum.

Regression Residual Analysis

These floras can be compared in two ways, by family and by habit of growth. Basic questions arise in making a comparison: How can we characterize the utilization of a flora? Which portions (if any) are more medicinal than others? Which portions are most likely (least likely) to be used as foods? For several reasons, this process is trickier than it might seem; the biggest problem is that the basic units of analysis—essentially, plant families—vary significantly in size. If we simply list the number of medicinal or food species by family, we find, unsurprisingly, that large families produce more than do smaller ones.

For example, the top three producers of medicinal species are Asteraceae (the sunflowers) with 304, Rosaceae (the roses) with 100, and Fabaceae (the beans) with 91. But these are very large families: Asteraceae has 2,231 species in the Flora North America checklist, Rosaceae 577, and Fabaceae 1,225. This suggests that the proportion of species, not the number, should be considered. However, seven small families in North America have only 1, 2, or 3 species, all of which were used medicinally; these families would be at the top of a list organized by percentage. In this arrangement, families that stood out in the first ordering are now lost in the crowd: Rosaceae is in the 75th position, Asteraceae is 87th, and Fabaceae is 124th. While a simple count of medicinal species overemphasizes large families, percentages or indices overemphasize small ones.

There are other problems. Neither the Acanthaceae (water willow family) nor the Zingiberaceae (the ginger family) has any medicinal species in North America; the two would share the same ranking on each of these lists (by count and by percentage, both zero on each list). There are, however, 65 species in the former family and only 1 in the latter in North America; it seems somehow more significant that Native Americans use none of the 65 Acanthaceae species than that they use none of the 1 Zingiberaceae species.

Nevertheless, researchers can effectively address these problems using the techniques of regression and residual analysis (Moerman 1991). Regression analysis, in effect, finds the one line closest to a set of data points. The three primary elements of a regression analysis are the intercept or constant (a), the coefficient or slope (b), and the correlation coefficient (r). The analysis generates a linear equation of the form $y = a + bx$, which allows us to predict the value of y given the value of x.

I subjected the data from MPNA and FNA to a regression analysis. The number of species per family used medicinally is regressed on the total number of species in each family according to FNA. The regression equation is MPNASPE

$$=1.3+.099x \text{ FNASPE}$$

where MPNASPE is the number of species from MPNA and FNASPE is the number of species from FNA. To predict the number of species used medicinally from a given family, then, multiply the number available by .099 and add 1.3. For the Asteraceae family, with 2,231 species, this equation predicts that 222 species of Asteraceae would be used medicinally. However, Native Americans actually used 305, many more than predicted. The difference between the predicted value and the actual value is called the residual and is a measure of the disproportionate use (or nonuse) of a particular taxon.

Figures 9.1 and 9.2 illustrate the data from the regression analysis for plant species having medicinal and food uses. In each graph, the residual is represented by the vertical distance between the actual data point and the regression line. The residual for Asteraceae on Figure 9.1 is 82, for example; the residual for Fabaceae is −31. The families can also be ranked by the size of their residual (Table 9.1). Asteraceae and Fabaceae appear first and last, respectively. The former is a major source of medicinal species, the latter is not. Similarly, the residual for Acanthaceae is −8, and for Zingiberaceae it is −1. They are no longer "tied." The small families with 100% usage also are no longer tied, and they now appear toward the middle of the list. (The complete data set on which this discussion is based is available on request of the author.)

Figure 9.1 displays the relationship between the total number of species in each family and the number of medicinal species in each family. Figure 9.2 displays the relationship between the total number of species in each family and the number of food species in each family. In a regression analysis, one seeks to determine if there is a relationship between two (or more) variables that can be measured. Is there a relationship between shoe size and income? Between family size and annual movie attendance? Between the amount of fertilizer applied and the yield per acre? Between femur length and stature? Typically, an investigator has a sample of a few dozen data points. If the variables exhibit a linear relationship (as in the femur/stature example), the data points, when graphed, will typically form a lens-shaped cloud, rising from lower left to upper right. In a negative relationship (car weight and miles per gallon), the cloud will range from upper left to lower right. The closer the relationship between the two variables (the higher the "correlation" between them) the narrower will be the cloud. Typically, too, the investigator wants to learn about these relationships to make *predictions:* having found a fossil femur, the investigator wishes to predict what the overall stature of this individual might have been (or, what might befall the movie industry as family size declines).

Like these typical cases, each data point here is a pair of numbers. What is the relationship between the size of a particular plant family (there are 232 in North America) and the number of those species that were used medicinally by Native Americans? Each data point on the graph in Figure 9.1 represents one pair of numbers. The total size of the family is plotted on the horizontal axis, and the number of medicinal species is on the vertical axis.

Here the regressions differ from the more normal situations. The medicinal plant data are, for all intents, a census of the data. Probably all but a handful of

Table 9.1 Number of Medicinal Species in Selected Families

Rank	Family	Medicinal Species	Total Species	Proportion Medicinal	Residual
1	Asteraceae	304	2,231	14%	81.8
2	Rosaceae	100	577	17%	41.6
50	Calycanthaceae	3	3	100%	1.4
63	Saururaceae	2	2	100%	0.5
79	Datiscaceae	1	1	100%	−0.3
142	Zingiberaceae	0	1	0%	−1.4
228	Acanthaceae	0	65	0%	−7.7
230	Fabaceae	91	1,225	7%	−31.3

Note: Families are ranked in order of residual, with families having similar residuals grouped together.

plants known to be used by Native Americans are represented in the data base. Were we to repeat the process of gathering the data, we would end up with essentially the same information as is reported here. The distance of a point from the regression line, then, is especially important information showing that the particular plant family (or habit group, or life form) is used much more, or much less, than is typical for other similar categories.

Analysis by Family

In Figure 9.1, we can see that Asteraceae (the sunflower family), Rosaceae (the rose family), and Lamiaceae (the mint family) lie well above the regression line and are therefore families that have a disproportionately large use as sources of medicines. Poaceae (the grass family), Cyperaceae (the rushes), and Fabaceae (the bean family) lie well below the line, showing that they are disproportionately small sources of medicines. In Figure 9.2, which shows the number of food species per family, Rosaceae and Liliaceae lie well above the regression line; they are substantial food producers. By contrast, Asteraceae, which is far above the line in the drug regression, here is very near the line, showing that while it produces many drugs, it produces only a few foods. Poaceae (the grasses) and Cyperaceae (the rushes) retain their positions well below the line on both graphs.

Figure 9.3 illustrates a further level of abstraction. From the two regression analyses shown in Figures 9.1 and 9.2, each of the 232 plant families can be

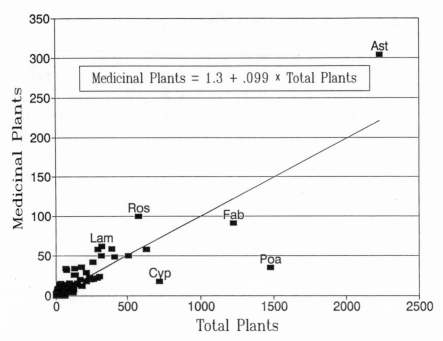

Figure 9.1. Regression of number of medicinal species on total species per family.

characterized by two residual values. The first residual describes the distance from the regression line on the drug regression analysis, while the second describes the distance from the line on the food regression analysis. Figure 9.3 plots those two values: the drug residual on the horizontal axis, the food residual on the vertical axis. A family that produces many drugs will be toward the right side of the graph (like Asteraceae); a family that produces few will be toward the left. A family that produces many foods will be toward the top of the graph (like Rosaceae); a family that produces few will be toward the bottom (like Poaceae). We can place these families into four categories exhibited in quadrants:

Top right, families that produce large numbers of both foods and medicines
Bottom left, families that produce few foods and medicines
Bottom right, families that produce medicines but not foods
Top left, families that produce foods but not medicines

We will consider each quadrant in turn. The plant families that are the sources of both foods and medicines are in the upper right quadrant. Notice the pattern of the graph: many families fall in the middle of the quadrant, good examples of the type, while only a few lie along the edges. Some important families of this type are Rosaceae (the roses), Liliaceae (the lilies, which includes the onions), Lamiaceae (the mints), Solanaceae (the nightshades), Apiaceae (the parsley family, which includes caraway and carrots), and Pinaceae (the pines).

Compare this with the lower right, the families that produce medicines but no foods. Asteraceae (the sunflowers) is the notable family here; it produces far more medicines than it does foods. Unlike the previous quadrant, however, there are no families out in the middle of the graph. There are only 30 families of this sort, and they hug the axes; there are no good examples of this type.

The shape of the distribution is similar in the upper left quadrant, the families that produce foods but no medicines. Again, the families hug the axes; there are no good examples of the type.

Consider the last quadrant, the lower left, which shows the families that are disproportionately small producers of both foods and medicines. This graph mirrors the upper right, albeit exhibiting only two examples out in the middle (more than the other quadrants). The two are the grasses (Poaceae) and the grasslike plants or sedges (Cyperaceae). This seems paradoxical. The grass family, as I have already noted, is the primary source of human foods—the grains (wheat, corn, barley, etc.). This discrepancy points out the difference between the volume of food produced and the variety of species eaten: people derive the vast proportion of their food (and feed grains) from a very few species.

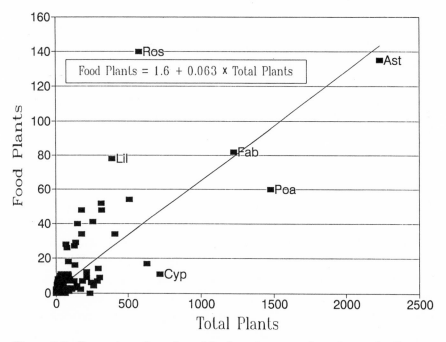

Figure 9.2. Regression of number of food species on total species per family.

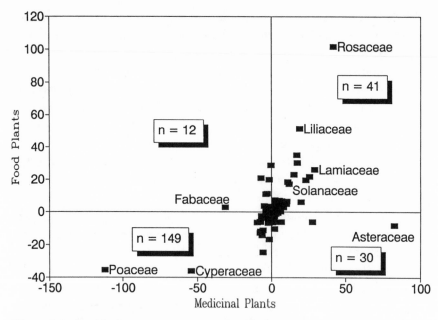

Figure 9.3. Residuals on two regressions by family.

In the most general terms, the pattern of few families in the upper left and lower right quadrants shows that if a family produces very few medicinal species, it will also produce very few food species (with the exception of Fabaceae); similarly, if a family produces many medicinal species, it will produce many food species (with the exception of Asteraceae).

The most striking and unexpected thing about this analysis is the substantial overlap of families in the upper right quadrant of Figure 9.3. That quadrant includes only 23% of the North American plant species but 41% of the medicinal species and 52% of the food species. A few of these families deserve closer attention.

Rosaceae

The rose family is a source of a broad range of both foods and medicines. Of 577 North American species in this family, 140 were used as foods by Native Americans, 100 as medicines, and 60 for both purposes. The medicinal uses are incredibly broad and range over the entire list of human ailments. For example, members of this family were used as cough and cold remedies (many commercial medicines today are "flavored" with cherry, one of the important members of this family; but the medicinal value of these drugs is never attributed to the cherry!). They also were applied externally on wounds and sores and were taken internally for parasites, as antidiarrheals, and for rheumatism. One member of the family, the genus *Spiraea*, produces methyl salicylate, a chemical precursor of aspirin; indeed, aspirin is named after *Spiraea*. Most of the naturally occurring salicylates seem to act as herbicides, deterring the growth of competing plant species.

The family is, of course, also an important source of a wide range of foods. Cherries, plums, rose hips, peaches, apples, prunes, apricots, nectarines, quinces, strawberries, raspberries, blackberries, loganberries, and almonds are among them.

The poisonous quality of this family is often not recognized, but it poses potential dangers. In addition to producing herbicides such as the salicylates, many species produce amygdalin that, when mixed with water, decomposes to produce prussic or hydrocyanic acid, a potentially lethal poison similar to cyanide. People have died from eating apple pits; livestock have suffered serious and occasionally fatal poisoning from eating chokecherry leaves; eight or nine bitter almond nuts are fatal for children, and three can cause severe cyanide poisoning (Bodin and Cheinisse 1970). Amygdalin and other toxins produced by other genera in this family probably inhibit sustained browsing by insects.

Liliaceae

The Liliaceae family contains a broad range of common ornamental flowers, notably the lilies, daylilies, and hostas. The family, with 393 North American species, clearly displays the overlap of food and drug species. Fifty-nine species were used as drugs, 78 as foods, and 39 for both purposes. The genus *Allium*, the onions, shows the same pattern: of 79 North American species, 14 were used as foods, 10 as drugs, and 8 for both purposes. The family contains two extremely poisonous species, the false hellebores (*Veratrum* spp.) and the death camas (*Zigadenus* spp.). A particularly interesting medicine from this family is the toxic alkaloid colchicine derived from the meadow saffron, *Colchicum autumnale*, long used as a highly effective treatment for gout. Plant breeders use the same alkaloid to induce genetic mutations in seeds as a source of new varieties (Claus et al. 1970:289; Deysson 1976).

Lamiaceae

The mint family Lamiaceae is also widely used for both food and medicine. There are 320 species in North America, of which 48 were used for food, 62 for drugs, and 29 for both purposes. Native Americans made the leaves of many species into aromatic "teas," and peoples of the Northwest Coast ate the roots of several species (Kuhnlein and Turner 1991:210–213). Most of the many medicinal uses were to alleviate pain, various lung conditions, colds, and headaches. The family produces a wide range of aromatic volatile oils, among them menthol and thymol. Several of these have been shown to reduce browsing by slugs and insects.

Solanaceae

The Solanaceae or nightshade family is unusual in that it produces many medicines, but also what we think of as a "staple food," the potato (*Solanum tuberosum*). Of 129 North American species in this family, 27 were used as foods, 26 as medicines, and 14 as both. Several of the food species are still widely utilized, such as tomatoes, chili and bell peppers, and eggplant. Drugs from the Solanaceae family include the alkaloids scopolamine, atropine, and hyoscyamine from a variety of toxic plants such as nightshade, mandrake, henbane, and jimsonweed, not to mention tobacco with its fascinating alkaloid nicotine. Timothy Johns, in an important book (1990) and in a chapter in this volume, discusses the implications of the human use of this complex and interesting family. He argues that potato toxicity increases crop yields but requires complex processing by human beings to enhance edibility (Johns 1990).

Summary of Families

These examples might be multiplied, but the point seems clear. Many food species come from families that produce highly toxic substances, and many food species themselves are toxic. This pattern of toxic characteristics has several consequences. At a formal level, it means that the list of food plants substantially overlaps that of drug plants. It also suggests that foods that are in some way toxic may be more reliable as part of a food supply than nontoxic ones: eating toxic foods might be better in the long run than eating no foods. It also implies an ecological foundation for the origins of cuisine in the sense of "an assortment of foods and a style of cooking" that is unique to each culture (Bogin 1991:161).

Analysis by Growth Habit

In addition to comparing these floras by family, we can characterize them by growth habit, whether grasses, forbs, shrubs, trees, ferns, and so forth. About 65% of North American plants are forbs, that is, herbaceous, nonwoody plants that are not grass or grasslike. Both medicinal and food species exhibit a similar proportion of forbs: 65% of 1,901 medicinal species, and 56% of 1,424 food species.

Each of the habit groups varies to some extent from its predicted values, as demonstrated by the residuals of two additional regression analyses plotted on Figure 9.4. The unit of analysis here is not the plant families but the plant growth habits. For example, according to FNA there are 984 species of trees in

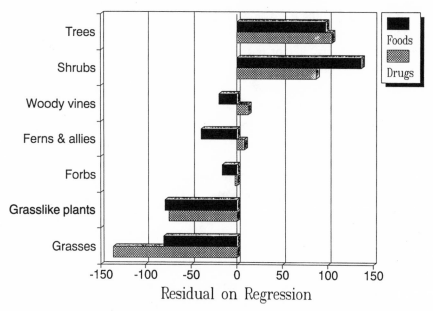

Figure 9.4. Residuals on two regressions by habit group.

North America. Of them, 201 produce drugs used by Native Americans; 217 produce foods. Similar data from the other six habit groups allow two regression analyses. The first shows, as has the previous analysis of families, that the grasses and rushes produce few drug species (Figure 9.4). This replication occurs because the plant habit and the taxonomy are the same. What is surprising is that there are so many medicinal trees and shrubs, something not at all evident to casual observation. What is even more surprising is that the regression residuals for the food regression take on almost exactly the same pattern as for the drug regression. The only apparent difference is that there are more food shrubs than medicinal shrubs. But the similarity of the food and drug pattern is the most obvious conclusion here.

Why trees? I have suggested elsewhere that, with respect to medicines, the underlying principle accounting for this distribution might have something to do with the complexity of plants (Moerman 1991). A tree with wood, bark, cambium, branches, leaves, seeds, roots, and so forth appears more complex than an herb such as plantain or a sunflower. The intermediate position of shrubs and vines seems reasonable here. All of those habit groups appear more complex than grass in the sense of number of distinct parts.

One may predict that more complex plants, with more parts to defend, would produce more defensive, biologically active chemicals that might be medicinally useful; this should be a testable proposition if one had the correct data set (which I do not). However, the most interesting and surprising attribute of the preceding regression analyses is that the pattern is generally the same for the food plants as for the medicinal plants. This suggests that people have, over millennia, sought out as foods those species that were likely to contain disproportionate quantities of secondary chemicals, many of which are poisonous.

Another factor may also be involved. Trees are by nature large and therefore easily seen, while forbs and grasses might be large but often are not. The sample may be biased toward trees because they are easy to find, examine, and find again "next season."

The practical principle here is, if you are looking for medicines, look first to trees and shrubs, then to vines and forbs, and last to grasses. Do the same for foods.

Analysis by Life Form

For most taxa in FNA, one can determine a life form; in particular, one can separate annuals from the rest, most of which can be designated perennial or biennial. Since the categories are of the same order of magnitude, one need not do a regression analysis but can simply compare the two groups.

Of the 16,270 medicinal and nonmedicinal plants listed in FNA, substantially fewer annuals are selected for medicines (253 medicinal species out of 3,484 annuals, or 7.3%) compared to the remainder (1,648 medicinal species out of 12,786, or 14.3%). I account for this difference in the same way as the differences relating to growth habit. Indeed, sorting species into life forms is in part redundant, since "annual tree" is an oxymoron (no species are so listed in the FNA checklist). Biennial or perennial plants are more complex than annual ones; ordinarily they can do all that annuals do, yet they can also survive for more than one year. For that reason, I suggest that they are more likely than annuals to produce biologically active chemicals to protect themselves against predators or competitors (this again is a potentially testable proposition if one had the appropriate data set, which, again, I do not). Furthermore, perennials must be adapted to long-term fluctuations in the incidence or severity of such threats as browsing, prepared for the most withering attack. Again, similar to the ease of studying larger plants in analyses by growth habit, people probably find it generally easier to study and experiment with perennials than annuals.

Although not as great, the pattern of difference in life form is the same for foods as for medicines: 227 (6.5%) of annuals are used as foods, compared to 1,197 (9.4%) of longer-lived species. Again, people seem to prefer to eat species that could be expected to have more than their share of biologically active secondary chemicals.

Conclusions

Many sources of medicines (be they sorted by family, growth habit, or life form) are also sources of foods. However, some sources of foods produce few medicines.

One may wish to recognize different kinds of vegetable foods. Some—like wheat—that are primarily sources of energy and are eaten in quantity generally produce very low levels of secondary chemicals and are commonly distinct from medicines. Some—like potatoes or manioc—are also sources of energy (and are eaten in quantity) but may in addition have heavy loads of secondary chemicals (perhaps making them more pest resistant and therefore producing higher yields). These will require complex processing (or agronomy) to make them edible in quantity; they will probably not be collected as "wild" plants but rather produced in some system of agriculture.

Many additional foods will be eaten largely because of their important secondary chemicals in addition to their more ordinary "nutritional" elements. There are orders of magnitude more of this type of food than of the others.

At a minimum, the situation is complex. On the one hand, Native Americans used many food plants, probably many more than in modern diet. On the other hand, they were very selective; they used only a small minority of the available species. Of the food species, some are quite nontoxic. But many are highly toxic, and for a variety of reasons: some toxins are insecticides or other substances that inhibit browsing, while some are herbicides that inhibit the growth of plant competitors. Other toxins are substances that retard evaporation of water, especially in desert regions.

The human strategy for dealing with these toxins is similarly complex. As one approach, especially under domestication, people have in some situations selected for nontoxic strains, possibly paying the price of smaller yields along with increased needs for weeding, fertilizing, applying insecticides, and the like—in a phrase, developing complex agronomies. Alternatively, they have developed complex processes for detoxifying foods: the classic case is manioc, but there are many others where nothing more complex than simple cooking renders toxic foods much more palatable. (From an evolutionary perspective, "simple cooking" is an oxymoron. For example, people simply could not eat raw, unground wheat in any significant quantity no matter how nutritious and nontoxic it might be; indeed, without appropriate technology for grinding and cooking, neither wheat nor corn would probably have been domesticated.) People often seem to have sought out and "eaten" these toxic substances in the same sorts of small quantities that they would have used had they "taken" them as medicines (the emic character of the verbs and their cultural origins are suggested by the quotation marks). The regular inclusion in prepared foods of small quantities of highly flavored spices is one form this may take. Many, probably most, of the herbs and spices in a contemporary kitchen cupboard were formerly or elsewhere used overtly as medicines; parsley, fennel, caraway, mint, sage, and ginger are common examples.

This analysis underscores the traditional reliance of Native Americans on a broad range of plant species providing various secondary chemicals as well as other nutritive components. Our contemporary reliance on a narrow range of foods (notwithstanding the aforementioned herbs and spices) may be too restrictive, failing to provide useful chemical compounds, a possibility on which many other researchers have commented (see Bogin 1991 for a review). The substitution of synthetic medicines and vitamins may or may not make up the loss.

REFERENCES

Balée, William
   1989   The culture of Amazonian forests. *Advances in Economic Botany* 7:1–21.
Bodin, F., and C. F. Cheinisse
   1970   *Poisons.* McGraw-Hill, New York.
Bogin, Barry
   1991   The evolution of human nutrition. In *The anthropology of medicine: From culture to method* [Second edition], edited by L. Romanucci-Ross, D. E. Moerman, and L. R. Tancredi, pp. 158–195. Bergin and Garvey, New York.
Claus, E. P., V. E. Tyler, and L. R. Brady
   1970   *Pharmacognosy* [Second edition]. Lea and Febiger, Philadelphia.
Deysson, G.
   1976   Microtubule inhibitors. *European Journal of Toxicology and Environmental Hygiene* 9:259–270.
Etkin, Nina L., and Paul J. Ross
   1983   Malaria, medicine and meals: Plant use among the Hausa and its impact on disease. In *The anthropology of medicine: From culture to method* [First edition], edited by L. Romanucci-Ross, D. E. Moerman, and L. R. Tancredi, pp. 231–259. Bergin and Garvey, New York.
Johns, Timothy
   1990   *With bitter herbs they shall eat it: Chemical ecology and the origins of human diet and medicine.* University of Arizona Press, Tucson.
Keith, Margaret, and George J. Armelagos
   1983   Naturally occurring dietary antibiotics and human health. In *The anthropology of medicine: From culture to method* [First edition], edited by L. Romanucci-Ross, D. E. Moerman, and L. R. Tancredi, pp. 221–230. Bergin and Garvey, New York.

Kuhnlein, Harriet V., and Nancy J. Turner

    1991   *Traditional plant foods of Canadian indigenous peoples: Nutrition, botany and use.* Gordon and Breach Science Publishers, Philadelphia.

Lewis, Henry T.

    1989   Ecological and technological knowledge of fire: Aborigines versus park rangers in northern Australia. *American Anthropologist* 91:940–961.

Moerman, Daniel E.

    1979   Symbols and selectivity: A statistical analysis of Native American medical ethnobotany. *Journal of Ethnopharmacology* 1(2):111–119.

    1986   *Medicinal plants of Native America.* University of Michigan Museum of Anthropology Technical Reports, No. 19. Ann Arbor.

    1989   Poisoned apples and honeysuckles: The medicinal plants of native America. *Medical Anthropology Quarterly* 3:52–61.

    1991   The medicinal flora of native North America: An analysis. *Journal of Ethnopharmacology* 31(1):1–42.

Shetler, S., and L. E. Skog

    1978   *A provisional checklist of species for Flora North America.* Monographs in Systematic Botany, Vol. 1. Missouri Botanical Garden, St. Louis.

Smith, H. H.

    1932   Ethnobotany of the Ojibwe Indians. *Bulletin of the Public Museum of the City of Milwaukee* 4:327–525.

Wrangham, R. W., and J. Goodall

    1987   Chimpanzee use of medicinal leaves. In *Understanding chimpanzees.* Chicago Academy of Sciences, Chicago.

Yanovsky, Elias

    1936   *Food plants of the North American Indians.* United States Department of Agriculture, Miscellaneous Publication 237. Washington, D.C.

❧ *Wild Plants in Prehistory*

10

Interpreting Wild Plant Foods
in the Archaeological Record

❧ FRANCES B. KING

Assessing the importance of wild foods in the diets of prehistoric peoples depends largely on the plant remains recovered from archaeological sites. Ethnologists have documented the historic use of many other plants; for example, Elias Yanovsky (1936) listed more than 1,100 plants used by North American Indians. However, investigators often ignore the role of wild plants in the aboriginal diet either because researchers have not documented nutritional information for a plant or because they have identified no archaeological evidence for its prehistoric use.

In many parts of the world, early human populations not only were apparently healthier than those living after the development of agriculture but also expended less energy in obtaining food (Harlan 1992:4–12, 27). Early non-agricultural diets appear to have been high in minerals, proteins, vitamins, and trace elements and relatively low in starch. As cultures developed plant cultivation, they placed a growing emphasis on starchy, highly caloric foods of high productivity and storability that would effectively have increased the carrying capacity of their geographic area but also promoted a decline in nutritional quality (Roosevelt 1984:568).

The development of agriculture often drastically affected more than diet. The clearance of forest lands for fields accelerated as diet became more secure and human populations expanded. Concomitantly, as habitat was destroyed, the availability of wild plant resources within relatively easy access decreased. Larger populations led to increasingly localized collector territories as well as escalating conflict and warfare, which in turn confined foraging to even smaller, better protected areas that often included little more than agricultural fields.

Tremendous changes occurred in the relationship between people and the environment as the level of human usage rose from casual exploitation to intense manipulation and management. Evidence of the speed and course of those changes can be found in many aspects of the archaeological record, but it is often fragmentary and enigmatic.

The Preservation of Archaeobotanical Remains

Many factors influence the preservation and subsequent recovery of material in archaeological sites. Some of these, such as the durability of various types of plant remains, remained unchanged through time while others, such as processing methods, evolved along with human culture. The significance of this variability is that the application of archaeological plant data to questions of cultural process requires the formulation of methods that minimize problems of differential preservation (Pearsall 1983). For example, preservability varies greatly among various plant materials depending on density and composition and is mediated by such characteristics of the physical environment as acidity, hydration, and microbial contamination.

Differential Preservation of Plant Parts

Saps and Nectars. Carbohydrate-rich plant secretions and circulating fluids leave no archaeological record, forcing us to draw inferences from historical and other accounts regarding what dietary roles these energy sources may have played in prehistoric subsistence. For example, India and the eastern tropics have a long tradition in the palm sugar industry, harvesting the sap of several palm genera (e.g., *Borassus* spp., *Phoenix* spp., *Arenga* spp., and *Cocos* spp.). Other peoples directly consume the nectars of various plants (e.g., South African honey-flowers, *Melianthus* spp. and *Protea* spp.) (Schery 1972). Central American groups ferment the exuded sap of agave (*Agave* spp.) into *pulque*, a beverage prized by the Aztecs but used today primarily as a precursor of tequila. In North America, a lack of archaeobotanical remains has not prevented a hot debate over the origin of the use of maple (*Acer saccharum*) sap (Holman 1984, 1986; Holman and Egan 1985; Mason 1985, 1986, 1987). One investigator attempted to end the controversy by suggesting that sap was collected and boiled to remove some of the water but that it could not be stored or transported and use was necessarily therefore limited (Munson 1989). Several possible maple sugar camps have been identified on the basis of topographic location, forest type, site organization, and artifactual remains (Holman 1984; Kingsley and Garland 1980; Pendergast 1974). One can only speculate regarding how the saps and nectars of wild plants might have contributed to the diets of prehistoric peoples.

Greens (Leaves, Herbaceous Plants). In view of their relatively high vitamin and mineral content, and easy access and collectibility during the growing season, herbaceous plants and the leaves of woody taxa are important dietary constituents with respect to both nutritional quality and food quantity. Unfortunately, their high water content makes preservation a rare occurrence, and evidence of their prehistoric use seldom appears in archaeobotanical assemblages. However, pollen of both food and medicinal plants may be present in coprolites if the flowers were ingested (Holloway and Bryant 1986; Reinhard et al. 1991), as may phytoliths and plant cuticles.

Roots, Tubers, Corms, Bulbs. These various underground structures all store carbohydrates in relatively large amounts and were potentially important energy sources for prehistoric peoples. Although many (e.g., manioc, *Manihot esculenta;* yams, *Dioscorea* spp.; potatoes, *Solanum* spp.) require detoxification (Johns 1990; Johns and Kubo 1988), others can be eaten with only minimal processing. These food resources are predictable and stable, available at any time of the year, and most roots and tubers can be easily vegetatively propagated; for these reasons, tropical "vegeculture" could potentially have predated seed agriculture (Harlan 1992:132). Unfortunately, because of their high water content and a tendency to become amorphous and friable when carbonized, roots and tubers are rarely found in archaeological sites, and the antiquity of their use is poorly represented by features such as earth ovens or the remains of processing tools such as manioc graters.

Fleshy Fruit. Because fleshy fruits have evolved to disperse seed, they tend to have attractively packaged, sweet and juicy flesh surrounding a seed that is either well protected and capable of surviving an animal's digestive system or too large to ingest. Although the fleshy portion of the fruit is seldom preserved in archaeological sites, the seed (or its enclosing structure) is often durable enough to survive in such contexts. Archaeobotanists may recover small seeds (e.g., grapes, *Vitis* spp.; raspberries, *Rubus* spp.) consumed with the fruit from somewhat different contexts than larger seeds (e.g., plum, *Prunus* spp.; mango, *Mangifera indica*) that are discarded before the fruit is eaten or those of fruits whose seed kernels are more valued than the pulp (almond, *Prunus amygdalus;* holly-leaved cherry, *Prunus ilicifolia*) (Timbrook 1982). Archaeologists may find their interpretation confounded by fruits such as those of squashes and pumpkins (*Cucurbita* spp.) from whose seed remains one cannot discern whether the plant was collected or grown for flesh, seeds, or both (F. King 1985:77–78).

Starchy or Oily Seeds. Most flowering plants produce seeds; although many are to some degree toxic and may require detoxification (e.g., rapeseed, *Brassica rapus;* chocho, *Lupinus mutabilis*), most can be eaten. Annual species are more likely to produce economically significant quantities of seeds than are perennial species, and the endosperm composition is dominated by either starches (e.g., maize, *Zea mays;* wheat, *Triticum* spp.; rice, *Oryza* spp.; beans, *Phaseolus* spp.) or oils (e.g., sunflower, *Helianthus annuus;* sesame, *Sesamum indicum*). Because these seeds are small, compact, and easily stored for long periods, and because they tend to be more palatable and nutritious when cooked (during which process they may become carbonized), they often exist in archaeological assemblages. Their representation may vary, however, depending on processing and preparation methods.

Nuts. Nuts contain large amounts of oils and provide an easily stored source of food energy used widely throughout the world (e.g., almonds; walnuts, *Juglans* spp.; Brazil nuts, *Bertholletia excelsa;* macadamia nuts, *Macadamia integrifolia*). Despite their high food value, nuts contain minimal amounts of many important nutrients, including calcium and ascorbic acid, and are better used as a dietary adjunct than as a staple (Keene 1981:188; Watt and Merrill 1963:34). Although nutmeats preserve poorly and are uncommon in archaeological sites, archaeologists commonly find nutshell debris, which provides fuel (Renfrew 1973:154–160; Talalay et al. 1984).

Barks and Woods. Food reserves manufactured by woody plants are transported by phloem cells in the inner bark. Rich in proteins and carbohydrates, these cells are thickest early in the growing season when tree tissues are differentiating; they are also relatively more abundant in young shoots than in older stems. Because tree growth begins at a time when most other plant foods are scarce, bark and young twigs were important foods among many historic groups and, one may presume, among prehistoric groups as well. In North America and Europe, indigenous peoples used the bark of several taxa (e.g., maples, *Acer* spp.; pines, *Pinus* spp.; elms, *Ulmus* spp.; lime or basswood, *Tilia* spp.) to produce "bark bread," and people with gastric disorders still use the bark of slippery elm (*Ulmus rubra*) as a highly nutritious and digestible food (Dimbleby 1967:30, 137–138; Yanovsky 1936). Although bark is readily preserved when carbonized, the remains of dietary bark in archaeological sites are undoubtedly obscured by bark remains associated with wood used for fuel. This would be especially true when a single species serves both purposes; the stripping of bark for food would shortly result in the presence of dead wood suitable for fuel. The relative paucity of bark in the diets of historic and contemporary populations used as the models for reconstructions of prehistoric plant use would also bias archaeological interpretations of the use of bark in diet (Kuhnlein and Turner 1991).

Processing Techniques

People process foods to reduce the amount of extraneous plant material, remove toxins, prepare food for storage or transportation, or enhance culinary enjoyment (Stahl 1989:172). Changes in food processing that reduce either the amount of fiber (thus increasing time in the intestine) or the particle size (thus increasing absorption of nutrients) provide an opportunity for intensification of subsistence that is independent of resource quantity (Stahl 1989:172). The methods employed in plant food processing (grinding, pounding, grating, soaking, leaching, fermentation, drying, heating) have important implications both for dietary quality and for the likelihood of plant remains being preserved in the archaeological record. A modification in processing or cooking such as a shift from baking on a hearth to boiling in a vessel may profoundly affect not only the nutritional value of the prepared food but also the presence of remains in the archaeological record (Buikstra et al. 1986).

Preparation or Consumption Location

The location at which food is processed is also important for its preservation and recovery. Archaeobotanists are more likely to discover and study food remains if the inhabitants of the study site consistently performed plant processing in an established area and incorporated refuse into a single large midden rather than leaving it at the collection point. In addition, an unknown, variable, and potentially large portion of the diet might consist of foods casually picked and eaten in the course of hunting or foraging. Although such foods may have formed a significant portion of the diet during certain seasons, they may also have been considered too perishable, too scarce, or too low in food value to carry home (Pulliam 1981). As a result, they may be absent from the archaebotanical record of primary habitation sites (other than possibly in coprolites), further biasing the record toward an illusionary low diversity of plant foods and types available during certain seasons.

Preservation Environment

Several very different types of environments share the characteristic of preserving uncarbonized organic remains by limiting chemical and microbial activity. Dry caves, rockshelters, and protected sites in arid climates produce some of the best-preserved material in the world (Fritz 1986; Gilmore 1931; Watson and Yarnell 1966). Preservation of organic material is also excellent in wet sites where deposits have been continually saturated and free from oxidation and bacterial action (Doran et al. 1990; Glob 1969; Kay et al. 1980). Organic remains may also be preserved in permanently frozen arctic and high alpine environments.

The poorer preservation environments of more humid areas require that material be carbonized or in association with an antimicrobial material such as copper (Heckenberger et al. 1990; Janaway 1985). Carbonization may either be purposeful (as in the burning of wood, nutshells, maize cobs, and other material as fuel or the discarding of food debris into a hearth or fire pit) or accidental (such as spillage, breakage of vessels, etc). At sites where both carbonized and uncarbonized remains are preserved, the two assemblages are often strikingly different and indicate the biased record presented by carbonized remains (King 1980).

Recovery Techniques

Our understanding of prehistoric plant use has changed radically over the past several decades simply because of improved sampling and processing techniques. In particular, the use of water flotation and finer screen mesh has allowed for the recovery of small-scale floral and faunal remains that investigators may overlook in hand excavation or lose while sieving with coarser screens (Struever 1968; Watson 1976). As a result, subsistence data from recent excavations are often far superior to those from most sites excavated prior to about 1965.

Advanced techniques today allow us to recover that small portion of plant material that meets a series of criteria: it must be relatively dense, collected in fairly large quantity, taken to a preparation site rather than processed in the field, and carbonized either before or after it was eaten or discarded. Conversely, we find little or no macrobotanical record for those plant materials that were less durable, were collected in small amounts, were eaten while hunting or foraging, or escaped carbonization.

Archaeological Evidence

Despite the many constraints acting on the preservation and recovery of archaeobotanical remains, archaeobotanists nevertheless (perhaps surprisingly) understand much about prehistoric plant use. This large body of current knowledge reflects an enormous amount of tedious and labor-intensive research coupled with creative research designs that circumvent the numerous problems. Researchers have employed many sophisticated methods to fill in the gaps and reconstruct prehistoric plant use; some of these, such as isotopic analysis of human skeletal remains, have become as important to understanding human subsistence as the analysis of macrobotanical remains themselves.

Macrobotanical Remains

The various factors affecting the preservation of plant materials often interact, further accentuating the apparent importance of some while only dimly reflecting the value of others. Table 10.1 lists types of plant foods, typical processing or preparation techniques, and the likelihood of finding botanical remains, diagnostic features, or utensils in archaeological contexts. This table clearly illus-

Table 10.1 Type of Plant Foods and Characteristic Archaeological Evidence Produced

Food	Processing	Features	Tools	Remains	Other
Sap (syrup)	boiling	+	−	−	context
Greens, buds, flowers	raw	−	−	−	−
	boiling	−	?	?	−
Roots	raw	−	−	−	−
	drying	−	−	−	−
	roasting	pit	−	?	−
	boiling	−	−	?	−
Fruit	raw	−	−	+	−
	drying	−	−	+	−
	boiling	−	−	+	−
Seeds	parching	?	+	+	−
	storage	?pit	+	+	−
	boiling	−	?pot	+	−
	grinding	−	+	+	−
	soaking	pit	?pot	+	−
Maize	parching	−	+	+	cobs
	storage	?pit	+	+	cobs
	boiling	−	?pot	+	cobs
	grinding	−	+	+	cobs
	roasting	?pit	−	+	cobs
Nuts	cracking	+	+	?	shell (pericarp)
	boiling	+	?pot	?	shell (pericarp)
	storage	pit	−	?	shell (pericarp)
	leaching	pit	?	?	shell (pericarp)
		bag	?	?	shell (pericarp)

Abbreviations: + = likely, ? = possible, − = unlikely

trates the problems caused by differential preservation and varying storage and preparation methods.

Although excluded from the table because they are nondiagnostic, hearths or fire pits are obviously the most common type of feature used in the preparation of food. Unfortunately, their construction and use are generic and multi-

purpose; archaeologists must base any interpretation of their use for the cooking of plant foods (rather than for heat, smoking hides, cooking meat, or heat-
treating lithic materials) on the recovery of plant or other remains. Combusti-
ble refuse such as maize cobs and nutshell debris is often present in hearth
features, indicating the probable importance of related foods in the diet. Wood
charcoal, by contrast, is ubiquitous and (although it may suggest environment,
catchment radius, wood preference, or the availability of potential plant foods)
is not in itself very informative about plants that might actually have been used
for food, including those with edible bark. Structures such as the earth ovens or
roasting pits used for some of the larger roots and tubers (Brown 1975:15) can be
more distinctive and therefore more informative.

Storage pits are another type of feature commonly associated with food.
With or without preserved remains, these indicate that the site inhabitants
were reserving something for future use and imply certain patterns of subsistence and site occupation. The most interesting and informative pit features are
those that burned after being filled or that were used for refuse disposal.

The most common type of utensil is vessels in which food could be stored,
soaked, fermented, or cooked. Such containers can be bark, stone, ceramic, or
metal; in addition, shape or composition may sometimes suggest the kinds of
food prepared or the preparation method (Stahl 1989:183). Unless a vessel
happens to break so that food spills into the fire, cooking in a container is less
likely to produce carbonized remains than cooking directly in the ashes. In the
midwestern United States, the abundance of seeds in archaeological sites dated
to after the development of efficient pottery cooking vessels suggests that the
site inhabitants were processing very large volumes of seeds or were using a
variety of cooking methods. Other commonly encountered utensils include
nutting stones, mortars and pestles, manos, and metates. Woven bags used for
gathering food, winnowing seeds, leaching, or other purposes are seldom recovered in more than fragmentary form.

Chemical Analyses

The application of accelerator mass spectrometry (AMS) to date minute samples heralded a recent expansion in the number of analysis methods that might
be applied to the study of prehistoric diet. Perhaps the most common new
technique is the use of stable carbon and nitrogen isotope ratios in human or
animal bone to determine the relative contributions of maize, beans, and marine foods to the diet (Schoeninger et al. 1983; Sillen et al. 1989; van der Merwe
and Vogel 1977). Numerous other methods being developed should enable
archaeobotanists and paleonutritionists to identify organic food residues on
cooking pots, grinding stones, and other artifacts (Hastorf and DeNiro 1985;
Hill and Evans 1989; Hillman 1989). The use of most of these techniques in the

reconstruction of past diets is still experimental and often problematic. The most serious obstacles to the development of such procedures are (1) the necessity of first compiling reference standards against which investigators can compare the residues for identification and (2) the destructiveness of these analyses, which, at least in the initial stages of development, require relatively large sample sizes (Hill and Evans 1989:421).

Coprolites

Coprolite analysis, although requiring special conditions for the preservation of fossil feces (such as in dry caves), is probably the best method of reconstructing diet because coprolites reflect the total diet as ingested. Seeds, nutshell, and wood charcoal inclusions are relatively easily identified and can often yield information about both diet and preparation techniques (Watson and Yarnell 1966). Other remains such as fruit skin or outer pericarp, leaves, roots, and bark may also be identifiable (Bryant 1974; Callen 1967a, b). Pollen and phytoliths may likewise be abundant and well preserved in coprolites. Analysis of parasite eggs in coprolites provides evidence of intestinal infestations that may also help in the reconstruction and interpretation of diet (Warnock and Reinhard 1992).

Pollen

Pollen, produced by virtually all flowering plants, is often genus or species specific (thus, readily identifiable when found in the archaeological record) and extremely long-lasting in environments shielding it from oxidation or microbial degradation (J. King 1985; King et al. 1975). Archaeological investigators have recovered pollen from various contexts including soils, lake and bog sediments, dry cave sediments, coprolites, adobe brick, and the residue on pottery or stone artifacts. People can ingest pollen intentionally by eating flowers or flower buds (in foods, beverages, or medicines) as well as inadvertently by consuming water or food on which pollen has settled or by inhaling pollen while processing plant materials (Reinhard et al. 1991). In addition to revealing dietary composition, analysis of coprolite pollen may yield information about seasonality and paleoenvironmental conditions (Bryant 1974; Bryant and Holloway 1983; Martin and Sharrock 1964).

Phytoliths

Phytoliths are resistant silica bodies that occur in the leaves, stems, and fruits of many kinds of plants and may be preserved in soils, clay, and daub; in crevices on the teeth of ungulates; and on the surface of stone tools or pottery vessels (Piperno 1988:114). Phytoliths vary tremendously in size, shape, and surface ornamentation; like pollen, many are genus or species specific. Pollen and phytolith analyses complement one another because they reflect differing aspects of the environment and of plant use. Pollen is generally more regional, while phytoliths are site specific; the two methods also differ in the level to which differing taxa can be identified. Although archaeobotanists apparently have made no attempt to recover phytoliths (distinct from nondiagnostic calcium oxalate plant crystals) from coprolites, this analysis technique may be possible (Piperno 1988:11, 114).

Other Indicators of Prehistoric Plant Use

Ecological Evidence

In the search for other types of information on prehistoric plant use, researchers have also moved beyond the area of the site. In regions subjected to minimal recent disturbance, relict populations of plants used by earlier people sometimes persist in the vicinity of archaeological sites (Harlan 1992; Hutterer 1983; Lundell 1938). For example, some food plant species in New Mexico are more common around prehistoric Pueblo Indian ruins than in adjacent undisturbed plant communities (Yarnell 1965). In Arizona, the majority of specimens of *Agave murpheyi* (agave) and all specimens of a previously undescribed *Agave* species are clearly associated with Hohokam fields or O'odham gardens (Delamater et al. 1989). Likewise, populations of ramón (*Brosimum alicastrum*) in the vicinity of Tikal, Guatemala, are atypical of the species, suggesting that the Maya may have practiced artificial selection (Peters 1983).

Ethnohistoric Accounts

Much of what we understand about prehistoric plant use is based on historic accounts by explorers, missionaries, anthropologists, and botanists—who have shared the assumption that, once established, plant use changed slowly. Many of the earliest observers were not trained in botany, and archaeobotanists may find it impossible to identify specific plants from their descriptions. This is unfortunate because historic plant use by native groups altered rapidly because of the incorporation of introduced foods into the diet and the abandonment of traditional foods. In eastern North America, for example, Native Americans apparently used marshelder (*Iva annua*) up to the time of European contact and then abruptly dropped the plant from their diet. The reconstruction of earlier prehistoric plant use is made more difficult because of (1) environmental changes that have occurred as a result of climatic shifts or human activity, (2) the evolution and transformation of human knowledge about useful plants, and (3) the replacement of wild with cultivated plant foods. Although researchers have produced many compilations of food plants used by the historic peoples, such as that by Yanovsky (1936) for North America, we lack even poor evidence about the early use of most plants. A few other sources also provide insights into the history of plant use, for example, linguistics (Munson 1973) and artistic depictions.

Optimal Foraging Models

Models derived from animal ecology and wildlife biology have also been successfully applied to the study of human plant use—for example, optimal foraging models of resource utilization (e.g., Krebs et al. 1974; MacArthur and Pianka 1966; Pulliam 1975) have aided in the interpretation of present or past hunter-gatherer subsistence (e.g., Cashdan 1990; Winterhalder 1990; Winterhalder and Smith 1981). Such assessments require understanding many aspects of diet and culture, including knowledge of the environment, distribution of various plant and animal resources, the energy involved in various harvesting and processing methods, the effects of processing on food value, and the total nutritional value of foods including not only protein, fat, and carbohydrate but also other nutrients present in significant amounts. Additional factors include resource aggregation (spatial concentration), ease of exploitation, nonfood yield, social value, taste, and changes in availability (Yesner 1981:163–167).

However, the application of optimal foraging models to reconstruct prehistoric human diet is considerably more difficult than the use of such models to interpret subsistence patterns of contemporary groups because so many values must be reconstructed or estimated rather than measured directly. Also, many of these may change through time because of climatic shifts, vegetational succession, disturbance, cultural evolution, shifting territories, and other factors. In particular, altered efficiency due to changes in abundance or in collecting and processing methods can significantly modify relative harvesting and processing costs (Stahl 1989). For example, we know of at least three ways to process hickory (*Carya* spp.) nuts, and two of these are approximately 17 times more efficient than the third (Ozker 1977; Talalay et al. 1984). If we assume that the study population used the less efficient method (bashing the nuts and picking out the nutmeats), then hickory nut utilization may appear to have been a poor subsistence strategy. However, if we instead assume that they employed one of the more efficient methods (throwing the mashed nuts into boiling water and skimming off the nutmeats or placing the pulverized nuts in the mouth and spitting out the shell fragments), then nuts become an optimum resource compared to other types of plant foods and we find it easier to understand why nuts are so common in archaeological sites in eastern North America (Watson and Yarnell 1966).

Medicinal Use

The number and diversity of medicinal plants used by indigenous peoples also reflect the evolution of human plant use. An enormous number of wild plants have pharmacological effects, and many of these were familiar to historic and contemporary peoples (Farnsworth 1992; Lewis and Elvin-Lewis 1977) as well as, presumably, to their prehistoric forebears. People may discover the medicinal properties of plants in the process of searching for edibles, especially in times of famine (Plowman 1984) or as a result of trial and error, guided perhaps by observable attributes that suggested a specific use (Etkin 1988). The use of a greater diversity of plants for medicine than for food by historic groups may reflect a wide variety of injuries and ailments that affected their prehistoric ancestors. Daniel Moerman (1986), for example, lists 2,147 species that historic groups in North America used for various medicinal purposes, while Yanovsky (1936) lists only 1,112 used for food. Although many of these plants had primarily magical or ceremonial value, they also contain compounds (secondary chemicals or allelochemicals) with important medicinal properties. When used in combination, as historic healers typically used them, their synergistic interactions may have enhanced their curative values over those of the same plants used alone.

Unfortunately, archaeobotanists find it nearly impossible to reconstruct the prehistoric use of plants for medicinal purposes, other than those plants found in specific contexts (e.g., medicine bundles) or those that were especially prominent such as tobacco (*Nicotiana* spp.), which was important socially as well as medicinally. Plant remedies consist typically of leaves, flowers, or roots used in small amounts and prepared in ways that do not lend themselves to preservation (e.g., infusions, poultices).

Nutritional Requirements

Studies of human nutritional requirements have implications for prehistoric diet and also help to interpret various types of deficiency diseases encountered in the archaeological record. Foods of animal origin provide complete protein and are important sources of several vitamins and minerals. However, protein is metabolically inefficient when processed by the human body, and the consumption of meat and protein may have an upper limit of safety, especially when other sources of calories (i.e., fats and carbohydrates) are lacking (Speth 1983). One researcher suggests that protein should constitute less than 50% of the diet and that no more than 1,200 kcal per person per day should be derived from meat (Speth 1983). Another researcher contends that prehistoric peoples in rich environments may have obtained 40 to 50% of their calories from meat with the amount falling to as low as 20% only in marginal, game-impoverished environments such as that of the modern San of southern Africa (Cohen 1989:170). An exception might be groups with relatively sophisticated high-meat diets, such as Inuit, that minimize the loss of nutrients such as vitamins

C, K, and E that occur at low concentrations in meat (Wing and Brown 1979:52–61).

Given the aforementioned data, at least half the diet of most prehistoric peoples was probably derived from plant foods. Although investigators have documented good evidence for heavy reliance on carbohydrate-rich plant foods by later prehistoric groups, the use of plant foods by Paleoindian hunters and other early peoples with highly mobile lifestyles remains speculative. Their use of plant foods was probably more opportunistic than that of later, more sedentary groups and probably included greater amounts of greens, seeds, fruits, and even nuts than is generally suggested by the archaeological record.

Botanical Characteristics

Plants themselves provide a good bit of information about their probable prehistoric use. Experimentation with new plant foods would most likely occur in times of food shortage or after prehistoric peoples entered unfamiliar environments. New plant foods would be selected, insofar as possible, for their similarity to plants already in the diet and their lack of resemblance to plants known to be distasteful or toxic. A good model for the adoption of wild plants might be the introduction of cultivated New World plants to Europe. Europeans quickly adopted maize, beans, squash, and chili peppers because of their similarity to already familiar Old World crops. Other crops such as potatoes, tomatoes, pineapples, and especially manioc were unlike anything then known in Europe, and Europeans accepted them with extreme reluctance (Davidson 1992).

Between 250,000 and 750,000 higher plants exist in the world. Of these, only about 3,000 have ever been important food plants and approximately 200 ever domesticated. Fewer than a dozen plant species feed most of the people in the world today, and the 4 major carbohydrate crops (wheat, rice, maize, and potatoes) feed more people than the next 26 most important crops combined (Heiser 1990:61; Plotkin 1988). Although food plants occur in practically every plant family, the important cultivated plant species contain only about 55 families, with the most important staples even more limited in distribution: the 3 most important crops in the world are grasses (wheat, rice, maize), as are 6 of the top 10 crops (Harlan 1992:57–78; Heiser 1990:61).

Gatherers around the world collect much the same types of plant foods: grass seeds, legumes, roots and tubers, oil plants, fruits and nuts, vegetables, and spices (Harlan 1992:11). Where families, genera, or species occur over a wide area, various peoples have often independently selected them for use as foods. One of many possible examples is that of wild yams (*Dioscorea* spp.), which include 50 to 100 species that are harvested in Africa, India, Southeast

Table 10.2 Important Crop Plant Families

Family	Crop Species	North American Species Used	Main Products
Fabaceae	41	69	pulses, tubers, edible pods
Poaceae	29	47	cereals, sugarcane
Solanaceae	18	26	fruits, spices, 1 tuber
Brassicaceae	13	27	leafy vegetables, oil, root crops
Rosaceae	11	102	mostly fruits
Liliaceae	11	90	edible bulbs
Apiaceae	9	42	spices and salad vegetables
Araceae	8	8	tubers

Asia, the South Pacific, Australia, and tropical America (Coursey 1972, 1976). The importance of specific families of food plants is shown in Table 10.2, which lists the number of crop species in the eight most important crop families (Harlan 1992:68), compared to the number of species in families used for food by the historic Indians of North America (Yanovsky 1936). Even this simple comparison of a few families illustrates that these families include many wild edible species that, for one reason or another, escaped being domesticated. A similar relationship would be apparent in comparisons between the important food plant families and the total diversity of food plants in any part of the world.

The 16 families for which Yanovsky listed at least 20 species are presented in Table 10.3. (Yanovsky's taxonomy was accepted for the table; some species may since have been reassigned.) These 16 families are 13% of the total of 120 families and 748 (67%) of the total of 1,112 species listed, even though some important North American aboriginal food plant families, such as Juglandaceae (walnut family), contain too few species to be included here. All of the families listed, and many subtaxa, have distinctive characteristics (e.g., leaves, flowers, growth form) by which they can be readily identified. They are all locally abundant, widely distributed, or both, and many thrive in disturbed habitats including those created by human activity. Although some of these families contain species that may be toxic if eaten in large quantities, few are actually fatal when ingested in small or moderate amounts (Kingsbury 1964). Those that are mildly poisonous can often be simply detoxified by leaching or heat treatment. The families that include species used as greens tend to have characteristically pungent flavors or odors (e.g., onion, mustard, mint) that promoted their use as flavorings as well as food. Most of these families were also important in the Old World, and many gave rise to at least one cultivated plant.

That people are not fastidious when hungry is underscored in Paul E. Minnis's (1991:232) list of only two minimal requirements for famine foods: they must be edible and they must be available when normal foods are not. Nevertheless, some characteristics are desirable in a food plant under more normal circumstances:

1. A good food source returns a relatively large amount of food energy for that expended in its collection and processing. Nutritional value correlates directly to the acceptable level of energy expended in the collection and preparation of a food resource. Although harvesting may require special tools (e.g., digging sticks), techniques, or scheduling, it should not conflict with the exploitation of other, more important resources that might be available at the same time.

2. A desirable food plant is readily recognized and widely available. It has characteristics making it easily distinguishable from superficially similar toxic species, and it either has a long season of availability or is storable.

3. A desirable food plant is palatable and nontoxic, or it can be detoxified and made palatable by cooking or other processing. However, the nutritive value must justify the amount of energy expended in processing.

4. A desirable food plant fills specific nutritional needs or complements other foods already in the diet. For example, a high-carbohydrate (grain) diet is improved by the addition of vegetable protein (legumes) and fats (nuts, sunflower seeds). Moreover, the proteins provided by the eating of grains and legumes together are complementary and the diet considerably improved over that consisting of either protein source eaten separately.

5. A desirable food plant provides a stable or predictable resource either seasonally or over the entire year. Disadvantages of nuts are that the quantity produced varies from year to year and that they are available at the same time as many other foods. In contrast, roots and tubers are available throughout the year even though the quality may decline during the growing season, a time when many other foods are normally available.

Conclusions

Plant foods formed the bulk of most prehistoric (and modern) human diets, as evidenced by the large number of important crop plants that were domesticated millennia ago. Unfortunately, we know relatively little about the evolution of human diet or about where and when specific plants might have been first used. The remains of some types of plant foods are seldom preserved,

Table 10.3 Important Food Plant Families of North America

Family	Morphology	Abundance	Distribution	Poisonous Members	Food	Availability
Rosaceae (102)* (Rose)	distinct	common	widespread: woods, prairie, edge	rare, occasionally seeds, leaves, or bark	succulent fruit	seasonal, can be dried and stored
Asteraceae (92) (Sunflower)	distinct	common	widespread: edge, prairie, disturbed	relatively few	oily seeds roots	seasonal all year
Liliaceae (90) (Lily)	distinct	common	widespread: forest, prairie	some extremely poisonous	bulbs berries	all year seasonal
Fabaceae (69) (Pea)	distinct	common	widespread: including disturbed	common, some can be detoxified with heat treatment	seeds roots/tubers	seasonal all year
Poaceae (47) (Grass)	distinct	common	widespread: esp. prairie, disturbed	rarely, some leaves	seeds	seasonal
Apiaceae (42) (Celery)	distinct	common: temperate	widespread: prairie, marsh, forest	some extremely toxic most not poisonous	seeds, leaves roots	seasonal, distinct flavor all year
Ericaceae (41) (Heath)	distinct	common: temperate	widespread: forest, bog	none	fruit	seasonal, can be dried & stored
Cactaceae (40) (Cactus)	distinct	often dominant	limited to desert	several hallucinogenic	fruit stems	seasonal all year

Family				Toxicity	Parts used	Seasonality
Pinaceae (33) (Pine)	distinct	common: temperate	widespread: forest	needles toxic in large quantities	seeds, bark	seasonal, all year
Chenopodiaceae (33) (Goosefoot)	distinct	common	widespread: esp. disturbed	none	seeds, greens	seasonal
Fagaceae (32) (Beech)	distinct	common: temperate	widespread: forest	mildly toxic, tannins and saponins may require detoxification	nuts	seasonal, can be stored
Lamiaceae (28) (Mint)	distinct	common	widespread: forest, prairie, disturbed	rarely	seeds, greens	seasonal
Brassicaceae (27) (Mustard)	distinct	common: temperate	widespread: alpine, disturbed	many toxic if large amounts eaten raw	leaves, seeds	seasonal, leaves have pungent taste
Grossulariaceae (26) (Currant)	distinct	common	widespread: forest, edge	none	fruit	seasonal, can be stored
Solanaceae (26) (Nightshade)	distinct	common	widespread	many poisonous, some psychoactive	fruit, tubers	seasonal, all year, may need detoxification
Portulacaceae (20) (Purslane)	distinct	common	widespread: esp. disturbed	rarely	roots, seeds	all year, seasonal

*Number of species listed in Yanovsky 1936

and the archaeological record is dominated by those plants that leave durable remains, especially those that produce burnable refuse.

The large number of plants used for food or medicine by historic groups illustrates that early peoples obviously had the occasion, and the need, to sample virtually every species. The use of optimal foraging models allows us to at least speculate about which plants may have been most desirable in any given environmental situation and forms a background against which to interpret prehistoric plant use as seen in the archaeological record.

Many other methods either are available or are being developed to enable archaeobotanists to study prehistoric diet. All are being continually refined and the possible applications constantly expanded. More significantly, investigators are becoming increasingly interested in the role of wild plant foods in the diets of early agricultural societies and in the relationship between dietary diversity, status, and health.

Contemporary diets largely comprise plant foods that people first chose to cultivate thousands of years ago because they fit specific lifeways. Ironically, although those primitive lifeways have in most cases evolved into something radically different, the food plants have generally changed very little. People have often sought wider distribution, increased yield, and decreased diversity in their food plants. Although the problem of identifying and protecting the ancestors of our modern crop plants is a subject of intense current concern, researchers have shown much less interest in nondomesticated plants. Advanced analytic technology and a sophisticated understanding of plant genetics mean that plant breeders now have a reservoir of many additional plants that could be developed for food, medicine, or other purposes, or that could contribute genetic material to the development of other plants. Because of the great number of plant species that exist in the world, understanding past and primitive plant use is a logical first step in exploiting the biodiversity still available in the modern world.

REFERENCES

Brown, Margaret K.
  1975   *The Zimmerman Site: Further excavations at the Grand Village of Kaskaskia.* Illinois State Museum Reports of Investigations No. 32. Springfield.
Bryant, Vaughn M.
  1974   The role of coprolite analysis in archeology. *Bulletin of the Texas Archeological Society* 45:1–28.
Bryant, Vaughn M., and Richard G. Holloway
  1983   The role of palynology in archaeology. *Advances in Archaeological Method and Theory* 6:191–224.

Buikstra, Jane E., Lyle W. Konigsberg, and Jill Bullington
1986   Fertility and the development of agriculture in the prehistoric Midwest. *American Antiquity* 51(3):528–546.

Callen, Eric O.
1967a   Analysis of the Tehuacan coprolites. In *The prehistory of the Tehuacan Valley.* Vol. 1, *Environment and subsistence,* edited by D. S. Byers, pp. 261–289. University of Texas Press, Austin.
1967b   The first New World cereal. *American Antiquity* 32:535–538.

Cashdan, Elizabeth [Editor]
1990   *Risk and uncertainty in tribal and peasant economies.* Westview Press, Boulder, Colorado.

Cohen, Mark N.
1989   *Health and the rise of civilization.* Yale University Press, New Haven.

Coursey, D. G.
1972   The civilizations of the yam: Interrelationships of man and yams in Africa and the Indo-Pacific region. *Archaeology and Physical Anthropology of Oceania* 7:215–233.
1976   Yams. In *Evolution of crop plants,* edited by N. W. Simmonds, pp. 70–74. Longman Scientific and Technical, Essex, England.

Davidson, Alan
1992   Europeans' wary encounter with tomatoes, potatoes, and other New World foods. In *Chilies to chocolate: Food the Americas gave the world,* edited by N. Foster and L. S. Cordell, pp. 1–14. University of Arizona Press, Tucson.

Delamater, G. L., Wendy Hodgson, and Gary Paul Nabhan
1989   Precolumbian agave cultivars rediscovered. *Journal of Ethnobiology* 9(2):238 (abstract).

Dimbleby, Geoffrey
1967   *Plants and archaeology.* Unwin Brothers, London.

Doran, Glen H., David N. Dickel, and Lee A. Newsom
1990   A 7,290-year-old bottle gourd from the Windover Site, Florida. *American Antiquity* 55(2):354–360.

Etkin, Nina L.
1988   Ethnopharmacology: Biobehavioral approaches in the anthropological study of indigenous medicines. *Annual Review of Anthropology* 17:23–42.

Farnsworth, Norman
1992   Screening plants for new medicines. In *Biodiversity,* edited by E. O. Wilson, pp. 83–97. National Academy Press, Washington, D.C.

Fritz, Gayle J.
1986   Prehistoric Ozark agriculture: The University of Arkansas rockshelter collections. Ph.D. dissertation, University of North Carolina at Chapel Hill. University Microfilms, Ann Arbor.

Gilmore, Melvin R.

1931   Vegetal remains of the Ozark bluff-dweller culture. *Papers of the Michigan Academy of Science, Arts, and Letters* 14:83–102.

Glob, P. V.

1969   *The bog people: Iron-age man preserved.* Ballantine Books, New York.

Harlan, Jack R.

1992   *Crops and man* [Second edition]. American Society of Agronomy and the Crop Science Society of America, Madison, Wisconsin.

Hastorf, Christine A., and Michael J. DeNiro

1985   Reconstruction of prehistoric plant production and cooking practices by a new isotopic method. *Nature* 315:489–91.

Heckenberger, Michael J., James B. Petersen, Louise A. Basa, Ellen R. Cowie, Arthur E. Spiess, and Robert E. Stuckenrath

1990   Early Woodland Period mortuary ceremonialism in the far northeast: A view from the Boucher Cemetery. *Archaeology of Eastern North America* 18:109–144.

Heiser, Charles B.

1990   *Seed to civilization: The story of food* [Second edition]. Harvard University Press, Cambridge, Massachusetts.

Hill, H. Edward, and John Evans

1989   Crops of the Pacific: New evidence from the chemical analysis of organic residues in pottery. In *Foraging and farming: The evolution of plant exploitation,* edited by D. R. Harris and G. C. Hillman, pp. 418–425. Unwin Hyman, London.

Hillman, Gordon C.

1989   Late Palaeolithic plant foods from Wadi Kubbaniya in Upper Egypt: Dietary diversity, infant weaning, and seasonality in a riverine environment. In *Foraging and farming: The evolution of plant exploitation,* edited by D. R. Harris and G. C. Hillman, pp. 207–239. Unwin Hyman, London.

Holloway, Richard G., and Vaughn M. Bryant

1986   New directions of palynology in ethnobiology. *Journal of Ethnobiology* 6(1): 47–65.

Holman, Margaret B.

1984   The identification of Late Woodland maple sugaring sites in the upper Great Lakes. *Midcontinental Journal of Archaeology* 9:63–89.

1986   Historic documents and prehistoric sugaring: A matter of cultural context. *Midcontinental Journal of Archaeology* 11:125–131.

Holman, Margaret B., and Kathryn C. Egan

1985   Processing maple sap with prehistoric techniques. *Journal of Ethnobiology* 5:61–75.

Hutterer, Karl L.

1983   The natural and cultural history of Southeast Asian agriculture: Ecological and evolutionary considerations. *Anthropos* 78:169–212.

Janaway, R. C.

1985   Dust to dust: The preservation of textile materials in metal artefact corrosion products with reference to inhumation graves. *Science and Archaeology* 27:29–34.

Johns, Timothy

1990   *With bitter herbs they shall eat it: Chemical ecology and the origins of human diet and medicine.* University of Arizona Press, Tucson.

Johns, Timothy, and Isao Kubo

1988   A survey of traditional methods employed for the detoxification of plant foods. *Journal of Ethnobiology* 8:81–129.

Kay, Marvin, Frances B. King, and Christine Robinson

1980   Cucurbits from Phillips Spring: New evidence and interpretations. *American Antiquity* 45:806–822.

Keene, Arthur S.

1981   Optimal foraging in a nonmarginal environment: A model of prehistoric subsistence strategies in Michigan. In *Hunter-gatherer foraging strategies: Ethnographic and archeological analyses,* edited by B. Winterhalder and E. A. Smith, pp. 171–194. University of Chicago Press, Chicago.

King, Frances B.

1980   Plant remains from Phillips Spring, a multicomponent site in the western Ozark highland of Missouri. *Plains Anthropologist* 25:217–228.

1985   Early cultivated cucurbits in eastern North America. In *Prehistoric food production in North America,* edited by R. I. Ford, pp. 73–97. University of Michigan, Museum of Anthropology, Ann Arbor.

King, James E.

1985   Palynological applications to archaeology: An overview. In *Archaeological geology,* edited by G. Rapp and J. A. Gifford, pp. 135–154. Yale University Press, New Haven.

King, James E., Walter E. Klippel, and Rose Duffield

1975   Pollen preservation and archaeology in eastern North America. *American Antiquity* 40:180–190.

Kingsbury, John M.

1964   *Poisonous plants of the United States and Canada.* Prentice-Hall, Englewood Cliffs, New Jersey.

Kingsley, Robert G., and Elizabeth B. Garland

1980   The DeBoer site: A late Allegan phase site in Allegan County, Michigan. *The Michigan Archaeologist* 26(1):3–44.

Krebs, J. R., J. Ryan, and E. L. Charnov

1974   Hunting by expectation or optimal foraging? A study of patch use by chickadees. *Animal Behavior* 22:953–964.

Kuhnlein, Harriet V., and Nancy J. Turner

1991   *Traditional plant foods of Canadian indigenous peoples: Nutrition, botany and use.* Gordon and Breach Science Publishers, Philadelphia.

Lewis, Walter H., and Memory P. F. Elvin-Lewis

   1977   *Medical botany: Plants affecting man's health.* John Wiley and Sons, New York.

Lundell, Cyrus L.

   1938   Plants probably utilized by the Old Empire Maya of Petén and adjacent low-
           lands. *Papers of the Michigan Academy of Science, Arts, and Letters* 24:37–56.

MacArthur, Robert H., and Eric R. Pianka

   1966   On optimal use of patchy environments. *American Naturalist* 100:603–609.

Martin, Paul S., and F. W. Sharrock

   1964   Pollen analysis of prehistoric human feces: New approach to ethnobotany.
           American Antiquity 30:168–180.

Mason, Carol I.

   1985   Prehistoric maple sugaring sites? *Midcontinental Journal of Archaeology* 10:
           149–152.

   1986   Prehistoric maple sugaring: A sticky subject. *North American Archaeologist*
           7:305–311.

   1987   Maple sugaring again: Or the dog that did nothing in the night. *Canadian
           Journal of Archaeology* 11:99–107.

Minnis, Paul E.

   1991   Famine foods of the northern American desert borderlands in historical
           context. *Journal of Ethnobiology* 11:231–257.

Moerman, Daniel E.

   1986   *Medicinal plants of Native America.* University of Michigan Museum of
           Anthropology Technical Reports, No. 19. Ann Arbor.

Munson, Patrick J.

   1973   The origins and antiquity of maize-beans-squash agriculture in eastern
           North America: Some linguistic implications. In *Variation in Anthropology:
           Essays in honor of John C. McGregor,* edited by D. W. Lathrap and J. Doug-
           las, pp. 107–135. Illinois Archaeological Survey, Urbana.

   1989   Still more on the antiquity of maple sugar and syrup in aboriginal eastern
           North America. *Journal of Ethnobiology* 9:159–170.

Ozker, Doreen B. V.

   1977   The nature of the Early Woodland adaptation in the Great Lakes region.
           Ph.D. dissertation, University of Michigan. University Microfilms, Ann
           Arbor.

Pearsall, Deborah M.

   1983   Evaluating the stability of subsistence strategies by use of paleoethnobotani-
           cal data. *Journal of Ethnobiology* 3(2):121–137.

Pendergast, James D.

   1974   The Sugar-bush site: A possible Iroquoian maple sugar camp. *Ontario Ar-
           chaeologist* 23:31–61.

Peters, Charles M.

   1983   Observations on Maya subsistence and the ecology of a tropical tree. *Ameri-
           can Antiquity* 48:610–615.

Piperno, Dolores R.
   1988   *Phytolith analysis: An archaeological and geological perspective.* Academic Press, New York.

Plotkin, Mark J.
   1988   The outlook for new agricultural and industrial products from the tropics. In *Biodiversity*, edited by E. O. Wilson, pp. 106–116. National Academy Press, Washington, D.C.

Plowman, Timothy
   1984   The ethnobotany of coca (*Erythroxylum* spp., Erythroxylaceae). *Advances in Economic Botany* 1:62–111.

Pulliam, H. Ronald
   1975   Diet optimization with nutrient constraints. *American Naturalist* 109:765–768.
   1981   On predicting human diets. *Journal of Ethnobiology* 1:61–68.

Reinhard, Karl J., Donny L. Hamilton, and Richard H. Hevly
   1991   Use of pollen concentrations in paleopharmacology: Coprolite evidence of medicinal plants. *Journal of Ethnobiology* 11:117–132.

Renfrew, Jane M.
   1973   *Palaeoethnobotany: The prehistoric food plants of the Near East and Europe.* Columbia University Press, New York.

Roosevelt, Anna C.
   1984   Population, health, and the evolution of subsistence: Conclusions from the conference. In *Paleopathology at the origins of agriculture*, edited by M. N. Cohen and G. J. Armelagos, pp. 559–593. Academic Press, New York.

Schery, Robert W.
   1972   *Plants for man* [Second edition]. Prentice-Hall, Englewood Cliffs, New Jersey.

Schoeninger, Margaret J., Michael J. DeNiro, and H. Tauber
   1983   Stable nitrogen isotope ratios of bone collagen reflect marine and terrestrial components of prehistoric human diet. *Science* 15:425–438.

Sillen, Andrew, Judith C. Sealy, and Nikolaas J. van der Merwe
   1989   Chemistry and paleodietary research: No more easy answers. *American Antiquity* 54(3):504–512.

Speth, John D.
   1983   *Bison kills and bone counts.* University of Chicago Press, Chicago.

Stahl, Ann B.
   1989   Plant-food processing: Implications for dietary quality. In *Foraging and farming: The evolution of plant exploitation*, edited by D. R. Harris and G. C. Hillman, pp. 171–194. London, Unwin Hyman.

Struever, Stuart
   1968   Flotation techniques for the recovery of small-scale archaeological remains. *American Antiquity* 33:353–362.

Talalay, Laurie, Donald R. Keller, and Patrick J. Munson

    1984   Hickory nuts, walnuts, butternuts, and hazelnuts: Observations and experiments relevant to their aboriginal exploitation in eastern North America. In *Experiments and observations on aboriginal wild plant food utilization in eastern North America*, edited by P. J. Munson, pp. 338–359. Indiana Historical Society, Indianapolis.

Timbrook, Jan

    1982   Use of wild cherry pits as food by the California Indians. *Journal of Ethnobiology* 2:162–176.

van der Merwe, Nikolaas J., and J. C. Vogel

    1977   Isotopic evidence for early maize cultivation in New York State. *American Antiquity* 42:238–242.

Warnock, Peter J., and Karl J. Reinhard

    1992   Methods for extracting pollen and parasite eggs from latrine soils. *Journal of Archaeological Science* 19:261–264.

Watson, Patty Jo

    1976   In pursuit of prehistoric subsistence: A comparative account of some contemporary flotation techniques. *Midcontinental Journal of Archaeology* 1:77–100.

Watson, Patty Jo, and Richard A. Yarnell

    1966   Archaeological and paleoethnobotanical investigations in Salts Cave, Mammoth Cave National Park, Kentucky. *American Antiquity* 31:842–849.

Watt, Bernice K., and Annabel L. Merrill

    1963   *Composition of foods.* Consumer and Food Economics Research Division, Handbook No. 8. United States Department of Agriculture, Washington, D.C.

Wing, Elizabeth S., and Antoinette B. Brown

    1979   *Paleonutrition: Method and theory in prehistoric foodways.* Academic Press, New York.

Winterhalder, Bruce

    1990   Open field, common pot: Harvest variability and risk avoidance in agricultural and foraging societies. In *Risk and uncertainty in tribal and peasant economies*, edited by E. Cashdan, pp. 67–87. Westview Press, Boulder, Colorado.

Winterhalder, Bruce, and Eric A. Smith [Editors]

    1981   *Hunter-gatherer foraging strategies: Ethnographic and archeological analyses.* University of Chicago Press, Chicago.

Yarnell, Richard A.

    1965   Implications of distinctive flora of Pueblo ruins. *American Anthropologist* 67:662–674.

Yanovsky, Elias

    1936   *Food plants of the North American Indians.* United States Department of Agriculture, Miscellaneous Publication 237. Washington, D.C.

Yesner, David R.

1981   Archeological applications of optimal foraging theory: Harvest strategies of Aleut hunter-gathers. In *Hunter-gatherer foraging strategies: Ethnographic and archeological analyses,* edited by B. Winterhalder and E. A. Smith, pp. 148–170. University of Chicago Press, Chicago.

11

Coprolite Evidence for Prehistoric Foodstuffs, Condiments, and Medicines

✾ HEATHER B. TRIGG, RICHARD I. FORD, JOHN G. MOORE, AND LOUISE D. JESSOP

Throughout the past century archaeologists trained in the United States have been interested in the diets of prehistoric inhabitants of this continent and elsewhere. This interest in food was first inspired by the desiccated plant remains, including maize, beans, and squash, from Mancos Canyon cliff dwellings in Colorado, which were exhibited at the 1893 World's Columbian Exposition in Chicago. The methods of field archaeology have changed since 1893, and our goal today is to learn about patterns of consumption and not simply to create lists of potentially edible plants and animals.

Various techniques in combination are useful for understanding the dietary practices of prehistoric peoples. We examined seeds, pollen, and odors from human coprolites from Bat Cave in New Mexico, as an example, to elucidate not only what plants these people used for food, but also how they prepared the plants, how they combined plant foods into meals, what condiments they added, and perhaps what medicines they used as well. Although we focus here on the plant taxa recovered from the coprolites, our analysis also yielded information on other dietary practices such as geophagy and entomophagy. The combination of analytical techniques, macrobotanical and pollen analyses, and odorgrams provides information about a much greater range of dietary practices than can be revealed by any single method.

Early field recovery techniques were limited and allowed for little more than the examination of large plant parts. Specialists were few, and archaeologists recorded only the most common food items. However, at the turn of the century examination of undisturbed deposits became more commonplace, and chance finds of pot contents or a mummy with intestines intact revealed the possibility of investigating prehistoric meals (Callen and Cameron 1960). During the past 60 years, researchers have directed concerted efforts toward recovering subsistence remains by sieving deposits, floating adobe bricks and daub, examining human paleofeces, and conducting water separation (flotation) of charred remains. These techniques have accelerated dramatically the quality and diversity of food remains recovered from archaeological contexts. Today, the inclusion of archaeobotanical analysis in archaeological research designs is customary, and site reports routinely include lists of plants and animals of potential dietary significance interpreted according to contextual analysis, associated remains, or ethnographic analogy.

Dietary assessment of what was ingested depends upon analysis of human skeletons and teeth, bone chemistry, and chance discovery of food spills or coprolites. Typically, only carbonized plant parts are preserved in open sites (Minnis 1981), and if we must rely on the limited lists of charred food remains from open sites, prehistoric meals would appear boring and highly redundant. Even pollen and phytolith analyses have not expanded our knowledge of the diet except to add new taxa. Bone chemistry does allow insight into quantitative differences in dietary composition; for example, isotopes of strontium and nitrogen permit relative measures of plants and meat in a prehistoric diet, and carbon isotopes and patterns of tooth caries indicate the importance of maize in a diet (Larsen 1987; Price et al. 1985). Yet, data supplied by these analytical techniques pose interpretive problems (Sillen et al. 1989). As valuable as the biochemical techniques are, we must use unusual finds to learn about meals. Human paleofeces are uncommon archaeological finds, but they are invaluable for learning about what people ingested during a limited period of time, usually less than 24 hours (Bryant 1974; Watson 1974).

Macroremains, pollen, and odor identifications from coprolites allow assessment of the passage of food through the dietary tract and offer evidence of prehistoric meals and perhaps medicines. Analysis of human coprolites generally includes identification of pollen (Williams-Dean and Bryant 1975), macroscopic seeds or tissues (Callen and Cameron 1960; Minnis 1989), or both (Williams-Dean 1978). Other researchers have more recently demonstrated the use of odorgrams to identify food items in coprolites that may have been so thoroughly masticated that visual identification is impossible (Moore et al. 1984). Additionally, particular methods of food preparation such as the steeping of leaves for a "tea" may not deposit seeds or pollen in the coprolite but would add odors. Thus, odorgrams complement data recovered from palynological and macrobotanical analyses and may prove to be the only method for recovering information about certain dietary items.

Our research on prehistoric meals and unusual patterns of consumption involves human paleofeces from Bat Cave. This famous shelter in west-central New Mexico has produced some of the earliest maize and squash in the Southwest, dating back some 3,100 years (Wills 1988). The coprolites examined in this research appear to be associated with the ceramic occupations of the Mogollon cultural period (A.D.200–1000).

The shelter lies at an elevation of 2,093 m and overlooks a Pleistocene lake bed. At the time of occupation, the basin floor was a playa supporting grasses and halophytes. Cattails surrounded pools of water, and pond weeds grew in deeper water (Hevly 1981); the hills and mountains surrounding this playa supported trees such as pinyon (*Pinus edulis*) and juniper (*Juniperus* spp.), shrubs such as hackberry (*Celtis reticulata*) and squawbush (*Rhus trilobata*), and herbaceous plants such as goosefoot (*Chenopodium* spp.). Botanical materials from archaeological contexts within the cave include seepweed (*Suaeda* spp.), reedgrass (*Phragmites communis* spp.), sunflower (*Helianthus annuus*), walnut (*Juglans arizonica*), pinyon, juniper, cattail (*Typha latifolia*), and cultigens such as maize, squash, and beans (Smith 1950; Wills 1985).

Methods

Seeds and Pollen in Coprolites

Investigators selected 11 human coprolites from Bat Cave for this study based on their shape, size, and contents indicating human origin. Initially, analysts divided each coprolite in half and curated one portion for future study. The other half they divided into samples for the identification of macroremains, pollen, and gastroenterological odors. Analysts identified the odors without knowledge of the results of the macroremains and pollen analyses.

The analysis of each coprolite for seeds and pollen began with weighing and reconstitution. Coprolites were soaked in a .5% solution of trisodium phosphate and agitated daily until disaggregated, typically 72 hours. Analysts recorded the color of the solution as an additional indication of human origin (Bryant 1974) and also noted the presence of bacterial colonies and fecal odors. After deflocculating the samples, they rinsed each one through a 150-micron screen to separate the macroscopic materials from the pollen-laden solution, which they retained for pollen extraction. The macromaterials were dried and sorted. Analysts then scanned the samples using a dissecting microscope at 10–30X magnification and identified seeds by correspondence with modern comparative collections housed in the University of Michigan Ethnobotanical Laboratory and published atlases (Delorit 1970; Martin and Barkley 1961).

Analysts extracted pollen using standard methods (Faegri and Iversen 1964; Williams-Dean and Bryant 1975). First they added a known number of club moss spores (*Lycopodium* sp.) and removed carbonate deposits using hydrochloric acid. They then soaked each sample in hydrofluoric acid for 48 hours to remove silicates. Next they rinsed samples to neutral pH and concentrated the samples by centrifuge. Acetolysis removed unwanted organics. Finally they stained the pollen samples with safranin O and made three slides from each sample for the identification of pollen.

Typically, palynologists count 200 pollen grains per sample (Barkley 1934), although some (Stephen Hall, personal communication 1986) believe that a 200-grain count is inadequate for proper representation of pollen types and prefer 300-grain counts. Following this criterion, analysts for this project identified 300 grains per sample except when one pollen type overwhelmed the assemblage. In such cases, they counted an additional 300 grains, excluding the dominant pollen type, to mitigate the statistical swamping effect. We made our identifications by comparison to reference slides and a published atlas (Kapp 1969).

Food Odors from Coprolites

Analysts for this project established odorgrams using gas chromatography (GC) and mass spectrometry to separate the component odors and also human olfaction to identify the odors (Moore et al. 1984, 1985). Samples were reconstituted in a .5% trisodium phosphate solution for 24 to 72 hours. Just before purging, laboratory assistants added 45 g of ammonium sulfate $((NH_4)^2SO_4)$ to the samples. They then purged the volatile compounds by bubbling helium gas through the solution. The volatiles were trapped on a collector, which was then connected to the GC column and desorbed of trapped components by heating to 220° C for 2 minutes. The eluted volatiles were swept off the head of the GC column by helium carrier gas. The column outlet had a 1:1 splitter; one branch of the splitter was connected to a flame ionization detector, the other to a sniffing port. The GC operator recorded the retention time of each eluted sample component peak and the characteristics of the odor emerging from the sniffing port.

Appendix 11.1 lists the odors recovered from each human coprolite and the identifications of macroremains and pollen in order of numerical dominance. Our interpretation of the identifications obtained by these analyses acknowledges three significant problems. First, in ethnographic situations, food and medicine usually represent categories along a folk classification continuum depending upon context of use and the social or cultural understanding of health (Etkin and Ross 1982; Johns 1990). Many groups do not recognize a distinction between plants used for food and those used medicinally such as tonics taken to promote health (Etkin 1988). Additionally, the same item could be both a food and a medicine. Second, evidence of food processing and medicinal usage may appear similar in a coprolite. For example, clay used to detoxify a solanaceous plant may also be used to relieve stomach problems (Johns 1990). The coprolite would have a signature of geophagy, but the purpose, whether food preparation or medicinal, may not be self-evident. Third, we remain wedded to some form of analogic reasoning either through laboratory assessment of the chemical properties of a plant or animal or through ethnographic reference to peoples' use, but neither necessarily confirms why an item was used.

Meals and Medicines Revealed

Despite these problems, coprolites contain a variety of data to enlighten us about subsistence activities: food selection and preparation, water consumption, and possibly medicinal use. The seeds recovered from the 11 human coprolites are a repetitious list of weedy plants. Although the seeds represented 10 different genera, a limited number of taxa predominated: pigweed (*Amaranthus* spp.), goosefoot (*Chenopodium* spp.), purslane (*Portulaca* spp.), alkali sacaton (*Sporobolus* spp.), and seepweed (*Suaeda* spp.). Further, within each coprolite, one taxon dominated the assemblage with the remaining seeds recovered in much lower quantities. This pattern, repeated in each of the coprolites studied, is suggestive of meals consisting of combinations of a few subsistence items, with one food type clearly dominating each meal. The macrobotanical remains were notably from wild, usually weedy plants whose seeds are starchy. None of the coprolites contained maize pericarps. Ethnographic data suggest that Southwestern peoples used these seeds in a similar manner as maize, and damage to the seeds recovered from the coprolites suggested that the population under study had used several methods to prepare these foods.

The samples exhibited evidence for a variety of food processing techniques. Two samples (17 and 20) revealed the parching of seeds from the genus *Sporobolus,* but the process must have been rapid because not all seeds were fire scarred. Similarly, the seed coats in several samples were striated, perhaps from grinding. Ethnographic evidence from the region indicates that various peoples used parching and grinding on many small annual plant seeds: pigweed, goosefoot, seepweed, dropseed, and panic grass (*Panicum* spp.). The Navajo parched the seeds of goosefoot and ground them like maize (Franciscan Fathers 1910). The Yavapai, too, parched seeds in a basket with coals and then ground them on a metate (Gifford 1936), and the Paiute parched the seeds of the genus *Sporobolus* before grinding (Palmer 1878).

Other possible evidence of food processing includes silts or clays found in several coprolite samples (5, 6, and 21). Project investigators submitted samples of the silt from each of these coprolites for scanning electron microscope (SEM) microprobe analysis. The clay that dominated sample 6 comprised illite, syngenite, and polyhalite; and the clay in sample 5 contained a few particles of syngenite. The silt in sample 21 appeared to be more typical of soil-type material. Ethnographic sources indicate that the Navajo, Hopi, and Zuni mixed clay with wild potatoes to detoxify the bitter alkaloids (Fewkes 1896; Johns 1990), but analysts recovered no evidence of potatoes or starch crystals in the macrobotanical remains in these samples. Thus, this silt may have served as a seasoning or possibly a medicine.

In addition to evincing plant consumption, analysis of coprolites provides a perspective on other dietary practices of these prehistoric people. Sample 20 contained numerous butterfly pupae that appeared to have been deliberately eaten: the shells, thoroughly masticated, were evident throughout the coprolite. Researchers have documented entomophagy not only for the Southwest but also for the Great Basin, where insects may have been an important seasonal source of protein. However, insect consumption there tended to be opportunistic (Sutton 1988).

In addition to macroscopic evidence, pollen evidence is useful for identifying plants used for food and medicines. Five pollen types dominated the pollen record for the 11 coprolites: grass (Poaceae), cheno/am (Chenopodiaceae or Amaranthaceae, difficult to distinguish from each other), composites, cattail, and pine. Since analysts found no fragments of cattails or pine in the coprolites, these pollen types probably had been blown into the drinking water. Similarly, the pollen from the aquatic genus *Potamogeton* (pondweed) would have originated in the water used for drinking. However, in sample 6, we found cattail pollen in clumps and in considerable quantity. Palynologists usually interpret this type of evidence as deliberate ingestion of the pollen, and ethnographic data suggest food, ceremonial, and medicinal uses of cattail flowering heads and pollen (Loud 1929; Train et al. 1957; Whiting 1939).

Where grass, cheno/am, or composite pollen dominated the assemblage, macrobotanical remains of these genera were more numerous than pollen in the coprolites. Generally, the dominant pollen type was from the same family as the most numerous seed in the feces. Thus, the study population had probably ingested the pollen accidentally as it adhered to the seeds or other plant parts. Other pollen types recovered in small quantities, such as juniper, are anemophilous and probably represent ingestion of airborne pollen.

The use of odorgrams in conjunction with more traditional pollen and macroremains studies enhances our understanding of the possible uses of medicines in archaeological contexts. The question of medicine in prehistory is an important issue but quite difficult to answer. For example, how often is a person ill? How often is a person treated with a plant, animal, or mineral medicine? And what is the chance of finding the stool of a sick person? Researchers recently addressed some of these difficulties through pollen studies and ethnographic analogy (Reinhard et al. 1991). Yet, other lines of evidence can also help to identify the use of medicine.

The detection of strong odors and the presence of clay in at least two samples (5 and 6) and the dominance of cattail pollen in sample 6 suggest possible examples of medicinal treatment. Sample 4 had a variety of smells with contemporary medicinal analogues: cough syrup, anise, menthol, etc. This sample also contained an odor tentatively identified as tobacco smoke, which modern groups in the area have used in curing ceremonies (Parsons 1936; Stevenson 1915). Sample 21 also had distinct odors but very few seeds and few pieces of bone, and the macrobotanical remains and pollen content were commonplace. Pollen consisted of only the basic five types (grass, cheno/am, cattail, composite, and pine) suggestive of drinking water as their source, and analysts noted only two odors: spicy woody and seaweed. However, a fine clayey silt dominated the sample and had to have been deliberately consumed to account for the quantity recovered. Perhaps it is an example of geophagy directed toward soothing the stomach or intestinal tract. Sample 21 was anomalous in many respects and may point to medicinal treatment.

The evidence presented by the odorgrams yields a much different picture of the diet than either the macrobotanical or the pollen data. The coprolites typically emitted a variety of food-related odors such as seaweed, anise, cherry, spice, and strawberry. This information sometimes corroborates and sometimes contrasts with the macrobotanical and pollen data. In some cases the macrobotanical and pollen data accorded with the odors noted. For example, Sample 12 contained both strawberry (cf. *Fragaria* sp.) pollen and a berry/ strawberry odor. Similarly, the ocean seaweed odor present in many samples may have derived from halophytic plants such as seepweed and alkali sacaton or perhaps from the drinking water from the playa. Another sample (17) contained a limited quantity of seeds of the genus *Lappula* (stickseed), but enough to give a pepperlike odor to the paleofeces. Samples 12 and 19 had the distinct smell of mint, and Sample 12 also contained Labiatae pollen, possibly an additional condiment. In addition to these correlations, the odorgrams indicated the use of plants other than those suggested by either the seeds or the pollen. Many samples gave off berry, mint, orange, and lemon odors that had no corresponding macrobotanical or pollen remains. These odors may have derived from plant parts prepared in such a manner that they did not leave visually identifiable traces such as teas or infusions.

One of the most important findings of this research is the characterization of plant consumption at Bat Cave. The macroremains suggested that meals had consisted of combinations of subsistence items, with one food type dominating each sample. The number of taxa consumed in substantial quantity is limited to a single type of grass and a few members of the Chenopodiaceae/Amarantha-ceae families. These foods tend to be bland, starchy seeds, often used by peoples of the Southwest in a similar manner to maize.

Although the Mogollon had maize in their subsistence economy, the coprolite evidence suggests negligible consumption, with maize (*Zea mays*) pollen and odors from one coprolite and only maize odors from two others. The presence of domesticated plants in an economy does not ensure they will be consumed as a staple at all meals. The availability, use, and importance of maize may vary seasonally, according to activity schedules, or as a matter of personal preference. All the coprolites contained ample evidence of many wild plant foods, especially small seeds, some fruits, and possible condiments. (Animal protein was present as well, including butterfly pupae.) While the starchy seeds appear to have been the main component of the diet, plants consumed as condiments may also have been of substantial dietary significance, adding vitamins and other nutrients.

Bat Cave was not a major occupational site, yet the unusual remains allow insights into the lifeways of the prehistoric inhabitants and illustrate a variability in dietary practices not evident in the remains recovered from open sites. At most, the site was occupied seasonally by a few family groups starting in the preceramic periods and possibly by groups of hunters or small gathering groups in the late summer during the succeeding Mogollon period. The maize consumed by Mogollon visitors may have been brought from elsewhere to the shelter. The other plant foods were probably gathered locally; all are present within an easy walk of the site today. The use of local foodstuffs, the small quantity of maize recovered, and entomophagy all point to opportunistic use of foods in the immediate area. Although the Mogollon opportunistically gathered plants, they apparently prepared their meals deliberately, attempting to enhance the flavor of an otherwise bland diet using seeds, plant condiments, and clays.

The methodological combination of pollen analysis, macrobotanical analysis, and odorgrams gives insight into dietary and perhaps medicinal practices that any single technique will not yield. Our use of these techniques suggests that the Mogollon were not interested merely in satisfying energy needs, but also in adding distinct flavors to their meals. Future research into prehistoric diets must recognize that reconstructions based on single variables such as caloric value are inadequate for characterizing a diet. Models must be developed that accommodate nutrients derived from nonstaple plants such as the condiments discovered here in our research, as well as such salient cultural features as taste preference.

REFERENCES

Barkley, Fred A.
    1934   The statistical theory of pollen analysis. *Ecology* 15:283–289.

Bryant, Vaughn H.
    1974   The role of coprolite analysis in archaeology. *Bulletin of the Texas Archaeological Society* 45:1–28.

Callen, E. O., and T.W.M. Cameron
    1960   A prehistoric diet revealed in coprolites. *The New Scientist* 8:35–40.

Delorit, Richard
    1970   *An illustrated taxonomy manual of weed seeds.* Agronomy Publications, River Falls, Wisconsin.

Etkin, Nina
    1988   Ethnopharmacology: Biobehavioral approaches in the anthropological study of indigenous medicines. *Annual Review of Anthropology* 17:23–42.

Etkin, Nina L., and Paul J. Ross
    1982   Food as medicine and medicine as food: An adaptive framework for the interpretation of plant utilization among the Hausa of northern Nigeria. *Social Science and Medicine* 16:1559–1573.

Faegri, Knut, and Johs. Iversen
    1964   *Textbook of pollen analysis.* Munksgaard, Copenhagen.

Fewkes, Jesse Walter
    1896   A contribution to ethnobotany. *American Anthropologist* 9:14–21.

Franciscan Fathers
    1910   *An ethnologic dictionary of the Navajo language.* Franciscan Fathers, St. Michaels, Arizona.

Gifford, G. W.
    1936   The northeastern and western Yavapai. *University of California Publications in American Archaeology and Ethnology* 34:247–354.

Hevly, Richard H.
    1981   Pollen analysis of the AKE site. In *The AKE Site: Collection and excavation of LA 13423, Catron County, New Mexico,* edited by Patrick H. Beckett, pp. 257–265. New Mexico State University Department of Sociology and Anthropology Cultural Resources Management Division Report 357. Las Cruces.

Johns, Timothy
    1990   *With bitter herbs they shall eat it: Chemical ecology and the origins of human diet and medicine.* University of Arizona Press, Tucson.

Kapp, Ronald

    1969   *How to know pollen and spores.* William C. Brown, Dubuque, Iowa.

Larsen, Clark Spencer

    1987   Bioarchaeological interpretations of subsistence economy and behavior from human skeletal remains. In *Advances in Archaeological Method and Theory,* Vol. 10, edited by M. Schiffer, pp. 339–411. Academic Press, New York.

Loud, Llewellyn L.

    1929   Notes on the Northern Paiute. In *Lovelock Cave,* edited by L. Loud and M. Harrington, pp. 152–164. University of California Publications in American Archaeology and Ethnology, Berkeley.

Martin, Alexander, and William D. Barkley

    1961   *Seed identification manual.* University of California Press, Berkeley.

Minnis, Paul

    1981   Seeds in archaeological sites: Sources and some interpretive problems. *American Antiquity* 46:143–152.

    1989   Prehistoric diet in the northern Southwest: Macroplant remains from Four Corners feces. *American Antiquity* 54:543–563.

Moore, John G., B. K. Krotoszynski, and H. J. O'Neill

    1984   Fecal odorgrams: A method for partial reconstruction of ancient and modern diets. *Digestive Diseases and Sciences* 29:907–911.

Moore, John G., R. C. Straight, and A. W. Wayne

    1985   Olfactory, gas chromatographic and mass spectral analysis of fecal volatiles traced to ingested licorice and apple. *Biochemical and Biophysical Research Communications* 131:339–346.

Palmer, Edward

    1878   Plants used by the Indians of the U.S. *American Naturalist* 12:593–606.

Parsons, Elsie Clews

    1936   *Taos Pueblo.* General Series in Anthropology No. 2. George Banta Publishing Company, Menasha, Wisconsin.

Price, T. Douglas, Margaret J. Schoeninger, and George J. Armelagos

    1985   Bone chemistry and past behavior: An overview. *Journal of Human Evolution* 14:419–447.

Reinhard, Karl J., Donny L. Hamilton, and Richard H. Hevly

    1991   Use of pollen concentration in paleopharmacology: Coprolite evidence of medicinal plants. *Journal of Ethnobiology* 11:111–132.

Sillen, Andrew, Judith C. Sealy, and Nikolaas J. van der Merwe

    1989   Chemistry and paleodietary research: No more easy answers. *American Antiquity* 54:504–512.

Smith, C. Earle, Jr.

    1950   Prehistoric plant remains from Bat Cave. *Botanical Museum Leaflets of Harvard University* 14:157–180.

Stevenson, Matilda
1915   *Ethnobotany of the Zuni Indians.* 13th Annual Report, Bureau of American Ethnology. Washington, D.C.

Sutton, Mark Q.
1988   *Insects as food: Aboriginal entomophagy in the Great Basin.* Ballena Press Anthropological Papers, No. 33. Ballena Press, Menlo Park, California.

Train, Percy, James R. Henrichs, and W. Andrew Archer
1957   *Medicinal uses of plants by Indian tribes of Nevada.* Contributions Toward a Flora of Nevada, No. 45. U.S. Department of Agriculture, Washington, D.C.

Watson, Patty Jo
1974   Theoretical and methodological difficulties in dealing with paleofecal material. In *Archaeology of the Mammoth Cave Area,* edited by P. J. Watson, pp. 239–241. Academic Press, New York.

Whiting, Alfred F.
1939   *Ethnobotany of the Hopi.* Museum of Northern Arizona, Bulletin No. 15. Flagstaff.

Williams-Dean, Glenna
1978   Ethnobotany and cultural ecology of prehistoric man in southwest Texas. Ph.D. dissertation, Texas A&M University, College Station.

Williams-Dean, Glenna, and Vaughn M. Bryant
1975   Pollen analysis of human coprolites from Antelope House. *Kiva* 41:97–111.

Wills, Wirt Henry
1985   Early agriculture in the Mogollon Highlands of New Mexico. Ph.D. dissertation, University of Michigan. University Microfilms, Ann Arbor.

1988   *Early prehistoric agriculture.* School of American Research Press, Santa Fe.

Appendix 11.1. Macroremains, Pollen, and Odors from Bat Cave Coprolites

Sample Number	Macroremains	Pollen Remains	Odors
2	*Amaranthus* sp. L.	cheno/am	faint green grass
	Helianthus annuus L.	Poaceae	
	Sporobolus sp. R. Br.	*Pinus* sp. L.	
	Portulaca sp. L.	long-spine Compositae	
	cheno/am	*Typha* sp. L.	
		short-spine Compositae	
		Juniperus sp. L.	
4	*Sporobolus* sp. R. Br.	Poaceae	maize
	Cleome sp. L.	short-spine Compositae	cherry/berry?

Sample Number	Macroremains	Pollen Remains	Odors
	cheno/am	cheno/am	lemon
	Helianthus annuus L.	*Ambrosia* sp. L.	orange
		Pinus sp. L.	tobacco smoke?
		Typha sp. L.	cough syrup
		long-spine Compositae	anise-like
		Celtis sp. L.	mentholatum
		unidentified	ocean seaweed
5	*Sporobolus* sp. R. Br.	Poaceae	orange
	Portulaca sp. L.	*Typha* sp. L.	spicy?
	Chenopodium sp. L.	*Pinus* sp. L.	earthy nutty
	Amaranthus sp. L.	short-spine Compositae	ocean seaweed
	Suaeda sp. Forsk.	*Ephedra* sp. L.	
	Panicum sp. L.	*Potamogeton* sp. L.	
	cheno/am	unidentified	
	clay		
6	*Rhus* sp. L.	*Typha* sp. L.	fishy
	Poaceae	*Pinus* sp. L.	green grass/apple
	Amaranthus sp. L.	Poaceae	ocean seaweed
	Panicum sp. L.	cheno/am	
	unidentified	long-spine Compositae	
	clay	short-spine Compositae	
		Celtis sp. L.	
		Ephedra sp. L.	
		unidentified	
9	*Sporobolus* sp. R. Br.	Poaceae	maize?
	Chenopodium sp. L.	cheno/am	berry/cherry
	Compositae cf.	*Pinus* sp. L.	ocean seaweed
	Helianthus sp. T. & G.	*Ribes* sp. L.	lemon
		unidentified	orange?
		short-spine Compositae	
		long-spine Compositae	
12	*Chenopodium* sp. L.	cheno/am	maize?
	Portulaca sp. L.	Poaceae	berry/strawberry
	Sporobolus sp. R. Br.	long-spine Compositae	green floral
	unidentified	cf. Labiatae	grasslike
		short-spine Compositae	fresh green apple

Sample Number	Macroremains	Pollen Remains	Odors
		Ambrosia sp. L.	floral
		cf. *Fragaria* sp. L.	butterscotch?
		unidentified	floral (cherry)
		Zea mays L.	mint
		Typha sp. L.	hot meaty
		fern	
		Pinus sp. L.	
14	*Suaeda* sp. Forsk.	fungi	gin (juniper)
	Helianthus annuus L.	cheno/am	ocean seaweed
	unidentified	*Pinus* sp. L.	
		Poaceae	
		cf. *Ambrosia* sp. L.	
		short-spine Compositae	
		long-spine Compositae	
		Typha sp. L.	
		cf. *Salix* sp. L.	
		unidentified	
17	*Sporobolus* sp. R. Br.	Poaceae	berry/cherry
	Lappula sp. Moench.	*Typha* sp. L.	green grass
	Poaceae	cf. *Ambrosia* sp. L.	ocean seaweed
	unidentified	*Pinus* sp. L.	pepperlike?
	bone	cf. *Nymphaea* sp. L.	
		cf. *Yucca* sp. L.	
19	*Suaeda* sp. Forsk.	cheno/am	fresh green grass
	Chenopodium sp. L.	Poaceae	mint
	Chenopodiaceae	*Pinus* sp. L.	orange/lemon
	Sporobolus sp. R. Br.	cf. *Ambrosia* sp. L.	ocean seaweed
	Helianthus sp. T. & G.	short-spine Compositae	
		unidentified	
20	*Sporobolus* sp. R. Br.	Poaceae	fresh green?
	Chenopodium sp. L.	*Typha* sp. L.	fresh green floral?
	butterfly pupae	*Pinus* sp. L.	floral berry
		cheno/am	old seaweed
		long-spine Compositae	
		short-spine Compositae	
		cf. *Potamogeton* sp. L.	

Sample Number	Macroremains	Pollen Remains	Odors
		cf. *Celtis* sp. L.	
		cf. *Ambrosia* sp. L.	
		unidentified	
21	few seeds	Poaceae	spicy woody
	bone	cheno/am	ocean seaweed
	silt	*Typha* sp. L.	
		short-spine Compositae	
		Pinus sp. L.	
		unidentified	

Note: Taxa are listed in decreasing order of abundance within each sample. Samples 1, 3, 7–8, 10–11, 13, 15–16, and 18 are from nonhuman coprolites and are not included in this study.

✽ *Plants and Nonhuman Primates*

12

Nonhuman Primate Self-Medication with Wild Plant Foods

✳ KENNETH E. GLANDER

Primate researchers generally view foraging strategies as a balance between acquiring the proper nutrients and avoiding toxins and digestion inhibitors (Glander 1982; Waterman 1984), but this view of optimal foraging may ignore potential benefits of certain plant secondary compounds. Unlike ethnobotanists studying human diets who often emphasize the "medicinal" aspects of plants rather than the selection of plant material for nutrients (Etkin and Ross 1991), primatologists may concentrate solely on the dynamic interaction between nutrients and secondary compounds as the explanation for primate foraging behavior. If a nonhuman primate can learn to avoid certain plant species or plant parts because ingestion reduces the animal's fitness (Glander 1975, 1978, 1981, 1982; Glander and Rabin 1983; Hladik 1978; McKey 1979; Milton 1979, 1980; Oates 1977; Oates et al. 1977; Wrangham and Waterman 1983), then nonhuman primates may also be able to learn to exploit the tropical forest medicine chest. Scholars familiar with the use of plants as effective drugs by humans worldwide as discussed elsewhere in this volume should not be surprised that nonhuman primates also use the wild plant medicines available to them in the natural pharmacopoeia of tropical forests.

The study of natural drugs and how they affect animals and people that ingest them is known as pharmacognosy. In 1991, Richard Wrangham and Eloy Rodriquez coined the term *zoopharmacognosy* to describe self-medication by

This research was partially supported by National Science Foundation grants BNS-8819733 and BNS-8819733-REU Supplement, Duke University Research Council grants, Duke University Biomedical Research Support grants, COSHEN-Pew grants, and grants from the Center for Field Research.

animals in general and nonhuman primates in particular. The first zoopharmacognosy symposium, titled "Zoopharmacognosy: Medicinal Plant Use by Wild Apes and Monkeys," was held in February 1992 at the American Association for the Advancement of Science meetings in Chicago.

The natural history literature is filled with anecdotal evidence that vertebrates use plant medicines. Malay elephants, for example, feed on certain legume creepers (*Entada schefferi*) just before walking long distances (Hubback 1941). Indian wild boars selectively dig and eat the roots of pigweed (*Boerhaavia diffusa*), which humans use as an anthelmintic (Janzen 1978). Mexican folklore suggests that pigs eat pomegranate (*Punica granatum*) roots because they contain an alkaloid toxic to tapeworms (Janzen 1978).

Daniel Janzen (1978) may have been the first to suggest that nonhuman primates are self-medicating when he linked the absence of protozoan parasites in Kibale Forest black and white colobus (*Colobus guereza*) and red colobus monkeys (*C. badius*) with their regular ingestion of plant secondary compounds. Only recently, however, have observations of wild chimpanzees (*Pan troglodytes*) provided the first direct evidence of self-medication by nonhuman primates (Huffman and Seifu 1989). Known and presumed cases of self-medication, as well as the use of nonfood plants by primates, involve chimpanzees (*P. troglodytes*), howling monkeys (*Alouatta palliata*), muriqui (*Brachyteles arachnoides*), black and white colobus monkeys (*C. guereza*), and baboons (*Papio anubis* and *P. hamadryas*), among others.

Chimpanzees and Plant Medicines

Chimpanzees in both Gombe Stream National Park and the Mahale Mountains National Park (both are located along the eastern shore of Lake Tanganyika in western Tanzania) eat leaves from the genus *Aspilia* in a highly unusual and characteristic manner (Nishida 1990; Wrangham and Nishida 1983). Normally, chimpanzees stuff leaves in their mouths as fast as they can and chew them into small pieces, but in the case of *Aspilia* spp., the Gombe and Mahale chimpanzees take only one or two of the young leaves at a time and roll them between the tongue and cheek before swallowing the leaves whole. The chimpanzees may be using *Aspilia* spp. in the same manner that humans do for stomach disorders (Wrangham and Nishida 1983). Moreover, ingestion of *Aspilia* leaves by chimpanzees in this manner increases during the time of year when the incidence of intestinal nematodes is highest (Nishida 1990). This nonchewing feeding method results in the *Aspilia* leaves passing through the chimpanzee digestive tract intact and appearing whole in the feces.

The curious method of holding *Aspilia* leaves in the mouth could possibly allow the medication to be absorbed through the cheek in a manner analogous to the administration of certain medications under the tongue or through the skin and mucous membranes, such as nitroglycerine to humans (Newton and Nishida 1994). This explanation by itself is unlikely since chimpanzees would not need to swallow the leaf if buccal administration were the sole purpose.

Chimpanzees on occasion ingest large quantities of *Aspilia* leaves, but when doing so, they always rapidly chew the leaves (Nishida 1990). Chewing subjects any medicinal compounds in the leaves to deactivation through breakdown and digestion in the stomach. Swallowing the leaf whole protects the compound from deactivation in the stomach and delivers it to the small intestines where it can be absorbed.

To test the hypothesis that *Aspilia* leaves contain a medicinal compound, researchers analyzed *Aspilia* leaves and found high concentrations (5 mg/leaf) of the potent antibacterial, antifungal, and antinematodal agent thiarubrine A (Rodriquez et al. 1985). They reported that this compound has a strong antibiotic effect on bacteria such as *Staphylococcus albus, Mycobacterium phlei, Bacillus subtillis,* and *Streptococcus faecalis* and is toxic to the nematode *Coenorphabitidis eleagans.*

Another case of apparent self-medication involved a female chimpanzee in the Mahale Mountains that ate the leaves of *Lippia plicata* at a time when observers judged her to be sick (Takasaki and Hunt 1987). The method of eating was similar to that for *Aspilia* spp. in that the chimpanzee took only one leaf at a time and appeared to suck on each leaf several times before swallowing it. A bioassay indicated potent biological activity, and the local Tongwe people use an infusion of leaves crushed and soaked in water to treat stomachaches (Takasaki and Hunt 1987).

Self-medication and recovery by a nonhuman primate are most convincingly linked in the description of a lethargic chimpanzee with dark urine and bowel irregularity that recovered after sucking the bitter juice from young stems of *Vernonia amygdalina* (Huffman and Seifu 1989). Chimpanzees only rarely consume this plant, known as "bitter leaf," which humans in tropical Africa use as an anthelmintic and antiscorbutic as well as a tonic to treat intestinal upset and appetite loss (Watt and Breyer-Brandwijk 1962). Several sesquiterpene lactones in *V. amygdalina* (vernodalol, vernolide, and hydrozyvernolide) have demonstrated anthelmintic properties (Koshimizu et al. 1994); these same sesquiterpene lactones, the steroid glucosides (vernonioside A_1, A_2, A_3, and B_1), and three of their aglycones in *V. amygdalina* have also demonstrated antischistosomal activities (Jisaka et al. 1992).

Researchers first conducted the antischistosomal tests in vitro using *Schistosoma japonicum.* All of the sesquiterpene lactones inhibited movement and egg laying by schistosomes at 200 ppm, but only vernodalin inhibited movement and egg laying at 20 ppm. The aglycones also all inhibited egg laying at 20 ppm.

When tested in mice, however, vernodalin was lethal to the mice when administered at levels clinically effective against the parasite *S. Japonicum*, while oral doses of nonlethal levels had no effect on the parasite (Jisaka et al. 1992). Clinical tests of a closely related plant (*V. anthelmintica*) on humans demonstrated the effectiveness of this plant against pinworm, hookworm, and *Giardia lamblia* (Singh et al. 1981). Although observers (Huffman and Seifu 1989) did not determine whether the aforementioned sick chimpanzee was infected by schistosomes, the above results suggest that vernonioside B_1 (and its aglycones) is effective against parasites such as *S. haematobium* and *S. mansoni*, which cause schistosomiasis, one of most problematic infectious diseases throughout Africa (Jisaka et al. 1992).

Analysis of *V. amygdalina* showed that the leaves have high levels of both vernolide and vernonioside B_1, while the pith from fresh stems contains similar amounts of vernonioside B_1 but only small amounts of vernodalin (Jisaka et al. 1992). Thus, the Mahale Mountain chimpanzee may ingest pith from young *V. amygdalina* stems instead of eating the leaves because the leaves, with their high levels of vernodalin, may be toxic to chimpanzees just as vernodalin was toxic to mice; by eating the pith from stems, the sick chimpanzee may have avoided the highly toxic vernodalin while still obtaining a clinically effective dose of vernonioside B_1. Also, research suggests that vernonioside B_1 may be metabolized into the more effective aglycones (Jisaka et al. 1992).

The toxic nature of many natural plant products must be balanced against the benefits of these products. The difference between life or death may be as simple as choosing stems over leaves from the same tree, as demonstrated by the Mahale chimpanzees. Primates apparently have to choose different plant parts as well as different plant species when medicating themselves. The evidence for self-medication by other nonhuman primates is more circumstantial, but an ever-increasing number of observations cannot be explained solely by the animals' nutrient requirements.

Howling Monkeys and Plant Medicines

During the past 22 years I have examined the teeth of more than 950 mantled howling monkeys (*Alouatta palliata*) and have found no cavities or gum disease. However, cavities and severe gum disease afflict chimpanzees (Kilgore 1989). This difference could be related to diet, since the diet of howlers consists mainly of leaves with occasional high levels of sugars from fruits and flowers (Glander 1981), while the diet of chimpanzees consists primarily of sugary fruit (Ghiglieri 1984).

Sugars provide an ideal environment for the bacteria that cause tooth decay. Since oral diseases caused by bacteria such as *Streptococcus mutans* are a serious problem for humans (Hamada and Slade 1980), the lack of oral diseases in howlers may be due to the incidence in their diet of plant parts (pedicels) from the cashew (*Anacardium occidentale*, of the family Anacardiaceae, which also includes poison ivy). These pedicels contain the phenolic compounds anacardic acid and cardol, which exhibit a narrow spectrum of activity against gram-positive bacteria such as *Streptococcus mutans* that cause tooth decay (Himejima and Kubo 1991).

Internal parasites are common in *A. palliata*, and it is not unusual to find 100% of the individual monkeys infested (Kuntz and Myers 1972; Stuart et al. 1990). Yet a comparison of populations in two different areas of Costa Rica (Hacienda La Pacifica and Santa Rosa National Park) has demonstrated significant differences in parasite loads: the La Pacifica howlers are heavily parasitized, while the Santa Rosa howlers and spider monkeys carry light parasite loads (Stuart et al. 1990). A major difference between these two populations is the availability of *Ficus* spp. None of the infected La Pacifica howlers has access to fig trees, while the Santa Rosa howlers have many fig trees available. Many human populations use the latex in *Ficus* spp. as an anthelminthic (Hansson et al. 1986; Lewis and Elvin-Lewis 1977), and consumption of fig leaves or fruit by the Santa Rosa primates may be keeping their worm load under control.

Twenty-two years of birth records suggest that some female mantled howlers in my study groups may be using plants to influence the sex of their offspring. While the normal sex ratio for the whole La Pacifica population is 1:1, one female had 4 of 4 male infants, another had at least 8 of 9 male infants (the sex of 1 infant was unknown); a third female had 4 of 5 female infants (1 unknown). In each case this represented the total number of infants that each of these females had during her life. These very skewed ratios suggest some extrinsic influence beyond mere chance, particularly when viewed in relation to other documented observations. For example, researchers have reported that naturally occurring phenolic plant compounds influenced reproduction in voles (*Microtus montanus*) and have suggested that these animals were using the plant chemicals to turn their reproduction on and off (Berger et al. 1977). A follow-up study verified that the plant chemicals acted as the ultimate cue to trigger reproductive effort in *M. montanus* (Berger et al. 1981).

I do not know the method of preselection being used by howler females, if they are indeed actively influencing the sex of their offspring, but the chemical composition of foods may be cuing the howler's reproductive efforts in a manner similar to what occurs in voles. The chemical components of food may also offer the female howler an opportunity to affect the sex of her offspring by controlling access of either X or Y sperm to the mature ovum that is shed into the oviduct. Because sperm carrying X or Y chromosomes can be distinguished as, respectively, electropositive and electronegative (Bhattacharya et al. 1979), researchers have successfully been able to separate X and Y chromosome–bearing human spermatozoa by electrophoresis (Sevinc 1968). If a female howler were able to produce an electrical charge and change it from positive to negative, she could control whether X or Y chromosome–bearing sperm passed her cervix and entered her uterus to fertilize ova in the oviduct.

To test this hypothesis, I measured the electrical potential at the entrance of the vagina and at the cervix of Costa Rican mantled howlers. The results grouped into two types: those individuals for whom the millivolt reading at the cervix ($\bar{x}=9.7$, $N=36$) was lower than the millivolt reading at the entrance of the vagina ($\bar{x}=32.5$, $N=36$); and those for whom the reading at the cervix ($\bar{x}=24.4$, $N=22$) was higher than the reading at the entrance of the vagina ($\bar{x}=11.2$, $N=22$). In both groups the readings at these two locations were significantly different ($F=14.72$, $p=.0004$ and $F=5.49$, $p=.024$). Several females also demonstrated a change from positive to negative in readings taken at different times during their reproductive cycles.

Since plant-produced chemicals can trigger the reproductive efforts of mammals (Berger et al. 1977, 1981), similar plant-produced chemicals could possibly change ion concentration in the vagina and affect gender determination. This might be accomplished by ingesting plant compounds that either block or increase the release of calcium, potassium, or sodium through the cell wall in the same manner that phytoestrogens either block or facilitate the release of follicle-stimulating hormone or luteinizing hormone in mammals (Hughes 1988; Labov 1977).

Muriquis and Plant Medicines

One of the world's rarest primates, the muriqui (*Brachyteles arachnoides*), may be using its forest pharmacopoeia to both reduce parasites and control fertility. In Brazil, perhaps as few as 500 individual muriquis are located in 12 isolated forests (Strier 1992, 1993). With the onset of the rainy season, the muriquis alter their feeding behavior by eating predominantly the leaves of two tree species in the legume family, *Apuleia leiocarpa* and *Platypodium elegans* (Strier 1993). The leaves of these legumes contain compounds that have antimicrobial activity as well as isoflavonoids similar in structure to estrogens. At the beginning of the rainy season, the muriquis make a special effort to eat the fruit of *Enterolobium contortisiliquim*, monkey ear (Strier 1993). This eating pattern may exhibit not a nutritional but a pharmacological perspective, since stigmasterol (a steroid used to synthesize progesterone and found in the monkey ear fruit) may influence the timing of fertility in muriqui (Strier 1993). The stigmasterol could function in the manner of the naturally occurring plant compounds that influence reproduction in voles (Berger et al. 1981).

Most primates carry intestinal parasites, but among four sampled populations in one study an anomalous group of muriquis were completely free of
parasites (Stuart et al. 1993). Whereas parasites normally are highest in primate
populations exhibiting high density and living in the most disturbed habitats,
in this case the parasite-free muriqui lived in a moderately disturbed habitat at
the second highest density, while muriqui from the least disturbed and lowest
density population had the most parasites. Another unusual finding is that the
brown howling monkeys (*A. fusca*) living at the same site as the parasite-free
muriquis also did not have any parasites (Stuart et al. 1993). A relationship may
hold between this parasite-free condition of the howlers and muriquis and the
food they eat (Strier 1992, 1993), since the monkeys appear to ingest some of
the same plant material that the Amazonian people eat to treat intestinal
worms (Strier 1992). These findings reinforce the potential importance of natural plant products and may prove to be another case of self-treatment by
monkeys.

Colobus and Plant Medicines

Several feeding behaviors of colobus monkeys cannot be explained solely in
terms of nutrient needs and may fit the idea of self-medication. The preferred
foods (young leaves) of black and white colobus (*C. guereza*) contain lower
amounts of tannin and higher amounts of protein than mature leaves that are
not eaten (Oates et al. 1977). The leaves of tree species with high concentrations
of tannins are never eaten by black and white colobus but are occasionally eaten
by red colobus, *C. badius* (Oates et al. 1977). The same pattern occurs in other
primates. For example, mantled howling monkeys usually select leaves that
have fairly high levels of protein but little or no tannin (Glander 1981; Milton
1979), but occasionally these same howlers eat leaves with relatively high levels
of tannin and phenolics. Plant secondary compounds such as tannin could be
beneficial, counteracting bloat and helping to detoxify alkaloids by precipitation (Oates 1977). Whereas most primatologists have been reluctant to accept
this self-medication explanation, they have been unable to offer other cogent
explanations for the occasional ingestion of tannin-rich plant material by primates such as red colobus and howlers.

Another unusual and controversial behavior is the ingestion of soil by some
primates. Arboreal primates are seldom found on the ground, but black and
white colobus have been observed on the ground eating clay (Oates 1978). Clay
is relatively high in kaolins, and the clay may be ingested to adsorb plant toxins
or to adjust the pH of the stomach (Oates 1978). These cases of clay feeding
cannot be explained in terms of nutrient gain, but they may be examples of self-
medication that find close parallels in the medical cultures and special diets of

many contemporary human groups who avail themselves of the adsorbent and other qualities of clay (Johns and Duquette 1991).

Baboons and Plant Medicines

The occurrence of schistosomiasis in baboons (*P. anubis* and *P. hamadryas*) near Awash Falls in Ethiopia may be decreased through the ingestion of *Balanites aegyptiaca* (Phillips-Conroy 1986). The fruit and leaves of this plant are eaten by baboons living below the falls but not by those living above, even though *B. aegyptiaca* occurs evenly distributed in both areas. Both the berries and the leaves contain the steroidal saponin diosgenin, which is active against *Schistosoma cercariae*. Snails surveyed above the falls were negative for schistosomes, while those below tested positive during the dry season. This feeding pattern may offset a higher risk for schistosomiasis in the baboons living below the falls that are more likely to come into contact with schistosome-carrying snails (Phillips-Conroy 1986). In effect, the baboons below the falls ingest plant material that protects them against a virulent parasite.

A follow-up study tested the hypothesis that diosgenin alters the host's hormonal milieu, which produces a less hospitable environment for the adult schistosomes (Phillips-Conroy and Knopf 1986). The study, conducted with mice, revealed that the disease actually increases in mice fed diosgenin. Thus, the hypothesis was not supported, but what is true for mice may not be true for baboons. The researchers in this study argue that generalizations cannot be made about a parasite when different hosts are involved and further suggest that the feeding behavior, ecology, and parasite load of primate species are indeed related (Phillips-Conroy and Knopf 1986).

The Implications of Nonhuman Primate Self-Medication

Although much of the documentation for primate self-medication remains anecdotal and circumstantial, good evidence indicates that chimpanzees may be using drugs from their forest medicine chest to treat themselves. This possibility has major implications. Primatologists generally perceive primate foraging strategy as a balance between obtaining sufficient nutrients and avoiding toxins and digestion inhibitors (Glander 1982; Waterman 1984). Except for recent interest, investigators have largely ignored the potential beneficial aspects of plant-produced secondary compounds, which may be the missing link in understanding the connection between primate foraging and social organization. Tropical forests present a complex mix of nutrients, toxins, and medicines. Does each chimpanzee, howler, muriqui, colobus, and baboon have to learn for itself the difference between food, medicine, and toxin? Or does each learn from older members of the social group?

The answers to these questions will provide important insights for primate social organization and have significant ramifications for understanding human evolution. The ubiquitous occurrence of toxic plant chemicals probably restricted our ancestors' use of plant products for food, and early humans were unable to use most plant material for food until the development of fire (Leopold and Ardrey 1972; Stahl 1984). In a similar manner, plant-based contraceptives and abortifacients almost certainly affected early humans, who could have been aware of and could have exploited these effects. Certainly, archaeological evidence and written records indicate that ancient and medieval people used plant products to control population size (Riddle and Estes 1992).

The rapid disappearance of forests, which exhibit a diversity of species, means that researchers have little time remaining to determine the effects of plant-produced chemicals on animal and human fertility. Earlier reports that fertility was sharply reduced when sheep fed on one species of clover, *Trifolium subterraneum* (Pope et al. 1960), and that Thai women used an extract from the root of *Pueraria mirifica* (a close relative of kudzu) to induce abortion were met with skepticism (Riddle and Estes 1992). However, evidence such as that from the vole study (Berger et al. 1981) strongly suggests that plants supply more than nutrients. We know that not everything that is green is food, and the nature of the complexity of plant chemicals requires skill and sophistication on the part of plant-eating primates (including humans) to survive.

Another benefit of understanding the primate's natural pharmacopoeia is the potential discovery of new medicines for human and veterinary use. Many modern drugs including aspirin, morphine, and penicillin can be traced directly to plant origins. Yet researchers have chemically analyzed only a very small percentage of the 250,000 flowering plants in the world (Farnsworth 1993). Investigators cannot test every one of those plants for pharmacologic potential, but we can utilize nonhuman primates to screen them for us. We should not ignore the possibility that our nonhuman primate relatives may provide us with clues for the development of potent new drugs. This possibility also emphasizes the importance of preserving the tropical forests of the world as potential future sources of human medicines.

REFERENCES

Berger, Patricia J., Norman C. Negus, Edward H. Sanders, and Pete D. Gardner
    1981   Chemical triggering of reproduction in *Microtus montanus*. *Science* 214:69–
            70

Berger, Patricia J., Edward H. Sanders, Pete D. Gardner, and Norman C. Negus
  1977   Phenolic plant compounds functioning as reproductive inhibitors in *Microtus montanus*. *Science* 195:575–577.

Bhattacharya, B. C., B. M. Evans, and P. Shone
  1979   Semen separation technique monitored with greater accuracy by B-body test. *International Journal of Fertility* 24:256–259.

Etkin, Nina L., and Paul J. Ross
  1991   Should we set a place for diet in ethnopharmacology? *Journal of Ethnopharmacology* 32:25–36.

Farnsworth, Norman R.
  1993   Ethnopharmacology and future drug development: The North American experience. *Journal of Ethnopharmacology* 38:145–152.

Ghiglieri, Michael P.
  1984   *The chimpanzees of Kibale Forest.* Columbia University Press, New York.

Glander, Kenneth E.
  1975   Habitat description and resource utilization: A preliminary report on mantled howling monkey ecology. In *Socioecology and psychology of primates,* edited by R. H. Tuttle, pp. 37–57. Mouton, The Hague.
  1978   Howling monkey feeding behavior and plant secondary compounds: A study of strategies. In *The ecology of arboreal folivores,* edited by G. G. Montgomery, pp. 561–573. Smithsonian Institution Press, Washington, D.C.
  1981   Feeding patterns in mantled howling monkeys. In *Foraging behavior: Ecological, ethological, and psychological approaches,* edited by A. C. Kamil and T. D. Sargent, pp. 231–257. Garland Press, New York.
  1982   The impact of plant secondary compounds on primate feeding behavior. *Yearbook of Physical Anthropology* 25:1–18.

Glander, Kenneth E., and Dori P. Rabin
  1983   Food choice from endemic North Carolina tree species by captive prosimians (*Lemur fulvus*). *American Journal of Primatology* 5:221–229.

Hamada, S., and H. D. Slade
  1980   Biology, immunology, and cariogenicity of *Streptococcus mutans. Microbiological Review* 44:331–384.

Hansson, Anders, Graciela Veliz, Cesar Naquira, Maud Amren, Miguel Arroy, and Guillermo Arevalo
  1986   Preclinical and clinical studies with latex from *Ficus glabrata* Hbk., a traditional intestinal anthelmintic. *Journal of Ethnopharmacology* 17:105–138.

Himejima, Masaki, and Isao Kubo
  1991   Antibacterial agents from the cashew *Anacardium occidentale* (Anacardiaceae) nut shell oil. *Journal of Agriculture and Food Chemistry* 39:418–421.

Hladik, C. M.
  1978   Adaptive strategies of primates in relation to leaf-eating. In *The ecology of arboreal folivores,* edited by G. G. Montgomery, pp. 373–395. Smithsonian Institution Press, Washington, D.C.

Hubback, T. R.

1941   The Malay elephant. *Journal of the Bombay Natural History Society* 42:483–509.

Huffman, Michael A., and Mohamedi Seifu

1989   Observations on the illness and consumption of a possibly medicinal plant *Vernonia amygdalina* (Del.), by a wild chimpanzee in the Mahale Mountains National Park, Tanzania. *Primates* 30:51–63.

Hughes, Claude L.

1988   Phytochemical mimicry of reproductive hormones and modulation of herbivore fertility by phytoestrogens. *Environmental Health Perspectives* 78:171–175.

Janzen, Daniel H.

1978   Complications in interpreting the chemical defenses of trees against tropical arboreal plant-eating vertebrates. In *The ecology of arboreal folivores*, edited by G. G. Montgomery, pp. 73–84. Smithsonian Institution Press, Washington, D.C.

Jisaka, Mitsuo, Masanori Kawanaka, Hiromu Sugiyama, Kazunori Takegawa, Michael A. Huffman, Hajime Ohigashi, and Koichi Koshimizu

1992   Antischistosomal activities of sesquiterpene lactones and steroid glucosides from *Vernonia amygdalina*, possibly used by wild chimpanzees against parasite-related diseases. *Bioscience, Biotechnology, and Biochemistry* 56:845–846.

Johns, Timothy, and Martin Duquette

1991   Detoxification and mineral supplementation as functions of geophagy. *American Journal of Clinical Nutrition* 53:448–456.

Kilgore, Lynn

1989   Dental pathologies in ten free-ranging chimpanzees from Gombe National Park, Tanzania. *American Journal of Physical Anthropology* 80:219–227.

Koshimizu, Koichi, Hajime Ohigashi, Michael A. Huffman, Toshisada Nishida, and Hiroyuki Takasaki

1994   Physiological activities and the active constituents of possible medicinal plants used by wild chimpanzees of the Mahale Mountains, Tanzania. *International Journal of Primatology* (in press).

Kuntz, Robert E., and Betty J. Myers

1972   Parasites of South American primates. *International Zoo Yearbook* 12:61–68.

Labov, Jay B.

1977   Phytoestrogens and mammalian reproduction. *Comparative Biochemistry and Physiology* 57:3–9.

Leopold, Carl A., and Robert Ardrey

1972   Toxic substances in plants and the food habits of early man. *Science* 176:512–514.

Lewis, Walter H., and Memory P. F. Elvin-Lewis

1977   *Medical Botany*. Wiley, New York.

McKey, Doyle
  1979   The distribution of secondary compounds within plants. In *Herbivores: Their interactions with secondary plant compounds,* edited by G. A. Rosenthal and D. H. Janzen, pp. 423–437. Academic Press, New York.

Milton, Katherine
  1979   Factors influencing leaf choice by howler monkeys: A test of some hypotheses of food selection by generalist herbivores. *American Naturalist* 114:362–378.
  1980   *The foraging strategy of the howler monkeys.* Columbia University Press, New York.

Newton, P., and Toshisada Nishida
  1994   Possible buccal administration of herbal drugs by wild chimpanzees. *Animal Behavior* (in press).

Nishida, Toshisada
  1990   A quarter century of research in the Mahale Mountains: An overview. In *The chimpanzees of the Mahale Mountains,* edited by T. Nishida, pp. 3–35. University of Tokyo Press, Tokyo.

Oates, John F.
  1977   The guereza and its food. In *Primate ecology,* edited by T. H. Clutton-Brock, pp. 276–321. Academic Press, New York.
  1978   Water-plant and soil consumption by guereza monkeys (*Colobus guereza*): A relationship with minerals and toxins in the diet. *Biotropica* 10:241–253.

Oates, John F., Tony Swain, and J. Zantovska
  1977   Secondary compounds and food selection by Colobus monkeys. *Biochemical Systematics and Ecology* 5:317–321.

Phillips-Conroy, Jane E.
  1986   Baboons, diet, and disease: Food plant selection and schistosomiasis. In *Current perspectives in primate social dynamics,* edited by D. Taub and F. King, pp. 287–304. Van Nostrand/Reinhold, New York.

Phillips-Conroy, Jane E., and Paul M. Knopf
  1986   The effects of ingesting plant hormones on schistosomiasis in mice: An experimental study. *Biochemical Systematics and Ecology* 14:637–645.

Pope, G. S., M. J. McNaughton, and H.E.H. Jones
  1960   Estrogens in pasture forage. *Nutritional Review* 18:14–15.

Riddle, John M., and J. Worth Estes
  1992   Oral contraceptives in ancient and medieval times. *American Scientist* 80:226–233.

Rodriguez, Eloy M., E. M. Aregullin, Toshisada Nishida, S. Uehara, Richard W. Wrangham, Z. Abramowski, A. Finlayson, and G.H.N. Towers
  1985   Thiarubrine A, a bioactive constituent of *Aspilia* (Asteraceae) consumed by wild chimpanzees. *Experientia* 41:419–420.

Sevinc, Afif

1968   Experiments on sex control by electrophoretic separation of spermatozoa in the rabbit. *Journal of Reproduction and Fertility* 16:7–14.

Singh, R. S., S. N. Pandey, L. H. Singh, and S. P. Sen

1981   Studies on *Centratherum anthelminticum* syn. *Vernonia anthelmintica* (Family: Compositae) in clinical cases of helminthiasis. *Journal of Scientific Research in Plants and Medicine* 2:47–54.

Stahl, Ann B.

1984   Hominid dietary selection before fire. *Current Anthropology* 25:151–168.

Strier, Karen B.

1992   *Faces in the forest: The endangered muriqui monkeys of Brazil.* Oxford University Press, New York.

1993   Menu for a monkey. *Natural History* 102:34–43.

Stuart, Michael D., Lisa L. Greenspan, Kenneth E. Glander, and Margaret R. Clarke

1990   A coprological survey of parasites of wild mantled howling monkeys, *Alouatta palliata palliata. Journal of Wildlife Diseases* 26:547–549.

Stuart, Michael D., Karen B. Strier, and Suzanne M. Pierberg

1993   A coprological survey of wild muriquis, *Brachyteles arachnoides*, and brown howling monkeys, *Alouatta fusca. Journal of the Helminthological Society* (in press).

Takasaki, Hiroyuki, and Kevin Hunt

1987   Further medicinal plant consumption in wild chimpanzees? *African Study Monographs* 8:125–128.

Waterman, Peter G.

1984   Food acquisition and processing as a function of plant chemistry. In *Food acquisition and processing in primates,* edited by D. J. Chivers, B. A. Wood, and A. Bilsborough, pp. 177–211. Plenum Press, New York.

Watt, J. M., and M. G. Breyer-Brandwijk

1962   *The medicinal and poisonous plants of Southern and East Africa.* E. & S. Livingstone, Edinburgh.

Wrangham, Richard W., and Toshisada Nishida

1983   *Aspilia* spp. leaves: A puzzle in the feeding behavior of wild chimpanzees. *Primates* 24:283–287.

Wrangham, Richard W., and Peter G. Waterman

1983   Condensed tannins in fruits eaten by chimpanzees. *Biotropica* 15:217–222.

13

Wild Plant Use by Pregnant and Lactating Ringtailed Lemurs, with Implications for Early Hominid Foraging

❊ MICHELLE L. SAUTHER

Before identifying important evolutionary factors in human-plant interaction, researchers may find it advantageous to determine how wild plant foods can shape the feeding behavior of our closest relatives, the nonhuman primates. Because the intimate relationship between these primates and plants is unfettered by cultural trappings, studies of their feeding behavior can provide comparative data on how ecological and physiological forces may have influenced early hominid foraging. Perhaps the most fundamental factor affecting feeding behavior is a female's reproductive state, and therefore, females and males should use different foraging strategies, at least during some periods. Yet there is little information on how male and female primates vary their use of wild plant foods. This basic difference does affect food selection and foraging in ringtailed lemurs and holds implications for the reconstruction of early hominid foodways.

Background Information and Methods

Study Habitat

I conducted my research in Madagascar's Beza Mahafaly Special Reserve, which was first established in 1978 and granted special reserve status in 1985. The reserve contains a wealth of birds, mammals, reptiles, and insects that are representative of southwestern Madagascar. The Mahafaly people who live in

This work was supported by grants from the National Science Foundation, the L.S.B. Leakey Fund, the National Geographic Society, the Collaborative Fulbright, the Boise Fund, and Sigma Xi and a fellowship from the American Association of University Women.

this area do not hunt lemurs there because it is *fady* (taboo) for them to eat lemurs, an injunction reinforced by guards in the employ of the reserve. The reserve does contain a natural complement of mammalian and avian predators, some of which feed on lemurs (Ratsirarson 1985; Sauther 1989). This is a strictly seasonal habitat having a hot/wet season (December–April), a cool/dry season (May–September), and a transitional period (October–November). The availability of wild plant foods used by ringtailed lemurs is influenced by this seasonal variation and is highest overall during the wet season.

The Ringtailed Lemur

During the 13-month study (October 1987 to November 1988) my research assistant and I followed two groups of ringtailed lemurs (*L. catta*). Close-range observations (1–2 meters) were possible as the animals quickly became used to our presence. I studied 16 lemurs (7 males and 9 females) and collected more than 1,800 hours of observations.

The ringtailed lemur is a social, diurnal prosimian that inhabits riverine forests of southern Madagascar (Tattersall 1982). At Beza Mahafaly ringtailed lemur group size ranges from 9 to 22 individuals (Sussman 1991). Males and females are similar in size, and adult females have first priority over males to all resources including food, water, and space (Kappeler 1990; Sauther 1992). *L. catta* forage opportunistically on a wide range of foods and at all levels of the forest, including ground level. In this species all females of reproductive age in a group mate during the same period. Thus, all adult females are pregnant and lactate at the same time (Sauther 1991). However, during this study some females lost their infants early after birth, and I could thus compare lactating and nonlactating females during the same time period. Females nursed during the hot/wet season, were pregnant during the cool/dry season, and gave birth during the transitional period.

Sampling Methods

My research assistant and I entered data directly into hand-held portable computers powered by solar-rechargeable batteries and saved data on $3^{1}/2''$ computer diskettes. For observation we used the focal animal sampling method (Altmann 1974), sampling behaviors at five-minute intervals. If the behavior was feeding or foraging, we also recorded the plant taxon and part used. In this study feeding was strictly defined as actual ingestion of food items and did not include handling and processing time. We sampled the behavior of each adult member one day per month for at least 7 hours. Each observation day each of us followed a different adult lemur; therefore, we always sampled two subjects simultaneously.

Furthermore, I determined the availability each month of fruits, leaves, and

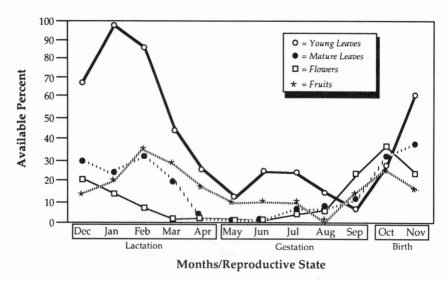

Figure 13.1. Presence of plant parts making up the diet of ringtailed lemurs, by month and associated reproductive state.

flowers as potential food resources for ringtailed lemurs by noting the presence or absence of these food parts on 31 species of trees, bushes, and lianas (N=119 samples). I collected samples of all ringtailed lemur foods and determined the weights of single food items based on the average of 100 food samples; I also dried samples of all foods for future chemical analyses. Of the identified food items, only *Tamarindus indica* (tamarind) fruit was too large for the lemurs to place the entire item into the mouth and chew. All other foods were of a small and roughly uniform size. Thus, each of the lemurs used its mouth to pluck leaves, leaf buds, flowers, and all fruits (except *T. indica* and *Catanaregam spinosa*) singly and consumed one part at a time directly from the source. I estimated food intake by multiplying the total number of times the subject fed on a particular species and part (with each time representing the ingestion of one such food item) by the mean wet weight for that species and part. This provides, for each lemur, the estimated minimum weight of a particular species and part ingested. I analyzed fruit of *T. indica* separately to avoid masking important differences between *T. indica* and other fruits. This fruit was qualitatively different from the others as it was available year-round, was heavier and more fibrous, and contained less water relative to other fruits, which were juicy drupes (based on percentage of water determined by weighing fruits before and after drying). *T. indica* fruit was also associated with low feeding competition, or agonism.

To determine the foraging efficiency of foods I used a ratio: the percentage of time spent feeding on a particular species or part divided by the percentage of time spent foraging for that same species or part. The higher the ratio, the more time spent feeding relative to foraging.

Statistical Analysis

I tested differences between males and females of varying reproductive states using the independent t test (Sokal and Rohlf 1981) and determined significance by a randomization test that employs 1,000 random permutations of the t statistic (Edgington 1980; Manly 1991). Significance was set at .05.

The Foraging Behavior of Males and Reproductive Females

Pregnant and lactating females exhibited different foraging strategies when compared to nonlactating females and to males. At Beza Mahafaly Reserve, female reproduction matched the seasonal availability of resources. Thus, females nursed and weaned their infants during the wet season, a time of greater food abundance; they were pregnant during the dry season, a period of reduced availability; and they gave birth during a transitional period when food availability began to increase (Figure 13.1).

Lactation

Activity Levels and Reproductive State: Although males and nonlactating females did not differ markedly in time spent resting, nursing females rested more than members of either of the other two groups (Figure 13.2). However, when time spent nursing was subtracted, the differences between these three classes were not significant, indicating that increased time resting was directly associated with lactation.

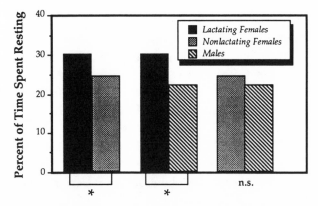

Figure 13.2. Comparison of time spent resting by lactating females, nonlactating females, and males during the wet season (*denotes p<.05; n.s.=no significance).

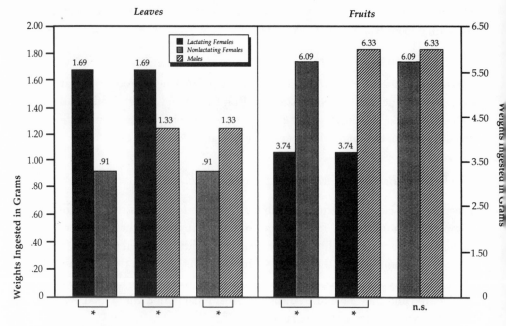

Figure 13.3. Mean minimum amount ingested (by weight) of young leaves and fruits by lactating females, nonlactating females, and males (*denotes p<.05; n.s.=no significance).

Feeding Behavior: Compared to males or nonlactating females, nursing females emphasized different plant parts, focusing more on young leaves, mainly herbaceous terrestrial species (Figure 13.3). Males ate more young leaves, by weight, than did nonlactating females. Nursing females and males also used, on average, more species of leaves than did nonlactating females (lactating females=3.95 species, males=3.54, nonlactating females=2.96; p<.05). In contrast, males and nonlactating females both fed more on fruits, ingesting more, by weight, than did lactating females.

Use of the Environment: Nursing females not only emphasized different foods but also foraged for wild plants in different ways. These females spent most of their time feeding on young leaves at all levels of the forest, whereas nonlactating females concentrated on fruit feeding in the trees (Table 13.1). Males spent more time than females feeding on fruits at ground level, especially the fruits of *T. indica,* which ripen and fall to the ground in large quantities. Males also fed more than nonlactating females on leaves at ground level.

I partitioned foraging into more active (climbing, running, leaping, hopping, jumping) and less active (walking) movement. Active foraging in the trees did not vary markedly between reproductive states, but nonlactating females and males used more active forms of foraging at ground level compared to lactating females. Nursing females also walked more than nonlactating females (Table 13.2).

Pregnancy

Feeding Behavior: Although total time spent feeding did not vary markedly between males and pregnant females, the sexes exhibited clear differences in the plant parts they emphasized. Females fed more on flowers and fruits (not including the fruits of *T. indica*), whereas males focused more on leaves during this period between May and September (Figure 13.4).

For many mammalian species, including humans, late pregnancy requires more energy because most growth of the placenta and fetus occurs during the third trimester (Stini 1988). To better discern feeding behavior during this time, I divided the pregnancy into two periods: early pregnancy (May–June) and late pregnancy (July–September). I then compared males and pregnant females for total time spent feeding and time spent feeding on fruits, leaves, and flowers. When feeding behavior is broken down into early and late pregnancy, a clear pattern emerges (Table 13.3). During early pregnancy females and males both searched out isolated pockets of herbaceous leaves, while females fed on the limited fruit available at this time. During late pregnancy, females

Table 13.1 Mean Time Spent Feeding at Different Levels by Lactating and Nonlactating Females and by Males

	Fruits			Leaves		
	Ground	Bush	Tree	Ground	Bush	Tree
Percentage of Time						
Lactating females	9%	3%	44%	16%	10%	18%
Nonlactating females	9%	6%	60%	10%	3%	12%
Males	14%	7%	48%	18%	5%	8%
Significant Difference						
Lactating vs. nonlactating females	n.s.	n.s.	p<.04	p<.05	p<.01	n.s.
Lactating females vs. males	p<.05	n.s.	n.s.	n.s.	p<.04	p<.002
Nonlactating females vs. males	p<.05	n.s.	p<.05	p<.01	n.s.	n.s.

Note: n.s. = no significance; significance at p<.05

Table 13.2 Type of Movement by Lactating and Nonlactating Females and by Males

	Active[a]		Less Active[b]	
	Ground	Tree	Ground	Tree
Percentage of Time				
Lactating females	3%	41%	37%	19%
Nonlactating females	9%	35%	29%	27%
Males	9%	30%	39%	22%
Significant Difference[c]				
Lactating vs. nonlactating females	p<.01	n.s.	p<.01	p<.05
Lactating females vs. males	p<.003	p<.015	n.s.	n.s.
Nonlactating females vs. males	n.s.	n.s.	p<.01	n.s.

[a]Includes climbing, running, leaping, hopping, jumping
[b]Walking
[c]n.s. = no significance; significance at p<.05.

focused more on new flowers and flower buds, and on fruits, whereas males fed more on mature leaves.

During this time males employed a feeding strategy not observed for pregnant females. Groups of three to four males went on "foraging expeditions": they split off from the main group, moved rapidly 6 or more hectares, and entered particular trees, presumably in search of early fruits. These were short forays, with the males rapidly rejoining their groups.

Use of the Environment: Ringtailed lemurs spent a variable amount of time walking or using more active forms of movement at different levels, and I could discern no pattern. Pregnant females did spend more time feeding in the trees on fruits and flowers, whereas males tended to feed on mature leaves at ground level (Table 13.4).

Foraging Strategies of Lactating Females

Energy Conservation

For most mammals, lactation is the costliest stage of reproduction and is associated with behavioral or dietary changes (Clutton-Brock et al. 1989; Sadleir 1969; Sauther and Nash 1987). In this study, lactating females proved to be discriminating feeders. By employing a variety of tactics, they were able to minimize foraging costs and yet still provide themselves with protein-rich foods. They conserved energy by spending more time resting, by using less active forms of foraging, and by focusing on young leaves that were easier to locate and digest. The processing costs associated with feeding on immature leaves versus fruits can be quite different with regard to the amount of energy needed to locate the food, prepare it, and metabolize nutrients after ingestion. In this study, young leaves were easier to locate than fruits. Thus, the foraging efficiency for fruits was much lower than for leaves (fruits=1.32, leaves=13.61), so that individuals spent less time feeding and more time searching for fruits. Fruits were also more expensive in terms of agonism, with mean agonistic displacements over fruit (47%) much higher than displacements over leaves (9%).

Leaves from deciduous bushes and trees provide a predictable and easily located food source because the foliage is all leaf flush, young leaves, or mature leaves at the same time. In contrast, evergreen species have a mix of leaf stages, requiring more effort to locate choice young leaves among mature ones. In this study the lemurs primarily utilized leaves from herbaceous species or deciduous trees. Of the 41 species of leaves used, 73% were from terrestrial or climbing herbaceous species, 20% were from deciduous shrubs and trees, and only 7% were from evergreen species. The herbaceous species often occurred in large, easily located patches.

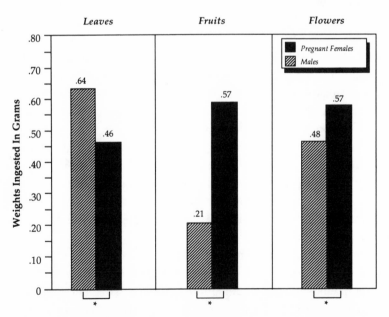

Figure 13.4. Mean minimum weights of fruits, leaves, and flowers ingested by males and pregnant females (*denotes p<.05). Fruit category does not include fruits of *Tamarindus indica*.

Table 13.3 Time Spent Feeding and Mean Minimum Weights (in grams) of Plant Parts Eaten by Males and Pregnant Females

	Total[a] Time		Leaves by Weight		Fruits[b] by Weight		Flowers by Weight	
	Early[c]	Late[d]	Early	Late	Early	Late	Early	Late
Pregnant females	12%	20%	.26	.18	.16	.41	0	.57
Males	11%	19%	.21	.43	.01	.23	0	.48
Pregnant females vs. males[e]	n.s.	n.s.	n.s.	p<.001	p<.01	p<.001	n.s.	p<.05

[a]Total time spent feeding as a percentage of all activities
[b]Not including fruits of *Tamarindus indica*
[c]Early pregnancy, May through June
[d]Late pregnancy, July through September
[e]n.s. = no significance; significance at p<.05

Nutrients and Food Choice

In terms of digestion, utilizing more young leaves than fruits was probably not more costly for lactating females. Nursing females fed only on young leaves and leaf buds, and while mature leaves are difficult for nonruminants to digest, young leaves and leaf buds are relatively easy to break down and do not necessarily contain more fiber than fruits (Rogers et al. 1990). Fruits can also vary in terms of processing costs. Some primate fruits are difficult to access because of hard coverings—for example, fruits used by *Cebus apella*, blackcapped capuchin (Lucas 1989; Terborgh 1983); they can vary in fiber content; and unripe fruits may contain higher percentages of phenolics (Rogers et al. 1990). Except for *T. indica*, the fruits used as food by ringtailed lemurs were all small and soft bodied, some occurring in clusters. When clearly distinguishable, ripe fruits were selected over unripe ones. Thus, although we did not measure digestibility directly, the digestibility of most fruits versus young leaves and leaf buds was probably similar (Rogers et al. 1990).

Focusing on immature leaves from herbaceous species may have provided lactating females the advantage of lower levels of digestion inhibitors and other secondary compounds and greater amounts of protein and micronutrients than are characteristic of leaves of evergreen trees (Coley 1983; Waterman et al. 1983). Lactating females also avoided an accumulation of any one type of secondary compound by feeding for only a short time on each of a variety of leaf species.

Nursing females focused on leaf stages that were both easier to process and nutritionally more valuable: young leaves and leaf buds rather than mature leaves. Nutrient availability from leaves of deciduous species varies with developmental stage, with young leaves exhibiting greater amounts of protein and energy (Baranga 1983). In addition, young leaves yield more accessible protein and micronutrients because their relatively weak cell walls afford easy digestibility, whereas mature leaves with tougher cell walls are difficult to digest without special morphological adaptations for rumination (Waterman and Choo 1981; Waterman et al. 1983). In some cases mature leaves contain higher percentages of secondary compounds, including digestion inhibitors (Waterman and Choo 1981; cf. Coley 1983).

Lactating females have higher protein and calcium requirements than do females in other reproductive states (Widdowson 1977). Young leaves provided these females with more of these nutrients than is normally available in fruits (Barton 1989; Coley 1983; Waterman et al. 1983). The wet season is marked by much higher availability of leaf buds and young leaves, and lactating females focused more on these food items than did nonlactating females and males. This pattern follows the general trend for a number of primate species in which nursing females either consume greater amounts or spend more time feeding on protein-rich foods (Fragaszy 1986; Gautier-Hion 1980; Harrison 1983).

Foraging Strategies of Pregnant Females

In general, the costs of gestation are less than for lactation (Sadleir 1969) and may explain why some species gestate during times of limited food availability (Gittleman and Thompson 1988). Ringtailed lemur females at Beza Mahafaly Reserve followed this pattern, as pregnancy coincided with the cool/dry season when food availability decreases. Although less dramatic, the tactics during this period tended to reflect behavioral adaptations of lactating females. In

Table 13.4 Mean Time Spent Feeding at Different Levels by Males and Pregnant Females

	Ground	Bush	Tree
Pregnant females	17%	13%	70%
Males	31%	15%	54%
Pregnant females vs. males	p<.02	n.s.	p<.02

Note: n.s. = no significance; significance at p<.05

general pregnant females decreased their activity levels by resting and by lessening social activity. Pregnant females fed more on fruits than did males, even though the availability of fruits was lower than during lactation. They also continued to exploit the diminishing patches of young leaves during early pregnancy; and when young leaves became scarce, large flowering trees provided pregnant females with a rich source of protein.

The findings discussed in this chapter provide one concrete example of how wild plant resources can mold nonhuman primate foraging behavior. In the case of ringtailed lemurs, who live in a highly seasonal environment with a fluctuating resource base, females pattern their reproduction to coincide with the availability of important plants. Hence, females nurse and wean their infants when they can exploit low-cost, high-protein plant resources such as young leaves, and pregnant females take advantage of the dramatic increase of flowers during the latter period of gestation. Males exhibit different foraging strategies by focusing on more costly foods when these are available but then feeding on lower-quality foods when other resources are reduced. Males are also able to make costly forays that potentially have a big payoff, that is, early access to seasonal fruit resources.

Implications for Early Hominid Foraging Behavior

Attempts to address the social and ecological adaptations of early hominids have often emphasized particular foraging behaviors such as meat eating or hunting (DeVore and Washburn 1963; Foley and Lee 1989; Tooby and DeVore 1987; Washburn and Lancaster 1968) or the gathering of wild plant foods (Zihlman 1981; Zihlman and Tanner 1978). Furthermore, models for hominid behavior have often been patterned on the feeding strategies of a single primate species (DeVore and Washburn 1963; Tanner 1987), an approach that other researchers have recently criticized (Tooby and DeVore 1987). A more promising method uses evolutionary principles to identify important ecological forces affecting behavioral ecology (Tooby and DeVore 1987). From this perspective, however, investigators need a clearer understanding of the basis of sex differences in primate foraging strategies. Although some researchers have posited greater female reproductive investment as one of the foundations for the development of food gathering (Tanner 1987; Zihlman 1981), there is little information regarding how this basic difference actually affects primate foraging behavior.

The ringtailed lemur (which is the most terrestrial of prosimians and is diurnal) inhabits mosaic forests similar to that of early australopithecine hominids (Van Couvering 1980). This species is directly influenced by its environment, as were early hominids, but the natural behaviors of lemurs have not been masked or modified by culture and technology. They encounter a range of environments within their habitat from tall canopy forest to more open bush and scrub to dry desertlike bioregions. Within this seasonal habitat ringtailed lemurs forage at all levels, including substantial terrestrial foraging and travel. Furthermore, they employ an opportunistic foraging strategy, using a wide range of food resources as each becomes seasonally available (Sauther 1992). As such, they can help to identify important behavioral adaptations for species living within seasonal, mosaic bioregions.

From an evolutionary perspective, the feeding behavior of ringtailed lemurs suggests that one critical advancement that set prehominid populations apart from other primate species was the development of behaviors that increased resource dependability. Given an increasingly seasonal savannah-mosaic bioregion (Van Couvering 1980), prehominids would have had to exploit these new feeding niches. Females would still have faced higher reproductive costs than would affect males. To exist in these seasonal environments, prehominids would have needed a more dependable resource base.

In this context, the high nutritional costs of lactating and gestation could have prompted early hominid females to expand their ecological niches in a variety of ways. Females may have broken free from some of the seasonal constraints on food availability by using tools to gather wild plants, insects, and small mammals (Boesch and Boesch 1983; McGrew 1981; Tanner 1987; Zihlman 1981) and thus could have provided a more reliable year-round resource base. For example, females may have employed digging sticks for underground tubers and used techniques similar to those observed in wild chimpanzees, such as using stone hammers to crack open nuts and employing termite and ant wands (Boesch and Boesch 1983; Goodall 1971; Tanner 1981). Such a perspective views high female maternal investment not as a burden (Tooby and De-Vore 1987) but rather as a catalyst for developing more efficient foraging techniques for maintaining adequate nutrition throughout all reproductive states. Because males do not incur these high reproductive costs, they are able to endure a more variable resource base, that is, they can exploit more costly food resources when food is abundant and thus employ more expensive modes of foraging but are then able to exist on low-quality foods when food availability is reduced.

This basic difference has important ramifications for understanding the basis for a sexual division of labor, with males exploiting less reliable resources such as meat through less efficient techniques such as hunting. Within this scenario, male reproductive success would have been closely tied to the female's ability to produce surviving offspring, and yet her reproductive costs within such an environment were probably higher than those of forest-dwelling species. Males (and nonlactating females) may therefore have contributed to resource dependability by locating new plant resources that were then added to the group's foraging path. This is consistent with the tendency for male primates to migrate out of a group and to travel more widely than females in many species (Wrangham 1986), as such behaviors would increase the male's chances of encountering new food patches. In addition, males could afford to engage in more costly foraging such as hunting, which would have provided an additional resource that could be obtained year-round. In this context, behavioral adaptations such as sharing meat and gathered wild plant foods would have a high adaptive value in terms of increasing both male and female reproductive success.

Dependable resources were also critical for the evolution of the human brain, for while we are a long way from understanding the essential factors that prompted hominid brain expansion, we do know that the modern human brain is metabolically expensive, using 20% of the body's calories in the form of glucose (Romero-Sierra 1986). The development of behaviors that allowed prehominids to maintain a more dependable resource base probably preceded hominid brain expansion.

In conclusion, ringtailed lemurs respond to seasonally available wild plant resources by patterning their most expensive reproductive events to coincide with optimal plant availability and also by focusing on foods for which foraging is less expensive. Similar data for other primates inhabiting seasonal environments could help to identify alternative or additional strategies used by reproducing females to exploit seasonal plant foods. For example, savannah baboons (*Papio cynocephalus*) live within a seasonal environment (in terms of rainfall) but do not show strict seasonal reproduction (Altmann 1980). These baboons have access to more dependable resources in the form of underground plant bulbs, rhizomes, and grass corms that are available throughout the year (Norton et al. 1987). Such a comparative approach may clarify the relationship between basic biological constraints and adaptive strategies, which researchers can then apply to the reconstructing of hominid lifeways.

REFERENCES

Altmann, J.
 1974 Observational study of behavior: Sampling methods. *Behaviour* 49:227–267.
 1980 *Baboon mothers and infants.* Harvard University Press, Cambridge, Massachusetts.
Baranga, D.
 1983 Changes in chemical composition of food parts in the diet of colobus monkeys. *Ecology* 64:668–673.

Barton, R.

    1989   Foraging strategies, diet and competition in olive baboons. Ph.D. dissertation, University of St. Andrews.

Boesch, C., and H. Boesch

    1983   Optimisation of nut-cracking with natural hammers by wild chimpanzees. *Behaviour* 83:265–286.

Clutton-Brock, T. H., S. D. Albon, and F. E. Guiness

    1989   Fitness costs of gestation and lactation in wild mammals. *Nature* 337:360–363.

Coley, P. D.

    1983   Herbivory and defensive characteristics of tree species in a lowland tropical forest. *Ecological Monographs* 53:209–233.

DeVore, I., and S. L. Washburn

    1963   Baboon ecology and human evolution. In *African ecology and human evolution,* edited by F. C. Howell and F. Bourliere, pp. 335–367. Aldine, New York.

Edgington, E. S.

    1980   *Randomization tests.* Marcel Dekker, New York.

Foley, R. A., and P. C. Lee

    1989   Finite social space, evolutionary pathways and reconstructing hominid behavior. *Science* 243:901–906.

Fragaszy, D. M.

    1986   Activity budgets and foraging behavior in wedge-capped capuchins (*Cebus olivaceous*): Age and sex differences. In *Current perspectives in primate social dynamics,* edited by D. Taub and F. King, pp. 159–174. Van Nostrand, New York.

Gautier-Hion, A.

    1980   Seasonal variations of diet related to species and sex in a community of Cercopithecus monkeys. *Journal of Animal Ecology* 49:237–269.

Gittleman, J. L., and S. D. Thompson

    1988   Energy allocation in mammalian reproduction. *American Zoologist* 28:865–875.

Goodall, J.

    1971   *In the shadow of man.* Dell, New York.

Harrison, C. M.

    1983   Age and sex differences in the diet and feeding strategies of the green monkey, *Cercopithecus sabaeus. Animal Behavior* 31:969–977.

Kappeler, P. M.

    1990   Female dominance in *Lemur catta:* More than just female feeding priority? *Folia Primatologica* 55:92–95.

Lucas, P. W.

    1989   A new theory relating seed processing by primates to their relative tooth sizes. In *The growing scope of human biology,* edited by L. H. Schmitt, L. Freedman, and N. W. Bruce, pp. 37–48. Proceedings of the Australasian Society for Human Biology No. 2. Centre for Human Biology, Nedlands, Western Australia.

McGrew, W. C.

1981   The female chimpanzee as a human evolutionary prototype. In *Woman the gatherer,* edited by F. Dahlberg, pp. 35–73. Yale University Press, New Haven.

Manly, B.F.J.

1991   *Randomization and Monte Carlo methods in biology.* Chapman and Hall, New York.

Norton, G. W., R. J. Rhine, G. W. Wynn, and R. D. Wynn

1987   Baboon diet: A five-year study of stability and variability in the plant feeding and habitat of the yellow baboons (*Papio cynocephalus*) of Mikumi National Park, Tanzania. *Folia Primatologica* 48:78–120.

Ratsirarson, J.

1985   *Contribution à l'etude comparative de l'eco-ethologie de Lemur catta dans deux habitats différents de la Reserve Spéciale de Beza-Mahafaly.* Université de Madagascar, Madagascar.

Rogers, M., F. Maisels, E. A. Willamson, M. Fernandez, and C.E.G. Tutin

1990   Gorilla diet in the Lopé Reserve, Gabon: A nutritional analysis. *Oecologia* 84:326–339.

Romero-Sierra, C.

1986   *Neuroanatomy: A conceptual approach.* Churchill Livingstone, New York.

Sadleir, R.M.F.S.

1969   *The ecology of reproduction in wild and domestic mammals.* Methuen, New Jersey.

Sauther, M. L.

1989   Antipredator behavior in troops of free-ranging *Lemur catta* at Beza Mahafaly Special Reserve, Madagascar. *International Journal of Primatology* 10:595–606.

1991   Reproductive behavior of free-ranging *Lemur catta* at Beza Mahafaly Special Reserve, Madagascar. *American Journal of Physical Anthropology* 84:463–477.

1992   The effect of reproductive state, social rank and group size on resource use among free-ranging ringtailed lemurs (Lemur catta) of Madagascar. Ph.D. dissertation, Washington University.

Sauther, M. L., and L. T. Nash

1987   The effect of reproductive state and body size on food consumption in captive *Galago senegalensis braccatus. American Journal of Physical Anthropology* 73:81–88.

Sokal, R. R., and F. J. Rohlf

1981   *Biometry.* W. H. Freeman, New York.

Stini, W. A.

1988   Food, seasonality, and human evolution. In *Coping with uncertainty in food supply*, edited by I. de Garine and G. A. Harrison, pp. 31–51. Clarendon Press, New York.

Sussman, R. W.

1991   Demography and social organization of free-ranging *Lemur catta* in the Beza Mahafaly Reserve, Madagascar. *American Journal of Physical Anthropology* 84:43–58.

Tanner, N. M.

1981   *On becoming human.* Cambridge University Press, Cambridge.

1987   The chimpanzee model revisited and the gathering hypothesis. In *The evolution of human behavior: Primate models*, edited by W. G. Kinzey, pp. 3–27. State University of New York Press, Albany.

Tattersall, I.

1982   *The primates of Madagascar.* Columbia University Press, New York.

Terborgh, J.

1983   *Five New World primates: A study in comparative ecology.* Princeton University Press, Princeton.

Tooby, J., and I. DeVore

1987   The reconstruction of hominid behavioral evolution through strategic modeling. In *The evolution of human behavior: Primate models*, edited by W. G. Kinzey, pp. 183–238. State University of New York Press, Albany.

Van Couvering, J.A.H.

1980   Community evolution in east Africa during the late Cenozoic. In *Fossils in the making*, edited by A. K. Behrensmeyer and A. Hill, pp. 272–298. University of Chicago Press, Chicago.

Washburn, S. L., and J. Lancaster

1968   The evolution of hunting. In *Man the hunter*, edited by R. Lee and I. DeVore, pp. 293–303. Aldine, Chicago.

Waterman, P. G., and G. M. Choo

1981   The effects of digestibility-reducing compounds in leaves on food selection by some Colobinae. *Malaysian Applied Biology* 10:147–162.

Waterman, P. G., G. M. Choo, A. L. Vedder, and D. Watts

1983   Digestibility, digestion-inhibitors and nutrients of herbaceous foliage and green stems from an African montane flora and comparison with other tropical flora. *Oecologia* 60:244–249.

Widdowson, E. M.

1977   Nutrition and lactation. In *Nutritional disorders of American women*, edited by M. Winick, pp. 67–75. Wiley, New York.

Wrangham, R. W.

1986   Evolution of social structure. In *Primate societies*, edited by B. B. Smuts, D. L. Cheney, R. M. Seyfarth, R. W. Wrangham, and T. T. Struhsaker. University of Chicago Press, Chicago.

Zihlman, A. L.

    1981   Women and shapers of the human adaptation. In *Woman the gatherer*, edited by F. Dahlberg, pp. 75–120. Yale University Press, New Haven.

Zihlman, A. L., and N. Tanner

    1978   Gathering and the hominid adaptation. In *Female hierarchies*, edited by L. Tiger and H. Fowler, pp. 163–194. Beresford Book Service, Chicago.

❧ Epilogue

In Search of "Keystone Societies"

❧ BRIEN A. MEILLEUR

Recent archaeological discoveries have destroyed the assumption that Eden's hunters were conservationists. —*Jared Diamond 1986:19*

Looked at from the point of view of other organisms, humankind . . . resembles an acute epidemic disease. —*William H. McNeill 1976:19–20*

The socioeconomic activities of virtually all societies have resulted in the simplification of their natural environments. —*Eugene Parker 1992:414*

Assessments of the depletion of biological diversity and of its social and biological implications bombard us today from nearly every type of public forum. Scholarly publications detail the ongoing levels of destruction (primarily in tropical forest ecosystems), predict future losses, and indicate which taxonomic groups will suffer the most (Davis et al. 1986; Ehrlich 1988; Raven 1988). Popular media such as radio and television inform us about endangered species, incite us to respect them, and sometimes ask us to contribute money to conservation organizations who will protect them for us.[1] This popularity is not lost on the advertising industry; multinational corporations increasingly use biodiversity-related themes to sell their products. As a result, hundreds of millions of people worldwide now understand fairly well some aspect of biological diversity and its loss.

People no longer limit their concern to the plight of large, exotic animals such as pandas, elephants, and whales, which were the focus of the upper middle class, urban "ecological" movement that began in the 1960s. Rather, the public has become increasingly aware that scores of species in groups as familiar as flowering plants and birds may soon be in equal (if not greater) danger of imminent extinction. In Hawai'i, for example, often called the endangered species capital of the United States, more than 20% of the native plants will soon be federally listed as threatened or endangered. More than 30 plant taxa in Hawai'i are now represented by fewer than ten individuals; 12 have only one remaining wild specimen (Center for Plant Conservation 1994)!

Indeed, important biological and physical changes to our environment are now under way. In all likelihood, we and our children will face in the near future a substantially different and probably less diverse and hospitable world as a result (Peters 1988). The obvious causes for these changes, in the most simple terms—humans in ever greater numbers, seemingly consuming resources and space at insatiable rates—appear to many people to be the most urgent political and social issues of our time.

But does the blanket condemnation of *Homo sapiens* and human economic activities, so graphically portrayed by Diamond, McNeill, and Parker, appropriately summarize the past and predict the future of the relationship our species has with the earth and its biota? Have humans of other times and other cultures invariably wreaked havoc on their worlds? Or does the history of humankind instead exhibit an array of environmental management strategies variably practiced over time and space, ranging in their effects from depletion of habitats and biodiversity to enhancement of these same, with one or more of these strategies gaining particularly destructive ascendancy in recent times?

A brief review of recent approaches to and results from the scientific study of the interrelationship between humans and wild plants may help us to address objectively the questions posed above. Because of the multifaceted nature and pervasiveness of the relations between humans and wild plants, researchers have studied human–wild plant issues through a spectrum of disciplines and subdisciplines, from archaeology to medicine, from nutrition to ethnobotany, not all of which can be addressed in this essay.[2] Taken as a whole, the evidence surveyed here leads to a rejection of the unequivocal statements of Diamond, McNeill, and Parker, which suggest that some sort of universal law of human nature invariably moves our species to engage in environmentally destructive behavior.

Before Biodiversity Was an Issue

Until the 1950s, researchers mostly studied the interrelationship between wild plants and humans through species-by-species investigations of plants useful to preindustrial peoples and through examinations of the transformation of some of these species into crops. The many and varied compendia of anthropologists and botanists documenting plant utility, called ethnobotany or economic botany, demonstrated the importance and the multiple roles of wild plants within indigenous societies practicing a range of subsistence modes. Plant domestication and breeding were similarly important areas of human–wild plant study, with much interest directed earlier in this century to the geographical origins of major crops and to the anatomical changes that wild species underwent as they became domesticated (Anderson 1954; de Candolle 1959; Sauer 1952).

During the 1950s, with the growth of scientific ecology (Odum 1953), investigations of human–wild plant interactions diversified within both ethnobotany and domestication research, while beginning to develop rapidly in other fields such as archaeology (i.e., paleoethnobotany: see Ford 1978; Jones 1957; Popper and Hastorf 1988). Ethnobotany became more cross-culturally comparative and ecologically responsive as it came under fire for its atheoretical nature and limited relevancy to the "real world" (Conklin 1954; Jones 1941), just as agriculture-related researchers increasingly viewed domestication as a process rather than as an event (Harlan 1992). Subdisciplines of anthropology and geography that had long described static aspects of human subsistence developed diachronic and processual views of human, plant (and animal), and environmental interactions, framed in ecological terminology, methodology, and theory (e.g., Anderson 1956; Bartlett 1955; Steward 1955). The field of "cultural ecology" was coalescing, with the best work of the period summarized in the authoritative volume edited by William L. Thomas, *Man's Role in Changing the Face of the Earth,* published in 1956.

Researchers within both the biological and the social sciences began to critically evaluate the relationships between human activities and natural environments despite the conservative stances of influential North American anthropologists such as Yahudi Cohen (1968), A. L. Kroeber (cited in Lewis 1977), and Robert Redfield (1953), which promoted more harmonious (although mostly unsubstantiated) views of preindustrial human-environmental relations. This work initially emphasized hunter-gatherer behaviors, as illustrated by the following examples.

Disruptions in vegetational and faunal patterns had long been associated with agriculture (Anderson 1954, 1956; Bartlett 1955, 1956; Sauer 1952), but investigators assembled evidence during the 1950s (Stewart 1956) that demonstrated beyond a doubt that hunter-gatherers had very substantially modified aboriginal vegetation patterns, especially through the use of controlled burning. This "discovery" motivated many researchers to carefully document indigenous fire use within their geographical areas of study (Lewis 1972, 1973, 1977; Norton 1979), and it stimulated wider skepticism of received notions on such diverse cultural phenomena as diet, gender roles in provisioning, subsistence base, and other forms of human-environment interaction.

A generalized inquiry developed during the 1960s and 1970s concerning whether so-called natural environments were indeed what researchers had so long presumed. Within anthropology, the new focus on human or cultural ecology produced a flow of influential publications on tropical agriculture, hunter-gatherer subsistence, and other forms of environmental management by indigenous peoples.

For example, major contributions (e.g., Hunn 1981; Lee and Devore 1968; Sahlins 1972) fundamentally changed several commonly held beliefs about hunter-gatherer subsistence. Perhaps the most important was that hunter-gatherers, except those living in extreme northerly or southerly climes, depended more on wild plant resources than on meat (or fish) for overall caloric intake—and thus more upon plant-gathering activities usually performed by women than upon the hunting activities of men.

Other publications (e.g., Conklin 1961; Geertz 1963; Harris 1971; Kunstadter 1978) further advanced the understanding of human–wild plant interaction by focusing on tropical forest environments, their wild plant resources, and management of both by indigenous peoples. For example, investigators found that swidden agriculture was a complex multiyear strategy of land management, often incorporating wild, gathered species into its later successional stages. More importantly, swidden agriculture was shown to be well adapted to many tropical climates and soils—contrary to prevailing opinion—and, in structural terms, was favorably compared to natural forest in species composition. More generally, despite widely held beliefs that hunter-gatherers had little effect on their environments (Clark 1952; Cohen 1968:394) and that agriculturalists invariably provoked simplifying and biologically negative consequences, research of this period produced findings that indigenous peoples may actually have had some positive effects on their environments.

This intellectual setting stimulated still others to investigate use of wild plants by agriculturalists, revealing that consumption of wild, gathered plants for food, medicine, and other purposes also commonly occurred within preindustrial farming societies (e.g., Berlin et al. 1974; Conklin 1954; Cox [this volume]; Etkin 1981; Etkin and Ross 1982, [this volume]; Meilleur 1982, 1986). As Annette Hamilton (1982:236) summarized, "to take up horticulture [in Highland New Guinea] does not automatically mean the abandonment of other production systems." Indeed, this inquiry eventually lead to an influential article arguing that folk inventories of wild plant taxa among agriculturists may actually be richer in species diversity than those of hunter-gatherers, presumably because of the "safety net" role that wild alimentary plants would play in times of below-average agricultural production (Brown 1985). Indeed, medicinal and other nonalimentary demands on wild plants may also expand as a result of the shift from foraging to nonintensive agriculture (Brown 1985:50; Logan and Dixon [this volume]). The study of famine foods (Huss-Ashmore and Johnston [this volume]) is also relevant here. Certainly a call for greater research into famine-related decision making and wild plant use is warranted, especially as it relates to the conjuncture between foraging and nonintensive agriculture. Biodiversity maintenance and depletion issues should also be explored in that context.

As some researchers were thus more carefully examining the relationship between humans and wild plants within emerging ecological paradigms through health, nutrition, fertility, and resource management contexts, other investigators were exploring aspects of the human–wild plant relationship from perspectives such as that of the newly differentiating anthropological field of ethnobiology. Driven in the 1960s and 1970s mostly by cognitively oriented research, ethnobiology is best known for expanding the scope and the theoretical value of human–wild plant studies by focusing on principles of folk biological classification (e.g., Berlin et al. 1974; Brown 1984; Conklin 1954; Hays 1976). However, by investigating the formal properties of folk knowledge more than its application, most ethnobiological research of this and later periods informs us more about the nature of the human mind as it classifies the biotic world than about the strategies adopted by people cross-culturally to manage resources. As we will see, in the late 1970s and 1980s ethnobiology developed a more pronounced ecological orientation that continues today.

But even as ecological method and theory permeated the biological disciplines and many cultural sciences in the 1960s and 1970s (Butzer 1982), scholars had yet to widely recognize (and hardly addressed) biodiversity problems as understood today. As few as 20 years ago—whether we look at the study of human–wild plant interactions in archaeology, ethnobiology, classical ethnobotany, cultural ecology, or domestication research—biodiversity depletion was simply not an issue. Indeed, until very recently, researchers and nonspecialists alike viewed mass extinctions as curious though certainly important events of prehistory. That contemporary human behavior could provoke species losses of the degree experienced by dinosaurs in the late Cretaceous or by North American mammals during the late Pleistocene (Martin and Klein 1974) has only been appreciated within the last 15 years or so (National Research Council 1978).

Although investigators within many disciplines have thus since the 1950s systematically recognized long-standing and often significant indigenous human effects on wild species numbers, distributions, and habitats, this work was not until recently contextualized in terms of biodiversity conservation or depletion. Even as late as the 1970s and early 1980s scientists undertook (and in many instances still undertake) much human–wild plant research in the absence of a well-developed appreciation of biodiversity issues. But as awareness of the severity of habitat and species losses grew, this changed quickly.

Biodiversity Becomes an Issue

By the time the biodiversity drama was revealed to an uneasy and oftentimes skeptical public in the 1980s, many scientists studying human–wild plant interaction had already begun framing new research and gauging results in terms of biodiversity concerns. For example, a resurgence in documenting wild plant use among indigenous peoples, most notably by botanists, has been under way for some time. But the motives of many contemporary ethnobotanists often differ from what they were earlier, where researchers usually attempted little more than to document aboriginal plant use among preindustrial peoples.

Today, biodiversity-related concerns commonly inform ethnobotanical research (Balick 1992). Emphasis has shifted to the urgency of plant and habitat conservation based on our need to accumulate traditional use data before the plants and the indigenous culture-bearers who use them are lost forever. This mostly Western viewpoint stresses the gaps in our biological knowledge of the natural world and its economic potential—usually as medicinal, crop, or forestry genetic resources—and then warns of the economic risks we take in allowing biodiversity depletion to progress unchecked (King 1991; McNeely et al. 1990; Plotkin 1988). "As we go into a period where rapid climatic change or other severe planetary stresses are likely" (Dasmann 1991:8), we are unwise, this literature repeats, to allow plant species to be extinguished before scientists have determined both their phylogeny and their potential for economic benefit.

In addition, observers of the nutrition and health of indigenous populations now widely hold that diminished health and nutrition among native peoples are corollaries of uncontrolled contact with Western markets and culture (Kuhnlein and Turner 1991; Norton et al. 1984; Vickers [this volume]). These investigators view continued consumption of local resources (both cultivated and gathered) as a positive feature of traditional life, with the archaeological record appearing to confirm this stance (King [this volume]). Therefore, the availability of traditional resources, to be ensured through biodiversity conservation, also has important consequences for human health.

I and others have described the value of preserving and engendering culturally sensitive, utility-based conservation ethics and actions among native peoples (Etkin and Ross [this volume]; Johns [this volume]; Meilleur 1991; Nabhan et al. 1991). The stewards of vast reservoirs of the world's biological diversity (Alcorn 1991), indigenous societies everywhere are now subjected to multiple acculturative forces. By encouraging local recognition of the value of native plants as "cultural identity symbols, ethnic foods, or objects of aesthetic and historical appreciation" (Nabhan et al. 1991:142–143), these authors argue, both indigenous leaders and government policy makers can promote conservation of biological diversity among native peoples by addressing their specific subsistence, health, and other cultural concerns. Such statements are illustrative of the now widely held notion that cultural and biological diversity are interdependent phenomena.

Very successful as a marketing tool in generating broad behavioral, philosophical, and monetary support for many conservation agendas, such an anthropocentric view of the value of plant (and animal) life nevertheless begs the question of what will become of species that hold no interest for humans. For example, funding is biased toward conservation programs involving species for which economic potential can be demonstrated (Plotkin 1988:106), although this linkage may be impossible to show for many species.

Other, less narrowly "anthropo-selfish" arguments must be found to increase concern for the plight of species having no apparent utility. Since the earlier ecologically sound argument of "diversity equals stability" (popularized as "rivets in an airplane wing" or "links in a chain") hardly caught on even with the Western nonspecialist public, conservation for its own sake is unlikely to occur on any substantial scale anywhere until urban industrial citizenries clearly comprehend the long-term consequences of their actions, accept responsibility for them, and adopt new ethical bases for environmental use and care (Alcorn 1991; Busch et al. 1989; Callicott 1990).

Many changes in direction have been proposed, such as development of heightened environmental respect through study and application of indigenous animistic precepts (Hunn 1990), management of land and resources using principles associated with the long-term common good rather than short-term individual gain (Daly and Cobb 1989; McCay and Acheson 1987), and respect for traditional ecological knowledge, tenure rights, and indigenous peoples' wishes for territorial and cultural exclusion of outsiders and nontraditional economic forms (Alcorn 1991:320–21, 332, 340–41; Hames 1991:189–90; Toledo 1991). Janis Alcorn (1981, 1984, 1991), especially, has taken the lead in proposing solutions that stress the need to empower successful indigenous resource managers in programs for the conservation of biodiversity worldwide, arguing that Western models of environmental protection are unlikely to work for a number of reasons in most situations in the developing world.

Not all contemporary ethnobotanical researchers are so directly involved in biodiversity issues. Nevertheless, individual as well as summary or statistical accounts of traditional plant use (e.g., Dufour and Wilson [this volume]; Kuhnlein and Turner 1991; Moerman 1986, 1991, [this volume]) do have considerable relevance for modern biodiversity decisions. By describing the importance of traditional plants over wide geographical and cultural areas, researchers can provide guidelines for near-term conservation of plants based on their real or potential utility or can furnish traditional ecological knowledge to (usually government) resource managers for both environmental monitoring and land management. Certainly, information on plant use derived from archaeological contexts would be of similar value (Ford et al. [this volume]). Moreover, this reasoning can be extended to the observation of nonhuman primate consumption of plants for self-medication (Glander [this volume]), a potential human benefit that has not escaped the interest of natural products chemists.

In some other plant-related disciplines—for example, those associated with domestication research (agronomy, genetics, horticulture, etc.)—researchers have long championed the value of genetic diversity and have warned of the dangers related to its loss (Frankel and Bennett 1970; National Academy of Sciences 1972). This awareness began in Europe by the late nineteenth century (Marchenay 1986:24–27). Indeed, recognition of genetic erosion penetrated the agricultural sciences well before it became generalized within botanical and ecological research,[3] where it nevertheless has gained greater attention. Not surprisingly, as awareness of the depletion of biodiversity in wild plants has grown, so has understanding of the threat to the world's food supply posed by reductions in potentially useful agricultural genes found within wild plants.

Ethnobiology has also changed in recent years, becoming more ecologically oriented and connected to biodiversity issues. Perhaps due to the emphasis of ethnobiology on the emic or native view of biotic environments, ethnobiologists have shown greater interest in studying indigenous practices of resource management as native biotic environments and their traditional managers have endured increasing encroachment (Hunn 1990; Meilleur 1986; Nabhan 1987; Posey 1984). Like plant-oriented archaeologists (e.g., paleoethnobotanists) and cultural ecologists, many ethnobiologists now employ a variety of ecological orientations (Ellen 1982) to finely analyze plant and animal and environmental management by indigenous peoples. Both its long-standing emic perspective and competence in biotic inventories position this form of ethnobiology to contribute to an understanding, and possibly the resolution, of some biodiversity problems.

Many ethnobiologists nevertheless maintain strong cognitive agendas within the discipline by focusing primarily on folk classificatory issues. Even then, the ethnobiological tradition of providing Linnean determinations for all culturally pertinent plants or animals, often also describing the biogeography and always the indigenous uses of folk taxa, has substantial value to contemporary biodiversity issues. Studies of vegetation cover, assessments of land-use change, and conservation decision making based upon real or potential plant utility are several applications that come to mind.

Thus, within the last 20 years or so, many archaeologists, cultural ecologists, human geographers, and ethnobiologists, among others, have abandoned the narrow documentation of functional interrelationships between wild plant species and indigenous peoples. A shift toward framing hypotheses and data recovery within ecological paradigms that can be linked to biodiversity-related problems increasingly ties these fields together. A substantial literature now stresses ecosystems and their biota as management challenges to the ingenuity of indigenous peoples past and present (e.g., Freeman and Carbyn 1988; Nietschmann 1973; Ruddle and Johannes 1985; Williams and Hunn 1982). Investigators now undertake analyses of social, functional, cognitive, and ecological interrelationships (within both hunter-gatherer and farmer ethnoeco-systems) in conjunction with detailed biotic inventories. Long the mainstay of ethnobotany, such inventories have now assumed roles supporting larger theoretical, social, and environmental studies.

In Search of "Keystone Societies"

A number of positive assessments of indigenous management practices and their effects on natural environments have resulted from this paradigmatic shift. Earlier statements were more general, describing such characteristics as mimicry of natural ecosystems by anthropogenic ones as a basis for stability and permanence (Geertz 1963; Harris 1971) or recognizing that preindustrial people modified their environments through burning or other techniques, thereby increasing the availability of certain game animals or other resources (Stewart 1956). But by the late 1970s and early 1980s, quantified arguments were emerging about biodiversity enhancement by indigenous peoples.

The anthropologists Henry Lewis and Peter Kunstadter, for example, produced early influential articles of this kind. Lewis (1977), describing traditional burning activities of Native American hunter-gatherers in northern Alberta, focused on indigenous management of vegetational regeneration after the firing of temperate grassland. Kunstadter (1978), working with Lua' farmers in northwestern Thailand, analyzed traditional ecological knowledge associated with swidden agriculture and other forms of land management that created clearings in the tropical forests.

Despite differences in subsistence mode and biotic background, the two indigenous peoples had nevertheless adopted similar strategies for enhancing habitat and species diversity through management of successional vegetation after initial burning. Variously stabilizing or prolonging naturally ephemeral community structures with fire or other techniques, each society promoted the growth and expanded the range of culturally valued wild plant species that then became readily available and more easily gathered. According to Lewis, "the hunter and gatherers . . . used controlled burning to increase and diversify natural resources" (1977:19), while Kunstadter stated that "the environment that is created and maintained . . . is more varied than would be found . . . if they [Lua'] were to give up swiddening" (1978:198).

Such claims are not limited to plant biodiversity. For example, using archaeological evidence from a coastal A.D. 1000 Amerindian site in northern Panama, one investigator analyzed links between shifting gardens and faunal richness in tropical rainforest (Linares 1976); another (Emslie 1981) studied archaeological faunal assemblages from several prehistoric Pueblo sites in the U.S. Southwest. Both authors describe augmented habitat diversities and wild animal species densities and ranges resulting from human environmental modification. Steven Emslie attributes much of this enhancement to the "ecotone" or "edge effect," the "tendency for increased variety and density [of organisms] at community junctions [or transitions]" (Odum 1953:278).

Drawing upon ethnography and ecology, Gary Paul Nabhan and colleagues (1982) investigated traditional Papago (now called Tohono O'odham) subsistence farming and land use and their effects on habitat and wild plant and animal diversity in the arid U.S. Southwest. Through detailed species comparisons of two desert oases, one of which was characterized by aboriginal human occupation, they concluded that the anthropogenic oasis was "more diverse in terms of [wild] plants, somewhat more diverse in birds, and not nearly as diverse in mammals" (Nabhan et al. 1982:139). According to Nabhan and his colleagues, the increased floral richness resulted from "Papago land and plant management practices [that had] created eight large scale and two small scale vegetation associations" (1982:124). In a later investigation of the Miwok of California, Kat Anderson and Gary Nabhan likewise found that "through burning or clearing to create 'ecotones' or 'habitat edges,' these people have hit upon the same processes that some professional foresters have discovered to increase wildlife abundance or diversity" (1991:29).

Claims of this nature have now accumulated, covering a variety of preindustrial societies and subsistence modes from different time periods and diverse geographical and environmental settings. In Central America, Janis Alcorn studied land and plant management among the Huastec, tropical forest gardeners of northeastern Mexico. She concluded that indigenous swidden agricultural activities "create a more diverse vegetational environment than would otherwise be available" (1981:410). Further south, Dominique Irvine found that Runa swiddeners of northern Ecuador "increase [wild] resource availability by exerting direct environmental control to enhance the habitat of desired . . . species" (1989:235). And Anthony Anderson and Darrell Posey concluded that the Brazilian Kayapo "enhance [environmental heterogeneity] by establishing and maintaining highly diversified vegetational 'islands' within a relatively less-altered environmental matrix" (1989:172). The foraging economies of Northwest Coast Indians have been similarly characterized (Norton et al. 1984:221).

Collectively, this body of work describes at least three outcomes of human behavior that singly or in combination appear to lead to enhanced biodiversity: production of ecotone or edge effects, provocation and then stabilization of vegetational succession stages, and the opening of forest gaps. Under natural conditions, each is a mechanism by which species distribution and diversity are determined (Hallé et al. 1978; Webb et al. 1972). Under human-induced conditions, whether consciously or unconsciously achieved, the expansion and condensation of desirable taxa into newly created niches can sometimes occur, resulting in their greater ease of removal by humans. Similarly adapted nonuseful taxa would also expand under such conditions, contributing again to overall species richness.

Human predation of wild plants and animals in these cases takes place at two levels. In the first, the people entirely or mostly remove the original vegetation through burning or some other technique; in the second, they cull (gather or hunt) the newly promoted or invasive taxa for sustained human use. The combined results of such behaviors are analogous to the effects of "keystone species" as these are described within the biological literature.

Keystone species are predators at high trophic levels that prey upon organisms at lower trophic levels within ecosystems that would be more uniform under nonkeystone conditions. In so doing, keystone predators create new ecological niches for invasion by an array of species that would otherwise be outcompeted for space and nutrients by the keystone prey, thereby increasing overall biodiversity within the ecosystem. Such predation "enhances the ability of other species to inhabit the area by keeping space open . . . [and] when the top predator is . . . removed or . . . absent . . . the systems converge toward simplicity" (Paine 1966:71). Thus, "predation [is] a diversity-causing mechanism" (1966:72). In terms of ecosystem conservation, "special efforts must be made to identify and preserve keystone species" (Pimm and Gilpin 1989:302).

Although the analogy is not isomorphic (keystone species may or may not prey upon the new arrivals and may or may not actively promote invasion), the environmental outcomes of the human behaviors described above and of the keystone species are remarkably similar. Indeed, in recent usage the concept of keystone species has expanded to include any species "on whose presence the whole structure and dynamics of a community depends" (Horn et al. 1989). It becomes the key to a resultant higher level of species richness within the ecosystem considered. Today, as human-induced loss of biodiversity approaches the dramatic, would we not be well advised to immediately inventory and protect what I call the biodiversity-enhancing keystone societies—several of which seem to be described by the writers above? At the same time, greater research funding must be applied to the study of the principles and practices of human groups that enhance plant and animal diversity.

Nevertheless, the general predominance of biodiversity-enhancing behaviors within preindustrial societies has yet to be demonstrated by researchers. Indeed, in numerous examples, preindustrial human activities clearly seem to have reduced biological diversity, sometimes on a substantial scale (Abrams and Rue 1988; Diamond 1986, 1992; McGovern et al. 1988). In Polynesia (Meilleur 1990; Vitousek 1988), for example, some of these activities might be instances of "frontier" or "pioneer" behavior (Curtis 1956; Janzen 1988) exerted by colonizing or technologically innovative populations, possibly for relatively short time periods (e.g., < 3,000 years) and sometimes within well-documented fragile environments. But certainly this negative effect on biodiversity was not everywhere the case.

Thus, we must also look at the substantial suggestive evidence that over longer periods, such as the 40,000 to 50,000 years of Aboriginal presence in Australia or the 10,000 to 15,000 years of human inhabitation of the Americas, many human cultures established stable, sustainable management regimes dominated by or heavily involving wild plant gathering. In Australia (Lewis 1989; Yen 1989) and in areas of the Pacific Northwest (Norton 1979), investigators have recognized no obvious negative effects on habitat or wild plant biological diversity provoked by aboriginal human populations.

What Have We Learned?

While it does not appear unusual for many, if not all, preindustrial human societies, whether hunter-gatherer or agricultural, to modify their biotic environments to facilitate improved gathering and ultimately to increase habitat and biological diversity within circumscribed areas, environmental degradation by preindustrial societies has also occurred. Many examples of both situations can be found, sometimes unequivocally under prehistoric conditions and thus not attributable to modern acculturative forces. Indigenous peoples thus exhibit behaviors that lead toward both the loss and the enhancement of biodiversity. Behavior resulting in biodiversity enhancement seems more likely to occur in two types of natural settings: (1) in species-depauperate biotopes, such as those found on isolated tropical low islands (Meilleur n.d.) and, possibly, in deserts (Emslie 1981; Nabhan et al. 1982); and (2) in regions of relative vegetational uniformity, examples of which may be certain natural forest communities in tropical and temperate settings (Kunstadter 1978; Norton 1979). Behavior of this type is comparable in some instances to that of the so-called keystone animal species, upon which enhanced biological diversity within many ecosystems depends.

Descriptions of preindustrial societies, especially agricultural ones, as biodiversity enhancers rather than biodiversity simplifiers have caught the imaginations of large numbers of people within and outside academia. Such evidence is attractive to conservation-minded individuals and scientists seeking support for contentions that indigenous resource managers have been more effective than industrialized societies in maintaining ecosystems at sustainable levels of serviceability. But I have also indicated numerous cases in which environmental simplification and outright destruction are also attributable to preindustrial societies. Greatly increased scrutiny of the scientific evidence surrounding these issues is warranted, not only because of the firm empirical foundation needed to maneuver through the emotional and political minefields generated by these issues, but also because of what may be learned about land and resource management from societies that have, in most instances, much more experience than we do. Preliminary results of this scrutiny are beginning to temper a number of growing popular beliefs associated with the concept of "primitive harmony" (Edgerton 1992; Hames 1991; Redford 1990), and this is to be expected.

The point here is not whether preindustrial societies have damaged their environments. Certainly it is useful to balance the record, as accomplished by recent books that focus on human maladaption and environmental degradation (Diamond 1992; Edgerton 1992). Yet one cannot help but wonder if these stances are not in some measure driven by a desire to justify or rationalize the damage inflicted by industrialized society—as if to say "indigenous people did it too, so we're not so bad." Rather, all human societies, industrialized or indigenous, must recognize the predicament confronting our species and our world and then promote human behaviors and management principles that may lead to biodiversity enhancement or at least to forms of longer-term stability of our natural ecosystems. If we were to dismiss evidence of what appears to be biodiversity-enhancing behavior because of previously held notions about the predisposition exhibited by our species toward environmental simplification, we would be foolish indeed.

NOTES

1. In March 1993, for example, I saw public announcements of this nature, paid for by the National Wildlife Federation, on the CNN television network. I also heard similar radio announcements attributed to the National Audubon Society during this period on National Public Radio.

2. It is not always obvious what a "wild" plant is, as opposed to tolerated, encouraged, or cultivated plants. Several contributors to this volume, and especially Dufour and Wilson, have explicitly recognized this problem. Good discussions of this issue appear in Alcorn 1981, Berlin et al. 1974, and Harlan 1992.

3. Crop genetic erosion began to dramatically accelerate with the development and widespread dispersal of genetically narrow "elite" cultivars in the late 19th century, the replacement of "landraces" or "peasant cultivars" by these new varieties, and the progressive conversion of locally adapted agricultural systems to energy-intensive, homogeneous modern systems (Marchenay and Meilleur 1983). Ironically, "the technological bind of improved varieties is that they eliminate the resource upon which they are based" (Wilkes 1984:134). An appreciation of domesticated germ plasm erosion thus has a substantially different origin than does that of genetic erosion in wild plant species.

REFERENCES

Abrams, E., and D. Rue
  1988   The causes and consequences of deforestation among the prehistoric Maya. *Human Ecology* 16:377–395.

Alcorn, J.
  1981   Huastec noncrop resource management: Implications for prehistoric rain forest management. *Human Ecology* 9(4):395–417.
  1984   Development policy, forest, and peasant farms: Reflections on Huastec-managed forests' contributions to commercial production and resource conservation. *Economic Botany* 38(4):389–406.
  1991   Ethics, economies, and conservation. In *Biodiversity: Culture, conservation, and ecodevelopment,* edited by M. Oldfield and J. Alcorn, pp. 317–349. Westview, Boulder, Colorado.

Anderson, A., and D. Posey
  1989   Management of a tropical scrub savanna of the Gorotire Kayapo of Brazil. *Advances in Economic Botany* 7:159–173.

Anderson, E.
  1954   *Plants, man, and life.* A. Melrose, London.
  1956   Man as a maker of new plants and new plant communities. In *Man's role in changing the face of the earth,* edited by W. Thomas, pp. 763–777. University of Chicago Press, Chicago.

Anderson, K., and G. Nabhan
  1991   Gardeners in Eden. *Wilderness* 55(194):27–30.

Balick, M.
  1992   Ethnobotany revisited. *Museum News* 70(1):45–48.

Bartlett, H. H.
  1955   *Fire in relation to primitive agriculture and grazing in the tropics: Annotated bibliography.* University of Michigan Press, Ann Arbor.
  1956   Fire, primitive agriculture, and grazing in the tropics. In *Man's role in changing the face of the earth,* edited by W. Thomas, pp. 692–720. University of Chicago Press, Chicago.

Berlin, B., D. Breedlove, and P. Raven
  1974   *Principles of Tzeltal plant classification.* Academic Press, New York.

Brown, C.
  1984   *Language and living things.* Rutgers University Press, New Brunswick, New Jersey.
  1985   Mode of subsistence and folk biological taxonomy. *Current Anthropology* 26(1):43–64.

Busch, L., W. Lacy, and J. Burkhardt
  1989   Culture and care: Ethical and policy dimensions of germplasm conservation. In *Biotic diversity and germplasm preservation,* edited by L. Knutson and A. Stoner, pp. 43–62. Kluwer, Boston.

Butzer, K.

1982   *Archaeology as human ecology.* Cambridge University Press, Cambridge, England.

Callicott, J.

1990   Whither conservation ethics? *Conservation Biology* 4:15–20.

Center for Plant Conservation

1994   *An action plan for conserving Hawaiian plant diversity.* Center for Plant Conservation, St. Louis.

Clark, J.G.D.

1952   *Prehistoric Europe, the economic basis.* Methuen, London.

Cohen, Y.

1968   *Man in adaptation: The biosocial background* [Second edition]. Aldine, Chicago.

Conklin, H.

1954   The relation of Hanunoo culture to the plant world. Ph.D. dissertation, Yale University. University Microfilms, Ann Arbor.

1961   The study of shifting cultivation. *Current Anthropology* 2(1):27–61.

Curtis, J.

1956   The modification of mid-latitude grasslands and forests by man. In *Man's role in changing the face of the earth,* edited by W. Thomas, pp. 721–736. University of Chicago Press, Chicago.

Daly, H., and J. Cobb

1989   *For the common good.* Beacon Press, Boston.

Dasmann, R.

1991   The importance of cultural and biological diversity. In *Biodiversity: Culture, conservation, and ecodevelopment,* edited by M. Oldfield and J. Alcorn, pp. 7–15. Westview Press, Boulder, Colorado.

Davis, S., S. Droop, P. Gregerson, L. Henson, C. Leon, J. Villa-Lobos, H. Synge, and J. Zantovska

1986   *Plants in danger: What do we know?* IUCN, Gland, Switzerland.

de Candolle, A.

1959   *Origin of cultivated plants* [Second edition]. Hafner, New York.

Diamond, J.

1986   The environmentalist myth: Archaeology. *Nature* 324:19–20.

1992   *The third chimpanzee.* Harper Collins, New York.

Edgerton, R.

1992   *Sick societies.* The Free Press, New York.

Ehrlich, P.

1988   The loss of diversity: Causes and consequences. In *Biodiversity,* edited by E. O. Wilson, pp. 21–27. National Academy Press, Washington, D.C.

Ellen, R.

1982   *Environment, subsistence and system.* Cambridge University Press, London.

Emslie, S.
1981   Birds and prehistoric agriculture: The New Mexican Pueblos. *Human Ecology* 9(3):305–329.

Etkin, N.
1981   A Hausa herbal pharmacopoeia: Biomedical evaluation of commonly used plant medicines. *Journal of Ethnopharmacology* 4:75–98.

Etkin, N., and P. Ross
1982   Food as medicine and medicine as food: An adaptive framework for the interpretation of plant utilization among the Hausa of northern Nigeria. *Social Science and Medicine* 16:1559–1573.

Ford, R.
1978   Ethnobotany: Historical diversity and synthesis. In *The nature and status of ethnobotany*, edited by R. Ford, pp. 33–49. University of Michigan Museum of Anthropology, Ann Arbor.

Frankel, O., and E. Bennett
1970   *Genetic resources in plants—Their exploration and conservation.* Blackwell Scientific Publications, Oxford.

Freeman, M., and L. Carbyn [Editors]
1988   *Traditional knowledge and renewable resource management in northern regions.* Boreal Institute for Northern Studies, Edmonton, Alberta.

Geertz, C.
1963   *Agricultural involution: The process of ecological change in Indonesia.* University of California Press, Berkeley.

Hallé, F., R. Oldeman, and P. Tomlinson
1978   *Tropical trees and forests.* Springer-Verlag, New York.

Hames, R.
1991   Wildlife conservation in tribal societies. In *Biodiversity: Culture, conservation, and ecodevelopment,* edited by M. Oldfield and J. Alcorn, pp. 172–199. Westview Press, Boulder, Colorado.

Hamilton, A.
1982   The unity of hunting-gathering societies: Reflections on economic forms and resource management. In *Resource managers: North American and Australian hunter-gatherers,* edited by N. Williams and E. Hunn, pp. 229–247. American Association for the Advancement of Science, Washington, D.C.

Harlan, J.
1992   *Crops and man* [Second edition]. American Society of Agronomy and the Crop Science Society of America, Madison, Wisconsin.

Harms, R.
1987   *Games against nature: An eco-cultural history of the Nunu of equatorial Africa.* Cambridge University Press, New York.

Harris, D.
1971   The ecology of swidden agriculture in the upper Orinoco rainforest, Venezuela. *Geographical Review* 61:475–495.

Hays, T.

1976   An empirical method for the identification of covert categories in eth-
        nobiology. *American Ethnologist* 3:489–507.

Horn, H., H. Shugart, and D. Urban

1989   Simulators as models of forest dynamics. In *Perspectives in ecological theory*,
        edited by J. Roughgarden, R. May, and S. Levin, pp. 256–267. Princeton
        University Press, Princeton.

Hunn, E.

1981   On the relative contribution of men and women to subsistence among
        hunger-gatherers of the Columbia Plateau: A comparison with *Ethno-
        graphic Atlas* summaries. *Journal of Ethnobiology* 1:124–134.

1990   *Nch'i-Wana, "The Big River": Mid-Columbia Indians and their land.* Univer-
        sity of Washington Press, Seattle.

Irvine, D.

1989   Succession management and resource distribution in an Amazonian rain
        forest. *Advances in Economic Botany* 7:223–237.

Janzen, D.

1988   Tropical dry forests: The most endangered major tropical ecosystem. In
        Biodiversity, edited by E. O. Wilson, pp. 130–137. National Academy Press,
        Washington, D.C.

Jones, V.

1941   The nature and status of ethnobotany. *Chronica Botanica* 6:219–221.

1957   The development and present status of ethnobotany in the United States.
        8ième Congrès International de Botanique: Comptes Rendus 15:52–53.

King, S.

1991   The source of our cures. *Cultural Survival Quarterly* 15(3):19–22.

Kuhnlein, H., and N. Turner

1991   *Traditional plant foods of Canadian indigenous peoples: Nutrition, botany and
        use.* Gordon and Breach Science Publishers, Philadelphia.

Kunstadter, P.

1978   Ecological modification and adaptation: An ethnobotanical view of Lua'
        swiddeners in northwestern Thailand. In *The nature and status of ethno-
        botany*, edited by R. Ford, pp. 169–200. University of Michigan Museum of
        Anthropology, Ann Arbor.

Lee, R., and I. DeVore [Editors]

1968   *Man the hunter.* Aldine, Chicago.

Lewis, H.

1972   The role of fire in the domestication of plants and animals in southwest
        Asia: A hypothesis. *Man* 7:196–222.

1973   *Patterns of Indian burning in California: Ecology and ethnohistory.* Ballena
        Press, Ramona, California.

1977   Maskuta: The ecology of Indian fires in northern Alberta. *Western Cana-
        dian Journal of Anthropology* 7(1):15–52.

1989   Ecological and technological knowledge of fire: Aborigines versus park rangers in northern Australia. *American Anthropologist* 91(4):940–961.

Linares, O.

1976   "Garden hunting" in the American tropics. *Human Ecology* 4(4):331–349.

McCay, B., and J. Acheson [Editors]

1987   *The question of the commons.* University of Arizona Press, Tucson.

McGovern, T., G. Bigelow, T. Amorosi, and D. Russell

1988   Northern islands, human error, and environmental degradation: A view of social and ecological change in the medieval north Atlantic. *Human Ecology* 16(3):225–270.

McNeely, J., K. Miller, W. Reid, R. Mittermeier, and T. Werner

1990   *Conserving the world's biological diversity.* IUCN, Gland, Switzerland.

McNeill, W.

1976   *Plagues and peoples.* Doubleday, New York.

Marchenay, P.

1986   *A la recherche des variétés locales de plantes cultivées.* Conservatoire botanique de Porquérolles/PAGE PACA, Porquérolles, France.

Marchenay, P., and B. Meilleur

1983   Anthropologie et biologie, le cas des cultivars locaux. *Nouvelles Breves* (special issue) July–October:1–10.

Martin, P., and R. Klein [Editors]

1974   *Quaternary extinctions.* University of Arizona Press, Tucson.

Meilleur, B.

1982   Du ramassage à la cueillette. *Etudes Rurales* 87/88:165–174.

1986   Alluetain ethnoecology and traditional economy: The procurement and production of plant resources in the northern French Alps. Ph.D. dissertation, University of Washington. University Microfilms, Ann Arbor.

1990   Forest and the Polynesian adaptation. Paper presented at the 89th Annual Meeting of the American Anthropological Association, as part of the Invited Session "Tropical Forest Ecology, The Changing Human Niche, and Deforestation," New Orleans, 28 November–2 December.

1991   The ethnobotanical garden and tropical plant conservation. In *Tropical botanic gardens: Their role in conservation and development,* edited by V. Heywood and P. Wyse Jackson, pp. 79–87. Academic Press, London.

Moerman, D.

1986   *Medicinal plants of Native America.* University of Michigan Museum of Anthropology Technical Reports, No. 19. Ann Arbor.

1991   The medicinal flora of native North America: An analysis. *Journal of Ethnopharmacology* 31:1–42.

Nabhan, G.

1987   *The desert smells like rain.* North Point Press, San Francisco.

Nabhan, G., D. House, H. Suzan A., W. Hodgson, L. Hernandez S., and G. Malda
 1991   Conservation and use of rare plants by traditional cultures in the U.S./Mexico borderlands. In *Biodiversity: Culture, conservation, and ecodevelopment*, edited by M. Oldfield and J. Alcorn, pp. 127–146. Westview Press, Boulder, Colorado.

Nabhan, G., A. Rea, K. Reichhardt, E. Mellink, and C. Hutchinson
 1982   Papago influences on habitat and biotic diversity: Quitovac oasis ethnoecology. *Journal of Ethnobiology* 2(2):124–143.

National Academy of Sciences
 1972   *Genetic vulnerability of major crops.* National Academy Press, Washington, D.C.

National Research Council (Committee on Germplasm Resources)
 1978   *Conservation of germplasm resources: An imperative.* National Academy of Sciences, Washington, D.C.

Nietschmann, B.
 1973   *Between land and water: The subsistence ecology of the Miskito Indians, eastern Nicaragua.* Seminar Press, New York.

Norton, H.
 1979   The association between anthropogenic prairies and important food plants in western Washington. *Northwest Anthropological Research Notes* 13(2):175–200.

Norton, H., E. Hunn, C. Martinsen, and P. Keely
 1984   Vegetable food products of the foraging economies of the Pacific Northwest. *Ecology of Food and Nutrition* 14:219–228.

Odum, E.
 1953   *Fundamentals of ecology.* W. B. Saunders, Philadelphia.

Paine, R.
 1966   Food web complexity and species diversity. *American Scientist* 100:65–75.

Parker, E.
 1992   Forest islands and Kayapo resource management in Amazonia: A reappraisal of the Apêtê. *American Anthropologist* 94(2):406–428.

Peters, R.
 1988   The effect of global climatic change on natural communities. In *Biodiversity*, edited by E. O. Wilson, pp. 450–461. National Academy Press, Washington, D.C.

Pimm, S.; and M. Gilpin
 1989   Theoretical issues in conservation biology. In *Perspectives in ecological theory*, edited by J. Roughgarden, R. May, and S. Levin, pp. 287–305. Princeton University Press, Princeton.

Plotkin, M.
 1988   The outlook for new agricultural and industrial products from the tropics. In *Biodiversity*, edited by E. O. Wilson, pp. 106–116. National Academy Press, Washington, D.C.

Popper, V., and C. Hastorf

1988   Introduction. In *Current paleoethnobotany,* edited by C. Hastorf and V. Popper, pp. 1–16. University of Chicago Press, Chicago.

Posey, D.

1984   A preliminary report on diversified management of tropical forest by the Kayapo Indians of the Brazilian Amazon. *Advances in Economic Botany* 1:112–126.

Raven, P.

1988   Our diminishing tropical forests. In *Biodiversity,* edited by E. O. Wilson, pp. 119–122. National Academy Press, Washington, D.C.

Redfield, R.

1953   *The primitive world and its transformation.* Cornell University Press, Ithaca, New York.

Redford, K.

1990   The ecologically noble savage. *Cultural Survival Quarterly* 15:46–48.

Ruddle, K., and R. Johannes [Editors]

1985   *The traditional knowledge and management of coastal systems in Asia and the Pacific.* UNESCO, Jakarta.

Sahlins, M.

1972   *Stone age economics.* Aldine-Atherton, Chicago.

Sauer, C.

1952   *Agricultural origins and dispersals.* MIT Press, Cambridge.

Steward, J.

1955   *Theory of culture change.* University of Illinois Press, Urbana.

Stewart, O.

1956   Fire as the first great force employed by man. In *Man's role in changing the face of the earth,* edited by W. Thomas, pp. 115–133. University of Chicago Press, Chicago.

Thomas, W. [Editor]

1956   *Man's role in changing the face of the earth.* University of Chicago Press, Chicago.

Toledo, V.

1991   Patzcuaro's lesson: Nature, production, and culture in an indigenous region of Mexico. In *Biodiversity: Culture, conservation, and ecodevelopment,* edited by M. Oldfield and J. Alcorn, pp. 147–171. Westview Press, Boulder, Colorado.

Vitousek, P.

1988   Diversity and biological invasions of oceanic islands. In *Biodiversity,* edited by E. O. Wilson, pp. 181–189. National Academy Press, Washington, D.C.

Webb, L., J. Tracey, and W. Williams

1972   Regeneration and pattern in the subtropical rain forest. *Journal of Ecology* 60:675–695.

Wilkes, G.

1984   Germplasm conservation toward the year 2000. In *Plant genetic resources: A conservation imperative,* edited by C. Yeatman, D. Kafton, and G. Wilkes, pp. 131–164. Westview Press, Boulder, Colorado.

Williams, N., and E. Hunn [Editors]

1982   *Resource managers: North American and Australian hunter-gatherers.* Westview Press, Boulder, Colorado.

Yen, D.

1989   The domestication of environment. In *Foraging and farming: The evolution of plant exploitation,* edited by D. Harris and G. Hillman, pp. 55–75. Unwin Hyman, London.

Contributors

EDITOR

Nina Etkin is Professor of Anthropology at the University of Hawaii, Honolulu. She has conducted ethnological field research in Nigeria and in Hawaii, combining inquiry in ethnomedicine, diet and health, pharmaceuticals, and the pharmacology of foods and medicinal plants. She is editor of *Plants Used in Indigenous Medicine and Diet* and coeditor of *Medicines: Meanings and Contexts;* her recent publications include "Anthropological Methods in Ethnopharmacology" (*Journal of Ethnopharmacology*). She also is Editor-in-Chief of the journal *Reviews in Anthropology*.

CONTRIBUTORS

Paul Cox is Professor of Botany and Dean of General Education and Honors at Brigham Young University. He has conducted ethnobotanical studies throughout the South Pacific and led efforts to raise funds for establishing rainforest preserves in Western Samoa; he has also worked with the chiefs of American Samoa to secure National Park status for their rainforests. He is coeditor of *Islands, Plants, and Polynesians* and President-Elect of the Society for Economic Botany.

Anna Dixon is a Ph.D. candidate in medical anthropology at the University of Hawaii, Honolulu. Her master's thesis addressed the acquisition of medicinal plant knowledge; her current research examines medicinal plant use by contemporary peoples of Hawaii and the use of "alternative" medicines by persons with HIV. A paleoethnobotanist by training, she has published numerous archaeological reports, focusing primarily on identification of botanical remains.

Darna Dufour is Associate Professor of Anthropology at the University of Colorado, Boulder. She has conducted fieldwork with the Tatuyo Indians in the Northwest Amazon. Her research has focused on problems related to cyanide toxicity and the processing of cassava. Her recent publications include "Nutritional Ecology in the Rainforests of Amazonia" (*American Journal of Human Biology*).

Richard Ford is the Arthur F. Thurnau Professor, University of Michigan, and Chair of the Department of Anthropology. He is also Director of the Ethnobotanical Laboratory in the Museum of Anthropology. He is editor of *The Nature and Status of Ethnobotany* and *Prehistoric Food Production in North America*, and has published widely on the ethnobotany of contemporary societies and paleoethnobotanical subjects.

Kenneth Glander is Professor of Biological Anthropology and Anatomy at Duke University and is Director of the Duke University Primate Center. He has done fieldwork in Brazil, Colombia, Costa Rica, and Madagascar concerning plant-primate interactions. His recent publications include "Dispersal Patterns in Costa Rican Mantled Howling Monkeys" (*International Journal of Primatology*) and "Selecting and Processing Food" (*The Cambridge Encyclopedia of Human Evolution*).

Rebecca Huss-Ashmore is Associate Professor of Anthropology at the University of Pennsylvania, Philadelphia. She has conducted research on food consumption, nutrition, and seasonal ecology in Lesotho, Swaziland, and Kenya. She is coauthor of *African Food Systems in Crisis, Coping with Seasonal Constraints,* and *Health and Lifestyle Change.* Her recent publications include "Agriculture, Modernisation, and Seasonality" (in *Seasonality and Human Ecology*).

Louise Jessop is a Laboratory Technician in the Gastroenterology Section at the Salt Lake City Veterans Administration Medical Center. Her research includes studies of gastrointestinal functioning and coprolite contents. She is currently investigating colon cancer in rats and the effects of alcohol on flow in the intestines. Her work has been published in both medical and anthropological journals.

Timothy Johns is Associate Professor of Human Nutrition at McGill University and Associate Director of the Centre for Nutrition and the Environment of Indigenous Peoples. He has conducted ethnobotanical studies in Bolivia and East Africa. He is an Associate Editor of *Economic Botany* and the author of *With Bitter Herbs They Shall Eat It: Chemical Ecology and the Origins of Human Diet and Medicine.*

Susan Johnston is a Ph.D. candidate in biological anthropology at the University of Pennsylvania, Philadelphia. She is a Physician Assistant with extensive practice and teaching experience. Her current research interests include nutrition, lifestyle change, and chronic disease in Native Americans of the northern Plains, and the contemporary use of wild plants as food and medicine by indigenous peoples of North America.

Frances King is a Research Associate in Anthropology at the University of Pittsburgh and at the Carnegie Museum of Natural History and Director of the Paleoethnobotanical Laboratory at the Center for Cultural Resource Research, University of Pittsburgh. Her research interests and publications include paleoecology, human ecology, and the origins of agriculture and domesticated plants.

Michael Logan is Associate Professor of Anthropology at the University of Tennessee, Knoxville. He has conducted field research in Guatemala, Mexico, and Brazil. His work focuses on the health of indigenous peoples, ethnomedicine, ethnopharmacology, and studies of ethnicity. He is coeditor of *Health and the Human Condition;* his most recent publications include "New Lines of Inquiry on the Illness of Susto" (*Medical Anthropology*), "Locus of Illness Control Beliefs Among Brazilian Herbalists" (*Human Organization*), and "The 'Ank'ohn Utz' of Chinaltenango" (in *A New Dawn in Guatemala*).

Brien Meilleur is President and Executive Director of the Center for Plant Conservation, headquartered at the Missouri Botanical Garden in St. Louis. He has conducted ethnobiological research in the Columbia Plateau of Washington State, in alpine France, and in Polynesia. He is currently Secretary-Treasurer of the Society of Ethnobiology and a member of the Plant Conservation Task Force of IUCN. He most recently coauthored "Genetic Diversity in Eastern Polynesian Eumusa Bananas" (*Pacific Science*).

Daniel Moerman is Professor of Anthropology at the University of Michigan, Dearborn. He has long-standing interests in human healing as a biochemical and symbolic process. He is the author of *Medicinal Plants of Native America* and coeditor of *The Anthropology of Medicine* (second edition). Recent publications include "The Medicinal Flora of Native North America: An Analysis" (*Journal of Ethnopharmacology*).

John Moore is Professor of Medicine at the University of Utah and Chief of the Gastroenterology Section at the Salt Lake City Veterans Administration Medical Center. He has conducted research in gastric functioning and analysis of coprolites and is currently researching gastric physiology, acid secretion, and circadian rhythms of gastric emptying. He is coeditor of *Ulcerogenesis: Chronobiological Considerations*. His publications on gastroenterological functioning include books and articles in medical and anthropological journals.

Paul Ross is a Research R.N. and Adjunct Instructor in the Department of Anthropology at the University of Hawaii, Honolulu. His field research in Nigeria centers on ethnomedicine, diet, and health. His published work includes "Should We Set a Place for Diet in Ethnopharmacology" (*Journal of Ethnopharmacology*), "The Greater Risk of Fewer Deaths: An Ethnodemographic Approach to Child Mortality in Hausaland" (*Africa*), and "Recasting Malaria, Medicine, and Meals: A Perspective on Disease Adaptation" (in *The Anthropology of Medicine*, second edition).

Michelle Sauther is a Research Associate in the Department of Surgery at the Washington University Medical School. She has done field research on prosimian primates in Kenya and Madagascar, focusing on how interindividual variability affects feeding and behavioral ecology. Her recent publications include "The Dynamics of Feeding Competition in Wild Populations of Ringtailed Lemurs (*Lemur catta*)" (in *Lemur Social Systems and Their Ecological Basis*).

Heather Trigg is a Ph.D. candidate in anthropology at the University of Michigan, Ann Arbor. Her master's thesis describes a methodology for distinguishing between cultural and noncultural sources of seeds in rock shelters. At present her research focuses on the analysis of prehistoric diets in the southwestern United States, and she has published several reports on the plant remains recovered from archaeological sites in the United States and Germany.

William Vickers is Professor of Anthropology at Florida International University. He has conducted ethnological fieldwork in Ecuador, Peru, and Mexico, focusing primarily on the human ecology of Native American communities and their land and civil rights. He wrote *Los Sionas y Secoyas: Su Adaptación* *al Ambiente Amazónico,* coauthored *Useful Plants of the Siona and Secoya Indians of Eastern Ecuador,* and coedited *Adaptive Responses of Native Amazonians.*

Warren Wilson is a Ph.D. candidate in biological anthropology at the University of Colorado, Boulder. His master's thesis explored the impact of parasitic infection on the nutritional status and work capacity of Colombian boys; his current research examines agricultural practices of the Tatuyo Indians in the Northwest Amazon.

Botanical Index

Brugmansia x *insignis* (Solanaceae), 151
Brunfelsia grandiflora (Solanaceae)
    ssp. *schultesii*, 151, 162
Bryoria fremontii, 68
Bursera simaruba (Burseraceae), 34
Byrsonima (Malpighiaceae)
    amazonica, 136
    cf. *nitida*, 136

Cactaceae, 74, 200
Cadaba farinosa (Capparaceae), 99
Caesalpinaceae. *See* Fabaceae
Caesalpinia pulcherrima (Fabaceae), 34, 35
Calamintha macrostema (Lamiaceae), 34
Calathea (Marantaceae), 160
Calycanthaceae, 171
Calyptranthes (Myrtaceae), 137
Campomanesia lineatifolia (Myrtaceae),
    164
Canarium (Burseraceae), 108
Capparis flexuosa (Capparidaceae), 34
Capsicum (Solanaceae), 15, 47, 49, 197
    annuum, 33, 34, 50
Carica (Caricaceae)
    cauliflora, 127, 128, 137
    microcarpa ssp. *heterophylla*, 155
    papaya, 33, 34, 100
Carnegiea gigantea (Cactaceae), 70
Carpotroche linguifolia (Flacourtiaceae),
    137
Carum carvi (Umbelliferae), 37, 180
Carya (Juglandaceae), 73, 195
Caryocar (Caryocaraceae)
    amydaliferum, 122, 123, 125, 137
    glabrum, 163
    villosum, 137
Caryodendron orinocense (Euphorbia-
    ceae), 122, 123, 124, 125, 137, 146, 147,
    148, 155
Cassia (Fabaceae)
    laevigata, 34, 35
    occidentalis, 35, 51, 52, 53
    tora, 101
Castanea americanum (Fagaceae), 73

Castilla elastica (Moraceae), 34
Catanaregam spinosa, 242
Cecropia (Urticaceae), 120, 137
Ceiba pentandra (Bombacaceae), 101
Celastrus scandens (Celastraceae), 73
Celosia trigyna (Amaranthaceae), 101
Celtis (Ulmaceae), 221
    cf. *Celtis* sp., 223
    reticulata, 212
Cercidium microphyllum (Fabaceae), 71
Ceriops candoleana (Rhizophoraceae), 11
Cetraria islandica, 69
Chamaedorea sp. aff. *integrifolia* (Palmae),
    164
Chamaesyce hirta (Euphorbiaceae), 160
Chenopodiaceae, 201, 215, 216, 217, 220,
    221, 223
Chenopodium (Chenopodiaceae), 9, 28,
    30, 70, 212, 214, 221, 222
    ambrosioides, 31, 33, 34, 151
    berlandieri, 31
    canihua, 50
    quinoa, 50
Chiranthodendron pentadactylon, 26
Chrysophyllum (Sapotaceae)
    cainito, 124, 125
    sparsiflorum, 137
Cicer arietinum (Fabaceae), 123
Cirsium (Asteraceae), 74
Cissus populnea (Vitaceae), 101
Citrus aurantium (Rutaceae), 37
Cladina, 68, 69
Cladonia rangiferina, 73
Clathrotopis villosum (Fabaceae), 137
Clavija lancifolia (Theophrastaceae), 137
Claytonia lanceolata (Portulacaceae), 74
Cleome (Lamiaceae), 220
    serrulata, 70
Clerodendrum (Verbenaceae)
    capitatum, 100
    uncinatum, 37
Clidemia (Melastomataceae), 120, 123
    octava, 137
Cnicus benedictus (Asteraceae), 37

Cocos (Palmae), 186
  nucifera, 107
Codonanthopsis dissimulata
  (Gesneriaceae), 152, 160
Colchicum autumnale (Liliaceae), 175
Colocasia (Araceae), 106
Commelina (Commelinaceae), 9
Commiphora africana (Burseraceae), 100
Compositae = Asteraceae, 169, 170, 171,
    172, 173, 174, 200, 201, 215, 216, 217, 220,
    221, 223
Corchorus tridens (Tiliaceae), 101
Cordia (Boraginaceae), 137
  africana, 99
Cordyline terminalis (Agavaceae), 106, 107
Coryphantha vivipara, 72
Cosmos diversifolius (Asteraceae), 34
Couma macrocarpa (Apocynaceae), 122,
    124, 125, 137, 155
Coumarouna odorata
  (Fabaceae/Papilionoideae), 137
Crotolaria brevidens (Fabaceae), 50, 51, 52,
    56
Cruciferae = Brassicaceae, 47, 198, 201
Cucurbita (Cucurbitaceae), 187, 197, 210,
    212
Cyperaceae, 171, 172, 173, 174
Cyrtosperma chamissonis (Araceae), 106,
    107

Dacryodes belemensis (Burseraceae), 123,
    137
Dahlia coccinea (Asteraceae), 8
Dalbergaria picta (Gesneriaceae), 160
Datiscaceae, 171
Datura (Solanaceae), 27, 28
  stramonium, 177
Daucus carota var. *carota* (Umbelliferae),
    28
Dialium guianense
  (Fabaceae/Caesalpinoideae), 127, 137
Dichelostemma, 71
Dicranopygium bolivarense (Cyclantha-
  ceae), 137

Dioscorea (Dioscoreaceae), 137, 187, 197
  alata, 107
  esculenta, 107
Dioscoreaceae, 102
Diospyros mespiliformis (Ebenaceae), 100
Diplopterys cabrerana (Malpighiaceae),
    151, 164
Dorstenia contrajerva (Moraceae), 34
Drymonia coriacea (Gesneriaceae), 160

Echinocactus (Cactaceae), 70
Elaeagnus commutata (Elaeagnaceae), 73
Eleusine corocana (Poaceae), 101
Empetrum nigrum (Empetraceae), 74
Encyclia fragrans (Orchidaceae), 161
Entada scheffera (Fabaceae), 228
Enterolobium contortisiliquim (Fabaceae),
    232
Ephedra (Ephedraceae), 221
Equisetum telmateia (Equisetaceae), 74
Eragrostis ciliaris (Poaceae), 94, 100
Ericaceae, 200
Erisma japura (Vochysiaceae), 122, 123,
    125, 129, 137
Erythronium grandiflorum (Liliaceae), 13,
    74
Erythroxylon = Erythroxylum (Ery-
  throxylaceae)
  coca, 120
  ulei, 152, 159
Erythroxylum. See *Erythroxylon*
Eupatorium odoratum (Asteraceae), 34
Euphorbia pulcherrima (Euphorbiaceae),
    34
Euterpe (Palmae), 119, 121, 123, 138
  derasia, 125
  edulis, 137, 147, 148, 157
  oleracea, 121, 137
  precatoria, 137

Fagaceae, 201
Ferocactus (Cactaceae), 70
Fevillea cordifolia (Cucurbitaceae), 163

Musa (Musaceae), 116, 117, 148
  acuminata, 107, 108
  acuminata var. *banksii*, 106
  x *paradisiaca*, 146, 148
Myrcia (Myrtaceae), 139
Myrciaria tenella (Myrtaceae), 139
Myroxylon balsamum (Fabaceae), 35

Neurolaena lobata (Asteraceae), 159
Nicotiana (Solanaceae), 177, 196
Nymphaea (Nymphaeaceae), 222
  lotus, 99

Ocimum sanctum (Lamiaceae), 37
Oenocarpus (Palmae), 140
  bacaba, 139
  distichus, 140
  mapora, 157
Ogcodeia ulei (Moraceae), 140
Opuntia (Cactaceae), 70
  durangensis, 8
  macrorhiza, 72
Oribignya (Palmae), 140
  phalerata, 119, 121, 140
  aff. *polysticha*, 122, 140
  spectabilis, 140
Ormosia cf. *amazonica* (Fabaceae), 164
Orthomene schomburgkii (Menisper-
  maceae), 156
Orthosiphon (Lamiaceae)
  aristatus, 37
  stamineus, 37
Oryza (Poaceae), 188, 197
Oryzopsis hymenoides (Poaceae), 70, 71
Oxalis tuberosa (Oxalidaceae), 50, 56
Oxytropis (Fabaceae), 74

Palmae = Arecaceae, 146
Pandanus tectorius (Pandanaceae), 104
Panicum (Poaceae), 214, 221
Papilionaceae = Lotoideae. *See* Fabaceae
Pariana (Poaceae), 164
  aurita, 164

Parkia (Fabaceae/Mimosoideae), 123, 140
  filicoidea, 100
Parmelia physodes, 73
Parthenocissus quinquifolia (Vitaceae), 73
Passiflora (Passifloraceae)
  cf. *nitida*, 140
  quadrangularis, 157
Paullinia (Sapindaceae)
  bracteosa, 140, 158
  yoco, 147, 158
Pedicularis langsdorfii
  (Scrophulariaceae), 69
Pennisetum americanum (Poaceae), 86, 87, 92
Pentagonia williamsii (Rubiaceae), 165
Persea americana (Lauraceae), 33, 35, 37,
  124, 125
Persea gratissima. See P. americana
Petrea peruviana var. Mold. (Verbena-
  ceae), 162
Petroselinum crispum (Umbelliferae), 180
Phalaris caroliniana (Poaceae), 31
Phaseolus (Fabaceae), 73, 188, 197, 210, 212
Phenakospermum guyanense (Strelitzia-
  ceae), 122, 123, 124, 125, 126, 140
Phoenix (Palmae), 186
  dactylifera, 99
Phoradendron juniperinum
  (Loranthaceae), 71
Phragmites communis (Poaceae), 212
Physalis (Solanaceae)
  angulata, 140, 147, 149, 158
  peruviana, 149
Phytelephas (Palmae), 140, 157
  microcarpa, 140
Phytolacca (Phytolaccaceae), 120, 125, 126
  isconsandra, 140
  rivinoides, 127, 128, 140, 147, 158
Pilea (Urticaceae)
  sp. aff. *hydrocotyliflora*, 162
Pinaceae (pine family), 173, 201, 216
Pinus (Pinaceae), 188, 220, 221, 222, 223
  contorta, 72
  edulis, 70, 212
  ponderosa var. *scopulorum*, 71

Sesamum (Pedaliaceae)
  indicum, 188
  radiatum, 100
Shepherdia canadensis (Elaeagnaceae), 73
Solanaceae, 174, 176, 198, 201
Solanum (Solanaceae), 50, 71, 177, 187, 197
  diffusum, 162
  incanum, 100
  kioniotrichum, 162
  leptopodum, 162
  liximitante, 141
  sp. aff. nemorense, 162
  nigrum, 51, 53, 56
  quitoensis, 123
  sessiliflorum, 141
  stramonifolium, 141
  triflorum, 71
  tuberosum, 176, 177
Solidago odora (Asteraceae), 37
Sonchus schweinfurthii (Asteraceae), 51, 53
Sorghum bicolor (Poaceae), 86, 87, 92
Spilanthes alba (Asteraceae), 159
Spinacia oleracea (Chenopodiaceae), 125
Spiraea (Rosaceae), 175
Spondias (Anacardiaceae)
  mombin, 122, 123, 124, 125, 127, 141, 155
  tuberosa, 141
Sporobolus (Poaceae), 214, 216, 220, 221,
  222
Sterculia fananiho (Sterculiaceae), 105
Sticta amplissima, 73
Strychnos spinosa (Loganiaceae), 100
Stylochiton warnecki (Araceae), 100
Suaeda (Chenopodiaceae), 212, 214, 216,
  221, 222
Syngonium podophyllum (Araceae), 159
Syzygium samaragense (Myrtaceae), 107

Tacca leontopetaloides (Taccaceae), 106,
  107, 108
Tagetes lucida (Asteraceae), 35
Tamarindus indica (Fabaceae), 47, 101,
  123, 242, 244, 248
Taxomyces andreanae, 15

Taxus brevifolia (Taxaceae), 15
Tephrosia piscatoria (Fabaceae), 108
Terminalia catappa (Combretaceae), 106,
  107, 108
Thelypteris sp. aff. T. berroi (Poly-
  podiaceae), 165
Theobroma (Sterculiaceae), 141
  cacao, 116, 127, 141
  grandiflorum, 141
  speciosum, 141
  subincanum, 141
Tilia (Tiliaceae), 188
  americana, 73
Tournefortia angustifolia (Boraginaceae),
  159
Tribulus terrestris (Zygophyllaceae), 101
Trifolium (Fabaceae), 27
  subterraneum, 235
Triolena pluvialis (Melastomataceae), 161
Triticum (Poaceae), 188, 197
Tropaeoleum tuberosum (Tropaeolaceae),
  50, 56
Tsuga heterophylla (Pinaceae), 74
Typha (Typhaceae), 220, 221, 222, 223
  latifolia, 70, 215, 216

Ullucus tuberosus (Basellaceae), 50
Ulmus (Ulmaceae), 188
  americanus, 73
  rubra, 188
Umbelliferae = Apiaceae, 173, 198, 200
Umbilicaria, 68, 73
Urena lobata (Malvaceae), 100
Urera (Urticaceae)
  baccifera, 162
  caracasana, 162

Vanilla planifolia (Orchidaceae), 33, 35
Veratrum (Liliaceae), 175
Vernonia amygdalina (Vernoniaceae), 229,
  230
Vigna unguiculata (Fabaceae), 86, 92
Vitellaria paradoxa (Sapotaceae), 100
Vitex doniana (Verbenaceae), 100

Vitis (Vitaceae), 187

Withania somnifera (Solanaceae), 37

Yucca (Amaryllidaceae), 222
   bacchata, 70
   glauca, 70

Zanthoxylum cf. *tachuelo* (Rutaceae), 161

Zea mays (Poaceae), 33, 35, 70, 71, 73, 148,
   188, 189, 191, 192, 197, 210, 212, 214, 217,
   222
Zephyranthes carinata (Amaryllidaceae),
   35
Zigadenus (Liliaceae), 175
Zingiber (Zingiberaceae), 180
Zizyphus spina-christi (Rhamnaceae), 101

Topical Index

Anthelmintic, 11, 55, 151–52, 159, 161, 167, 174, 228–34

Anthraquinones, 51

Antibacterial, 229

Antibiotic, 167

Antidiarrheal, 127, 128, 159–63, 174

Antiemetic, 128

Antifungal, 229

Antimalarial, 52, 92, 167

Antinematodal, 229

Antioxidant, 55

Antipyretic, 128, 151, 161

Antischistosomal, 229, 234. *See also* Anthelmintic

Antiscorbutic, 128, 229

Antispasmodic, 127

Archaeobotanical analysis: in dietary reconstruction, 10–11, 185–202, 210–18, 220–23; of coprolites (*see* Coprolites); and differential preservation, 186–90; and evidence for medicinal plant use, 195–96, 210–18, 220–23; methods, 190–99, 202, 210–14, 265; of plant macroremains, 186–92, 211–12, 220–23; of pollen, 193, 210–13, 215, 220–23; of phytoliths, 193–94

Asia, 50, 186, 197–98

Aspen, 71

Australia, 270

Avalanche lily, 74

Avocado, 33, 35, 37

Bamboo, 146

Banana, 116, 117; dwarf, 146

Barberry, 37

Barrel cactus, 70

Basswood, 73, 188

Bat Cave (New Mexico), 210, 212, 217

Batemi, 50, 52, 54, 55. *See also* African indigenous peoples

Beach morning glory, 110

Bean/pea family, 169, 171, 172, 173, 174

Beans, 73, 188, 197, 210, 212

Biodiversity, 2, 13–15, 57, 85, 88, 96–97, 115, 152, 202, 235, 259, 263–67, 268–71; "anthropo-selfish" view of, 14–15, 264–65; and ethnobotanical research, 263–64; and "genetic erosion," 265–66; and human health, 264–67

Black pepper, 47, 49

Black tree lichen, 68

Bluedick, 71

Bog orchid, 70, 71

Bracken fern, 74

Brazil nut, 122–125, 136, 146, 188

Breadfruit, 102, 108, 147

Broccoli, 15

Bulrush millet, 86

Bush morning glory, 72

Butternut, 122, 123, 125, 137

Cabbage, 125

Cacao (chocolate), 116, 127, 141

Cactus, 70, 200

Calories. *See* Proximate composition

Cancer, 15, 27, 29, 55

Candlenut, 104, 106, 110

Capsaicin, 47, 49

Caraway, 37, 180

Carbohydrates. *See* Proximate composition

Cardol, 231

Carolina maygrass, 31

Cashew, 125, 127, 128, 136, 231

Cassava, 86, 122

Cat's whiskers, 9

Cattail, 70, 215, 216, 220–223

Chestnut, 73

Chickpea, 123

Children, 54, 75; as gatherers, 4, 5, 52, 106, 130

Chili pepper, 15, 33, 34, 47, 49, 50, 197

Clay-eating. *See* Geophagy

Climbing bittersweet, 73

Clover, 27, 235

Club moss, 213

Colchicine, 175

Gayfeather, 72
Ginger, 180; family, 169, 170, 171
Geophagy: and humans, 11, 12, 48, 55, 210, 215, 216; and nonhuman primates, 13, 55, 233–34; types of clay ingested, 215, 233
Glucosinilates, 47, 51
Glycoalkaloids, 47, 50, 51
Glycosides, 26, 64; luteolin, 26; quercetin, 26; steroid glycosides, 229–30
Goosefoot, 70, 212, 214, 221, 222; family, 201, 216, 217, 220, 221, 223
Gout, 175
Grape, 187
Greenstripe, 70
Groundnut. *See* Peanut
Groundsel, 71
Guatemala, 33, 52
Guava, 115, 122–25, 127, 128, 140
Guinea corn, 86
Gynecological aids. *See* Fertility-affecting plants

Hackberry, 212, 221, 223
Hallucinogens. *See* Psychoactive plants
Hand-flower tree, 26
Harmine (and related compounds), 25, 250
Hausa (Nigeria): definitions of "wild" and "domesticated," 88–89, 95, 97; diet, 86–87, 91–94, 99–101; health status, 92–93; medicinal foods, 91–94, 95, 99–101, 167; medicinal plants, 32, 89–97; nosology (beliefs about illness), 90; "wild" plant use, 4, 6, 7, 10, 85–97
Hawaii, 103, 259. *See also* Polynesia
Headache, 15, 52, 159, 160, 175
Hemlock, 74
Henbane, 177
Herbivores: plant defenses against, 12, 48, 53, 65, 127, 129, 166, 176, 178, 179. *See also* Allelochemicals
Hickory nut, 73, 195
HIV (Human Immunodeficiency Virus):

plants active against, 110–11. *See also* AIDS
Holly-leaved cherry, 187
Horseradish, 49
Horsetail, 74
Hunter-gatherers. *See* Foragers
Hyacinth bean, 54
Hyoscyamine, 176

Iceland lichen, 69
Indian millet, 71
Indian ricegrass, 70
Isohumulones, 49
Isothiocyanates, 47
Isotopic analysis, 190, 211

Jerusalem artichoke, 72
Jimson weed, 177
Juniper, 71, 212, 215, 220
Juniper mistletoe, 71

Keystone societies, 259–71
Keystone species: and biodiversity, 269–70; concept in ecology, 269

Lactic acid, 151
Lamb's quarters, 31
Lapita culture (ancestral Polynesians), 102, 106, 108
Laxative, 52, 127
Lemur, ringtailed (*Lemur catta*), foraging behavior: and implications for early hominid studies, 250–52; among lactating females, 246–49; among male vs. reproductive females, 243–46, 247, 248; among pregnant females, 249–50; and wild plants, 12, 240–52
Licorice, 10, 37
Lime, 188
Locoweed (*Oxytropis*), 74
Lodgepole pine, 72
Lousewort, 69
Lua' (Thailand), 32, 33, 267
Luteolin, 26. *See also* Glycosides

Maasai, 50, 51, 52, 55. *See also* African indigenous peoples
Macadamia nut, 188
Maguey, 26, 34, 37
Maize, 33, 35, 70, 71, 73, 148, 188, 189, 191, 192, 197, 210, 212, 214, 217, 222
Managed plants ("controlled plants"), 31–45, 88, 115–16
Mandrake, 177
Mango, 187
Mangrove, 11
Manioc, 115, 122, 148, 179, 187, 197
Marquesas Islands, 103. *See also* Polynesia
Marshelder, 194; large-seeded, 31
Meadow saffron, 175
Mescal, 70
Mesoamerican indigenous peoples: Aztec, 25, 26; Huastec Maya, 268; K'ekchi, 52; Maya, 25
Mesquite, 71
Mexico, 25; fertility-affecting plants of, 33–36; flora, 36. *See also* Mesoamerican indigenous peoples
Millet, 92
Minerals, 8, 51, 57, 75, 149, 180
Mint, 180, 199; family, 171–75, 201, 216, 221
Monkey ear, 232
Mustard, 49, 199; family, 201

Narcotics. *See* Psychoactive plants
N,N-dimethyltryptamine, 151
Natural selection, 3, 235
Nicotine, 176
Nigeria. *See* African indigenous peoples; Hausa
Nightshade, 177; family, 174, 176, 198, 201
Noncultigens. *See* Weeds; Wild plants
Nonhuman primates: baboon (*Papio* spp.), 228, 234; blackcapped capuchin (*Cebus apella*), 248; chimpanzee (*Pan* spp.), 12, 13, 55, 228–30, 234; colobus monkey (*Colobus* spp.), 228, 233–34; feeding behavior of, 12–13, 48, 55, 227–

35, 240–52; mantled howling monkey (*Alouatta palliata*), 12, 228, 230–32, 234; medicinal plant use among, 7, 12, 13, 167, 227–35, 265; muriqui (*Brachyteles arachnoides*), 228, 232–33, 234; ring-tailed lemur (*see* Lemur, ringtailed)
North America: ecological zones, 63, 66, 67; economic flora, by family, 168–76; economic flora, by growth habit, 176–78; economic flora, by life form, 178; floral diversity, 168; food and drug plants, 166–80, 185–202
North American indigenous peoples: Algonkians, 68; Apache, 71; Assiniboin, 72; Blackfoot, 73; Chipewyan, 69; Coast Salish, 73; Dakota, 72; Eskimo, 68; food plants of, 166–80, 185–88, 191–92, 195, 198, 200–2, 210; Gitksan, 73; Hidatsa, 72; Hohokam, 194; Hopi, 70, 215; impact on the environment of, 186; Inuit, 196; Iroquois, 72–73; Kiowa, 72, 73; Kumeyaay, 67; major crop plants of, 198; medicinal flora of, 168–80, 196; medicinal plant use among, 170, 171; Mogollon (prehistoric), 217; Mojave, 71; Navajo, 70, 71, 214; Nlaka'pamux (Thompson), 74; Omaha, 72; Paiute, 70, 214; Pima, 8, 70; Pueblo, 70, 71; San Felipe, 70; Shoshoni, 70; Slave, 69; Stoney, 73; Tohono O'odham (Papago), 70, 194, 268; wild plant use among, 8, 10, 13, 50, 62–77, 214–15, 267; Woods Cree, 68, 69; Yavapai, 214; Yuma, 71; Zuni, 71, 215
Nutrients: in cultivated plants, 51–52; in "weeds," 51–52; in wild plants, 8–9, 51–52, 64, 66, 68, 72, 73, 75, 114, 117, 120–22, 126, 149, 218. *See also* Dietary reconstruction; Minerals; Proximate composition; Vitamins

Oak, 50, 68
One-seeded juniper, 71
Onion, 47, 199

Optimal foraging: and hominid evolution, 250–52; model in archaeological analysis, 10, 193, 202; by nonhuman primates, 227, 240–52
Oregon creeping grape, 73
Orinoconut, 122–25, 137

Palatability: concept of, 46, 199; cultural variations in, 6, 49–50, 54, 64, 125; and medicinal plant selection, 6, 31–33, 46–57, 64, 65, 76, 91, 176, 218; odor and taste, relation to, 7, 46–57, 199, 217. *See also* Perceptual salience; Polymorphisms; PROP; PTC
Paleobotanical analysis. *See* Archaeobotanical analysis
Paleofeces. *See* Coprolites
Palynology. *See* Archaeobotanical analysis, of pollen
Panic grass, 214, 221
Papaya, 33, 34
Paper birch, 69
Parsley, 173, 180
Parturients, 29. *See also* Fertility-affecting plants
Peach-palm, 4, 148
Peanut (groundnut), 86, 123–25
Pepper. *See* Black pepper; Chili pepper
Perceptual salience, role in plant selection, 26–28, 31–33, 35, 96, 198–99, 218. *See also* Palatability; Selection
Pharmacognosy, defined, 227. *See also* Zoopharmacognosy
Phenolics, 46, 64, 151, 231, 233, 248. *See also* Flavonoids
Phytoliths. *See* Archeobotanical analysis, of phytoliths
Pigweed: *Amaranth*, 10, 70, 214, 220, 221, 222; *Boerhaavia*, 11, 228; family (Amaranthaceae), 216, 217, 221, 223; prostrate, 72
Pine, 188, 220–23; family, 173, 201, 216
Pineapple, 197
Pinyon, 70, 212

Piperine, 47
Plantain: *Musa*, 148; *Plantago*, 177
Plant foods, processing: detoxification of famine foods, 62–80; techniques, 12, 48, 50, 64, 65, 68, 74–76, 123, 125, 129, 179, 186, 187, 189, 190, 191, 200, 201, 211; tools for, 191, 192, 214. *See also* Famine foods; Palatability; Wild plants, as food
Plant knowledge: acquisition of, 6, 9, 25–37, 54, 88, 109–10, 149–50, 196; acquisition of, among nonhuman primates, 234–35 (*see also* Nonhuman primates); traditional, 53–54, 88–89, 96, 109–10, 168, 263; transmission of, 5, 7, 53–56, 76, 96–97, 109–10, 149–50, 197; transmission of, among nonhuman primates, 12, 234–35 (*see also* Nonhuman primates)
Plants: multicontextual use of (as food, medicine, etc.), 5, 6, 9–10, 30–33, 36, 52–53, 76, 85, 93, 96, 127–29, 174–76, 180, 213, 214, 262; ritual use of, 163–65, 196, 215, 216 (*see also* Psychoactive plants)
Plum, 187
Polymorphisms, role in taste perception, 49. *See also* PROP; PTC; Palatability; Perceptual salience
Polynesia: ethnomedicine, 108–11; floral diversity, 105; Hawaii, 103, 259; major crop plants, 102, 104, 106; Marquesas Islands, 103; Samoa, 10, 103, 105–11; settlement of, 102–5, 106, 108 (*see also* Lapita); subsistence economy, traditional, 102–4; Tonga, 103; wild plants, 105–11
Pomegranate, 11, 228
Pondweed, 215
Potato, 50, 176, 177, 187, 197
Prairie turnip, 72, 73
Prickly pear, 8
PROP (6-n-propylthiouracil), 49. *See also* Palatability; Perceptual salience; Polymorphisms

Protein. *See* Proximate composition

Proximate composition (calories, carbohydrate, protein, etc.): of famine foods, 75–76; of foods in general, 8, 9, 75, 123–26, 148–49, 167, 188, 196. *See also* Dietary reconstruction; Diet survey; Famine foods; Minerals; Nutrients; Vitamins

Psychoactive plants, 25, 27–28, 127, 143, 149–51, 162, 164, 200, 201. *See also* Plants, ritual use of

Psychotropic plants. *See* Psychoactive plants

PTC (phenylthiocarbamate), 49. *See also* Palatability; Perceptual salience; Polymorphisms

Puffed shield lichen, 73

Purgative, 128, 151, 159, 160, 161, 162

Purslane, 214, 220, 221; family, 201

Quechua, 25, 50. *See also* South American indigenous peoples

Queen Anne's lace, 28

Quercetin, 26. *See also* Glycosides

Quinic acid, 151

Quinine, 47

Quinoa, 50

Ragweed, 34, 35

Ramon nut, 194

Rapeseed, 187

Raspberry, 187

Reedgrass, 212

Reindeer lichen, 69

Reindeer moss, 68, 73

Rice, 188, 197

Ritual use of plants. *See* Plants, ritual use of; Psychoactive plants

Rock tripe, 68, 73

Rocky Mountain bee plant, 70

Rose, 72; family, 167, 169, 171, 172, 174, 175, 198, 200

Rubber tree, 123, 124

Rue, 31

Sage, 180

Saguaro, 70

Salicylates, 175

Salicylic acid, 151

Samoa, 10, 103, 105–11; medicinal plants, 108–11; subsistence economy, traditional, 105–11. *See also* Polynesia

Sand bunchgrass, 71

Saponins, 12, 47, 201, 234. *See also* Allelochemicals; Palatability

Schistosomiasis, 230. *See also* Anthelmintics; Antischistosomal

Scopaletine, 151

Scopolamine, 176

Screwbean, 71

Secondary chemicals. *See* Allelochemicals

Secoya. *See* Siona-Secoya

Seepweed, 212, 214, 216, 221, 222

Selection: 2–4, 6–7, 14, 32–33; of economic plants, as an evolutionary process, 1–2, 48–49, 96, 202; of food plants, 1–2, 46–57, 64, 74, 85, 93, 125, 178–79, 218; by nonhuman primates, 233; odor, taste, and related qualities, roles in, 26–28, 32, 35, 46–57, 64, 74, 93, 178, 198–99, 217, 218, 233. *See also* Natural selection; Palatability; Perceptual salience

Semidomesticates, 115–16, 145–46. *See also* Domesticates; Managed plants; Weeds; Weed-wild continuum

Sesame, 188

Sesquiterpene lactones, 151; vernodalol (and related compounds), 229–30

Silverberry, 73

Siona-Secoya (Amazonia), 10, 118, 120, 126–27, 128, 138, 139, 140, 141, 142, 143–65; cultural/ecological setting, 144–46; health of, 149–52; health of, vs. colonists in the area, 143–44; illness concepts, 149–52; indigenous ecological concepts, 146, 147; subsistence economy, 143–44; wild plant use, health significance of, 143–65

148–49, 185, 248–49; in production of
durable goods, 105–6, 120, 143, 152
Willow, 73, 222
Women: as curers, 36, 109; early hominid, 251–52; and food procurement,
4–6, 36, 87–88, 126, 130, 262; medicines
for, 36 (*see also* Emmenagogue;
Fertility-affecting plants; Galactagogue); use of wild plants, 4–6, 7, 88,
126
Woodbine, 73

Yam, 102, 187, 197
Yellow dogtooth violet, 13
Yellow mombin, 122–25, 127, 128, 141
Yucca, 70

Zooarchaeology, 267–68
Zoopharmacognosy, 11, 12, 13, 55, 227–28.
See also Allelochemicals; Herbivores;
Animals; Nonhuman primates